Flow

OXFORD STUDIES IN MUSIC THEORY
Series Editor Steven Rings

Flow

The Rhythmic Voice in Rap Music

Mitchell Ohriner

OXFORD
UNIVERSITY PRESS

Oxford University Press is a department of the University of Oxford. It furthers
the University's objective of excellence in research, scholarship, and education
by publishing worldwide. Oxford is a registered trade mark of Oxford University
Press in the UK and certain other countries.

Published in the United States of America by Oxford University Press
198 Madison Avenue, New York, NY 10016, United States of America.

CIP data is on file at the Library of Congress
ISBN 978-0-19-067041-2

1 3 5 7 9 8 6 4 2

Printed by Sheridan Books, Inc., United States of America

CONTENTS

LIST OF EXAMPLES

LIST OF TABLES

LIST OF ACRONYMS

API	Application Programming Interface, a means of accessing the data of a web service
AAVE	African-American Vernacular English, also termed African American Language
BUR	Beat-upbeat ratio, coined by Fernando Benadon to describe swung durations
CA	Correspondence analysis, a statistical analysis similar to PCA for categorical data
CMA	Computational music analysis
CMUPD	Carnegie Mellon University Pronouncing Dictionary
COCA	Corpus of Contemporary American English
GTTM	*A Generative Theory of Tonal Music*, a book by Fred Lerdahl and Ray Jackendoff
IAI	Inter-accent interval, a duration of time
IRI	Inter-rhyme interval, a duration of time
MIDI	Musical Instrument Digital Interface
MST	Metrical Stress Theory, a branch of phonology pioneered by Bruce Hayes and Elisabeth Selkirk
OHHLA	The Online Hip-Hop Lyrics Archive
PCA	Principal component analysis, a statistical analysis of variance in continuous data
TUBS	Time-Unit Box Series, an ethnomusicological notation system

ACKNOWLEDGMENTS

Without the work of countless artists, producers, and instrumentalists in hip hop's first forty years, there would be nothing to write about in this book. Their work appeared prior to and enables my own.

I have been fortunate to be able to address rap music in the college classroom, and I am grateful for the discussions I have had with students at Shenandoah University and the University of Denver. Whatever I know about rap music post-2005 is thanks to them, and their recommendations and enthusiasm keep me engaged in teaching.

My colleagues Keith Salley, Kristin Taavola, Laurie McManus, and Jack Sheinbaum provided much needed guidance at various stages of this work. Kyle Adams showed me that music analysis of hip hop was viable and generously read early versions of the book proposal. Chris Brody told me to let the scope of the idea shape the scope of the work, which was the permission I needed to write a book in the first place. Christopher William White wrote a very helpful signed review of that proposal. I am also grateful for two anonymous reviews written for Oxford University Press. The team at OUP, including Suzanne Ryan, Steven Rings, Dorian Mueller, Andrew Maillet, Jamie Kim, Patti Brecht, and Emma Clements has been unfailingly helpful and responsive throughout this process.

The ideas in Chapter 8 were presented at the 2016 meeting of the Society for Music Theory's Popular Music Interest Group, the 2017 meeting of the Rocky Mountain Society for Music Theory, and the 2017 annual meeting of the Society for Music Theory. At all these events, I received invaluable feedback and am especially grateful to Noriko Manabe, Jim Bungert, Robin Attas, and John Mattesich for their input on that work. Nathaniel Condit-Schultz reviewed a related article of mine in *Empirical Musicology Review* and provided commentary that I have incorporated here. I have also had the privilege of presenting this work outside of my "home discipline" of music theory, especially at the 2015 annual meeting of the United States Chapter of the International Association for the Study of Popular Music and at the 2016 Dagstuhl Seminar on Computational Music Structure Analysis. Participants at both these events provided generous and understanding perspectives of non-specialists in music theory.

Though I've not met most of them, many authors, journalists, and podcasters have been indispensable in my education in rap music and hip-hop studies, especially H. Samy Alim, Adam Bradley, Jon Caramanica, Jeff Chang, Martin Connor, Zach Diaz, Michael Eric Dyson, Paul Edwards, Kyra Gaunt, Steven Gilbers, Mickey

Hess, Byron Hurt, Cheryl Keyes, Bakari Kitwana, KRS-One, Serge Lacasse, Felicia Miyakawa, Chris Molanphy, Ali Shaheed Muhammad, Halifu Osumare, Imani Perry, James Braxton Peterson, Tricia Rose, Kelefa Sanneh, stic.man, and Justin Williams.

Since 2017, I have spent time at Youth On Record, a Denver-based non-profit that provides music education and access to recording studios to young Coloradans. I am grateful for the many discussions I've had on making hip-hop music with Brent Adams, Devin Urioste (Mace), and Jesus Rodriguez, an extraordinary multitasker. I am in awe of what the young artists do there.

Lastly, my son Nadav's birth was a wonderful reason to set this work aside for a time, and my son Zev's birth was a wonderful and motivating reason to finish it. My wife Taliah Weber made possible them, this book, and everything else good in my world.

INTRODUCTION

This book addresses the rhythm of the rapping voice, a phenomenon widely termed "flow" by emcees and fans alike. As such, it extends and converses with work by Adam Krims (2000); Felicia Miyakawa (2005); Serge Lacasse (2006); Noriko Manabe (2006); Kyle Adams (2008, 2009, 2015a, 2015b); Martin Connor (2011–2017); myself (Ohriner 2013, 2016); Paul Edwards (2015); Oliver Kautny (2015); and Nathaniel Condit-Schultz (2016). Flow presents challenges to understanding rhythm not encountered anywhere else. On the one hand, flow is rhythmic in the same way other music is rhythmic, including other music on a rap track. But on the other hand, rapping differs from singing: the rhythm of flow is related to the rhythm of speech. Listeners engage perceptual systems related to both these rhythmic systems in understanding and interpreting the rhythm of the rapping voice. While flow exists in a rhythmic space between music and speech, existing theories of rhythm in these two domains, as well as the domain of lyric poetry, are framed quite differently, addressing different features and making different assumptions. Key rhythmic concepts such as meter, periodicity, patterning, and accent are treated independently in scholarship of music- and speech-rhythm, and an analysis of flow must reconcile these theories. While examining flow through these different lenses enhances our understanding of what emcees do, the particularities of flow-as-rhythm also offer the promise of refining our understanding of rhythm more generally in popular music, speech, and the singing voice. Moving that understanding forward is a primary aim of this book.

A second aim of this book is to bring the full force of the tools of computational music analysis (CMA) to bear on questions of flow. CMA begins by representing a large collection of music—rap flows, in this case—in a digital format called a corpus. As I practice it, CMA then seeks to ground the assertions of humanistic analysis and close reading in formal characterizations of the data. I view this sort of analysis as an extension of Leonard B. Meyer's distinction between style analysis and critical analysis (1973, p. 6). The former seeks to identify the "rules of the game" operating in a style; the latter seeks to explain the individual choices of an artist by identifying the range of possibilities available to her and speculating on the reasoning that led her to one possibility over the others. The corpus approach formally identifies this field of possibilities and can characterize the exceptionality of artists' choices given the tendencies of the style. Not only does the computational approach greatly expand the range of music that characterizes the style, but it avoids a host of implicit biases and praxes in human analysis by forcing the analyst to define methods of analysis in machine-readable code (Marsden 2016, p. 25).

I remain surprised at the slow adoption of computational methods in music theory specifically and in the humanities more broadly. Following Patrik Svensson (2016), I distinguish here between "humanities computing" and "the digital humanities." While the digital humanities enjoy widespread attention, their use of computers emphasizes the storage and retrieval of large amounts of information (e.g., images, concert programs, etc.). As such, they are more apt to analyze the metadata of that information—its origin, chronology, etc.—than the information's content. Why does computational analysis remain a rather small segment of humanities scholarship and the digital humanities? In a comment to the Humanist Discussion Group in 1992, Mark Olsen argues that practitioners of computational methods in the humanities have consistently failed "to produce results of sufficient interest, rigor, and appeal to attract a following among scholars who *do not* make extensive use of computers."[1] This statement, though provocative, still rings true in 2019. In my own discipline of music theory, those who engage in CMA continue to struggle in generating interest from those who employ more conventional methods. Part of the challenge is undoubtedly the learning curve necessary to critique CMA at the professional level, but more so is the reticence of computational analysts to engage in data-supported close reading of texts or other kinds of scholarship essential to humanists. Emblematic of this issue are computational analyses that, while making valuable data available, deliver little more than descriptive statistics. While I hope scholars will extend this work by drawing on the datasets I publish here, my primary aim is to enable and ground close readings of the rhythms of rap delivery.

The questions regarding flow that I subject to CMA include the following: What musical features do artists refer to when they flow "about flow"? What are the most typical and least typical ways of flowing? What is accent in flow, and how is it patterned? Can rap flows have a structure that transcends the individual verse? In what ways can an emcee interact with the surrounding instrumental beat? What is the meaning of the rhythm of speech in the context of rap music? I address these questions in this book in two parts. The first part begins in Chapter 1 by sketching what rhythmic features emcees seem to refer to by the word "flow." The discourse around flow, both in interviews with artists and in existing scholarship, construes flow in a wide variety of ways. Rather than align myself with only one of these, I turn to the artists themselves. Since few of them are asked what flow is, I instead observe what they do when they flow, specifically, what they do when they announce within a verse that the flow has changed or "flipped." By examining flipped flows, I hone in on a set of features that one ought to represent in an analysis of flow.

The second chapter represents those features within the genre as a whole by defining and building a corpus of rap verses. Representative corpus construction requires careful sampling, and much of the chapter details how the sampling was

---

1. See http://dhhumanist.org/Archives/Virginia/v06/0365.html, cited in Svensson (2016, p. 181).

undertaken and how the features are represented. Of particular importance is the concept of "accent" in rap music and how it is patterned in and between verses. (I use "accent" as a synonym for prominence or emphasis, not regional differences in speech.) Chapter 3 details my conception of accent and how I automatically annotate it in verses, drawing from independent and somewhat contradictory theories of accent found in scholarship on the rhythm of speech and the rhythm of music. The latter part of the chapter addresses my model of rhyme in similar terms. Chapter 4 defines what I consider the most essential feature of flow: what I term vocal groove, reiterated patterns of durations between accents. To direct this concept of vocal groove at analyses of verses and tracks, I introduce a model of "groovy listening" that segments a verse into a succession of grooves heard by listeners with varying tolerance for inexactitude in patterning.

The second part of the book consists of three case studies that, drawing on the model of Part I, address pressing questions in the theories of rhythm, meter, and interaction through the work of three artists. Specifically, I explore how vocal grooves relate to narratives in the lyrics of Eminem, how the rhythm of Black Thought of the group The Roots interacts with the other instrumental streams he flows over, and how the rhythm of speech and the rhythm of music are reconciled (or not reconciled) in performances by Talib Kweli. Throughout, I argue that the methods most appropriate to the analysis of these artists offer new avenues of understanding to artists in related genres, or perhaps anyone who flows or sings against a steady beat.

Music Analysis, Advocacy, Fieldwork, and Identity

As may already be clear, the choice to use a computational approach means that for some readers this work will be stridently formalist and culturally detached. These critiques of music theory have been made for some time, though the stakes may be higher for music-theoretical work on hip hop. In discussing the recent flourishing of hip-hop scholarship, the self-described "journalist, activist, and political analyst" Bakari Kitwana (2017) aligns hip-hop scholarship with political advocacy:

> Hip-hop studies should build on this tradition of Black Studies, which was rooted in [making] a commitment, in the study, to advance the lifestyle of the people that created the music and the culture. So returning back to those black and brown communities, how can the study uplift the lifestyles of those people? That has to be central in any study of hip hop, rather than simply folks writing dissertations and advancing their own personal careers.[2]

---

2. This quote can be heard seven minutes into the broadcast. "Hip-hop" and "hip hop" are both standard in the literature. I use the hyphen only with the adjectival form, for example, "hip-hop scholarship."

I have been trained in music theory and music analysis, disciplines that remain largely focused on repertoires whose composers are no longer living, and thus the perspective that analysis might improve the lifestyles of artists was not one I encountered in my training. Still, in my experience, engaging with unfamiliar musical repertoires or unfamiliar scholarly techniques serves as training for engaging with other people across lines of difference. But that is certainly not what Kitwana is calling for, and this book will disappoint those who view scholarship as a means of advancing broad policy goals. Ultimately, and regardless of my support for many of those goals, this is not an ambition I share. Instead, I seek to answer what I believe are important questions about important music, even if those questions are not encountered in everyday political or cultural discourse. In my understanding of academic freedom, a scholar's right to pursue social justice through scholarship must be defended and strengthened, as must my own right not to.

As this book is not focused on advocacy, neither is it focused primarily on the relationship between African American culture and rap music. To be sure, the voices of the "Hip-Hop Nation" permeate the book, from interviews with artists, to fan comments on YouTube videos, to the work of hip-hop journalists. But this book differs from scholarship that is focused mainly on the relation of rap music to earlier black cultural forms, or the ways rap music operates in the wider culture as a means of resistance. Previous authors have related rap music to expressive forms such as the dozens (Wald 2012), the spoken word recitations of The Last Poets (Kopano 2002), the games played by black girls such as double-dutch (Gaunt 2006), and the singing of West African griots (Keyes 2002).[3] Other authors have stressed how urban geography (Krims 2007) and social policies targeting or excluding specific communities gave rise to hip hop (Rose 1994). Like Krims (2003, p. 3), I acknowledge that these matters of cultural meaning and history are crucial in understanding rap music's expressive power. I am grateful for the many titles I have read addressing these topics, and I have incorporated them into this work where relevant. But I also concur with Krims that "the vast majority of rap and hip-hop scholarship . . . takes the music seriously but gives little, if any, attention to its musical organization." While studies of rap music presented at and in music-theory conferences and journal articles have burgeoned in the last decade, Krims's statement remains true of hip-hop scholarship more broadly. In this regard, I echo Joseph Schloss's objectives, if not his methods:

> It does no disservice to previous work to say that it has tended to focus on certain areas (such as the influence of the cultural logic of late capitalism on urban identities, the representation of race in popular culture, etc.) to the exclusion of others (such as the specific aesthetic goals that artists have articulated). Nor is it a criticism to say that this is largely a result of its methodologies, which have, for the most part, been drawn from literary analysis. We must simply note that there are blank

---

3. Sajnani (2013) offers important context on the similarities and dissimilarities between the hip-hop emcee and the griot.

spaces and then set about to filling them in. Ethnography, I believe, is a good place to start. (2004, p. 2)

For Schloss, starting with ethnography means an emphasis on fieldwork. I have not undertaken fieldwork in preparing to write this book. The reasons for this are more practical than ideological, and I would not argue that this project would not benefit from an informant-based approach. Fieldwork doubtless provides information that cannot be accessed any other way. Nevertheless, I would argue that surely one of the reasons scholars like Schloss undertake fieldwork is so that other scholars with different training and perspectives might use that fieldwork to inform their own work. And furthermore, as Cheryl Keyes (2002, pp. 10–12) points out, the line between an insider and an outsider is fuzzy for hip-hop scholars, and the various components of one's identity alternately increase and decrease access. Keyes describes how her male consultants were more subdued in their responses to her than in the responses to other men she witnessed. Alternatively, those who considered her an outsider (as a non-participant in the music industry) could be more forthcoming without fear of consequence.

Although I have not undertaken "on-the-ground" fieldwork, I would argue that in our current moment a kind of virtual fieldwork is possible and valuable, and thus much of the book engages with large collections of rap lyrics, comments on YouTube videos and discussion boards, and blog posts and articles of the online hip-hop media. I am also mindful of the disconnect that can arise between scholarly and popular considerations of a topic, and thus I address the hazards of an insular view on topics such as "conscious rap," the impact of misogyny and homophobia in rap lyrics, and the value of complexity in flow.

For many, responsible hip-hop scholarship hinges not just on scholarly methods but also on a consideration of the scholar's identity. While fieldwork forces this kind of self-reflection, some might argue that methods like computational analysis—with their supposed objectivity—obviate the need to interrogate how the researcher's identity affects the results. But this would be a mistake, as undertaking work of this kind necessitates countless decisions, small and large, that may (perhaps unwittingly) be the result of the analyst's lived experience. Because rap music is forever implicated in issues of cultural resistance and appropriation, the identity of the hip-hop scholar is all the more crucial. As the video director Hype Williams related to Debi Fee (1988, R21), "You've got to be from the streets to know what rap is about, or at least be out there to know what's going on."

To the extent that the reader needs an account of the identity of an author in order to evaluate an analysis of rap music, I offer the following: I identify as Jewish, and most Americans would understand my race as white. I am the third generation of men in my family who have avoided the systematic denial of opportunities in education, employment, housing, and lending still to this day experienced by most people of color in the United States. I attended public schools in suburban Knoxville, Tennessee, in a system that, according to court findings, still actively segregated students by race in my years there (*Middlebrook v. Knox County School District*). To say the least, I was not surrounded by rap music as a child.

As a composer in training, I admired its dissonance, its repurposing of musical material, the rhythmic vitality of its voices, and its wordplay. Yet I did not listen to it exclusively, nor did I wear hip-hop fashions or attend hip-hop performances. Indeed, my interest in rap music quickened because I came to view it as an ideal ecosystem in which to pose important questions about rhythm, music, and speech. The amount of rap music I listened to over the five years of researching and writing this book likely exceeds that which I had heard before.

Music Theory, Music Analysis, and Rap Music

Another key aspect of my identity is my identity as a music theorist. This has a profound impact on how I approach rap music, as much if not more so as my identity with regard to race or gender. Many hip-hop scholars view music theory with deep suspicion, a suspicion confirmed by experiences like those of Tricia Rose, who writes:

> In the spring of 1989, I was speaking animatedly with an ethnomusicology professor about rap music and the aims of [her book, *Black Noise*]. He found some of my ideas engaging and decided to introduce me and describe my project to the chairman of his music department [NB: the chair's identity as a composer, performer, theorist, musicologist, etc. is unspecified]. At the end of his summary the department head rose from his seat and announced casually, "Well, you must be writing on rap's social impact and political lyrics, because there is nothing to the music." (1994, p. 62)

Rose goes on to argue that rap music's complexity was denied "by a mainstream cultural adherence to the traditional paradigms of western classical music as the highest legitimate standard for musical creation" (p. 65). As someone trained in the analysis of that music, and as someone who spends a significant portion of his working life teaching students the tools and methods necessary to analyze that music, it is essential to consider how these "traditional paradigms" inform my analyses of rap music. For starters, I do not consider them "the highest legitimate standard for musical creation." Music communities determine aesthetic values by making music together. In most cases, the tools of classical music analysis are unhelpful in understanding popular music generally and rap music specifically. A great many of those tools are concerned with harmony and voice leading, the ways independent musical lines relate to each other. Rap's aesthetic ideal of "hardness" and preference for harmonic dissonance diminishes the usefulness of these tools. But what of the more abstract values of classical music?

The analysis of Western classical music is an analysis of texts, namely, musical scores. These scores fix the details of a musical work into a single version that can be analyzed. I, like many others, treat rap music, especially verses, as a fixed text represented by a commercial recording. Others construe rap as an oral or post-literary form for which textual analysis is inappropriate. It is true that some rap performances are improvised, and some emcees of recorded verses claim not to write their verses down. But most emcees acknowledge that their verses are texts before they are performances (Rose 1994, p. 88). Still, my focus on commercial recordings means that I miss some features or meanings of verses that are not commercially released. I address this issue in my consideration of several live performances of The Roots's "You Got Me" in Chapter 7, but most of the analyses in this book treat a single commercial recording as a text.

Another focus of Western classical music that weighs on my analytical approach is the single authorial perspective. When analysts study classical scores, they attribute whatever meaning they find there to the composer. Similarly, I attribute the musical decisions that make up a flow to the emcee. This might overstate the extent to which the emcee "owns" the musical decisions that contribute to a verse. Keyes (2002, p. 124) cites the "cipha," a competitive and improvisational activity of maintaining a rhyme in a group, as a central activity of emcees. In this collaborative atmosphere, emcees respond to each other's rhymes and energy, and it may be that some portion of recorded verses arise through collaborative composition.

Even if emcees are the sole creators of the (rhythmic) content of their verses, other agents can intercede. The most jaw-dropping example I have encountered is Talib Kweli's verse on Kanye West's "Get 'Em High" from *The College Dropout*. Kweli recorded the verse "from Norway, or wherever I recorded at," only to discover upon hearing the album that his verse fell "on the wrong part of the beat." In an interview a decade later (VladTV 2015), he remains ambivalent about the result:

> [Kanye's] a musical genius. It was a beautiful mistake. It fit, for him. It didn't make sense for me for the first few months. Because I knew how I laid it, and it sounded off to me. But people liked it, and I had to learn how to appreciate it.

This episode might give pause to attributing aspects of musical organization solely to the emcee. And it also highlights the influence of alternative conceptions of authorship, since Kweli, in essence, surrenders his control, even of the final product, to others. Yet in his hesitancy ("I had to learn how to appreciate it") I sense an attitude toward ownership that is not so different from the composers of classical music. This sense of ownership is also supported by the common strictures against copying another artist's style (i.e., "biting").

Two other values in my analyses stem from my training in classical music. The first is a value placed on complexity. This value is by no means foreign to rap music, and I will demonstrate a host of ways in which rap music partakes in complexity. But there is plenty of rap music that does not aspire to complexity, and, especially in the case studies, that music is not given as thorough an examination.[4] The second is a value placed on clarity. A key aesthetic of rap music, probably more so of early rap music, is what Rose (1994, p. 74) calls "working in the red," recording and producing sounds outside the "recommended" technical specifications of the

4. I address the problematic status of complexity in rap music at the end of Chapter 6.

equipment. This often leads to beats with extremely loud and bass-heavy instrumental streams and vocals that are relatively hard to find in the mix. In order to access the rhythmic features of this music, I use transcriptions of lyrics and digital production techniques to change the sonic features or speed of verses in order to hear the rhythms of flow more clearly. I concede that doing so works against the aesthetic preferences of the producers, but I would imagine that emcees who craft verses would want the sonic details of their verses to be accessible.

Readers will find that this book differs from those discussed so far in several other ways as well, such as lack of emphases on geography or the influence of capitalism. As rap music becomes more geographically integrated in the United States, understanding the geographical particularities can explain the appeal of emcees who blend diverse styles. For example, Imani Perry (2004, p. 65) hails Biggie Smalls for "adopting and reinterpreting the symbols of West Coast hip hop through an East Coast style." Similarly, she praises 50 Cent for "integrating Southern and Western hip-hop sensibilities into his style." But symbols and sensibilities are not necessarily rhythms. As will be clearer later, the computational approach I adopt here does not find significant differences in the flow of rappers of different regions. This might be because the dataset is not large enough, and it might be because the features that would reveal these differences are not part of the analysis. But it might also be that the markers of regionalism in rap music are not rhythmic, but rather sonic, phonetic, or dispositional. More glaring is my exclusive focus on rap music in the United States. Hip hop has sprung from American roots to become a truly global phenomenon, and studies of global hip hop document how it can operate as a means of resistance abroad (e.g., Mitchell 2002, Manabe 2015, etc.) and how hip hop's rhythmic priorities translate into other languages and cultures (e.g., Osumare 2003, Condry 2006, Alim, Ibrahim, & Pennycook 2008, etc.). The emphasis on hip hop in the United States is a product of my limitations, but also a response to the challenge of sampling global hip hop through the methods appropriate to sampling hip hop in the United States (e.g., Billboard charts, mentions in the hip-hop press, etc.).

For the purposes of this study, the influence of corporate, market, and political forces is similar to geographical influences. Their influence is hugely important for telling the history of rap music and for understanding the meaning of its lyrics and its cultural force, but less certain when studying its rhythms. In particular, one cannot understand rap music as a cultural product without understanding the long history of censorship of its depiction of violence, explicit sexual discussion, and even political discourse. Rose's interview with producer Gina Harrell (1994, p. 14) documents the baroque censorship at work in music videos, where at that time one could show a gun and a body but not the gun shooting the body. The censorship of political speech includes very public episodes like Body Count's "Cop Killer" as well as all the similar episodes that never see the light of day. The same corporate forces that censor violence and sexual depictions also act to amplify those same instincts in rap music, as Byron Hurt's documentary film *Hip Hop: Beyond Beats and Rhymes* (2006) shows. These corporate encouragements feed what Stuart Allen Clarke (1991, p. 40) terms "the U.S. political culture's enormous appetite for images of black men misbehaving." But the title of Hurt's documentary is revealing: the corporate forces are beyond flow and, in my view, apart from it.

How to Read This Book

As previously discussed here, this book introduces a model of flow in rap music and rap music analysis and addresses several questions of rhythm, meter, and groove through close readings of specific emcees using that model. The model itself is computational, in that it takes symbolic transcriptions of rap performances (as opposed to audio recordings) as input and delivers analyses, graphical representations, and statistical descriptions as output. The value of this output vitally depends on the integrity of the transcriptions and the clarity of the steps the computer undertakes to analyze them.

This book, therefore, must provide a technical account of all the decisions that were made in constructing the model so that the work can be verified, replicated, and extended. At the same time, the model is subservient to humanistic ends, namely, analysis of rap-music discourse and close readings of performances. The challenge in writing the book, then, was navigating between technical exposition and critical analysis for the varied audiences that might encounter it. I have tried to meet this challenge in a number of ways:

- The analyses employ consistent technical language and a visual grammar detailed in the "Conventions" section that follows.
- A glossary defines all terms encountered in boldface.
- The section "On Reproducible Research" details the contents of the datasets prepared for this book (hosted at github.com/mohriner/flowBook) and information on verifying the many claims to come.

Even with these efforts, readers less interested in technical details and more interested in the issues explored in the case studies of Part II will not find each chapter equally inviting. Chapters 2–4 are the most technical, as their task is to detail the model of groovy listening employed in the case studies. Respectively, these will be of greatest interest to corpus analysts; scholars interested in accent in music, speech, and poetry; and those interested in meter and groove from a mathematical and cognitive perspective. While these chapters are indeed technical, they do not assume any familiarity with conventional music theory (e.g., knowledge of scales, chords, etc.), nor do they assume an ability to read Western music notation. The technical skills required to produce this work, while substantial, are not in my view unattainable for scholars already working in the humanities. Indeed, I did not start developing my own technical skill set until I was well into graduate training. My greatest hope for this book, and the reason I have not only adopted a computational approach but also made efforts to document the process of the analysis, is that other scholars might adopt a similar framework of using the power of digital computing to inspire, guide, and ground the humanistic inquiry they are already undertaking.

ON REPRODUCIBLE RESEARCH IN THE HUMANITIES

In the physical, social, and computer sciences, reproducibility refers to the ability to acquire the data used in an experiment, run the analyses described or furnished by the researchers, and get the same result. In the humanities, expert peer-review substitutes for reproducibility. The work in this book, in some ways, takes place at the intersection of these domains. While many chapters present close readings that must be assessed through the prism of hermeneutics, many of these analyses proceed from and are supported by the conclusions of computation. I have not encountered discussions of reproducibility in music scholarship, including recent and broad overviews such as David Beard and Kenneth Gloag's *Musicology: The Key Concepts* (2016) or Nicholas Cook and Mark Everist's *Rethinking Music* (1999). And I should stress my belief that humanistic endeavors supported by the expertise of the author or the utility of the reading are not in need of reproducibility. But a telling analogy from music composition illustrates the benefits of reproducible research where applicable in the humanities.

In 1981, the composer David Cope begin designing computer programs to aid his composition. He describes his impetus this way:

> My initial idea involved creating a computer program which would have a sense of my overall musical style and the ability to track the ideas of a current work such that at any given point I could request a next note, next measure, next ten measures, and so on. My hope was that this new music would not just be interesting but relevant to my style and to my current work.[1]

In the decades since, Cope has designed programs to automatically generate musical works in the styles of various composers, including himself. While the music has been convincing, interesting, and even beautiful, Cope has been criticized (e.g., Wiggins 2008, p. 111) for not making these programs available for scrutiny, presumably because the software contains a great deal of his intellectual property. Without access to his code, one cannot definitively refute the charge that he intervenes in creative work he ascribes to the computer. To be clear, there would be nothing wrong with editing the output of the computer if one's sole ambition

---

1. See http://artsites.ucsc.edu/faculty/cope/experiments.htm.

was to spark new compositional ideas. But the authority of the music—its claim to a certain kind of value—is that it is the result of unfettered computation.

This book is not a work of musical composition but one of musical analysis. Yet Nicholas Cook (1999, p. 255) points out a wealth of correspondences between musical composition, performance, and analysis. Each creates meaning by assembling, ordering, and/or interpreting musical material. In this sense, I view the "computational" part of computational music analysis as an analogue of Cope's original ambition, something with "a sense of [an] overall style." That part of the work is automatic, and it serves to contextualize my intuitions, find counterexamples, and establish significance. But the interested reader must know both how those results are derived and also where the computation ends and the interpretive act begins. Only by making the code available can an interested reader find those borders.

In addition to the code underlying the analysis, this book is accompanied by the publication of several corpuses containing roughly 200 transcriptions of rap verses in total. The concurrent publication of the corpuses and the book invites the reader to think of them as a one-to-one mapping. While this is certainly better than not publishing the data at all, Christine Borgman (2015) points out many pitfalls to this approach. Scholars have spent much longer perfecting the process of manuscript publishing than that of data publishing, and Borgman notes that

> for such a one-to-one mapping to be effective, it must be supported by a larger knowledge infrastructure that includes peer review of datasets, the availability of repositories, journal policies, and technologies to facilitate linking, and access to the necessary hardware, software, and other apparatus for reproducibility. (p. 49)

Of these different infrastructures, the one I am most concerned with is the peer review of the data. The corpuses have not undergone such a review, which would be difficult, tedious, and costly. I am very confident in nearly all aspects of the corpus, but the most uncertain aspect is the validity of onset quantization, wherein I decide which proportional rhythms best represent the rhythm as I hear it. This is an essentially interpretive act (see Chapters 2 and 8). A more rigorous verification of the corpus, perhaps in a format that accommodates different expert hearings of the rhythm, would be as burdensome as it would be welcome.

Even if one accepts the data, one might still be skeptical of the analytical process I put it through. I sympathize with the unnamed "respected scholar of pre-Islamic Arab history" who avowed to Tara Andrews (2015, p. 344) that "just about anything can be 'proven' by marshalling the correct evidence and ignoring what does not fit, and this 'scientific method' . . . [is] simply a process of legitimation of an argument that [makes] it difficult, rhetorically, to refute." It seems to me that reproducibility is the only protection against the very real danger the historian identifies. Incorrect or misleading empirical results abound in the published literature; these have generated the "reproducibility crisis" of recent years. Such results can be refuted by refuting the data or the method, but only if those are accessible.

The reproducible work in this book is of three varieties: (1) the source data of the transcriptions of rap verses themselves, (2) the analytical code performed on that data such as annotating accented syllables or segmenting verses into sequences of grooves, and (3) the visualizations that appear throughout. All these data, code, and visualizations are available at github.com/mohriner/flowBook, and can be revised and extended in the future by myself or others. The source data (namely, transcriptions) are stored in a spreadsheet structure, and I have strived to employ the concept of "tidy data" defined in Wickham (2014). In these transcriptions, each row is a syllable of flow, and each column is a feature of the syllable such as its metric position, accent specification, participation in rhyme, etc.

The analytical code is undertaken in the programming language R, a language that has emerged as the bedrock of modern data science. R is free, powerful, continually developing, and relatively easy to learn for newcomers to coding. The Scripts/DataScrubbingScripts directory in the github repository stores the functions used in preparing the data for analysis. Many of these functions require some pre-defined constant. For example, in Chapter 5, when characterizing the patterning of durations between rhymes, I decided that the upper limit of duration at which a listener can hear two rhyming words *as a rhyme* is eight beats. That variable is defined as upperLimit within the function in Scripts/AnalysisScripts/RhymeEntropyFunction.r. If one thinks the value ought to be different, or if subsequent research empirically supports a different value, the code can be changed. Additionally, some of the analyses involved in this book (e.g., the detection of grooves) take a very long time to compute, partly because they are computationally expensive but probably because the code is inefficient. Thus, some objects are stored as tab-separated data in the DerivedData directory of the repository.

Lastly, each chapter has two associated R scripts: a plotting script and an analysis script. The plotting script contains code to produce all the examples in the book. The analysis scripts, beginning with Chapter 3, contain code to reproduce each data-centered assertion in the book. These chunks of code are labeled by the footnote they address. Correspondingly, many footnotes in the text ask the reader to "see the analysis script." The repository also contains audio excerpts, corresponding to nearly all the examples in the book. Examples and their corresponding excerpts share numbering.

CONVENTIONS

Labeling Positions in the Measure and Durations between Them

Throughout this book, I necessarily refer to moments within rap verses. Some of these moments are very brief, even durationless, while others are longer. Music theory offers language for describing moments of music by identifying their measure number, and sometimes even which beat within the measure is of interest. My needs are more fine-grained and locutions like "the third sixteenth note of the fourth beat of measure one" are both too cumbersome and rely on language from Western music notation. The system I adopt for describing rhythm in this book is both precise and detached from that notation.

My labeling of rhythmic positions takes advantage of the fact that every track discussed in this book has a similar metric structure: there are four beats in every measure and emcees generally divide these beats into four parts, yielding sixteen relevant **metric positions.** (All boldfaced words in this book are defined in the Glossary.) I term the duration between these sixteen positions **units** of time in rap music. The common practice termed the **boom-bap** in rap discourse—placing bass drum events on beats one and three and snare events on beats two and four—makes finding these beats straightforward. For a clear example of some flow that places a syllable on each of the sixteen positions in the measure, one might consult the beginning of Eminem's verse on Jay-Z's "Renegade" (2001, hear Excerpt 0a 🔊).

To refer to specific positions, I number the sixteen positions from **0** to **15.** In work primarily on twentieth-century classical music (Mead 1987, Cohn 1992), these positions have been called "beat classes," but because "beat" already has two familiar meanings in rap music, I use "position" instead. When referenced in the text, these positions are always boldfaced. Conventionally, the first position in the measure, the "downbeat," would probably be numbered as **1** not **0.** But the computation of rhythm is much clearer if we start from 0. As we will see, the positions that start the measure (i.e., **0**), or bisect the measure (i.e., **0** and **8**), or divide it into four beats (i.e., **0, 4, 8,** and **12**), or even those that bisect the beats (i.e., **0, 2, 4, 6, 8, 10, 12,** and **14**) have a special status. Counting from 0 means that even numbers reflect this status.

Example A The positions within the measure (indicated as "|") and within the beat (numbered from 1) under *moduli* 16, 4, and 2.

```
                 |                                              |
beat:     1  •   •   •   2   •   •   •   3   •   •   •   4   •   •   • |1
mod 16:   0  1   2   3   4   5   6   7   8   9  10  11  12  13  14  15 |0
mod 4:    0  1   2   3   0   1   2   3   0   1   2   3   0   1   2   3 |0
mod 2:    0  1   0   1   0   1   0   1   0   1   0   1   0   1   0   1 |0
```

Often a position's relationship to the beat is especially important. Positions **1**, **5**, **9**, and **13** all share the feature of being just after a beat (i.e., positions **0**, **4**, **8**, and **12**). Each of these positions is equivalent under addition *modulo* 4. Readers are familiar with modular arithmetic even if they do not know it: for example, think of the time six hours after 9:00 a.m. The answer is 3:00 p.m. (not 15:00 p.m.), because $(9 + 6)_{mod 12} = 3$.[1] Often, we will think of rhythm in rap music as *mod* 16 because there are sixteen positions in the measure. But it can also be useful to think of those positions as the integers *mod* 4 because there are four positions in each beat. Thus, position $1_{mod 4}$ (without boldface) refers to all the positions that are just after the beat, that is, positions 1, 5, 9, and 13. It will also be useful to contrast those positions that are on a beat or bisect one with those that are just after or just before. Considering the positions *mod* 2, that is, evens vs. odds, accomplishes this: all the $0_{mod 2}$ positions are on the beat or bisectors, while the $1_{mod 2}$ positions are neither. Example A shows each position under these different *moduli*.

Sometimes the same set of positions will be important (e.g., by virtue of accent placement) from measure to measure. I will refer to those sets as **position class sets** and notate them with parentheses, for example, the position class set (0, 3, 5, 8). Other times, the durations between these positions (termed **duration segments** or **dsegs**) are important, and these are notated with square brackets. The dseg of the position set class (0, 3, 5, 8) is [323] with square brackets, found by subtracting each position from the one before. In Chapter 4 and afterward, I will introduce the concept of a groove class, a segment of 2-unit and 3-unit durations that sum to 16. Groove classes encompass rotational equivalence: [323323] is in the same groove class as [332332] and [233233]. To capture this rotational equivalence, I use angle brackets, that is, <332332>. Groove classes are notated such that the 3-durations are packed to the left.

Visualizing Rap Flows

As I will discuss in Chapter 1, I resist using Western music notation to transcribe rap verses because I feel most of its conventions are unnecessary for the task; the results are not only cluttered but also obscure important features. Example B ◐ here reprints part of Example 15b, showing a short excerpt of a transcription,

---

1. In my own thinking, "*modulo* 12" indicates a world of thinking in which the number 12 and everything higher do not exist. When one ascends past 11, one must return to 0. Negative numbers also do not exist in modular arithmetic, so when one descends past 0, one must return to 11.

Example B Salt 'N' Pepa, "Whatta Man" (1993, 0:36–055).

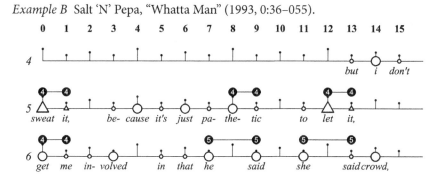

Example C Groove segmentation of "Go to Sleep" at two rates of effort.

Accent swaps per bar: 0

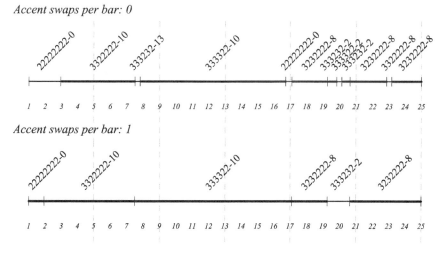

Accent swaps per bar: 1

from Salt 'N' Pepa's "Whatta Man" (1993). In the audio files on the github.com/mohriner/flowBook repository, one can find a recording of the excerpt. All the transcriptions and other verse visualizations in the book have paired recordings with corresponding labels.

The boldfaced numbers at the top of the transcription indicate the positions *mod* 16 within the measure; the italicized numbers on the left indicate the measure number within the verse, counting from 1. Each line of the transcription is a measure, laid out on what looks like a ruler. The tallest hashes of the ruler correspond to 0_{mod4} positions; the hashes for 2_{mod4} positions are slightly shorter and those for 1_{mod2} (i.e., 1_{mod4} and 3_{mod4}) positions are shorter still. Each syllable is indicated by a small or large circle; large circles indicate accents. These accents are annotated through the algorithm described in Section 3.1. In some cases, I manually override the results of the algorithm; this is indicated through triangles. The numbers within black circles above some syllables indicate rhyme classes within the verse (see Section 3.2). Black lines connect syllables within a multisyllabic rhyme (e.g., *picture* and *with ya*).

In later chapters, I will plot the groove segmentation of an entire verse on a single line. Example C reprints Example 6.7 and demonstrates this visualization. The diagonal numbers refer to groove classes and the number after the hyphen refers to the position in which the rotation of the groove class starts. The italicized numbers are measure numbers. The darker horizontal line indicates a groove that is maintained at the next lower level of accent swapping. (The meaning of accent swapping will become clearer in Chapter 4.)

Lastly, text that refers to file names or computer code is presented in a fixed width font.

ABOUT THE COMPANION WEBSITE

www.oup.com/us/flow

Oxford University Press has created a website to accompany *Flow: The Rhythmic Voice in Rap Music*. The site contains audio excerpts that correspond to each transcription in the book. The reader is also advised to visit https://github.com/mohriner/flowBook. That archive contains the datasets and metadata described in the book as well as R scripts for reproducing the book's examples and many of its data-driven conclusions.

PART I

Representing Flow

CHAPTER One

Flow in Rap Music: Sources of Confusion and a Strategy for Clarity

1.1 Defining the Scope of Flow

> "Now my rep grows like the nose of Pinocchio,
> Just because I mastered the art of braggadocio"
>
> —Akrobatic, "U Can't Fuck Wit It" (2004)

There are few topics as pervasive in rap lyrics as the boast. Entire verses might consist exclusively of displays of swagger, separating the emcee on the mic from his or her perceived rivals. Rap is indeed the "art of braggadocio," a word whose prevalence was on the decline for a century until beginning a new ascent in 1987 (Google Ngram Viewer 2017). Often emcees boast of what they have, rhyming necklace with Lexus. Or, they may boast of what they do, their romantic or violent conquests. But when emcees wants to boast of something more central to their identity, not of what they *have* or what they *do* but what they *are*, they will inevitably talk about their flow. Indeed, Akrobatic, in the very next line, chides his competitor's flow as "like molasses." And unlike boasts of material wealth, which gravitate toward the same luxury brands again and again, the language with which emcees describe their flow is incredibly diverse and evocative.

But when emcees boast of their flow, what are they boasting about? A definition that enables us to differentiate the flow of different tracks or artists continually eludes scholars, and not for lack of trying. Scholars differ mainly on the proper scope a definition of flow should address. What is flow a feature of? A line? A verse? An artist? An era? A region? What musical parameters are involved? Many authors define flow narrowly as something like "the rhythm of the words in a rap verse." Erik Pihel (1996, p. 253), in describing the evaluation of freestylin' emcees at a rap battle, cites three criteria: emcees are evaluated on "[their] flow (the *rhythm of the rap*), the clarity of his or her words, ... and the cleverness of his or her punch lines [emphasis added]."[1] Paul Edwards (2009, p. 63) expands the

---

1. "Freestylin'," as used by Pihel, refers to spontaneously improvised rapping, either in a live rap battle or as recorded in the studio. Interestingly, the definition of this term has changed substantially over the years. Big Daddy Kane relates to Paul Edwards (2009, p. 181) that in the 1970s and

definition somewhat, albeit using similar language, stating that "the flow of a hip-hop song is simply the rhythms and rhymes it contains." Yet such a narrow definition is not simple at all. Pihel and Edwards both call forth "rhythm," a word with very different connotations in the scholarly discourses surrounding speech, poetry, and music. In speech, "rhythm" refers to the number of unstressed syllables between stressed syllables or the duration between stressed syllables. For example, phoneticians describe languages like English as having "stress-timed" rhythm because the durations between stresses are often similar, while languages like French are said to be "syllable-timed" languages, in which the durations of syllables themselves are similar (Ladefoged & Johnson 2011, p. 249). In poetry, "rhythm" refers to the distinctions between the actual accentual pattern of a line and an idealized pattern of stressed and unstressed syllables called "the poetic meter" (e.g., iambic pentameter). In music, "rhythm" characterizes the variable durations of events in contrast to the normally equivalent durations of the beats of a musical meter.[2] Rapping exists in the spaces between speech, poetic recitation, and music. If flow is the "rhythm of rap," then it is some amalgamation of all of these. This is not a simple matter.[3]

Others offer a more expansive definition of flow. For Adam Bradley (2009, p. 6), flow "relies on tempo, timing, and the constitutive elements of linguistic prosody: accent, pitch, timbre, and intonation." Kyle Adams (2009, para. 6) casts a similarly wide net, defining flow as "all of the rhythmical and articulative features of an emcee's delivery of the lyrics." He later draws an analogy between flow in rap and other kinds of musical performances, writing that flow "may be thought of as the rap equivalent to what instrumentalists call 'technique,' a set of tools enabling the performer to most accurately convey his or her expressive meaning" (para. 7).[4] For Adams, this expansive definition is strategic, as it enables him to interpret the forms, narratives, and prosody of verses all under the banner of flow. Although such a sweeping definition is interpretively useful, it also hazards equating flow with "rapping in its totality."

Whether broad or narrow, these definitions complicate basic questions about flow. Consider the narrow view, that flow is "simply the rhythms" a rap verse contains, paired with the earlier issue of scope. Under this narrow view, is flow a property of an artist, a verse, a set of lines, or somehow all of the above? If flow

---

1980s the term meant a verse that was free of typical topics of verses (e.g., boasts, partying, etc.)—the style of the lyrics was free.

2. The different meanings of rhythm in speech, poetry, and music, especially in relation to the concept of "accent," is the subject of Section 3.1 in this book. An excellent overview of how these disciplines approach the concepts of meter and rhythm is given in Patel (2008, pp. 95–181). A more specialized overview of rhythm and meter in a poetic sense may be found in Attridge (1995).

3. In a further complication, some scholars coming from the standpoint of literature argue that the flow of rap music has nothing to do with rhythm of any sort. For Alexs Paté (2009, p. 115), flow is when "all of the images, rhymes, and ideas held within the body of a rap/poem . . . coalesce into a whole." For James Braxton Peterson (2016, p. 46), flow "concerns itself with aesthetics related to tone, articulation, word choice, and vocabulary."

4. In this music-instrumental analogy, "articulative features" refer to features like the hardness or crispness of consonances, the lengthening of vowels, and the like.

were the rhythm of the words in a verse, then it would seem that every flow, like the words of every verse, is unique. But hip-hop heads and critics alike speak of flow as though a single flow or kind of flow could encompass many verses.[5] Emcees are said to have their own distinctive flow, each different from another but applicable to many of an artist's verses. And emcees are often accused of stealing or "biting" the flow of another emcee, so "flow" must have some reality beyond the rhythm of the words in a particular verse. The broad view, that flow is made up of all the rhythmic, articulative, and prosodic features of a verse, is equally debilitating. Under this view, are there any aspects of rapping that do not pertain to flow? Is "the flow" any different from "the music"? In sum, how can one represent the flow of a verse such that one can compare it to that of another verse by the same artist, in the same subgenre, or originating in the same geographical or historical locale?

To address this challenge of representation, we must identify which parameters of rapping constitute flow and, even more importantly, we must create a consistent and formal-symbolic representation of those parameters. Identifying these constituents is the project of this chapter; formally representing them is the project of the next three. The better we understand the challenge in defining flow, the easier it will be to settle which parameters flow encompasses. Defining flow is difficult for two reasons beyond the initial problem of scope. First, the word itself permeates rap lyrics and scholarship. Many of its usages do not relate to music, at least not to musical rhythm. Second, scholars and emcees who talk about flow have conflated *prescriptions* for how to flow with *descriptions* of what emcees actually do. As I will show, these prescriptions are not borne out by expressive practice, and thus confuse flow's definition.

After sketching why defining flow in rap is so difficult, I will pursue a new strategy for construing flow in a way that enables meaningful comparisons later on. What makes this strategy new is that I am less concerned with what emcees or scholars say flow *is* and more concerned with what emcees *do* when they rap about it. Specifically, I will examine what musical features change when an emcee explicitly announces that their flow has changed, thereby piecing together flow's most central constituents. At the end of the chapter, I will present a model for how these constituents give rise to flow.

1.2 Sources of Confusion in Representing Flow

1.2.1 The Multiple Meanings of "Flow"

One looking to understand what is meant by "flow" in rap music would, rightly, start by looking at how emcees use the word. This is a large task. Some token of the word *flow*—for example, *flow, flows, flowin, flowin', flowing, flown, flow'n,*

---

5. Adam Krims (2000, p. 48) also notes this ambiguity of scope: for him, flow "marks several dimensions of rap music at once for artists and fans—history, geography, and genre all at once, not to mention the constant personal and commercial quest for uniqueness."

flo, flo', or *flowed*—occurs in roughly 20 percent of the 55,000 user-generated transcriptions of rap lyrics held in the Original Hip Hop Lyrics Archive as of 2016.[6] In comparison to the American National Corpus, a collection of texts that includes transcriptions of telephone conversations, government documents, magazines, fiction, and non-fiction, "flow" and related words occur 8 times more frequently in rap lyrics.[7] Within rap lyrics, it is the most common noun that relates topically to music, although some musical verbs like *play, rap, drop*, and *spit* are more common.[8] Yet many instances of the word have nothing to do with rhythm, musical or otherwise. Clichés like *go with the flow* or *cash flow* saturate rap lyrics and are irrelevant this discussion. *Flow* also appears in connection to liquidity, as in the following two lines:

> Blood can flow in ma veins, it feels the tightness
>
> —Werd n Deeko, "Let's Talk" (2007)

> To rebirth a nation, water distilled / so when she break water spill, catch the flow
>
> —Rapsody, "Believe Me" (2009)

Neither of these artists is talking about the rhythmic delivery of their words, but the connection of "flow" to liquidness permeates the musical connotations of the word. When emcees do use flow in connection to musical performance, they usually do so in a way that makes "flow" indistinguishable from "the ability of an emcee" when used as a noun and "to perform rap music" when used as a verb. As context makes clear, these abilities more often relate to an emcee's lyrical inventiveness, choice of subject matter, and the persona they present through their verses rather than any musical feature. When Jay-Z (2009) raps *my flow is like the Cuban Missile Crisis / Even my hand misses are priceless*, he's talking about the overall quality of the music he releases, not anything pertaining to its rhythm.[9]

6. The lyrics were collected from www.ohhla.com by a web crawler in November 2013. The webmaster for the site is Steve Juon (DJ Flash), who also contributes many of the transcriptions. The archive identifies transcription authors by email address in the fourth line of each transcription. While the ohhla.com lyrics are an invaluable resource, they are also imperfect. Spelling and orthography are constant issues. The archive includes more than 200 words starting with "bitc-"; in comparison, the American National Corpus (www.anc.org) has three. Transcribers differ on attention to phonetic details and also include many words that are not lyrics (e.g., details of musical form, names of emcees and transcribers, etc.). Still, the OHHLA constitutes perhaps the largest corpus of spoken **African American Vernacular English**. (All boldfaced terms in this text appear in the glossary at the back of the book.)

7. There are roughly 10,000 instances of forms of "flow" in 14 million words of rap lyrics, compared with 2,000 instances of forms of "flow" in the 22 million words of the American National Corpus.

8. Many instances of "flow" are verbs, so its usage as a noun is slightly less frequent.

9. In such comments, the meaning of "flow" in hip-hop lyrics approaches that of "flow" in the work of Mihaly Csikszentmihalyi (1991), as in a "flow state," the kind of experience in which one is wholly immersed in an activity. Writers on both improvised rapping (Weinstein 2008, p. 279) and DJing (Butler 2014, pp. 225–229) draw a connection between "flow" in rapping and Csikszentmihalyi's "flow as optimal experience." There are aspects of flowing (in rap) that are

Example 1.1 Classified, "Still Got It" (2009, 0:40–0:52). Boldfaced numbers refer to metric positions (i.e., "sixteenth-notes"), indexed from 0. Italicized numbers refer to measure numbers, indexed from 1. Circles represent syllables of rap delivery in my own interpretive quantization.

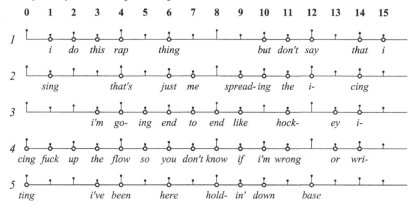

In other instances, it is clear that emcees refer to their actual verses in discussing their flow, rather than general descriptors of their identity or process. But even then, flow may not signify musical rhythm. When Hopsin (2009) raps *My label tryna make me switch the flow / Just because Oprah don't want me saying bitch no mo'*, he is referring to the opposite of what scholars like Adams and Bradley interpret as flow: the semantic meaning of the words themselves, not their rhythmic delivery.

Classified (2009) shows another way in which "flow" pertains not to the rhythmic delivery of the words but to their semantic meaning. Example 1.1 ◉ transcribes five lines from the middle of the first verse of "Still Got It." These lines celebrate ambiguity in word identification. The homophones *I sing* and both instances of *icing* all differ in meaning. Ambiguity is particularly pronounced at the end of the fourth line. The sound "right" could be an entire word (*right*) or the beginning of a longer word (*writing, writer*, etc.). The stylistic convention in rap music to align ends of sentences with ends of measures, as well as the cliché "wrong or right" encourages listeners, at first, to hear the sound "right" as the word "right," only to be mistaken by the following "ing" sound, clarifying the identity of the word. If this is a "fucked up flow," then flow has less to do with rhythm and more to do with the listener's ability to match sounds to words continually and with ease.

especially reminiscent of Csikszentmihalyi's writing, for example, the suspension of conscious interference and the changed quality of the passage of time. Yet as far as I can tell, the shared use of the word "flow" is independent and coincidental. And many aspects of Csikszentmihalyi's conception of flow are not apt in the context of rap music: the temporal frame of the verse (usually less than one minute) is shorter than what he describes and flowing to a beat emphasizes differentiation as much as repetition.

Since the Classified example is the first of many transcriptions to follow, I will now describe the somewhat novel methods I use to transcribe rap verses and reference various positions within the measure. These methods are also discussed in the "Conventions" section following the introduction to this book. And I will spend considerable time describing how the transcriptions are made because visualization is important. The music that analysts transcribe becomes the evidence in their arguments. If poorly designed, these displays of evidence can be corrupting, cherry-picking parameters to make an argument convincing or burying evidence that would lead to other conclusions. Thus, Edward Tufte (2006, p. 141) argues that "making a presentation is a moral act as well as an intellectual activity."

In the short history of musical analysis of rap music, scholars have employed a wide variety of transcription methods. Some transcribe rap through conventional Western music notation, developed over centuries in Europe.[10] Other transcribers avoid Western notation, either because they do not want to presume their audience can read it or because they find it lacking with respect to rap's particularities. But this can result in rhythmic vagueness in transcription. Edwards (2009, p. 68), for example, prints lyrics in four columns, one for each beat. Tabs indicate beat-beginning rests, but otherwise he does little to indicate rhythmic subtleties. This approach is adopted by Adams (2009) as well.

Still other scholars, borrowing from ethnomusicological writings on African music, employ a transcription method conceptually similar to James Koetting's "Time Unit Box System (TUBS)" (1970). In TUBS, the time of each measure is represented as a series of equally spaced boxes, some of which are filled in. Adam Krims (2000, p. 138) introduces this method to the analysis of rap music, conceptually if not visually, by creating a two-level grid (for beats and divisions of beats) and placing an x at each part of the grid occupied by a syllable. He then prints the text below, making it somewhat difficult to determine which syllable aligns with which x. Adams (2008, 2009) adapts Krims's method, creating boxes inscribing syllables so that he can divide the beat by divisions besides four if necessary.[11]

In writing about African music, Kofi Agawu (1995, pp. 185–187; 2014, pp. 48–53) advises scholars to employ conventional Western music notation in cases where it illuminates musical practice and to avoid it in cases where it does not. Namely, the design of Western notation is optimized to convey information about pitch, so long as there are twelve discrete notes per octave, and information about rhythm, so long as all the durations are ratios of 2:1 or 3:1. While the rhythmic features of Western notation might be useful in transcribing rap music, the resulting transcription has far more dots, lines, beams, and flags than would seem necessary to convey rhythmic structure. And while I do not address the pitch content of rap flows here, Western notation's approach to pitch would seem unhelpful as well.

---

10. See Robert Walser (1995, p. 201), Cheryl Keyes (1996, p. 230 and *passim*), Keyes (2002, p. 130), Justin Williams (2014, p. 28), Olivier Kautny (2015, p. 105), and Adams (2015b, p. 14 and *passim*). In his blog www.rapanalysis.com, maintained since 2011, Martin Conner has made several dozen transcriptions with conventional music notation.
11. Kautny (2015) adopts a similar approach, as well as conventional Western music notation.

To maximize the encoded information while minimizing the necessary ink, I, too, avoid Western music notation. Each line of the transcription in Example 1.1 ◐ is a measure of rap music, divided into four beats by the tallest hash marks topped by black dots. The shorter hash marks divide each of those beats into four **positions** within the beat.[12] In Western rhythmic notation, the duration between each hash mark would be a sixteenth note, because there are 16 of them in the measure. I number these divisions **0** through **15** and I will refer them by number, always in boldface to distinguish them from other uses of integers. Thus, the word *thing* in the first measure of Example 1.1 ◐ falls on position **6**. While numbering from zero may be initially confusing, I hope the reader quickly finds this intuitive. There are four divisions of each beat, and, numbering from zero, the positions that are "on the beat" are those divisible by four, namely, **0**, **4**, **8**, and **12**. In another sense that I will discuss later, all the positions that are "on the beat" or "between the beat" are metrically stronger than those just after or just before the beat. These stronger positions are all the even integers.

When I need to refer to an entire beat, such as *Yeah, I do this* on the first beat of the first measure in Example 1.1 ◐, I will number the beats 1 through 4 and refer to them as, say, beat 1. When I need to refer to a particular position relative to the beat, such as the position just before the beat, I will number those positions 0_{mod4} through 3_{mod4}. The *mod* 4 refers to modular arithmetic and reflects the idea that there are only 4 divisions of the beat. If one starts counting at zero and returns to zero when a beat is reached, one cannot count higher than three. Thus, 0_{mod4} includes positions **0**, **4**, **8**, and **12**. Likewise, 3_{mod4} includes positions **3**, **7**, **11**, and **15**. Referring to all the positions that share a relationship to the beat (e.g., on the beat, just after it, etc.) will enable important observations about rhythmic practice. In the Classified example, we can count how many times each of these *mod* 4 positions is voiced and get a sense of the character of meter in the example. Classified voices the even positions, 0_{mod4} and 2_{mod4}, 11 and 12 times, respectively; he voices the odd positions, 1_{mod4} and 3_{mod4}, 9 and 8 times, respectively. This corresponds to the notion of metric strength on even-numbered positions. We can also go one step further, describing positions as 0_{mod2} for the even positions (voiced 23 times) and 1_{mod2} for the odd positions (voiced 17 times), refining the connection between voice and meter.

Returning to the meaning of flow, Hopsin and Classified are exceptions, to be sure. Many instances of *flow* in rap lyrics speak to what might be called "the purely musical," in contrast to aspects of rap music that relate to the lexical meaning of the words themselves. When Earl Sweatshirt raps that *I sit in thought 'til the flow is right / then throw some D on all available open mics*, he implies that the words are already written (or at least formulated, if not actually written down on paper). Determining the way in which he will perform them—their musical features, rhythmic or otherwise—is a final consideration to address before sharing

---

12. All boldfaced terms appear in the glossary.

a verse with the public. Similarly, Kinetik distinguishes the content of his raps and their sound:

> I let the track play and after 30 minutes
> I had my raps straight, the hook and verse were finished
> Then I recited them to make sure the flow was tight
>
> —"London Mornings" (2013)

Cale Sampson makes the same point from another angle, rapping:

> If there's no content, then it's not impressive.
> To me, it's less about the flow and more about the message.
>
> —"The Big Picture" (2013)

1.2.2 An Inapt, Prescriptive "Law of Flow"

"Flow" is difficult to define because emcees use the word in so many ways. But the biggest difficulty in conceptualizing flow relates to an issue with which music theory has struggled for decades if not centuries: the difference between prescriptive theories and descriptive theories of music. A prescriptive theory of music tells composers and artists how to create "good" music in the opinion of the theorist. A descriptive theory of music defines the common practices exemplified in existing music. Most writers on flow opt for prescriptive theories, detailing what I call, somewhat facetiously, "the law of flow." This prescriptive view is favored by the growing number of rap pedagogues and creators of instructional videos. Edwards's book *How to Rap* states a version of the law:

> Rap is not just poetry spoken aloud, because unlike the rhythm of a poem, a song's flow *has to be in time with the music*—the rhythm of the lyrics must fit with the basic rhythm of the music [emphasis added]. (2009, p. 63)

The esteemed Chuck D of Public Enemy confirms the law of flow in an interview with Samy Alim:

> C: Poetry makes the beat come to it, and rap is pretty much subservient to the beat.
> A: What do you mean by that?
> C: Well, you know, if you have a beat, you *have to pretty much follow the beat* in some kind of way [emphasis added]. (2006, p. 96)

The law of flow is also affirmed in how emcees describe their own flows as something controlled, smooth, and continuous. Consider the following four ways by which emcees have described their flow:

> Yeah I know, accurate flow, I'm blessed with the gift.
>
> —Wiley, "Welcome to Zion" (2012)

I'm on time with the flow, not a minute nor second late.

—Ludacris, "Southern Gangsta" (2008)

When I spill, I regulate a flow like chicks on birth control pills.

—Bahamadia, "3 Tha Hard Way" (1996)

I shine like gold ingot, control the flow like a spigot, come swig it.

—Virtuoso, "Crematorium" (2004)

The last two descriptions, by Bahamadia and Virtuoso, place particular emphasis on continuity. By relating flow to periodic sequences of events, like water flowing from a spigot at a constant rate or regulated menstrual cycles, flow for these artists is a continuous stream of syllables, one after another after another. Alim himself echoes this conception of flow when he defines the verb *to flow* as

> to have a smooth current of rap lyrics. If a person [in a rap battle] messes up their rap lyrics while sayin' them, then they ain't flowin. (2006, p. 98)

Here, "messes up" presumably means, for example, tripping over a consonant and thus delaying the next syllable, undermining the continuity.

Furthermore, the frequent proximity of lyrics about flow and lyrics about intoxication affirms the law of flow. Rapping, at the most basic level, requires extremely precise control of the muscles and tissues involved in speech production, and those at greatest risk for "messing up" their lyric delivery are those with impaired motor function. Thus, on Krayzie Bone's "Ride If Ya Like" (2001), LaReece complains that *them drunk ass n*ggaz they always seem to fuck up the flow* while Ludacris, who boasted of his accuracy, concedes that it can be impeded:

> And you know how far one drink could go, start slurrin' my speech slowin' up the flow.

—Ludacris, "One More Drink" (2008)

Like any other law, violating the supposed law of flow has consequences. Mighty Casey spells these out when he compares flowing to a beat to musical ensemble performance:

> Like if you're a trumpet player and you're off [the] beat, you're not a good trumpet player. If your melodies and your rhythms don't sound good and you're a musician, you're not a good musician. (Edwards 2009, p. 64)

Notice how much Mighty Casey stakes on being "on-beat": if not on-beat, not only is the rhythm wrong and poor sounding, but even the quality of the melody is affected. His analogy, however, gives a hint as to how complicated enforcing the law of flow might be. "If you're a trumpet player and you're off [the] beat," you might be a *very* good trumpet player. As scholars have documented over the last couple of decades, live performance is replete with very small intervals of time that anticipate or delay the beat. Placing events exactly on the beat is referred to as playing

Example 1.2 Ice-T, "I Ain't New Ta This" (1993, 1:14–1:20).

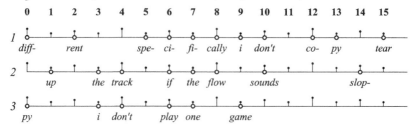

"in the pocket" of the beat.[13] A trumpet player, perhaps one in a jazz combo, might be slightly ahead of the beat, while other musicians (e.g., the drummer) might be behind. Performers speak of these relationships to the beat as "different feels" or "different grooves."[14] Scholars call this phenomenon **microtiming**, and they generally agree that it is what gives an artist his or her rhythmic particularity.[15] I will explore microtiming in the flow of Talib Kweli in Chapter 8. For now, suffice it to say that an emcee's flow can be poor, but not solely because syllables are not well aligned with the beat.

The issues involved in non-alignment of syllables and the beat can be much larger than the tiny intervals of microtiming (or inebriation). Ice-T relates the alignment of syllables to his own artistic integrity as a competent and original emcee:

> Different, specifically I don't copy,
> Tear up the track if the flow sounds sloppy.
>
> —Ice-T, "I Ain't New Ta This" (1993)

Ice-T's delivery of these lines (see Example 1.2 🔊) is a clever example of ruining a flow in order to clarify what it was in the first place. In the transcription, I have obscured the exact placement of each syllable by **quantizing** syllable onsets to the 16 positions as I hear them—this was the case in the Classified transcription as well, and will be the case in all the transcriptions until Chapter 8. Quantizing is an interpretive act, one any transcriber of music routinely undertakes.

---

13. Bradley (2009, p. 6) uses the "in the pocket" metaphor in service to his own articulation of the "law of flow," writing that "emcees boast about staying in the pocket of the beat, finding the place where their voices are rhythmically in sync with the drums." But Bradley is keenly aware of how often emcees intentionally stray from the beat to create "moments of calculated rhythmic surprise."

14. My own use of the word "groove" does not depend on microtiming; this is indeed a major source of confusion as to what "groove" is. See Chapter 4 for a broad discussion.

15. There is a large and growing literature on the relationship between microtiming and the perception of groove. For research relevant to microtiming in the popular music of the African diaspora, though not specifically rap music, see Alén (1995), Ashley (2014), Butterfield (2010b), Chor (2010), Davies et al. (2013), Iyer (2002), and Kilchenmann & Senn (2011). I have also written an overview of expressive timing with less of an emphasis on groove (Ohriner 2018).

Example 1.3 "I Ain't New Ta This," recomposed to align *copy* and *sloppy*.

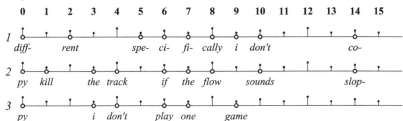

In my hearing, none of the syllables are especially "offbeat" in the way that Mighty Casey means; those kinds of errors are not what makes *sloppy* sloppy. The first syllable of *sloppy* is "off-beat" in the sense that it falls on position **14**, not a member of the group of 0_{mod4} positions. Indeed, both the syllables of *tear up* are on the especially weak positions of **15** and **1**. If avoiding these weak metric positions were critical, Ice-T could easily shift the word one position forward to **0** and **2**. One can imagine how this would sound by saying *tear up the track* with the same rhythm as *track if the flow*. But this adjustment is much too square: syllables do not need to be on the beat or even near it.

What, then, is sloppy about *sloppy*? Or, put another way, how is *sloppy* a violation of the law of flow? Partly, it is the performance of the "s" sound, which is considerably longer than the "s" at the beginning of *sounds*. But the larger issue, in my view, is that while *sloppy* rhymes with *copy*, these two words fall on different positions. The first syllable of *copy* is on position **12**, while the first syllable of *sloppy* is on **14**. Because **12** is "on the beat," it carries its own sense of weight, and therefore the placement of *copy* with respect to the beat conforms with the accentual pattern of the word in everyday speech (as "cópy"). *Sloppy*, which places the second (not the first) syllable on the beat, resists that pattern. From this example, it seems that following the law of flow does not mean "place syllables exactly on the beat." Rather, a more apt description of Ice-T's flow would translate as "place similarly accented or rhyming syllables at similar metric positions."

In the "I Ain't New Ta This" example, it is hard to tell whether *sloppy* errs because the accented syllable is off the beat or because it is not on the same position as *copy*. The confusion is that *copy* itself falls on a beat. We might clarify the situation by shifting *copy* to where *sloppy* falls and, to make room, removing a syllable, as in Example 1.3. Try rapping this a few times to yourself.[16] Is the flow still sloppy? I am somewhat unsettled by the implied accentuation of *-py* over *co-* or *slop-*, but

---

16. A reviewer of an earlier version of this chapter objected to the idea that a reader could simply "rap this passage to themselves," feeling such a directive devalued the effort of emcees. To be clear, I think most people, freed from their inhibitions, can learn to recite a few lines of rap music in time with a beat, but *very few* people can write dozens of rap verses, create a stage persona, perfect a voice, and perform those verses convincingly in front of audiences from memory. As a music theorist, I am very familiar with hacking through an impoverished version of a classical piece to understand something of its melody or harmonies; there is no risk anyone would confuse me for a concert pianist.

I think this thought experiment suggests that the shared alignment of rhyming syllables to particular positions is more important than the alignment of syllables to beats.

Another example, one that should put to rest the idea that flowing "to a beat" requires placing syllables on or near beats, comes from Eminem, the subject of Chapter 6. Example 1.4 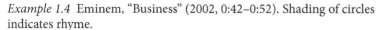 transcribes the first four measures of the first verse of "Business" (2002).

In this transcription, I have shaded each syllable one of three shades. The grey dots all have the vowel heard in "oat"; the black dots have the vowel heard in "hop." The white dots, primarily, have the vowel in "in," though some, like *the* and *but* are the unstressed schwa vowel. The consistency of rhythm in these lines is immediately apparent: the same positions are either occupied or vacant from line to line. But another kind of consistency emerges when you rap the lines yourself. Once you have practiced performing the verse, rap it aloud keeping your thumb on your chin. Phoneticians describe the vowel in "oat" (represented by black dots) as "back" and "open" (Ladefoged & Johnson 2011, pp. 88–89), meaning that your jaw is likely to drop on those syllables.

A patterning emerges in the movement of the jaw, and the regularity of this patterning—which is not the same as the meter of the music!—demonstrates an independence of rap delivery and beats that is clearly outside the jurisdiction of "the law of flow." To understand why, let us return to the different conceptions of rhythm and meter in scholarship directed at music and poetry. Recall that meter in poetry is a pattern of accentuation and rhythm in poetry is the discrepancy between the stress pattern of the words themselves and the pattern of the prevailing meter. In rap music, the meter is the strong/weak relationships of the four beats of each line: beat 1 (position 0) is very strong, beat 3 (8) is somewhat strong, and beats two (4) and four (12) are weak (Lerdahl & Jackendoff 1983). For Adam Bradley and other scholars coming to rap music from the perspective of lyric poetry, these two formulations of meter are easy to conflate. The

Example 1.4 Eminem, "Business" (2002, 0:42–0:52). Shading of circles indicates rhyme.

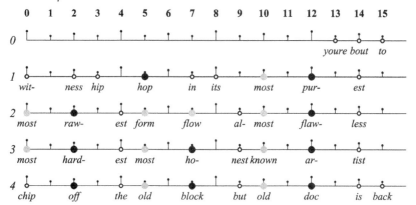

innovation of rap music, in Bradley's view, lies in how rap music sounds the poetic meter through the beat: "Rap makes audible a rhythmic relationship that is only theoretical in conventional verse" (2009, p. 8). Because of this relationship of the words and the meter-made-audible, rap music can "achieve an organic unity of rhythm that is more powerful than most literary verses can likely achieve" (p. 7). At the same time, the beat constrains the creativity of the emcee because "the rhythms of rap are governed by something outside of the emcee's own literary conceptions" (p. 12).

In its way, Bradley's dual conception of rhythm-of-lyrics and meter-of-music is a modification of the law of flow. Emcees do not have to align syllables to the beat, but we are to understand the discrepancies between syllables and beats as a roughness that gives texture to the flow of rap, just as (poetic) rhythm gives texture to (poetic) meter. But when we rap Eminem's verse while attending to the changing position of the jaw, I do not believe we are marking discrepancies between syllables and beats, but rather between the sounds of the words and a pattern of durations, albeit a pattern that differs from the (musical) meter. This is the pattern of durations between all those back, open vowels. These durations have all the hallmarks of poetic (and not musical) meter. Starting with *pur-* in *most purest*, every third syllable (almost) shares the same back, open vowel. Understanding these vowels as stressed, and borrowing the terminology of poetic meter, the lines could be viewed as an amphibrachic trimeter, da-DA-da—da-DA-da—da-DA-da. From the perspective of poetic rhythm, the rhythm of these lines—what makes the flow *almost flawless*—is the discord between the amphribrachic trimeter and Eminem's word choices. For example, it is difficult to read the first line in the meter as *witNESS hip hop IN its most PURest*. The other two lines scan more easily as *most RAWest most HONest known ARTist* and *chip OFF the old BLOCK but old DOC is*. Furthermore, the word *form*, as the noun of the long prepositional phrase *in its most purest, most rawest form*, wants more duration when read aloud than Eminem accords it. The concept of poetic rhythm is useful in identifying these discrepancies, but they are discrepancies in relation to the patterning Eminem presents, not in relation to "the beat."

Again, the poetic meter that emerges from the lyrics is at considerable odds with the musical meter. While the repeated back, open vowels occur in the same place from measure to measure, they are in no simple relationship with the beats of each measure. Starting with *purest*, they are separated by a cycle of 6, 5, and 5 beat divisions; we can represent this cycle as a **durational segment** (or **dseg**) of [655]. (I will refer to all the **rhyme instances** of the rhyme as the **rhyme class** of these lines.) Some instances of the rhyme in these lines (e.g., *purest, flawless, artist, Doc is*) are on the beat, at position **12**. Others (e.g., *rawest, hardest, off the*) are off the beat, at **2** or **7**. But in my hearing, they all equally feel like instances of stress caused by the dropping of the jaw to make the vowel. What is *almost flawless* about this flow, in my view, is not its relation to the four beats of the measure, but rather its own fierce integrity and insistence on durational repetition. This integrity undoubtedly constrains where Eminem can place syllables and what sounds those syllables must have. But the constraint is not the musical meter, something "outside the literary conception" of the emcee, but rather *a pattern of durations and vowels Eminem himself created*. While we can describe the durational pattern of his flow in reference to the beat as 6, 5, and 5 divisions, no law of flow demanding subservience to the beat constrains an emcee like Eminem.

1.3 A Source of Clarity: Flipping the Flow

I hope by now the meaning of flow—the word, the idea the word signifies, and the purpose of defining it—is no longer obvious. Which musical parameters constitute flow? How can they be represented? In my own view, a large part of the problem has been the attempt to describe a musical concept in writing or conversation. In trying to determine what musical parameters constitute flow, I will in this section prefer to attend to emcees' actions rather than their words. Stated simply, what do emcees *do musically* when they are flowing?

One could answer this question by observing the entirety of rap music, but I would like to constrain the search. There is an inherent contradiction in the ways emcees describe flow. Emcees flow over **instrumental streams** (usually called "the beat") that, within verses, change very little.[17] Samples and drum patterns repeat endlessly. To flow over the instrumental streams accurately and continuously implies matching this stasis. But emcees also clearly value originality and inventiveness. These two values—fidelity and invention—must be constantly rebalanced to maintain the integrity of the flow while avoiding boredom. The necessity for change gives rise to the concept of "flipping the flow," where the flow—whatever that is—is altered midverse. In most cases, emcees flip the flow without comment, but occasionally they call attention *in the lyrics themselves* to the change in flow. In those cases, we can examine what changes musically when the flow flips, in order to determine which musical parameters constitute flow. Identifying these parameters, in turn, clarifies how we ought to represent rap music in transcriptions in order to enable comparisons between verses and artists. I will focus on four such parameters in this section: syllable duration, position of rhyme, the durations that separate rhymes, and the durations that separate accented syllables.

1.3.1 Flipping Syllable Duration

Very often, "flipping the flow" means drastically changing the number of syllables in each line. In the eyes of many hip-hop heads, The Notorious B.I.G. pioneered the ability to switch from a fast flow to a slow flow and back again (Kelley 2010). Afterward, if you want to compliment an emcee on his flow, you might start with

---

17. Here, I use the term "instrumental stream" in place of what is usually called "the beat." I wish to distinguish between "beat" in the sense of an abstract time point within the meter of the music from "beat" in the sense of the instrumental sounds of a rap verse, minus the rapping.

the range of tempos at which he or she can perform. Thus, Fredro Starr says of Jay-Z that he's "a master of the flow—he can flow fast, he can flow slow" (Edwards 2009, p. 112). But The Notorious B.I.G. was known for being able to rap fast or slow *on different verses*, not necessarily on the same verse. Later, emcees will boast of their ability to flip the flow by changing the density of syllables in their lines abruptly, and even calling attention to the change, as Big Bói does in his verse from Outkast's "Flip Flop Rock" (2003, see Example 1.5 ◉). Here, "flipping the flow" from slow to quick involves inserting syllables in metric positions that were previously silent. With the newly inserted syllables, the duration between syllables is lessened. I will call these durations **inter-syllable intervals**, or ISIs. While this term is a bit of a mouthful, it will be useful later on in distinguishing the durations between syllables from those between rhyming syllables or accented syllables.

In "Flip Flop Rock," the inserted syllables still fit in the grid of 16 positions per measure. We can call this grid a metric space whose **cardinality** is 16. I will signify this metric space with the notation C_{16}. (Here, in music notation, "C" represents a whole note.) All the examples we have seen so far, and almost all those to come, use the C_{16} metric space. When the flow flipped from slow to fast in "Flip Flop Rock," the cardinality of the metric space was preserved and previously empty positions were filled in. Flipping the flow can also mean changing the cardinality of the metric space. In Example 1.6 ◉, a couplet from A$AP Rocky's "Purple Swag: Chapter 2" (2011), the cardinality switches from a C_{24} space (i.e., triplet sixteenth notes) to a C_{32} space (i.e., thirty-second notes). In order to determine the cardinality of the metric space, one needs to be clear about which duration is the **tactus** (the level of the metric grid to which a listener primarily entrains and is likely to tap along). In "Purple Swag: Chapter 2," some listeners might argue that the tactus is twice as fast as I have shown in Example 1.6 ◉—that the tempo of

Example 1.5 OutKast featuring Jay-Z and Killer Mike, "Flip Flop Rock" (2003, 1:42–2:02).

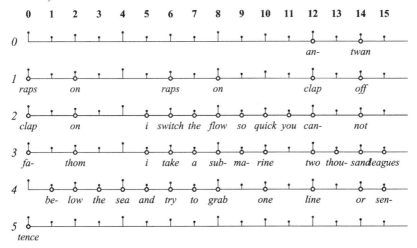

Example 1.6 A$AP Rocky featuring ASAP Nast and Spaceghost Purrp, "Purple Swag: Chapter 2" (2011, 0:54–1:03).

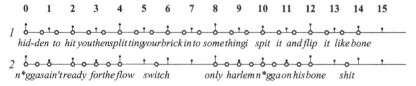

Example 1.7 Eminem, "Take from Me" (2011, 2:03–2:16).

the song is 104 beats per minute rather than 57. The faster tactus would be more common in a rap track, but as a rule of thumb, I understand the tactus as the tempo that orients snare hits to positions 4 and 12 while orienting bass drum hits to positions 0 and 8. This drum pattern is so common in rap music it gets its own name: the **boom-bap**.[18] In this case, the slower rate maintains the boom-bap structure. The effect of switching from slow to fast remains, although A$AP Rocky was flowing pretty quickly to begin with.

Another example of increasing syllable rate to flip the flow comes from Eminem's "Take from Me" (Example 1.7 ●). Syllable durations are highly patterned throughout most of the excerpt: Eminem places a syllable on all positions except 1, 3, and 11, and occasionally adds a syllable in between positions (e.g., *give a fuck, just to give*, etc.). Where the delivery rate changes is in the third measure, at the text *people who don't even appreciate flows*. Here, Eminem packs in ten syllables in just over a second. As we will see later, this is some of the fastest rapping possible. By including this virtuosic flourish in an argument against music piracy, Eminem argues for the value of the ability to change speeds, and we, in turn, should attend to such changes in a construal of flow.

---

18. Boom-bap also refers to styles of hip-hop in which the snare and bass are especially prominent in the mix, such as KRS-One's *The Return of the Boom Bap* (1993).

Example 1.8 Lil' Wayne featuring Nikki, "Weezy Baby" (2005, 0:37–0:50).

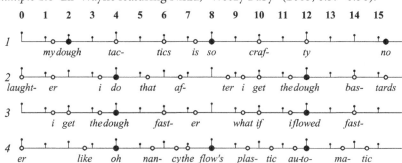

1.3.2 *Flipping Rhyme Duration*

Sometimes when emcees claim to flow "faster," they refer not to the rate of syllables but to the rate of rhymes. Lil' Wayne raps about flowing faster in Example 1.8 🌑. Here, I have used solid dots rather than open ones to show the repetition of the vowel heard in *dough, so, no*, etc. Note that in most cases, this vowel is followed by some variation on *-tastic* (e.g., *crafty, laughter, bastards, faster, plastic, -matic*, etc.). When he "flows faster" in the last line, the flow does indeed have more syllables than other lines, but not by much: from *like* to *I'm*, he places 13 syllables in the span of around three beats, compared to 11 syllables in three beats in the previous line. Rather than just the rate of syllables, I think he is referring to the rate of *the repetition of the rhyming vowel*. In the first line, roughly a beat and a half separate these vowels. In the second, if one stretches to hear *do* as rhyming with *dough*, two beats separate reiterated vowels. In the last line, the durations between *oh, flow's*, and *to-* reduce to just one beat. In order to squeeze in more instances of the vowel, he limits the number of syllables not related to the rhyme of *dough tactics* with each successive line. Lil' Wayne is flowing faster, but only if flow means "the rate of rhyme" and not just "the rate of syllables." Another constituent of flow, then, is the duration not only between syllable onsets but also between rhyming words. I call these durations **inter-rhyme intervals** or **IRIs**.

1.3.3 *Flipping Position of Rhyme*

Most rap verses settle into a pattern of IRIs, usually four beats, and, as a consequence, a consistent position for those rhymes (usually near position **12**, i.e., beat 4). Shifting either the beat of rhymes or the IRIs can change the flow. For example, Tung Twista's "Say What?" (1992) strives for the consistency that is a hallmark of early rap. The sixteen lines of the verse are organized into rhyming quatrains that place rhyming syllables on positions **6** and **10** (e.g., *ping pong, swing wrong, ding dong*, and *flow . . . song*). Example 1.9 🌑 transcribes the last four lines. Twista's crew claims position **8** as their own with their reiteration of *what?* in each line.

Example 1.9 Twista, "Say What?" (1992, 1:16–1:21).

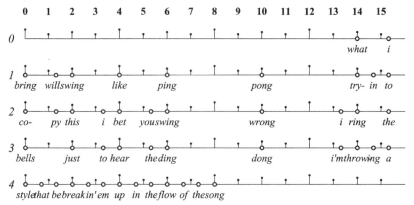

Example 1.10 Fat Joe featuring The Game, "Breathe and Stop" (2006, 2:18–2:30).

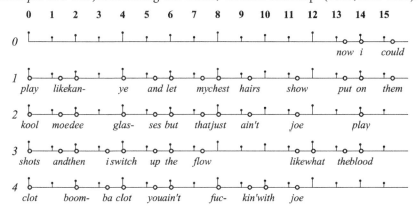

The final line of the verse, *I'm throwin a style that be breakin' 'em up in the flow of the song*, breaks up the flow in two different ways. First, as in the "Flip Flop Rock" and "Purple Swag" examples, "breakin' up" the flow means changing the metric space from C_{16} to C_{24}. Second, Twista interferes with the reiterated *what* by placing *song* on **8**, thereby anticipating the expected rhyme of **10**. The metric position of rhymes, **6** and **10** for much of the verse, ought to be a constituent of a model of flow.

The flipped flow in "Say What?" seems to arrest the verse entirely, but often flipping the flow means only momentarily changing the metric position of the rhyme. Example 1.10 ◐ transcribes a quatrain from Fat Joe's "Breathe and Stop" (2006). Here, *switch up the flow* parallels *chest hairs show* and *just ain't Joe*, but flips the flow by falling a beat earlier. Yet the flow is regained by beginning *fuckin' wit Joe* once again on position **8**.

So far we have seen the flow flipped by shifting one rhyme instance of a series of rhymes to an unexpected beat. The flow can also flip by revising the predominant

Example 1.11a Flobots, "Airplane Mode" (2010, 3:14–3:40).

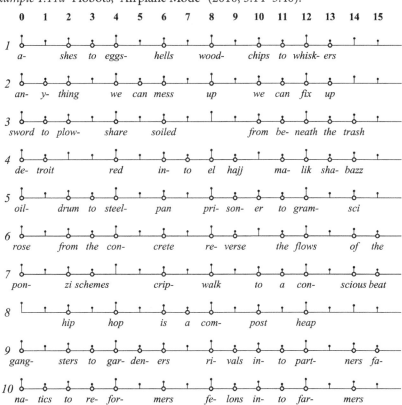

IRI from four beats to something else—either a pattern of different intervals or a series of rhymes with no consistent IRIs between them. The Flobots, in their 2010 track "Airplane Mode," call out a change in flow while changing durations between rhymes; the first ten lines of the third verse are transcribed in Example 1.11a ◐. The schematic outline below the transcription (Example 1.11b ◐) shows the IRIs of the verse. The first four lines are rhyming couplets with rhymes on beat four. The fifth line introduces an internal rhyme by rhyming *concrete* on beat two with *Gramsci* heard at the end of the previous measure. But beginning with *concrete*, as the flow is "reversed," the durations between the rhyming words *concrete, ponzi, conscious,* and *compost* are all three beats. A continuous three-beat IRI pattern is relatively unusual in rap music because of the way such a pattern drifts apart from the four-beat measure, losing one beat per measure.[19] The Flobots cycle through enough three-beat rhymes to again "catch up" with the meter with *gardeners* in

---

19. In the literature on meter in nineteenth-century European music, Harald Krebs (1999, p. 31) calls this a "grouping dissonance," because the grouping of beats in the meter (presumably four) is "dissonant" against the grouping of beats on the surface (in this case, three).

Example 1.11b Flobots, "Airplane Mode," inter-rhyme intervals (IRIs).

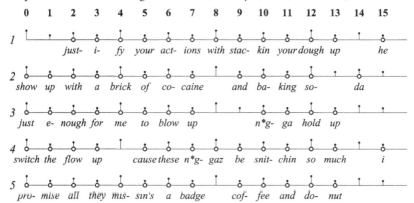

Example 1.12a T.I. featuring André 3000, "Sorry" (2012, 2:11–2:26).

m. 8 (i.e., measure 8). From that point onward, two-beat and four-beat IRIs predominate for the remainder of the verse.

Example 1.12a 🌑 shows another instance of "flipping the flow" coinciding with a change in IRIs, from T.I.'s "Sorry" (2012). Again, a schematic view below

Example 1.13a KRS-One, "Don't Get So High" (2008, 1:05–1:17).

Example 1.13b KRS-One, "Don't Get So High," inter-rhyme intervals (IRIs).

(Example 1.12b 🌀) measures IRIs in the transcription. The repeated IRI of four beats across *dough up, soda, hold up, so much*, and *donut* misrepresents the instability of duration wrought by *blow up* and *flow up*, which suggest a new IRI pattern of 1.5 beats. This would be highly unusual and cannot be maintained for long.[20]

1.3.4 Flipping the Consistency of Inter-Rhyme Intervals

In "Airplane Mode" and "Sorry," one could argue that to "flip the flow" means "switch to a different IRI pattern," even if that pattern informs only a small portion of the verse. In other cases, such patterning never emerges. Example 1.13a 🌀 transcribes part of KRS-One's "Don't Get So High" (2008). In most of the previous 14 bars that are not transcribed, rhymes fall on position **12**, or on **4** and **12** if there are two rhyming syllables in one measure, as is the default in rap music. Two measures before the transcription starts, KRS-One announces that he is *flippin' the sound, flippin' the flow*. In these measures identified as a flipped flow, the consistency of the four-beat IRI pattern disintegrates without another durational pattern taking its place. Durations of two and three beats roughly alternate, but many of these are a quarter-beat unit shorter or longer than the integer-length IRIs I have identified (Example 1.13b 🌀).

---

20. For an example of a persistent beat-and-a-half duration segment between rhymes, see the beginning of the first verse of Talib Kweli featuring Dion, "More or Less" (*Eardrum* 2007, Excerpt 1A).

Example 1.14 KRS-One, "Don't Get So High," recomposed to maintain a consistent three-beat duration between rhymes.

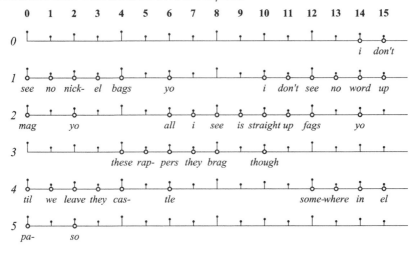

In my view, KRS-One flips the flow in two distinct ways in these lines. First, he approximates a series of three-beat IRIs, which already distinguishes the verse from rap's conventions. Second, he declines to maintain this pattern, as the Flobots or T.I. might have. Example 1.14 shows a slight recomposition on my part that normalizes KRS-One's delivery—now there are three beats between syllables rhyming with *bags yo*. The normalization loses some shades of meaning, but I do not believe these are critical. Because KRS-One is clearly capable of stringing together a great many lines with the same number of syllables, I believe he could have remained consistent here as well, along the lines I have, had he wished to do so. For me, the variability he introduces by displacing the arrival of rhymes demonstrates that flow pertains to not only the durations between rhyming words, but also the extent of variation in those durations. And that variation takes place on two levels: IRIs can change in their quantity of beats (e.g., 2 or 3) and their "roundness" of beats, that is, how close each IRI is to a whole number of beats.[21] In comparing the flow of different verses, we should aim to represent both aspects of IRI consistency.

Thus far, I have demonstrated a link between what emcees conceive of as flow and four rhythmic and metric features: metric space cardinality, position of rhyme, IRIs, and the variability of IRIs. A final example, by the emcee Tech N9ne, densely demonstrates several other aspects of flow that arise in a "flipped flow." The excerpt comes near the end of N9ne's feature on Krizz Kaliko's "Strange" (2012), and the flipping is called out in the lyrics in the middle of m. 13, inviting us to contrast mm. 9–12 with mm. 13–14 (Example 1.15). Unlike previous examples, here the "flipped

21. In later chapters, I will draw on the concept of entropy for examining the variability of durations between rhymes.

Example 1.15 Krizz Kaliko featuring Tech N9ne, "Strange" (2012, 4:08–4:31), mm. 9–14.

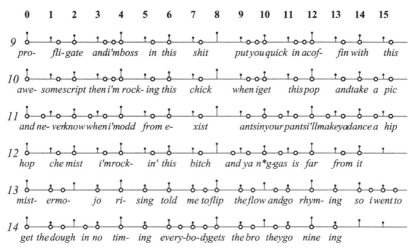

flow" means a switch in rhyme classes all together, not just altering durations between rhymes. The complexity of the rhyme classes themselves makes it difficult to even say what these durations are. The rhyme class of mm. 9–12 merges a pair of syllables (as in *obli-, bossin', coffin, awesome,* etc.) with a near rhyme for *it* (as in *-gate, this, with, script,* etc.). But this three-syllable rhyme does not simply repeat. If we represent the paired syllables as "A" and the *it*-rhymes as "B," the scheme Tech N9ne uses in mm. 9–12 is ABABB, repeating twice per measure.[22] Measures 13–14 rotate among three sets of vowels, including those heard in *Mi*ster (also *flip,* etc.), *Ri*sin' (also *rhymin',* etc.), and *Mo-* (also *jo, flow, go,* etc.). Defining these as A, B, and C, respectively, the pattern is ABBCB, also repeating twice per measure.

These two groups of measures differ substantially in their rhythm, both in the way rhythm relates to the meter, and in the way prominent durations are patterned. The example transcribes mm. 9–12 in a C_{48} metric space, with 12 positions per beat (i.e., 3 positions per C_{16} point in the grid), and transcribes mm. 13–14 in a C_{32} space, with 8 positions per beat (i.e., 2 positions per C_{16} point in the grid).[23] Many of the positions in the first group of measures—for example, those just after the beat, or those just after the midpoint of a beat—are never used. Example 1.16 ◐ presents another transcription of mm. 9–14, this time quantized to a uniform C_{32} space. In effect, this change in cardinality attracts syllables that fall just after

---

22. The beginnings of these repetitions (i.e., the downbeats and midpoints of the measure) vary slightly, but I believe we are still intended to hear something repeating twice per measure.

23. The tempo of "Strange" might suggest a transcription at twice the rate I've chosen, with metric cardinalities of 24 and 16 instead of 48 and 32. I chose the slower tempo according to the rule described earlier: I always choose a tactus such that the snare is on 4 and **12**. I recognize some readers will not endorse this practice, but ambiguity of tactus will rarely figure into later discussions.

Example 1.16 Krizz Kaliko featuring Tech N9ne, "Strange," mm. 9–14, re-quantized to unified C_{32} metric space (i.e., without swing).

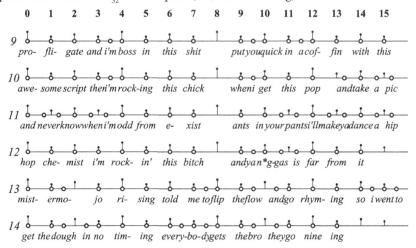

1_{mod2} positions in C_{16} space onto those positions, such as *-li-, and, in,* and *shit* in the first two beats of m. 9. The delay of these 1_{mod2} positions in N9ne's performance indicates his use of **swing**, a topic I address in Chapter 8.[24] This editorial change in quantization affects one group of measures but not the other.

Compared in a similar metric space, the two groups of measures differ in their patterning of duration. Within the groups, they present similar durations, but a few minor differences must be reconciled in order to contrast them. Consider the beginnings of mm. 9 and 12, *Profligate, and I'm boss in this shit* vs. *[hip-] hop chemist, I'm rockin' this bitch.* Although the rhythm of these two phrases is very similar, it is not identical; the first phrase has an extra syllable compared to the second, *I'm,* falling just before position 8. While not ignoring this distinction, I would argue that this additional syllable is unaccented, and that in terms of durations between **accented** syllables, the two phrases are the same. I will call these durations the **inter-accent intervals**, or **IAIs**, in contrast with inter-rhyme intervals, or **IRIs**. "Accent" is a famously loose word in scholarship on speech, music, and poetry. Sometimes "prominence" or "salience" is used instead. Whichever word is chosen, one must be very specific about the intended meaning, and I will provide a formal definition of accent particular to rap music in Chapter 3.

Example 1.17 transcribes the excerpt once more, again in a unified C_{32} metric space, and this time it draws the circle that represents accented syllables larger

24. The quantization of mm. 9–12 to a C_{32} space does not account for the rhythm of m. 11, where Tech N9ne presents three syllables per half beat, rather than the long-short pair of syllables indicative of swing. Measure 11 is thus transcribed in a C_{24} space with six positions per beat. Swing in rap music is common; in fact, we have already encountered swing in the first three measures of the Lil' Wayne transcription in Example 1.8 🌑, the first three measures of the Tung Twista transcription in Example 1.9 🌑, and throughout the Fat Joe transcription of Example 1.10 🌑.

Example 1.17 Krizz Kaliko featuring Tech N9ne, "Strange," mm. 9–14, with larger circles representing accented syllables.

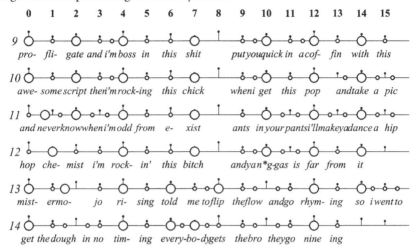

Example 1.18 Krizz Kaliko featuring Tech N9ne, "Strange," mm. 9–14, schematic outline of inter-accent intervals (IAIs).

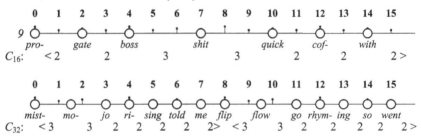

than those representing unaccented syllables. Example 1.18 makes a schematic outline of the inter-accent intervals of the two groups of measures. The first group of measures, in the un-swung C_{32} space, presents an IAI duration segment (dseg) of [4466444] in each bar; note these durations sum to 32. In contrast, the second group of measures presents an IAI dseg of [33244] repeating twice per measure. I call this kind of patterning of inter-accent duration in the voice, and its relation to the meter, **vocal groove**. For me, vocal groove is among the most essential aspects of flow.

While these two grooves differ in their durations, they are related in a subtle way. Although the first group of measures necessitates a C_{32} space, the accented syllables in those measures all occur on C_{16}-space positions. Thus, the dseg of [4466444] in C_{32} space could be represented as [2233222] in C_{16} space. Furthermore, if one emphasized the syllables on positions 5, 7, 13, and 15 in the second group of measures (e.g., *[ris-]in'*, *me*, *[rhym-]in'*, and *went* in m. 13), the dseg of those measures would change from [33244] to [3322222]. Notice that this is a rotation of the [2233222] dseg of the first group of measures—the first two 2s in [2233222] are shifted to the end, creating [3322222]. Thus, the groove of the second set of measures is the same as the first, rotated and doubled in speed. As I will argue later, this is not uncommon, as there is a finite number of vocal grooves and many of them can be related in much the same way as the grooves of the "Strange" example. Changing the groove is a powerful way of flipping the flow and Chapter 4 formalizes these procedures.

1.4 Representing Flow

These instances of flipped flows reveal that flow encompasses phrasing, rhythm, meter, rhyme, accent, patterning, and groove, not to mention the relations among these parameters. Flow also occurs on different scales. Each decision of an artist contributes to the flow of a verse of rapping, but all the verses of an artist, and the central tendencies that emerge from them, also constitute a flow. And further- more, all the verses of all the artists contribute to what it means to flow. These levels constantly interact as well. We know the tendencies of an artist by care- fully listening to all of his or her verses, and these tendencies, in turn, guide our perceptions of a new verse by that artist. And when we characterize an artist's flow, we do so against the backdrop of all the flows of the genre.

A primary aim of this book is to present a uniform representation of flow in a digital format. This enables us to transition among perspectives of the specific as well as the generic. By representing the flows of many verses of many artists, we can investigate how a verse relates to the output of an artist and how an artist relates to the genre. In considering how to construct such a representation, some of the constituents of flow precede and give rise to others. For example, you cannot determine which syllables of a flow are accented without knowing its rhythm. One must also know those accents before the relationship between groove and meter can be characterized.

These dependencies give rise to what I call primary and derived constituents of flow. The primary constituents are the flow's words, phrasing, and rhythm. These constituents are not primary because they are more important, but rather be- cause they generate other constituents. Primary constituents are also defined with less contention—there are fewer disagreements regarding the words of a verse, where phrases begin and end, and how the rhythm is quantized.[25] The derived constituents of flow are rhyme, accent, and groove, fuzzier phenomena that re- quire greater attention. With these primary and derived constituents in place, I de- fine flow as the interaction between the derived constituents and meter. Example 1.19 visualizes this construal of flow.

---

25. Of course, fewer disagreements should not be misunderstood as no disagreements, and Chapter 2 will elaborate points of contention.

Example 1.19 The derivation of flow from primary and derived constituents.

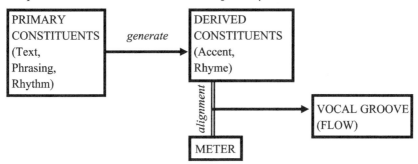

Construing flow as the interaction between derived constituents and meter enables a common method of inquiry into many aspects of flow. The "looseness" or "tightness" of flow can be characterized by the repetitiveness of this interaction. "Flipping the flow," even when not announced in the lyrics, can be characterized as an abrupt change in a pattern of interaction. To formalize comparisons between verses, by one artist or many, I will in later chapters introduce a number of global features of flow, features that represent some aspect of the flow of a verse or artist as a single number. Those features are listed in Table 1.1, though I will introduce more compact names for many of them when they are formally defined in Chapter 5.

With these global features of flow defined, statistical methods might reveal similar flow practices among artists not usually associated with each other. Other methods might document shifts in expressive practice across eras or highlight anomalous verses. Much work remains to realize these analytical possibilities, and the next four chapters expand on and formalize the method of Example 1.19 and the features of Table 1.1. If characterizing an artist requires making reference to the totality of rap music, then a representative sample of rap music must be gathered. That is the project of Chapter 2, which also details the representation of the primary constituents of flow in rap. Chapter 3 does the same for the derived constituents of accent and rhyme. The interaction between derived constituents and meter creates vocal groove, the subject of Chapter 4. Thereafter, Chapter 5 uses the processes of Chapters 2–4 to detail the general tendencies of flow in rap music and demonstrate how the flow of a particular artist can be contextualized within the genre.

Formalizing flow in this way is a considerable undertaking, and a reader may well question whether it is worth the effort. I undertake this project to open new avenues of inquiry into rap music. This music has been with us for at least forty years. It has been a part of scholarly discourse for at least twenty-five years. Yet studies of its musical features remain scarce, especially in comparison to the many fine works on its interaction with race, gender, culture, technology, and language. Why does this continue to be the case?

A comparison with the analysis of rock music is telling in this regard. In comparison to rap, rock music enjoys an abundance of scholarship on its musical

Table 1.1 Global features of delivery

Syllables per word
Syllables per second
Phrase length
Variation in phrase length
Proportion of positions occupied in the measure
Line-to-line variation in this proportion
Position of line or phrase ending in the measure
Global features of rhyme:
Number of instances in rhyme classes
Number of syllables in rhyme instances
Overlapping of rhyme classes
Rhyme scheme complexity
Variation in quantities of IRIs at the level of the beat
Variation in IRIs below the level of the beat
Global features of rhythm:
Tempo
Patterning of inter-accent intervals (i.e., groove)
Exactitude of that patterning
Typicality of that patterning
"Evenness" of inter-accent intervals
Extent of syncopation
Extent of 1_{mod2} accents

materials and conventions. But analyzing any sort of popular music, in the view of Allan Moore, requires resisting the widespread mystification of music in popular and scholarly writing:

> Listeners everywhere are encouraged to conceptualize the invention of music as a branch of magic, to believe that musical actions and gestures cannot be subject to any level of explanation, and hence understanding, beyond the trivially biograph-ical. . . . [This] view seems only too natural to those who have never made note-to-note musical decisions, and only too absurd to those who reflect upon spending their lives doing so. (2003, p. 7)

Explaining the decisions of emcees, either from moment to moment or in consideration of their larger output, faces yet another hurdle beyond those Moore mentions: characterizing these decisions as "note-to-note" is obviously inappropriate. In my view, until we have analytical tools that conform with rap's unique position at the intersection of music and speech, we will continue to view the expressive practice of emcees as outside the purview of analysis.

CHAPTER Two

A Corpus for Rap Music Analysis

2.1 Motivating the Need for a Corpus

In the last chapter, I discussed a number of instances of "flipping the flow" called out by the lyrics of a verse. One instance was the flipped (or "reversed") flow of Jonny 5's verse on The Flobot's "Airplane Mode" (see Example 1.11a 🔊). The flip involved changing the inter-rhyme intervals (IRIs) from predominantly two and four beats to three beats. Those three-beat durations culminate with the line "hip hop is a compost heap," an image that motivates the rest of the verse. Here, Jonny 5 imbues hip hop with an ability to convert objects of waste and harm into objects of use and value: *swords into plowshares, gangsters into gardeners*, etc. And the implication is not only that these conversions should be made, but also that they should be made specifically through the expressive power of hip-hop music.

The utility of my interpretation of the verse rests on several claims—that I understand the meaning of Jonny 5's use of "compost heap," that most of the "x to y" constructions in the verse can be understood as gaining value, etc. But the most important claim is that the line "hip hop is a compost heap" is a focal point of the verse. My argument that it is rests on the idea that the flow leading up to the line has certain internal consistencies that differ from the surrounding context and, furthermore, that the three-beat IRIs are a relatively rare occurrence in The Flobot's music and in rap music generally, marking them as significant in this case. But, at this stage, these claims are only intuitions gleaned from listening.[1]

These matters of interpretive process—salience, meaning, and value—encouraged Leonard B. Meyer to theorize two distinct analytical approaches for music that he termed **style analysis** and **critical analysis** (1973, p. 6). Style analysis documents the norms of a given repertoire of music, distinguishing between

---

1. Although the method for documenting this claim will not be clear until later chapters, the claim is nonetheless true: the Jonny 5's use of four rhymes, each three beats apart, sets him apart from other emcees. This pattern of inter-rhyme intervals occurs in five other verses I examined for this project, all in the work of the three artists whose case studies form Part II of this book, and never in the collection of verses I consider representative of the genre as a whole. See footnote 14 in Chapter 5, and the corresponding section of Chapter 5's analysis script, for details.

features so universal that they take on the character of laws from those features that are common but not inviolable. Critical analysis, on the other hand, identifies the ways in which an individual piece within a repertoire differs from and responds to the norms uncovered through style analysis. These two analytical orientations are inseparable: critical analysis motivates most music analysts who want to learn more about a specific piece or our reaction to it, but that project cannot begin until the norms, expectations, and constraints that confront artists are understood.

At the intersection of style analysis and critical analysis are the choices of an artist. While one could argue that every aspect of a rap verse is the result of the choice of the emcee, Meyer sees choice differently, and his view is worth quoting at length:

> The word *choice* tends to suggest conscious awareness and deliberate intent. Yet only a minute fraction of the choices we make are of this sort. For the most part human behavior consists of an almost uninterrupted succession of habitual and virtually automatic actions: getting out of bed in the morning, washing, dressing, preparing breakfast, reading the mail, driving to work, conversing with colleagues, playing the violin, and so on. . . . By far the largest part of behavior is a result of the interaction between innate modes of cognition and patterning on the one hand, and ingrained, learned habits of discrimination and response on the other. (Meyer 1989, p. 4, emphasis in original)

Moments at which artists transcend the constraints of learned behavior and modes of cognition—and I believe the IRIs of three beats in "Airplane Mode" represent such a moment—are especially significant and invite interpretation. This is the payoff of critical analysis. The payoff of style analysis goes beyond making a statistical description of the repertoire. For Meyer, the constraints uncovered in style analysis are not arbitrary, but rather represent "innate modes of cognition." Style arises as a compositional community replicates specific decisions when confronting similar circumstances. Details of cognition motivate these decisions because the options that best concord with human cognition will be most frequently replicated (Meyer 2000, p. 229). Thus, the study of style, such as the typical habits of emcees, is as much a study of how the mind works as it is a study of how the emcee raps.

In order to undertake style analysis, on must first collect a number of texts to stand in for the repertoire. This collection constitutes a **corpus**. With a collection of texts in hand, one can see how a number of artists approached a given scenario and interpret the decisions of the specific artist. But the practical difficulties of conducting corpus studies by hand limited Meyer's use of the corpus studies method to only one published study (Meyer 2000). There, he documents the prevalence of a particular phenomenon in classical music, the cadential six-four progression.[2] He undertakes the study partly to show a historical trend toward increasing use of the progression into the nineteenth century and a subsequent

---

2. A "cadential six-four progression" refers to a cadence in classical music wherein the dominant chord of the cadence—the one built on the fifth scale degree in the bass—includes two notes that are each a step higher than notes that belong in the dominant. These notes resolve down by step.

decline. But he is equally concerned with examining the shifts in ideology that motivate these changes in style. Because the cadential six-four came to signify definitive closure, its prevalence in the late eighteenth century further demonstrates the importance of hierarchy and balance in Enlightenment-era music, just as its decline in the nineteenth century demonstrates the Romantic dismissal of convention (Meyer 2000, pp. 244–250). Finding significant historical trends in the use of, for example, three-beat IRIs in rap music, would be a similar invitation to speculate on changing ideologies among emcees.

Meyer understood that corpus studies substantiate claims about style change on the basis of two conditions. First, the corpus must contain works "considered to be stylistically representative"; second, the phenomenon traced must be rigorously defined (p. 238). But going beyond manual corpus studies introduces a third challenge: the difficulty of representing musical phenomena in a digital format. As Alan Marsden (2016) summarizes, scholars conceptualize music on an ontological spectrum. At one side of this spectrum are those who view music fundamentally as an activity, such as Christopher Small's (1998) concept of musicking. This ontology holds that musical objects like scores and recordings are representations, abstractions, or even distortions of those activities. When I perform or listen to live music, I find this view deeply appealing. But as Alan Marsden points out, computational music analysis lives at the other end of this spectrum, considering music "to be a distinct 'object' with an abstract existence made manifest in various ways in the scores, recordings and performances of the piece, not to say also in the imagination of its composer and the memories of those who read the scores or hear the recordings and performances" (2016, p. 4). The forced ontology of computational music analysis places the analyst at a distinct disadvantage compared to those analysts who do not employ a computational method. A human analyst can proceed as though the music is a "distinct object" and undertake an analysis without determining what features that object might or might not have. The chosen features might change as the analysis proceeds, and retrofitting the analysis to comment on them is not too burdensome. But the computational music analyst must commit not only to the idea that a piece has a distinct existence, but also that it has a set of features:

> Provided they show some due concern for the nature of the materials they use, [music analysts] are able to proceed with their activities, and to produce useful insights, without having to commit themselves on the finer points of ontological debate. The computational music analyst, on the other hand, is not so free to use diffuse conceptions of a piece of music. The input to analytical software must be, ultimately, a binary code, in which every bit is unequivocally 0 or 1. (Marsden 2016, p. 5)

Eleanor Selfridge-Field similarly emphasizes the immediate challenge of representation, writing that

> feature or attribute selection is the single most important aspect of a scheme for representing music. No matter how elegant the design or how numerous the attributes included, if one attribute essential for a particular purpose is not present, the representation cannot be used for the intended application. (1997, p. 569)

While I would argue that one can analyze rap music as a product without denying its power as an activity, the choice of features to include in that analysis will necessarily silence other features that might have been chosen. Encoding features is costly to both the human encoder and the computer processor, and this creates an incentive to be frugal. In committing to a computational approach, I recognize that much of the experience of rap music as an activity, both from the perspective of artist and listener, is lost. And some obvious features of rapping (e.g., pitch modulation, regional accent, affective cues in speech, etc.) will be inaccessible in the analyses to come. Committing to reproducible research (see the "On Reproducible Research in the Humanities" section in the Introduction) means that one could later append these features to the corpus, but for now they remain absent.

These issues of ontology and representation seem to have delayed corpus studies of music (and not just rap music) in comparison to, say, computational linguistics. Furthermore, a chief aim of computational music studies to date has been to interrogate the assumptions and conclusions of conventional music theory, historically focused on questions of harmony and form in classical music. For this reason, most musical corpus studies—digital and manual—have addressed the same questions of harmonic usage as Meyer did. In the past two decades, researchers have gone beyond counting chord frequencies to counting chord progressions, employing various schemes for representing musical scores (Pardo & Birmingham 2001; Conklin 2002; Quinn & Mavromatis 2011; White 2013, 2014). As music theory has come to embrace the study of popular music (mainly Anglo-American rock music), corpus studies of harmony have expanded their repertoires of concern (Moore 1992; de Clercq & Temperley 2011; Burgoyne, Wild, & Fujinaga 2013).

The remainder of this chapter and the next two address the three tasks of a Meyerian corpus study of rap music: identifying representative material, representing that material digitally, and defining phenomena of interest rigorously. In this chapter, I will detail the construction of several corpora of rap verses, including a genre-wide corpus that mirrors the geographical, chronological, and stylistic diversity of a mature genre, as well as corpora of individual emcees collected so that specific verses can be understood not only in comparison to the genre as a whole but also in comparison to the rest of an emcee's output. I will then describe a representation of those corpora's primary constituents of text, onset, and phrase. Ultimately of greater interest is the treatment of derived constituents (accent, rhyme, and groove) and their alignment with the meter. The next two chapters provide formal definitions of these attributes.

2.2 Building a Corpus of Rap Verses

Performing Meyer's critical analysis of a rap verse—comparing a verse to others that share an artist or era—requires the kind of corpus construction pioneered in computational linguistics. In that discipline, corpora draw on two different kinds of collections of texts, known as populations and samples. A population of texts consists of all the texts within certain parameters. For example, an early corpus known as the Brown Corpus (Francis & Kucera 1964) consists of all examples of American English printed in 1961. Often the population is divided into categories (e.g., fiction, non-fiction, academic non-fiction, poetry, etc.). The samples in a corpus are random selections of the population designed to maintain the proportions of subcategories in the population. In recent decades, as both the availability of digital texts and computational power expands, sampling is rarer. Instead, entire populations of texts are used in very large corpora.

Existing corpus studies of music, however, still rely on sampling. In general, that sampling is not random. Rather, a corpus of classical music in a digital format is emerging through the combination of smaller corpora originally encoded for computational music analysis or the digital preservation of scores.[3] The roughly 400 four-part chorales of J. S. Bach comprised the earliest of these corpora and spawned much of the original music corpus research. But the Bach chorales are neither a population nor a sample. They are part of the population of European classical scores of the eighteenth century, but that population includes tens of thousands of other scores. And they are not a random sample of that population, but rather a specific body of work particular to one composer, locale, and genre.

The emerging corpus of classical music has been encoded manually through the efforts of countless researchers and volunteers. Some sites, like the Choral Public Domain Library (cpdl.org), encourage users to upload music notation files from which data can be extracted. Others (such as classicalarchives.com) encourage users to upload performances in the Musical Instrument Digital Interface (MIDI) format, generated by playing a MIDI keyboard. Still others, such as the Josquin Research Project, involve academic groups generating data. In relation to corpus studies of texts, music corpus studies are at a technological disadvantage. Since the early 2000s, researchers studying language and its interaction with culture have used techniques of optical character recognition to automatically encode texts, resulting in corpora like the Corpus of Contemporary American English of 455 million words or the Google Books corpus of 155 billion words (Davies 2013). Researchers hope that methods of optical music recognition will improve and provide corpora of similar size, but automatic scanning of music notation presents severe obstacles, as it contains hundreds of symbols whose meaning depends on precise placement, size, context, and interpretation.

Even within music corpus studies, rap music presents special challenges. There is no rap analogue for the MIDI protocol. While rap enthusiasts (and sometimes emcees themselves) reliably transcribe lyrics, they do not transcribe other primary constituents like rhythm and phrasing. There is, however, a rap analogue for the promise of optical music recognition: perhaps at some point, the analysis of the rhythm and phrasing of a rap verse could be performed by computer. The most promising approach to the problem is through text-to-speech alignment. The Penn Phonetics Forced Alignment program (Yuan & Liberman 2008) takes a text file and an audio file of that text being spoken. This approach is successful because the computer

---

3. The ELVIS project (http://database.elvisproject.ca/) attempts to gather all existing symbolic representations of musical scores in one place.

only has to find the phonemes in the text in order, rather than recognize an arbitrary sequence of phonemes. Yet two challenges complicate using the P2FA with rap music. First, rap music contains much else besides the rapping voice—namely, the music. The sounds of the instrumental streams often compete with the phonemes of the rap, making them hard for the computer to recognize. The second challenge is cultural. The P2FA works through techniques of machine learning. First, researchers manually annotated the phoneme onsets of a corpus of speech with the aligned text. They then train the computer model on this corpus, and in the future what happened in that corpus will help the computer recognize phonemes in new speech. In order to build the corpus in the first place, the researchers needed a large collection of recorded speech that, preferably, had already been transcribed. They found this in the work of the OYEZ project (www.oyez.org) that transcribed and manually aligned seventy-eight hours of oral arguments heard in the Supreme Court of the United States.

The language heard in rap music, of course, is quite different from such arguments, both in terms of words used and in terms of phonetic features. In my own informal tests of the P2FA for rap music, the program can locate the onsets of syllables within a span of several seconds, provided one substantially increases the vocabulary of the program to include that of rap music. Still, it frequently fails to locate the syllables within the more relevant window of human perception, a window on the order of hundreds of milliseconds. I suspect the failures are due to the interference of the instrumental streams, but they may also reflect phonetic differences between emcees and Supreme Court justices. As of this writing, and for the foreseeable future, manual annotation of rhythm and phrase is the only viable means for constructing a corpus of the rapping voice.

Because the construction of the corpus must be undertaken manually, the corpus obviously cannot contain the entire population of rap verses. The music metadata site Discogs.com lists 50,000 "masters" of hip-hop music, and the documentation explains that a master is

> a display function that gathers two or more matching releases together. It can be thought of as a folder that holds two or more Discogs releases. An example would be gathering several versions of an album, such as Michael Jackson's *Off the Wall*.[4]

There is surely some overlap in tracks between these different masters, and rap releases, more than other genres, frequently have tracks without verses (e.g., skits, instrumentals, etc.). Still, conservatively estimating eight songs with rapping per release and two verses per song suggests a population of 400,000 verses.[5] Transcribing four verses per hour, encoding the population would require fifty years of skilled labor.

How then should the population be sampled? Typically, one identifies the population and determines a number of subpopulations. Subsequently, one samples the population so that the relative proportions of the subpopulations are

4. See https://www.discogs.com/help/submission-guidelines-master-release.html.
5. This, in turn, suggests that the aforementioned Original Hip-Hop Lyrics Archive (OHHLA) contains roughly half of the verses in the genre.

maintained. What would these subpopulations be in rap music? Forty-five years after Kool Herc's first parties in the shadow of the Cross-Bronx Expressway, rap music is a highly diverse genre. Those who might identify as emcees may range from age 10 to 60 and live anywhere in the world. They might be part of a group, collective, or band. They might have contracts with major record labels, release music themselves online, or only rap in cyphers and battles.

Representing such a diverse population requires careful sampling. As a first approximation, we could sample files from the corpus of lyrics contained in the OHHLA and take the first verse from each selected track. But the practicalities of transcription limit us to something like one one-thousandth of the population, and using a random process with such a small sample would likely overrepresent some segments of the population and underrepresent others (Biber 1990). For example, the geographic diversity that rap celebrates would be lost if our random sample included too few West Coast or southern emcees. We might also lose diversity in what Robert Hatten calls "stylistic register" (1994, p. 14) if we overrepresent commercial rap, battle emcees, or underground emcees. Worst of all, the lyrics of the OHHLA are not tagged by locale or stylistic register. Thus, we do not know the distributions of these parameters in rap music as a whole, so we would not know if our sample was unrepresentative.

Indeed, rap music is in some ways more than one genre. Or, perhaps more clearly, it is a genre that has undergone a sustained trajectory of development. Lena and Peterson (2008) model the trajectory of a genre like rap music in four stages: avant-garde, scene-based, industry-based, and traditionalist. In the life cycle of a genre, the avant-garde stage occurs when a small number of artists, away from the spotlight, create a new genre in contrast to existing modes of expression. As they attract attention, a scene arises and establishes social conventions such as fashion (p. 704). Some genres then progress to the industry-based phase, in which music is distributed through corporations and made by professionals. Finally, after popular taste moves on and commercial opportunities recede, some genres enter a traditionalist phase, where a dedicated group of fans maintain a genre's history and aesthetics and compete to define it and set boundaries around it (p. 706). Rap music as a whole has gone through this complete cycle, but now aspects of the genre simultaneously exist in all these stages, for example, as seen in the (virtual) scene-based SoundCloud rap community of the mid-2010s (Caramanica 2017).

What is needed is a sample of emcees that captures all this diversity in terms of chronology, geography, stylistic register, and genre type. The popular hip-hop media provides an approximation of this diversity by regularly producing lists of "the best emcees." For differentiation, publications will often ascribe a different focus to these lists. I selected six such lists from which to build a corpus of rap music, described in Example 2.1. Among the six lists are 225 emcees; some emcees recur on multiple lists (see Appendix 1). Some lists (e.g., the *Complex* magazine bestsellers or the B.E.T. list of most influential rappers) track rappers at the top of the industry-based phase of the genre. Others include emcees at the height of (mainstream) critical acclaim. The "most slept-on" list includes emcees with limited success in the industry-based phase of the genre, such as the Bay Area emcee

Example 2.1 Six lists of "the best emcees" used in the construction of the corpus.

1. The Source Magazine (Various authors, 2012), "Top 50 Lyrical Leaders"
2. Complex Magazine (Ross, 2013), "Best Selling Albums of All Time"
3. B.E.T. (Gale, 2011), "The Fifty Most Influential Rappers"
4. Complex Magazine (Drake, Martin, Baker, & Ahmed, 2012), "Fifty Most Slcpt-On Rappers of All Time"
5. XXL, "Freshman Class," 2008–2014
6. All artists with albums receiving a score higher than 85 (out of 100) on metacritic.com.

Note: The "Freshman Class" is published in various issues. A list of lists, archived by Wikipedia.org, is available at https://en.wikipedia.org/wiki/XXL_(magazine)#XXL_Annual_Freshman_List. Metacritic aggregates critical reviews and converts their assessments into a percentage. "Metascores" for releases are averages of these percentages, weighted by the site's assessment of the critic's importance. The site allows for filtering by genre and ranking by metascore, which is how the top tier of rap releases was determined. It is likely biased towards more recent reviews that are available online.

The Jacka. Finally, the "Freshman Class" lists identify talented emcees who may or may not have achieved later success.

Individually, none of the lists are ideal. Each reflects the biases of its editors. "Slept-on" and "influential" are fuzzy terms that would be interpreted differently by a different set of editors. The Freshman Class lists also have a somewhat controversial history, as seven emcees declined to join them after being invited. Furthermore, the chronological distribution of the lists is somewhat bimodal. The "top," "bestselling," and "influential" emcees skew toward rap's golden era of the 1980s and early 1990s, while the Freshman Class lists include much more recent emcees. Emcees who began their careers around 2000–2005 are slightly under-represented. Also excluded are the artists who never garner the attention of the hip-hop media. In particular, this applies to rappers who rarely record, such as freestylists and battle rappers. Furthermore, it is likely these lists constitute a rap canon that subsumes any number of collective biases and prejudices. Writing about canonization of the blues, John Dougan states that canons "represent the essence of the tradition, and the connection between the texts and the canon reveals the veiled logic and internal rationale of that tradition" (2006, p. 45). I suspect that part of the "veiled logic" of rap canonization works to exclude women and non-black rappers. For example, in the ranker.com list of "The Best Latin Rappers/Groups," generated by user votes, the top five entries as of this writing are, in order, Big Pun, Cypress Hill, Immortal Technique, Snow Tha Product, and B-Real. Of these, only Big Pun appears in the corpus. Ralf Von Appen and Andre Doehring (2006) show similar biases in the canonization of rock music.

Furthermore, I have not exerted any editorial control on the artists in the corpus, some of whose membership in the genre may be contested. For example, the corpus includes white, southern rappers like Bubba Sparxx and Yelawolf because they appear in the XXL Freshman Class lists. Yelawolf is especially problematic as a white rapper who has worn Confederate garb and defended that choice at length shortly following the murder of nine black worshippers at the Emanuel African Methodist Episcopal Church in Charleston, S.C., in 2015. Facets of the hip-hop community might consider these artists interlopers rather than members of the genre (Carter 2017), but I have not attempted to legislate who belongs in hip hop. Lastly, these lists were all compiled around 2011–2013, so the most recent generation of rappers (representing perhaps the last tenth of rap's history) are not represented.[6]

Having selected the emcees who will be in the corpus, songs must be selected for each emcee. For this task, I used the now-defunct Echo Nest Application Programming Interface (API), a repository of music metadata and derived measures.[7] The Echo Nest developed a measure of a song's popularity it termed "hotttness" (Lamere 2009). While the exact formula for measuring hotttness was proprietary, it took into account the mentions of a song on the Web and in social media, as well as the number of downloads and streams. In my view, the hotttness measure is more valuable than competing measures like positions on the Billboard charts because hotttness documents the popularity of a track in comparison to other tracks by the same artist, and it does so even after the initial popularity of a track has worn off. The Echo Nest assigned each song a hotttness value between 0 and 1, and I determined the hotttest song of each artist in the population. I also queried Echo Nest for the artist's city of origin and the year of the artist's first credit.[8]

At this stage, there are 225 songs in the corpus, still too many to transcribe at one time. Thus, I randomly sampled 75 of the artists, ensuring that the sample maintained the chronological and geographical distributions of the population. I also randomly decided to transcribe the first, middle, or last verse of the chosen tracks. The geographical and chronological distribution of the population and the sample is shown in Example 2.2. A table of the artists included is given in Appendix 1; also, see the Discography listing for complete information on recordings.

In addition to this genre-wide corpus, I also constructed three corpora of specific artists discussed in Part II: Eminem, Black Thought, and Talib Kweli. As with the genre-wide corpus, I aimed for a representative chronological distribution for these artists. In the case of the first two, I maintained the distribution of their verses between those they record for their own projects and those that are featured in the work of others. Furthermore, I maintained the distribution of their verses recorded for tracks released as singles and those not released as singles.[9]

---

6. While the lists are a few years old, because the XXL Freshman List aims for the latest talent, many of the biggest current names in rap music (e.g., Future, Kendrick Lamar, Kevin Gates, Logic, etc.) are represented, their careers having blossomed.

7. The Echo Nest was a music data platform in operation from 2005 to 2014, when it was acquired by Spotify. After acquiring Echo Nest, Spotify developed an API that reproduces most of Echo Nest's features, although methods of calculation may well have changed. The sampling I undertake should be replicable through the Spotify API, but I have not attempted to do so.

8. The Echo Nest API did not include artists' birth years, which might be more useful in constructing a representative corpus. Still, the year in which an artist enters music metadata, usually in their late teens or early twenties, is a good proxy for their age.

9. As will be clearer in Chapter 8, my concern with Talib Kweli is how his placement of syllables relates to the instrumental streams. It was therefore necessary to work with verses with available a cappella recordings, and the maintenance of the chronological distribution was sacrificed for this requirement.

Example 2.2 Histogram of chronological and geographical distribution of the corpus sample (*n* = 225) and subsample (*n* = 75).

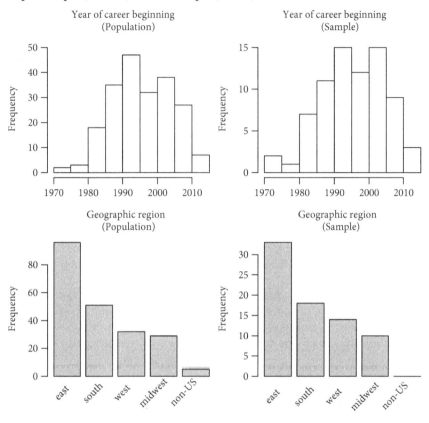

2.3 Representing Flow's Primary Constituents

2.3.1 Representing Text

Having decided what verses will be in the corpus, the next step is to decide how to represent the primary constituents of their flow: text, rhythm, and phrasing. Again, I mean "primary" in the sense that these features give rise to the derived features of accent, rhyme, and groove I will address in Chapters 3 and 4, not in the sense that I consider these features more valuable than others, even those I have not represented. I gather the text from online sources, predominantly from the Original Hip-Hop Lyrics Archive. Since I am interested in the rhythmic expression of the emcee, I tend to remove words and sounds in the lyrics that are not made by the main emcee of the verse. Many of the OHHLA transcriptions also strive to represent slang and (regional/cultural) accent through their orthography, resulting in words like *rhymin* instead of *rhyming*. Capturing the particularities of the emcee's speech through this kind of orthography pays respect to the emcee's authority to determine the representation of his or her own language. When I can, I try to pay the same respect, but I must balance the added complication of my need for computing phonetic similarity as a constituent of rhyme. As I will describe here, I use the syllabized version of the machine-readable Carnegie Mellon University Pronouncing Dictionary (hereafter CMUPD; Lenzao & Rudnicky 2007). The CMUPD uses a phonetic alphabet called Arpabet, which represents phonemes using regular letters, in contrast to the International Phonetic Alphabet. A typical entry to the CMUPD looks like this:

MUSIC   M Y UW1 - Z IH0 K

The 1 and 0 after the two vowels (UW1 and IH0) indicate stressed and unstressed syllables. The hyphen between UW1 and Z indicates a new syllable (Bartlett, Kondrak, & Cherry 2009). The CMUPD has *rhyming* but not *rhymin*, so I often change the spelling to the version that the dictionary will have. I also keep an addendum to the dictionary of about 1,000 African American Vernacular English words (e.g., *I'mma, gon, tryna*, etc.) and neologisms in rap lyrics (e.g., *livest, lipping*, etc.).[10]

2.3.2 Representing Rhythm

After retrieving the lyrics and dividing them into syllables, I manually annotate the duration of each syllable using two integers. The first integer represents the cardinality of the metric space; the second represents the number of such divisions occupied by the syllable. Example 2.3 ◑ shows this representation for part of the "Weezy Baby" transcription seen in Example 1.8 ◑. Notice that the pair of integers representing duration is insufficient to make the transcription; one must also represent when the first syllable occurs with respect to the meter. This information is also a pair of integers, one representing the measure of the first syllable (counting from 0) and the other representing the beat of the first syllable (also counting from 0); any "pickups" occur in measure −1.[11] From this information, we can compute the beat index (i.e., the number of beats that have elapsed since the beginning of the verse) of any syllable by multiplying the quantities of all the syllables by the inverses of the cardinalities of all the syllables, summing those values for all previous syllables, and adding the beat index of the first syllable.[12]

As mentioned in connection to Ice-T's "I Ain't New Ta This" in Chapter 1, there is a subjective element to determining the rhythm: I posit a cardinality and

10. See SourceData/PhoneticData/cmudict-syls-addendum.txt.
11. See SourceData/verseMetadata.txt.
12. See Scripts/DataScrubbingScripts/GenerateCorpus.r, lines 19–39.

Example 2.3 Lil' Wayne, "Weezy Baby" (2005, 0:37–0:44), with representation of syllable duration (below).

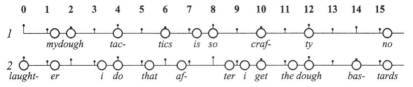

word	syllable	cardinality	quantity		word	syllable	cardinality	quantity
my	my	24	1		i	i	24	1
dough	dough	8	1		do	do	12	1
tactics	tac-	8	1		that	that	12	1
tactics	tics	12	1		after	af-	8	1
is	is	24	1		after	ter	24	1
so	so	8	1		i	i	24	1
crafty	craf-	8	1		get	get	12	1
crafty	ty	24	5		the	the	24	1
no	no	24	1		dough	dough	8	1
laughter	laught-	12	1		bastards	bas-	12	1
laughter	er	8	1		bastards	tards	8	1

measure durations in that cardinality. In most cases, this should not be controversial, as most emcees strive to place syllables in a C_{16} space. Still, quantizing a verse is an interpretive act that, depending on the emcee, can distort the rhythm to a greater or lesser extent. Of all the tracks discussed in the last chapter, I subjectively found Lil' Wayne's "Weezy Baby" hardest to quantize—this is reflected in the variety of cardinalities in Example 2.3 ◗. Example 2.4 ◗ reproduces the audio signal at the beginning of the excerpt and, using the program Audacity, marks the onset of a number of events. The first level of annotation marks the onsets of the vowels of each syllable, as can be best determined through the interference of the instrumental streams. The accompanying audio excerpt inserts clicks at these moments. The next lower level, which also includes the text of the syllables, marks where the quantization asserts these syllables begin. Such onsets are determined by marking the two bass drum events and the two snare drum events that constitute the boom-bap as defining the metric space. All the syllables seem to occur after the quantization suggests, and some occur considerably later. Perhaps

Example 2.4 Lil' Wayne, "Weezy Baby," beginning, wave form (top) with four levels of annotations, marking (1) the onsets of vowels, (2) the onsets of syllables implied by my quantization, (3) the onsets of C_{16} positions implied by the boom-bap, and (4) the onsets of the boom-bap (i.e., bass drum and snare).

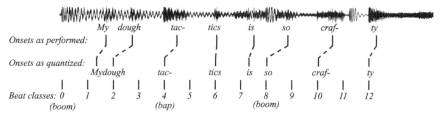

another analyst would assert a different quantization, but no quantization will line up exactly with where the syllables begin, and furthermore, a difference may exist between where I have annotated the syllable onsets and where listeners hear the syllables beginning. These are complex issues, and in Chapter 8, I will attempt to reclaim what has been lost in the quantization through an examination of Talib Kweli, an emcee who makes the most of the tension between the regularity of rap music's meter and the freedom of rhythm in speech. In the meantime, the reader can compare recordings of verses to my transcriptions in order to affirm or dispute the validity of the quantization.

2.3.3 *Representing Phrasing*

The third primary constituent of flow is phrasing. Phrasing is how emcees segment their verse into smaller units. The boundaries of these units are relevant in analyzing the verse, as we might note, for example, which beat in the measure tends to coincide with a phrase ending. Dai Griffiths refers to phrase endings metaphorically as the **central pillars** of a song, "as posts on a fence along the song's ongoing road" (2003, p. 43). The shifting of these pillars can be moments of drama, as might be an increasing rate at which they occur. Griffiths avoids specifying "what one takes to *be* a musical phrase" and suggests there are two prominent and sometimes conflicting criteria by which we can segment a verse: the ends of phrases as indicated by the performer's breathing and the ends of lines as indicated by an analysis of the lyrics, especially their rhyme structure. In many cases, these two criteria arrive at the same segmentation of a verse. For example, in Bubba Sparxxx's "Deliverance" (see Example 2.5 ●), every measure contains a line of rapping that starts at or just before the downbeat and ends with a rhyme on the fourth beat, at which point the emcee breathes.

In cases like "Deliverance," whether one attends to breathing or lyric analysis makes no difference. But in many cases, one's segmentation of a verse indicates one's theoretical orientation. At one end of the spectrum is Adam Krims, who

Example 2.5 Bubba Sparxxx, "Deliverance" (2003, 1:05–1:15).

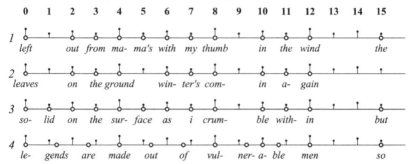

prints the lyrics of rap verses so that the first word heard in each measure begins the line, regardless of semantic or grammatical factors.[13] At the other end of the spectrum are listeners and scholars who align rap music with lyric poetry, placing line endings in a way that highlights lyric-poetic devices. Adam Bradley voices this perspective clearly, writing that "line breaks are the skeletal system of lyric poetry. . . . [R]ap poets are no different" (2009, p. xii). Thus, he and his co-editor Andrew Lee Dubois adopt this segmentation method in their *Anthology of Rap*:

> Many of the transcriptions found online tend to follow a practice in which the line breaks signal a pause in the rapper's delivery. Whenever the flow stops, the line breaks. . . . This anthology follows a principle of transcription that takes its cue from rap's lyrical relationship in rhythm to the beat. Each measure (or bar) in a typical rap song consists of four beats, and a lyric line consists of the words one can deliver in the space of that bar. Therefore, one musical bar is equal to one line of verse. . . . Preserving this fundamental relationship makes it possible to discern a host of formal qualities in the verse. It allows us to distinguish between end rhymes and internal rhymes, to appreciate effective enjambment, to note the caesural pauses within lines, and to perceive a host of formal elements that might otherwise escape notice. (2010, p. xlvii)

The lyrics Bradley transcribes in many cases were never printed before; it is therefore somewhat artificial to argue that the lyrics have "lines." I appreciate Bradley's attempt at consistency through equating measures and lines, but when the relationship between measures and lines is complex, his practice can yield strange segmentations. Example 2.6 ◐ shows three transcriptions of the first quatrain of Black Thought's first verse of The Roots' track "You Got Me" featuring Erykah Badu.[14] The first transcription is from *The Anthology of Rap*. The second is from the OHHLA. The third is my own transcription and breaks lines when Black Thought breathes. In each, I have used italics and underlining to indicate rhyming

13. See, for example, Krims (2000, pp. 100–102).
14. For a discussion of Black Thought's live performances of "You Got Me," see Chapter 7.

Example 2.6 The Roots featuring Erykah Badu, "You Got Me" (1999, 0:29–0:39), emceed by Black Thought.

> *Bradley & Dubois (2010, p. 495)*
> Somebody | told the that this planet was *small*, we use to live
> In the same | building on the same *floor* and never met be*fore*
> Un-|til I'm over<u>seas</u> on *tour* and <u>peep</u> this Ethiopian
> |<u>Queen</u> from Philly taking classes a*broad*

> *ohhla.com*
> Somebody | told me that this planet was *small*
> we use to live in the same | building on the same *floor*
> and never met be*fore*
> un|til I'm over<u>seas</u> on *tour*
> and <u>peep</u> this Ethiopian | <u>Queen</u> from Philly
> taking classes a*broad*

> *Segmented by where Black Thought breathes*
> Somebody | told me that this planet was *small*
> we use to live in the same | building on the same *floor*
> and never met be*fore* un|til I'm over<u>seas</u> on *tour*
> and <u>peep</u> this Ethiopian | <u>Queen</u>
> from Philly taking classes a*broad*

syllables and a vertical bar ("|") to indicate which syllables fall on or immediately after the first beat of the measure.

In the transcription of Bradley and Dubois, the beginning of the measure falls toward the beginning of the line, and there are the same number of measures and lines, but the beginnings of each certainly do not coincide. Indeed, their placement of a line break after *live* in the first line seems designed to keep the prepositional phrase *in the same building* together rather than align line endings with measure endings. Furthermore, the transcription disperses instances of rhyme throughout the lines. The ohhla.com transcription, which is similar to my breathing segmentation, effectively highlights rhyme. In my view, this transcription also does more to capture the changing pace of the flow than the lyric-poetic transcription of Bradley and Dubois.

My own practice uses both the breaths of an emcee and the grammatical structure of the lyrics to create two segmentations of a verse, one of which segments lyrics at every breath (I call these **phrase endings**) while the other segments lyrics to create as many closed grammatical segments as there are measures (I call these **line endings**). In general, I prefer phrase endings because segmenting according to breath follows an empirical feature of the audio signal. I also believe the emcees intend their breathing to perform this kind of segmentation: emcees breathe when they believe their breaths will be unobtrusive, that is, when their listeners will not expect the completion of an ongoing idea. Still, I also track line endings for two reasons. First, some emcees use studio manipulations to create phrases longer than would be possible otherwise—in such cases, other features articulate the flow. And second, although I cannot think of an example, I can imagine emcees using breaths for expressive purposes such as hyperventilation. In future transcriptions, unless otherwise noted, I place commas after syllables preceding breaths.

At this stage, the primary constituents of flow are digitally represented. The payoff is limited, as most of the questions we would ask about a verse or artist concern derived parameters of accent, rhyme, and groove. There are challenges to representing primary parameters—orthography, rhythmic quantization, segmentation, etc.—and I hope I have handled those challenges responsibly. But the lack of basic definitions of the derived parameters make their digital representation much more challenging. The next chapters take up that challenge, and in the course of designing a representation of derived parameters, distinctions among music theory, phonetics, and cognition come to the fore.

CHAPTER Three

From Rhythm to Accent, from Sound to Rhyme

3.1 Representing Accent

Example 3.1a 🜨 and Example 3.1b show two measures of rap from the genre-wide corpus and a bit of their surrounding context. The first plot centers on the third measure of Jean Grae's "My Crew" (2003); the second centers on the fifth measure of Logic's "Under Pressure" (2014). Syllable onsets saturate every position in both measures. In each, I have annotated some accents in the central measures with larger circles; these accents reflect only my own way of hearing the excerpts. The instrumental streams to these tracks are rather similar. In particular, both have a higher-register sound on all the 0_{mod2} positions. In "My Crew," a synthesizer leaps between two notes some distance apart; in "Under Pressure," a sample of Michel'le's singing from Eazy-E's "Eazy Duz It" (1988) meanders through a scale on the on-beat and midbeat positions. Yet the flow of the measures is quite different. In "My Crew," a prominent syllable of a multisyllabic word aligns with the last three beats of the measure. The 1_{mod2} positions, in contrast, support either unaccented syllables like -re- of *serenade* and -*light* of *moonlight* or short "function words" like *the* and *to*. In "Under Pressure," the accented syllables of multisyllabic words are always on 1_{mod2} positions, inverting the tendencies of "My Crew." In effect, Jean Grae uses her voice to support the instrumental streams by placing accents in positions that already carry them. Logic, in contrast, opens up a distance between himself and the instrumental streams by placing his accents apart from positions emphasized by those streams.

Already in the last several analyses of Chapter 1, I plotted some syllables with larger circles to reflect accent. In several cases, a change in durations between accents or the position of accents constituted "flipping" the flow. In many more, like those in Example 3.1, an identifying feature of a verse is the relationship between accent and meter. Thus, any stylistic analysis of flow employing a corpus should, as a prerequisite, annotate which syllables an emcee accents in a verse. This annotation can be (and usually is) determined by ear, but an automated method of annotating accent makes the features that indicate accent explicit. Furthermore, if such a method is publicly available, other researchers can adapt it to accord with their own view of how accent arises. The first part

Example 3.1a Jean Grae, "My Crew" (2003, 0:45–0:50).

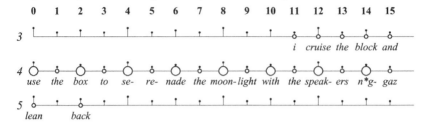

Example 3.1b Logic, "Under Pressure" (2014, 0:36–0:43).

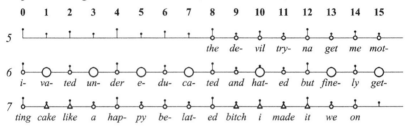

of this chapter presents such a method. Yet "accent" (or its synonyms "stress," "prominence," and "emphasis") is an especially problematic term in discussions of rhythm, meter, and flow, because it has been employed by so many disciplines surrounding music and speech, often for very different purposes. Thus before introducing a method of annotating accent in the corpus, I will begin by recounting some of these usages, noting their utility and liability in the analysis of the rhythm of the rapping voice.

3.1.1 Accent in Music

Perhaps the most widely known consideration of accent in contemporary music theory is Lerdahl and Jackendoff's *A Generative Theory of Tonal Music* (1983, hereafter referred to as *GTTM*). Lerdahl and Jackendoff describe three kinds of accent, arising from different sources. **Phenomenal accents** are those that arise from acoustic emphasis, i.e., moments that are louder, higher, or markedly different from their surrounding context. The workings of Western tonal harmony can give rise to **structural accents**, as melodies and harmonic progressions reach points of arrival. Finally, a hierarchy among the beats of the measure (e.g., the beat 1 understood as stronger than beat 2) gives rise to **metric accents** (p. 17). The different accents, though they remain distinct, relate in various ways. For example, the metric grid that confers metric accent emerges through an initial consideration of phenomenal accents. A series of well-formedness rules and preference rules specify how accent structures arise. For example, well-formedness

Example 3.2 Transcriptions of m. 10 of Eminem's second verse on Jay-Z's "Renegade": (a) studio version at left (2001, 1:32–1:36) and (b) live performance at right (2010, 1:43–1:47), in conventional Western music notation. Notated pitches indicate the closest equal-tempered pitch to the highest frequency within a syllable. In syllables without note heads, the accompanying parts obscure the pitch of the voice.

(a) Studio version (2001)   (b) Live version (2013)

May -be it's beau -ti -ful -mus -ic I made for you to just che -rish   May -be it's beau -ti -ful mus -ic I made for you to just che -rish

rules prohibit consecutive metric accents within a level of the metric grid (p. 69). Grouping preference rules similarly encourages the formation of larger groups of proximal events (p. 43). In the decades after *GTTM*, music psychologists have affirmed these three different types of accent in tonal melodies (Drake & Palmer 1993).

The formalism of Lerdahl and Jackendoff's well-formedness rules and preference rules suggests that they could be implemented as a system that detects accent in musical scores. Efforts to design such a system have tended to focus on detecting metric accents and determining the time-span reduction of a piece (the way in which groups form hierarchical relationships based on features of tonality).[1] In contrast, John Roeder (1995) has tried to integrate these various kinds of accent. In Roeder's view, accent arises from the effort involved in intensifying a parameter of music like pitch or loudness (p. 15). The time points of higher pitches are more accented than those of lower pitches because it takes more work to make them in many instrumental and vocal contexts. Importantly, in Roeder's system, the accent associated with a given time point takes into account not only the amount of intensification, but also the duration of that intensification. A large leap is accented; a quick large leap is more accented.

These prior approaches have limited relevance to rap music for at least four reasons. First, they invariably rely on discrete pitch content. Speech, including rapped speech, of course has pitch content, and in rap music that content is often more determinate than one might think. Example 3.2 ◐ shows transcriptions in staff notation of two performances of a line from Eminem's verse on Jay-Z's "Renegade." The first is from the album *The Blueprint*, released in 2001. The second (Jay-Z 2010) is from a live performance from the summer of 2010. The indicated pitches refer to the highest approximate pitch Eminem attains for each

1. Lerdahl and Jackendoff themselves (p. 55) dismiss the computability of *GTTM* because the "understanding of many difficult musical and psychological issues" was insufficient in their view. For implementations of grouping well-formedness and preference rules, see Stammen & Pennycook (1993), Temperley & Sleator (1999), and Temperley (2001). For a more complete implementation of grouping, meter, and time-span organization, see Hamanaka, Hirata, & Tojo (2006).

Example 3.3a Distribution of event durations less than four beats in Beethoven, Opus 18, no. 1 (*n* = 4,467).

Example 3.3b Distribution of event durations less than four beats in the genre-wide corpus (*n* = 13,973).

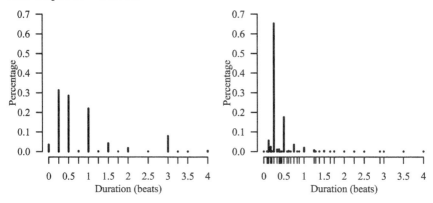

syllable.[2] In performances separated by ten years, the highest pitch in the line is on *beau-* of *beautiful*; it is even the same pitch. But while rap has melody, this melody rarely exhibits the kind of stability that would enable us to represent the pitch of each syllable with a number.[3] Such a representation of pitch is assumed by prior approaches to accent in music.

Second, many of these existing measures rely on differences in duration, but the durations of syllables in rap music are more uniform than the durations of notes in Western classical music. Example 3.3 demonstrates this difference. Example 3.3a measures the durations of events in a melody from Beethoven's first string quartet. Example 3.3b plots the distributions of durations in that movement (in all four voices) as well as the rap corpus. In the Beethoven plot, three different

---

2. Some syllables do not have transcribed pitch because other sounds in the accompaniment forestall an analysis of the pitch of the voice.

3. There is a long history of denying that rap music has melody. For example, Mark Costello and David Foster Wallace (1990, p. 82) identify rap's primary feature as "no melody besides canonized fragment w/o progression." On the other hand, emcees frequently use language evocative of melody to describe their art. In interviews with Cheryl Keyes (2002, p. 128), Afrika Bambaataa describes rapping as creating "a melody in itself," while Melle Mel describes rapping as "rhythmic chanting." More recent rapping also tends toward discrete pitch, sometimes with the aid of Auto Tune.

durations (a quarter beat, a half beat, and one beat) all occur more than a fifth of the time; in the rap plot, durations of a quarter beat make up two-thirds of the distribution. Very few syllables are neither a quarter nor half a beat. Because existing models address a repertoire that has these varied durations, duration is often a key criterion in accent discovery (Lerdahl & Jackendoff 1983, p. 19; Roeder 1995, p. 15; Lester 1986, p. 15). But in rap music, most of the events (syllables) are the same quantized duration. Duration, on its own, is therefore much less useful in determining accent in rap music.

Third, music theorists and psychologists have, through considering primarily Western classical music, come to view meter as a construct in the mind of the listener that persists even when no events articulate its structure. As Lerdahl and Jackendoff (1983, p. 18) put it, "Metrical accent . . . is a mental construct, inferred from but not identical to the patterns of accentuation at the musical surface." Locating meter in the listener's mind, rather than the "sounding surface" of the music, is critical in defining concepts I will address later, such as syncopation. But rap music reifies the metric structure in virtually every measure through the boom-bap of the bass drum and snare. Put another way, there is a much greater correlation between phenomenal accents and metric accents in rap music than in other repertoires. In an environment where every beat carries both a metric and phenomenal accent, and where most of the available metric positions carry syllables as well, the distinction between metric and phenomenal accent is less useful.

Finally, and most significantly, rap listeners employ an additional system of accent discovery not relevant in most classical music: the perception of accented syllables in connected speech. The differences in the meaning of accent in the domains of speech and music are stark. Yet as with theories of accent in music, theories of accent in speech can inform an accent-detection method for rap music. But these theories, like those of accent in music, have been developed for an environment that differs from rap in important ways.

3.1.2 Accent in Speech

The idea of accent in speech begins with the concept of the phonological hierarchy, a hierarchy whose levels extend from the phoneme, a basic unit of sound like a vowel or consonant, through the syllable, foot, word, phonological word (discussed at length later), phonological phrase, intonational phrase, and ultimately the utterance (see Example 3.4 🌑).[4] At each of these levels, some elements

---

4. An early theory of phonological hierarchies may be found in Mark Liberman and Alan Prince (1977). Not all phonologists consider each of these levels part of the hierarchy. The phonological word, a constituent between the syllable and phrase, remains controversial. A strong appeal for such a level can be found in Hall (1999). My account of accent and the phonological hierarchy is slanted toward American English as well as African American Vernacular English because they are found in the corpus. Phonologists recognize other levels of the phonological hierarchy in other languages; the mora encountered in Japanese is a classic example.

Example 3.4 The phonological hierarchy of the spoken sentence "The music theory course was entertaining," as spoken by the author. Boldface indicates a primary accent beginning at Level 3 (feet). Italics indicates a secondary accent beginning at Level 4 (words).

7. The utterance	the**mu**sictheory*course* wasenter**tain**ing						
6. Intontational phrases	the**mu**sic*theory*		**course**was		*en*ter**tain**ing		
5. Phonological words	the**mu**sic	*theory*	**course**was		*en*ter**tain**ing		
4. Words	the	**music**	*theory*	course	was	*en*ter**tain**ing	
3. Feet	the	**music**	**theo**ry	course	was	**en**-ter-	**tain**-ing
2. Syllables	the	mu- sic	theo-ry	course	was	en- ter-	tain- ng
1. Phonemes	th e	m u s i c	th eo r y	c ou r	se w a s	e n t er t	ai n i ng

are more prominent. For example, at the level of the syllable, some phonemes are more prominent (e.g., louder, higher, or longer) than others. Beginning at the level of the foot, that prominence may be termed "accent" or "stress." I will not give a complete account of all the various approaches to accent in speech, but I would emphasize two themes in this literature: first, the concept of accent becomes more controversial as one ascends the hierarchy. For example, Elisabeth Selkirk (1986) and Bruce Hayes (1995) describe methods for identifying the accent of a sentence. In contrast, Peter Ladefoged and Keith Johnson (2011) resist applying the term "accent" to anything above the phonological word.[5] For them, one syllable in a sentence may be the "tonic" syllable—most often, the highest syllable—and that syllable may also be the accented syllable of a word, but it is not the accented syllable of the sentence (pp. 113–116)

A second theme in the phonological literature is the non-correspondence between features of sound and perceived accent. Anatomically, syllabic stress is associated with an increase of activity in the production of speech, such as pushing more air through the lungs or producing more laryngeal activity (Ladefoged & Johnson 2011, 294). Acoustically, this means that stressed syllables tend to be spoken more loudly, and their vowels are longer and pitched higher. But the relationship between features of sound and accent is much more complicated. As Hayes puts it,

> It is certainly true that pitch and duration are both intimately linked with stress. However, because the relation between stress and pitch/duration is both indirect and language-specific, it is impossible to "read off" stress contours from the phonetic record. (1995, p. 8)

In English, syllables within a multisyllabic word are grouped into metrical feet; because English is a "left dominant" language, the first syllable of a foot is stressed and the others are unstressed (p. 75). In longer words with multiple feet, the stressed syllables of feet may be further distinguished into a single primary

---

5. Gussenhoven and Jacobs (1998, pp. 186–232) provide a thorough introduction to the complex relationship between accent and different levels of the phonological hierarchy.

Example 3.5 Distribution of primary accents, secondary accents, non-accents, and monosyllabic words among the four metric positions of the beat in the rap corpus. Syllables not on a sixteenth-note position (6.6 percent of the corpus) are discarded.

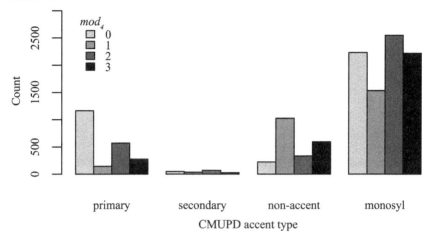

stress and one or more secondary stresses. Primary stresses are conventionally indicated with the high vertical line (ˈ) before the syllable, secondary stresses with the low vertical line (ˌ). For example, the lyrics in the corpora contain several six-syllable words, such as *underestimated* stressed as ˌunderˈestiˌmated, and *extraterrestrial* stressed as ˌextraterˈrestrial. A specification of a word's primary and secondary stresses is called its citation form (p. 107). The CMUPD, the machine-readable pronouncing dictionary cited in the previous chapter, gives the citation form of more than 125,000 English words. I will call the primary stress of a word in the CMUPD its **word accent**. The CMUPD assigns primary stresses a value of 1 and secondary stresses a value of 2. Thus, it represents the accent contour of *underestimated* as <201020> and *extraterrestrial* as <200100>.

In a moment, I will discuss several reasons why we cannot equate the word accents of citation forms with musical accents in rap delivery, even though doing so considerably simplifies accent discovery. While word accent and musical accent are not the same, they are strongly related in rap music, insofar as word accents tend to fall on the beat. Example 3.5 shows the frequency of four kinds of CMUPD accents—primary accents, secondary accents, non-accents in multisyllabic words, and monosyllabic words—in each of the four *mod* 4 positions.[6] Most primary accents fall on 0_{mod4} and 2_{mod4} positions, while few fall on 1_{mod2} positions; non-accents reverse this situation, falling primarily on 1_{mod2} positions.

But equating word accent with musical accent is unviable for three reasons. First, the accent structure of a word in citation form does not always map onto accent structure in connected speech, let alone in rapped speech. The surrounding

6. See the analysis script.

Example 3.6 The Roots, "I Remember" (2011, 0:22–0:34). Numbers in circles indicate rhyme class; horizontal lines connect syllables of a rhyme class.

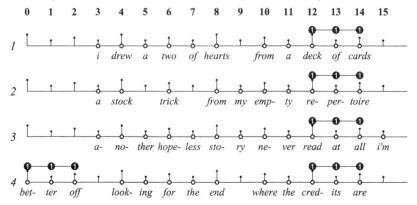

context can alter accent structure, for example, to encourage a more even distribution of accents. Thus, *bam'boo*, usually accented on the second syllable, can sometimes receive an accent on the first syllable, as in "the table made of *bam'boo* is a *'bamboo* table" (Wells 2007).

The second problem with equating citation-form accent and musical accent is that most words in rap music, as in speech, are monosyllables. By default, the only syllable of a monosyllabic word is accented in its citation form.[7] Phonologists recognize that when several monosyllables are spoken consecutively, we do not perceive several consecutive stresses. Instead, these words merge together to form **phonological words**, also called p-words (Hall 1999, p. 2). P-words contain a single stress, like multisyllabic words with a single foot. P-words would seem especially relevant to rap music because of its profusion of what scholars of lyric poetry call mosaic rhyme, a rhyme that pairs a multisyllabic word with several rhyming monosyllables. The first rhyme class of Black Thought's first verse of "I Remember" (2011, Example 3.6 ◆) is a mosaic rhyme, though, given the prevelence of mosaic rhyme in rap music, virtually any verse could serve as an example. The class has five instances (*deck of cards, repertoire, read at all, better off,* and *credits are*), but only one of these instances (*repertoire*) consists of a single word with a single word accent. Yet given their sonic and metric similarities, we should assign them a similar accent structure, the <102> contour of *'reper,toire.*

Determining the rules by which monosyllables merge to form phonological words is the project of Hayes, Selkirk, and other scholars of meter in speech, a project termed by Hayes "Metrical Stress Theory" (hereafter referred to as MST). Like Lerdahl and Jackendoff, these scholars tend to offer general principles rather than computable formalisms. For example, Hayes notes that if the

7. More precisely, the CMUPD often lists two versions of monosyllables, one with accent and one without. When alphabetized, the one without takes precedence.

vowel of a syllable is shortened to a schwa, as in the case of function words like "a," "of," and "the," then those syllables cannot be the accents of phonological words (1995, p. 12). Usually at the level of the phonological word, stress is determined as much by meaning as by sound. In many cases, stress accrues to words that present novel information or clarify ambiguities. Yet one practical challenge is that MST has not been completely formalized. Even if it were, current versions of MST do not address the practices of African American Vernacular English, and it would seem more difficult to do so. Scholars of AAVE assert that a rule-based approach to phonetics is inappropriate for AAVE because speakers often vary the accent structure of words. For example, they might switch between ꞌpolice and poꞌlice depending on formality, among other reasons (Thomas 2015).

Incorporating metrical stress theory into a theory of accent in rapping faces a larger issue: rappers emphasize syllables for reasons that go beyond phonological explanations of conveying information or resolving ambiguity. Two examples of Black Thought's rapping demonstrate the distance between MST and rap delivery. Example 3.7 ◓ shows the first five measures of a verse from "Walk Alone" (2011). In two of these measures, position 8 is a word accent (i.e., ꞌprobly and eꞌnough). Two of the others contain monosyllables surrounded by words with shortened vowels and are thus accented in MST (i.e., ꞌfin surrounded by I'm and to, as well as ꞌif surrounded by as and it). In the last measure, MST would not accent of because it has a shortened vowel and is surrounded by words that would receive more stress in speech (i.e., ꞌboys and Siꞌerra). Yet its metric placement and resonances with earlier position 8 accents, as well as participation in rhyme, elevate it to a musical accent.

Example 3.7 The Roots featuring Dice Raw, P.O.R.N., and Truck North, "Walk Alone" (2010, 1:43–1:58), verse 3, emceed by Black Thought.

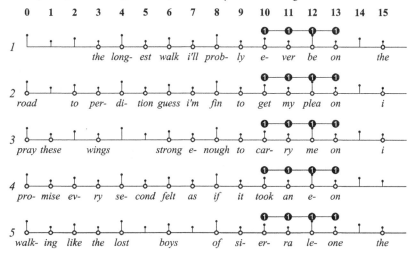

Example 3.8 The Roots featuring Dice Raw and Phonte, "Now or Never" (2010, 1:14–1:20), verse 1, emceed by Black Thought.

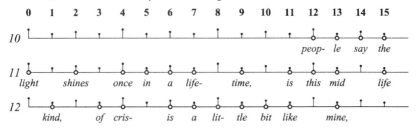

Example 3.8 🌓 prints the lyrics of a couple of measures from Black Thought's verse on The Roots's "Now or Never" (2010). If one were to read the second line having not heard the rap, I would imagine an accent structure like this: *Is this ˈmidlife kind of ˈcrisis a ˈlittle bit like ˈmine?* Such a structure places three or four syllables between accents and emphasizes words most informative of the meaning of the sentence. But Black Thought raps *like ˈmine* to highlight its rhyme with ˈ*lifetime*, placing the emphasis on ˈ*like* as was heard on ˈ*life*. This demonstrates that expressive purposes—creating rhythmic motives or highlighting rhyme structure—can often overrule the expectations of MST.

I hope I have demonstrated the shortcomings of theories of accent in both music and speech in terms of their utility for accent discovery in rap music. Musical theories of accent have been developed for very different repertoires and do not intersect with the accent discovery methods we use when hearing speech. On the other hand, phonological theories of accent are less determined at levels above the word and do not recognize the creative power of rap to reshape the pronunciations encountered in speech. What is needed is a method of determining accents in rap that draws on the most useful features of both these fields of inquiry; I will detail such a method in the next section.

3.1.3 Accent in Rapped Speech

These previous sections document the many features of rapping that bear on perceived accent: rhythmic features like metric position and duration; basic phonetic features like pitch height, intensity, and vowel length; higher-level phonetic features like word accent and p-word accent structure; and musical features like rhyme and rhythmic motives. Yet many of these are impractical for inclusion in a system of accent discovery for rap music. The basic phonetic features are recoverable only in the rare cases of high-quality a cappella recordings, and at any rate there is no simple mapping between these and accent. The higher-level phonetic features like p-word structure are generally not computable with existing methods. How, then, can we formally determine which syllables in a verse are musical accents using only the features that are readily available?

A first approximation might accent syllables coincident with a beat, particularly if those syllables are also word accents or especially long in duration. The
algorithm given here, which is the first of a three-phase method, takes into account five features of a syllable, all of which are either TRUE or FALSE, i.e., they are
Boolean values:

1. `zeroMod2?`, which is TRUE if a syllable is on a 0_{mod2} position, i.e., on or
   midway through a beat
2. `long?`, which is TRUE if a syllable is more than .34 beats, i.e., longer than
   an eighth-note triplet
3. `wordAccent?`, which is TRUE if a syllable is a multisyllabic accent in
   the CMUPD
4. `wordNonAccent?`, which is TRUE if a syllable is a multisyllabic non-
   accent in the CMUPD
5. `monosyllable?`, which is TRUE if a syllable is a monosyllabic word

All syllables will have a value of TRUE for one of the last three variables, i.e.,
all syllables except secondary accents in the CMUPD. Around a fifth of the words
in the dictionary have secondary accents. These include two-syllable words that
are annotated as primary-then-secondary, such as *gateways, birthright*, and *ram-
page*, or those annotated as secondary-then-primary, such as *oneself, misheard*,
and *typhoon*. Entries with secondary accents also include longer words where the
primary and secondary accents are not adjacent, such as *pistachio, exemplify*, and
intoxicate, in which the second syllable is primary and the last is secondary. My
aim is the determine whether a syllable is or is not accented, so I eliminate the
category of "secondary accent." If a secondary accent is adjacent to a primary accent, I convert it to a non–word accent; otherwise, I convert it to a (primary) word
accent.[8]

The object of the algorithm is to determine if a final variable, `accent?`, is
TRUE or FALSE. In pseudo-code, the second phase of the algorithm determines
the `accent?` value for each syllable through the following steps:[9]

```
1 For each syllable i,
2 if
3    zeroMod2?ᵢ is TRUE
4 and
5    wordAccent?ᵢ is TRUE, or
6    monosyllable?ᵢ is TRUE, or
7    wordNonAccent?ᵢ is TRUE and long?ᵢ is TRUE,
8 then
9       accent?ᵢ is TRUE.
```

---

8. The code for removing secondary accents appears in `Scripts/DataScrubbingScripts/`
   `BuildCMU.Objects.r`.
9. `Scripts/DataScrubbingScripts/AppendAccent.r` implements this code.

```
10 otherwise,
11   if
12      zeroMod2?ᵢ is FALSE and wordAccent?ᵢ is TRUE, or
13      long?ᵢ is TRUE,
14   then
15      accent?ᵢ is TRUE.
```

Stated in prose, the first nine lines accent syllables whose positions are 0_{mod2}, so long as they are not short, unaccented syllables of multisyllabic words. Lines 10–15 accent syllables' positions on 1_{mod2} positions if they are longer than .34 beats or the accented syllables of multisyllabic words. Example 3.9a 🖲 and Example 3.9b 🖲 reprint the transcriptions of Jean Grae and Logic given in Example 3.1 with the algorithm applied.

In "My Crew," the algorithm replicates my intuition of accent in Example 3.1a 🖲, but in "Under Pressure," the algorithm has produced consecutive accents in three different locations, beginning on positions 8 and 14 of m. 5 and position 12 of m. 6. In each case, the word accent of a bisyllabic word follows a 0_{mod2} monosyllable. In a rare moment of agreement, both music theorists and phonologists express skepticism toward such adjacent accents. Spoken English seems to avoid consecutive accents through the phenomenon of "stress-shift," such as the

Example 3.9a Jean Grae, "My Crew" (2003, 0:45–0:50), with accent discovery algorithm applied.

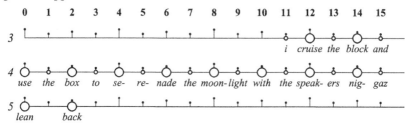

Example 3.9b Logic, "Under Pressure" (2014, 0:36–0:43), with accent discovery algorithm applied.

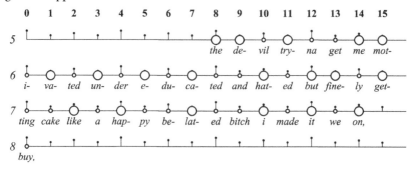

shift described by Wells (2007) in the utterance "the table made of *bam*'*boo* is a '*bamboo* table" mentioned earlier. Lerdahl and Jackendoff (1983, p. 69) enshrine an avoidance of successive accents as their Metric Well-Formedness Rule #3: "At each metrical level, strong beats are placed either two or three beats apart." And if accent is understood as a local maximum in work (as in Roeder) or in laryngeal activity (as in Ladefoged & Johnson), then consecutive accents could not be perceived as such.

Of two adjacent accents, one must be deemed more accented, the other a non-accent in comparison to the first. A second phase of the algorithm prevents successive accents by removing accents whose positions are adjacent to word accents or long monosyllables on 1_{mod2} positions. This correction removes the accent from the first syllable of each pair because the second syllable is a word accent, returning the transcription seen in Example 3.10a. Removing the consecutive accents has left a separate problem: a dearth of accent in positions 12–14 of m. 5. This span without accents will occur when word accents fall on consecutive 1_{mod4} or 3_{mod4} positions, as is the case here. A final phase of the algorithm finds strings of five syllables of which the first and last are accented, and accents the middle one, producing the transcription of Example 3.10b.

At this stage, the algorithm no longer returns consecutive accents or gaps without accent, but it still produces what I consider errors. These errors affect less than 4 percent of the syllables, and they arise from three distinct sources.[10] The first category of errors derives from the structure of the CMUPD that determines word accents. The dictionary often contains multiple entries for a word reflecting pronunciation variants. Some of these variants have different phonemes (e.g., "po-tay-to" vs. "po-tah-to"), while others have different accent structures (e.g., the noun '*contest* vs. the verb *con*'*test*). Since the parts of speech in the dictionary are not tagged, I arbitrarily choose the first listing, which is sometimes wrong.

A second, more common source of discrepancies is rap's long sequences of monosyllables. In the absence of surrounding multisyllabic words, monosyllables on 0_{mod2} positions are accented and those on 1_{mod2} positions are not. More than half of discrepancies between the algorithm and my own analysis of accent concerns the treatment of monosyllables. In m. 7 of Example 3.10b, while there are no consecutive accents, I tend to hear the noun *cake* on position 1 as more accented than the preposition *like* on position 2; similarly, I hear the verb *made* on position 11 as more accented than the pronoun *it* on position 12. In both these cases, the 0_{mod2} positioned syllable is a function word (e.g., a preposition, determiner, conjunction, etc.) and the 1_{mod2} positioned syllable is a content word, a noun or verb. Example 3.11 corrects the transcription by asserting accents on these 1_{mod2} positions. To show that the resulting accents were not discovered by the algorithm, they are plotted with triangles. In fact, among monosyllables, many of the algorithm's "false positives" are function words. Few syllables need manual adjustment, but an accented monosyllabic function word is more than

10. See the analysis script.

Example 3.10a Logic, "Under Pressure," pruned of adjacent syllables.

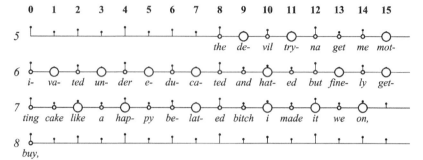

Example 3.10b Logic, "Under Pressure," without spans with no accents (note new accent on position 13 of m. 5).

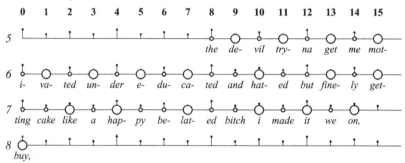

Example 3.11 Logic, "Under Pressure," with manually corrected accents indicated by triangles.

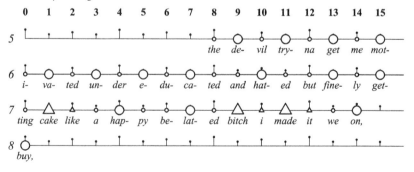

Example 3.12a Esham, "Sunshine" (1993, 0:12–0:19), with accent discovery algorithm applied.

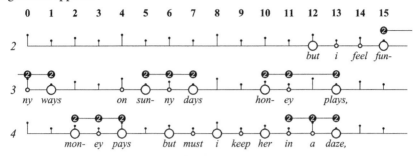

Example 3.12b Esham, "Sunshine," with manually corrected accents.

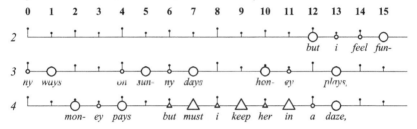

12 times as likely to require revision than an accented monosyllabic content word.[11]

Finally, rhyme contributes to some discrepancies between the algorithm's output and my own sense of accent. As I will next discuss in more detail, emcees often alter words' pronunciations in response to rhyme. Example 3.12a 🌑 transcribes part of Esham's "Sunshine" (1993), applying the algorithm. The lines include five instances of a rhyme class: *funny ways, sunny days, honey plays, money pays,* and *in a daze.* Unlike many verses, these rhyme instances do not share a rhythmic structure—notice that *money pays* is the only instance to end on a 0_{mod2} position, and that the second syllable of *honey plays* is longer—but they all would seem to accent the first and third syllables. The output of the last instance, *in a daze,* differs from the others because *in* is a 0_{mod2} short monosyllable. In my hearing, *in* is accented even though it is a function word because of its participation in rhyme. Hearing *in* as accented changes the preceding accents as well, accenting *must* and *place* and de-accenting *but* and *her.* (The alliteration of *must* and the preceding *money* also contributes to its accent.) Example 3.12b 🌑 shows

11. To make this calculation, I gathered a list of 225 function words from Cook (1988), removed multi-syllabic words, and added another 30 function words encountered in hip-hop lyrics (e.g., *cuz, ain't, wit', gon',* etc.). In the genre-wide corpus, I have toggled 208 of 2,301 function words to remove detected accents, compared with 44 of 5,382 nonfunction words. $(208 \div 2{,}301)/(44 \div 5{,}382) = 12.5$. See the analysis script.

these manual corrections and exemplifies the complex set of features that makes manual correction necessary.

Without manual correction made in light of features not represented in the corpus, the algorithm is "right" 96 percent of the time. However, it might be that I have designed an algorithm to annotate my own idiosyncratic hearing of accent. While no one has yet undertaken a large-scale study in which participants annotate accent in transcriptions of rap music, I can report that the algorithm compares well to other published analyses of rap music verses. To my knowledge, the only rap verse extant in multiple published transcriptions that annotates accent is Kurtis Blow's "Basketball" (1984), transcribed in Adams (2009) and included in the corpus constructed for Condit-Schultz (2016). Example 3.13 🞊 transcribes the first verse, annotating accent as described here. The correspondence between Adams, Condit-Schultz, and the algorithm is very high. Every unaccented syllable is unaccented in all three; every accented syllable found by the algorithm is also accented in Condit-Schultz. While Adams annotates accent more sparingly, he does not mark an accent unmarked by Condit-Schultz and the algorithm. The only other discrepancy is reflected in the triangles of mm. 3 and 7, at the lyrics *king on, pick and*, and *give and*. Each of these cases has long, 1_{mod2} function words whose accents I have toggled

Example 3.13 Kurtis Blow, "Basketball" (1984, 0:20–0:39). Large dots indicate syllables accented by both the algorithm described here and in Condit-Schultz (2016). ">" indicates further annotation of accent in Adams (2009). Triangles show the author's corrections to the algorithm.

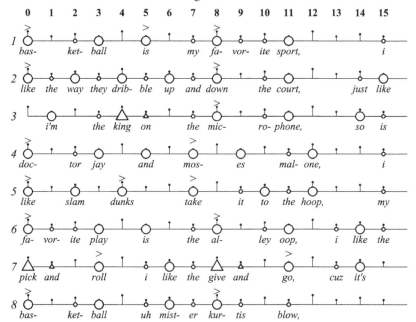

manually. These scholars did not intend for their accent analyses to be compared to an algorithm, nor were they trying to formalize accent discovery. Still, the other analyses lend support to the algorithm I have presented here.

3.2 Representing Rhyme

3.2.1 Rhyme, Memorization, and Segmentation

The second derived constituent of flow in need of formal representation is rhyme. Example 3.14a 🔊 and Example 3.14b 🔊 show two couplets of rapping by Black Thought on tracks by The Roots, one from the second verse of "The Fire" (2010), the other from the second verse of "Lighthouse" (2011). The flow of the lines is very similar: they are at nearly identical tempos and have identical accent structures. But the couplet from "Lighthouse" seems more self-similar than that of "The Fire" because of their differing rhyme schemes. Both couplets have rhymes at the ends of lines, but only "Lighthouse" also has interior rhymes. The inner rhyme of "Lighthouse," pairing *breaking out in a sweat* with *paying up on my debt*, articulates the flow of that couplet at a moment where the couplet of "The Fire" seems more continuous.

As virtually every observer of the genre has noted, rhyme permeates rap music more than any other expressive form. Adam Bradley (2009 p. 52) argues that "rap

Example 3.14a The Roots featuring John Legend, "The Fire" (2010, 1:56–2:01), emceed by Black Thought.

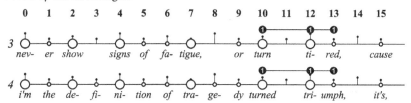

Example 3.14b The Roots featuring Dice Raw, "Lighthouse" (2011, 2:20–2:27), emceed by Black Thought.

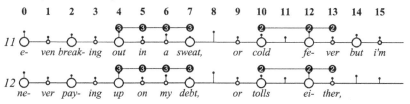

rhymes so much and with such variety that it is now the largest and richest contemporary archive of rhymed words." Indeed, rap rhymes to such an extent, even more so than its rhyme-dense precursors such as blues, toasts, and the dozens (Keyes 2002, pp. 17–39), that the verses themselves are often called rhymes, as though there was nothing else in them (Edwards 2009, p. 81). Rhyme serves many purposes in rap, but perhaps the most critical in relation to flow is its facilitation of memorization.

Rap lyrics are astonishingly verbose. In a cross-genre study of the textual features of song lyrics, Rudolf Mayer, Robert Neumayer, and Andreas Rauber (2008) find hip hop to have nearly twice as many words per minute as any other genre. At the same time, many emcees—for example, Jay-Z (Rodriguez 2015), Kanye West (Ryon 2012), and The Notorious B.I.G. (Gale 2012)—insist that they never write their verses on paper. And the memorization of lyrics extends to listeners as well. In his documentary *Something from Nothing: The Art of Rap*, Ice-T describes a performance strategy for memorization that relies on the audience (Ice-T & Baybutt 2012). As he begins a concert, he looks for someone adjoining the stage rapping along. If he forgets a line, he positions the microphone in front of the audience member, disguising his own memory lapse as an act of audience participation.

Rap's density of rhyme aids in memory recall for both performers and listeners who have memorized the lyrics and are rapping along. This economy of sounds explains rhyme's appeal to emcees, but it does not explain rhyme's relation to flow. That connection is better explained through current theories of emotion in music. David Huron (2006) locates music's emotional power in the predictive nature of listening. As we listen to a piece of music, we are constantly predicting what will happen and when. These predictions are not unlike the predictions we make about the unfolding of events in the rest of our lives. In some contexts, our survival depends on these predictions being correct. Therefore, our brain rewards correct predictions with positively valenced emotions—and punishes incorrect predictions with negatively valenced emotions—in order to refine our predictive abilities.

When we recite a rap verse, we are constantly monitoring our abilities to remember the words and speak them at the right time. When our memory is accurate, we are consistently rewarded by the brain for these correct predictions. When memory stumbles, we may experience the negatively valenced emotions associated with incorrect predictions. These peaks in felt competency are most likely to align with rhyming words, and these shifts in the performance of our memory enhance the segmentation conferred by the rhyme scheme and thus contribute to the articulation and character of the flow of a verse.

3.2.2 Determining Rhyme Classes: Phonetic Similarity and Temporal Limits

In order to document this articulation of flow and memory through rhyme, one must identify which time points listeners experience as rhymes. As I will show, this cannot be formalized in the same manner as accent. Intuitively, rhyme is a kind of pattern recognition: if syllables are conceptualized as *CVC*, where the initial and terminal *C* indicates one or more consonants and the interior *V* indicates a vowel, then syllables sharing the vowel and final consonant(s) rhyme.[12] But listeners seem rather permissive in judging whether two syllables "share the vowel and final consonant." Consonants made through similar manners of articulation, like the plosives sounds of "t" and "d," may sound similar enough to qualify as rhyming.[13] These possibilities for substitution create what Terry Brogan calls "equivalence sets" of consonants and vowels (2012, p. 1187). How individual listeners construct these sets of equivalence is the first way in which their perception of rhyme may differ.

Beyond the similarity of vowels and final consonants, other features of syllables affect their prospects for rhyming. Position of stress may be implicated: does *ag'hast* rhyme with *'ballast*? And, most relevant to rap, the syllables' similarities in their citation form may belie their similarity in pronunciation. As Emcee Escher and Alex Rappaport (Escher & Rappaport 2006, p. 59) relate, "Some artists use line after line of slant rhyme, but because of their flow and the way they pronounce the words, you don't even hear the words as being slant rhymes."

So far, we have addressed only the complications of identifying monosyllabic rhymes. But rap also relishes in rhymes extending over many syllables. Perhaps all paired syllables rhyme, perhaps not. Perhaps the syllables of the rhyme are not even contiguous. Consider the following quatrain:

> Where I'mma start it at? Look I'm a part of that
> Downtown Philly where it's realer than a heart attack.
> It wasn't really that ill until the start of crack.
> Now it's a body caught every night on the Almanac.

> —The Roots, "Game Theory" (2006)

The last four syllables of each line form a rhyme class, provided one is willing to hear *Al-* rhyme with *part, heart,* and *start* and *that* rhyme with *-tack, crack,* and *-nac.* The first three lines feature clear internal rhyme as well (*start it at = part of that, Philly = realer; real- = ill*). But I hear internal rhyme in the fourth line as well, between *body* and *caught (eve)ry,* even though the first syllable of *every* intervenes.

Brogan argues that rhyme is about more than phonological correspondence, writing "it is essential that the definition not be framed solely in terms of sound, for that would exclude the cognitive function" (2012, p. 1184). One aspect

---

12. The difficulties inherent in defining and classifying rhyme—and the basis for much of my account of rhyme—are discussed in Brogan (2012). Brogan also discusses relationships between initial consonances (i.e., "alliteration"). Scholars, especially in the lyric poetry tradition, highlight alliteration in rap lyrics. For example, Yasin (1997, p. 120) correlates the preponderance of fricatives in a particular verse to "the harshness of life for some in America" described in the lyrics. It is my own view that vowel-final-consonant rhyme is much more prominent in rap music than initial-consonant alliteration. See also Bradley (2006, p. 66) and Edwards (2009, p. 86).

13. Brogan (2012, p. 1186) documents this distinction between "perfect" and "near," "slant," or "inexact" rhyme. Because emcees use near rhyme so profusely, the distinction between "perfect" and "near" seems less relevant in this genre.

Table 3.1 Line-ending rhyme classes in "The OtherSide," mm. 5–16

m. 5	positive	*m.* 6	promises	*m.* 7	comics is
m. 8	complements	*m.* 9	tolerance	*m.* 10	consequence
m. 11	inventions	*m.* 12	intentions	*m.* 13	life sentence
m. 14	an entrance	*m.* 15	omelets is	*m.* 16	Thomas is

affecting this cognitive function is duration. In the second line of "Game Theory," the two syllables of *Downtown* share aural features, but I doubt anyone hears these as rhymes functioning in the same way as *start of crack* and *Almanac*. Thus, the duration between syllables in a prospective rhyme would seem to have a lower limit.

Rhyme would seem to have an upper limit as well. Table 3.1 shows the ends of mm. 5–16 of Black Thought's first verse of "The OtherSide" (2011). The ends of mm. 5–10 rhyme, as do the ends of mm. 11–14. The last two measures end-rhyme with each other, but they also rhyme with the earlier rhyme class of mm. 5–10. Is that rhyme perceptually relevant? That question can only be addressed by raising two others: How long can a listener maintain attention on a past rhyme class in order to link another instance to it? And, second, can a listener maintain attention on two rhyme classes simultaneously? The answers to these two questions will certainly vary, and introduce another source for interpersonal difference in rhyme detection.

3.2.3 Automating Rhyme Detection: Prospects and Limits

These complications of phonetic similarity, duration, and cognition present severe challenges in defining rhyme in such a way that a computer could detect the rhymes of a verse. First, the computer would need to be able to measure the phonetic similarity between two syllables. Then, it would need a model of cognition and attention capable of distinguishing the pseudo-rhyme of *downtown* from the actual rhyme of *heart attack* and *start of crack*. Hussein Hirjee and Daniel Brown (2010) go a long way toward solving the first problem, presenting a method for measuring phonetic similarity. For any two syllables i and j, the method compares how often rappers match the vowels and terminal consonants of the syllables at line endings in comparison to random pairs of syllables. The "rhyme score" of two consonants or two vowels is the natural log of the likelihood of their being matched in a rhyme divided by the likelihood of their being matched by chance. Where the rhyme score is positive, the two phonemes are said to rhyme. For example, the vowels of "cod" and "coy," while not identical, have a rhyme score of 1.6.[14] By summing the rhyme scores of the vowels and final consonants of two

---

14. The score of 1.6 represents the exponent of the log-likelihood of being matched; $e^{1.6} = 4.95$, meaning that these two vowels are 5 times more likely to be matched at the ends of consecutive lines than at the ends of a random pair of lines (Hirjee & Brown 2010, p. 126).

syllables, the method can quantify the extent to which the syllables rhyme given a certain threshold of rhyme score, which they set at 1.5.

Hirjee and Brown use their measurement of syllabic rhyme score to find internal rhymes (i.e., those syllables that have positive rhyme scores with the final syllable of the line) and multisyllabic rhymes (i.e., sequences of syllables that all have positive rhyme scores).[15] By automatically finding internal and multisyllabic rhyme, they are able to make a number of observations about the history of rhyme in rap music: over time, rhyme density increases, the percentage of rhymes that are monosyllabic decreases, and the percentage of rhymes that are "perfect" also decreases. Most provocatively, their method also enables them to speculate on one of rap's most severe taboos, the practice of ghostwriting (2010, p. 137).

Yet Hirjee and Brown's method is less successful in capturing Brogan's "cognitive function" of rhyme. They begin with lyrics that are already segmented into lines that presumably rhyme, and they only look for rhymes that either are found at ends of two consecutive lines or correspond to the last syllable(s) of their line. These constraints will miss rhymes in at least four scenarios. First, some rhyme classes consist only of internal rhymes, as in the couplet from "Lighthouse" in Example 3.14b ⬣. Second, some rhyme instances have intervening internal syllables that are not part of the rhyme; Alim (2006, p. 153) highlights such a rhyme when The Notorious B.I.G. rhymes *spectacular* with *neck [to yo] back then ya*. Third, some rhymes extend over nonconsecutive lines, as in the rhyme of *[un-] holy music* and *so confusing* in the first quatrain of Black Thought's first verse of "Baby":

> Your ma don't like to jitterbug,
> says this unholy music.
> Hip hop just so ridiculous,
> everything sounds so confusing.
>
> —The Roots featuring John-John, "Baby" (2006)

A fourth scenario that plagues automated rhyme detection are rhymes asserted by scholars not strictly on the basis of sonic similarity. David Caplan (2014) appreciates rhyme in hip hop because it takes a device that is often "stale and obvious" and uses it to bring disparate ideas in contact. When rappers boast of material wealth, they seem unable to resist the rhyme of "Lexus" and "necklace"; seventy lyric files in the OHHLA contain both of these words. When stic.man of Dead Prez rhymes "Lexus" with "justice," the triteness of the "necklace" rhyme heightens the rhetorical force: "To rhyme 'Lexus' and 'justice,' though, is to contrast two competing values and distinguish the artists who espouse them" (p. 10). But under Hirjee and Brown's model, "Lexus" and "justice" do not rhyme at all.

The model could be adjusted to accommodate stic.man's rhyme by lowering the threshold of phonetic similarity. Yet doing so would greatly expand the number

---

15. Hirjee and Brown allow for an interior syllable of a multisyllabic rhyme to have a negative rhyme score without affecting the identification of rhyme.

of detected rhymes to include word pairs surely not perceived as rhyming. And even with the higher threshold constraints, their method still labels some syllables or groups of syllables as rhyming when they do not (false positives) and as not rhyming when they do (false negatives). Raising the threshold raises the false negatives but lowers the false positives; lowering the threshold does the opposite. A final limitation of Hirjee and Brown's automated rhyme detection method is that it is constrained by the pronunciations encoded in the CMUPD, which is unaware of the way emcees alter conventional pronunciations to coerce rhyme.

3.2.4 A Machine-Readable Representation of Rhyme

I admire Hirjee and Brown's contribution, and I should note that the constraints they have established and the error rate their model registers (false positive rates of 5 percent and false negative rates of 15 percent) probably do not affect the broad claims they make about changes in rap lyrics over time. But these constraints and errors do make the model unusable for a critical analysis of rap—manual correction of model output would take as much time as doing the analysis manually. Thus in the corpus created for this study, "rhyme" is my own annotation of sound patterning in the rap verses. I make this annotation after annotating the rhythm, by which point I can already recite the verse from memory. I suspect my perception of rhyme is quite permissive in terms of phonetic similarity, especially if the pronunciation of a word is more similar to a rhyme class than its citation form would suggest. I am also willing to hear rhyme over long durations.

Like the metric positions of syllables, I annotate the rhyme of a syllable with two integers. The first describes the cardinal position of the rhyme class within the verse (i.e., the first rhyme class is 1, the second is 2, etc.). The second describes the ordinal position of the syllable within the rhyme class (i.e., the first syllable is 1, the second is 2, etc.). In the first line of "Game Theory," for example, *start it at* and *part of that* are both annotated as ((1,1), (1,2), (1,3)). This double-numbering enables me to align syllables of similar position within the rhyme and also to indicate instances of the rhyme that do not have every syllable.

Example 3.15a 🜺 and Example 3.15b 🜺 demonstrate the advantage of using two integers to represent rhyme. In Example 3.15a 🜺, from Kool Moe Dee's verse on the Treacherous Three's "Feel the Heartbeat" (1981), each pair of measures has a monosyllabic rhyme on position **11**. Rhyme in the second excerpt, from Salt-N-Pepa's "Whatta Man" (1993), is much more involved, with a combination of monosyllabic and multisyllabic rhyme classes (compare classes 1–3 to 4–5). Another aspect of the complexity of Salt's rhyme is the overlapping of classes, the way *girl* of Class 2 follows four instances of Class 3. Also more variable in Salt's flow, compared to Kool Moe Dee, are the durations between rhymes (the inter-rhyme durations or IRIs introduced in Chapter 1). While always four beats in "Feel the Heartbeat," they range from less than one beat (*ho's* to *flows* in m. 3) to more than two measures (*word* to *girl* across mm. 2–4).

Example 3.15a The Treacherous Three, "Feel the Heartbeat" (1981, 0:34–0:43).

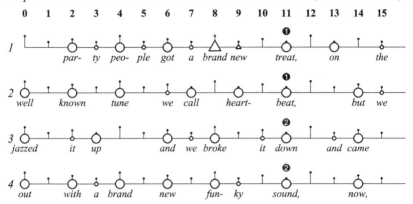

Example 3.15b Salt 'N' Pepa, "Whatta Man" (1993, 0:36–055).

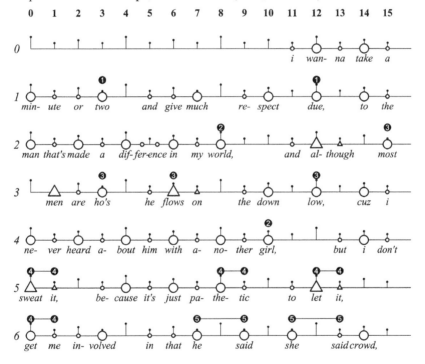

Less clear are the IRIs of the multisyllabic rhyme classes; in order to measure the inter-rhyme interval, we must specify a unique onset for each rhyme instance. In a monosyllabic rhyme, the time point of the perception of rhyme is obviously the time point of the only syllable of the rhyme. In a multisyllabic rhyme, I maintain that the perception of rhyme is still aligned with a single time point. If the rhyme is four syllables, the feeling of hearing a rhyme completed does not begin anew with each syllable. Instead, as a heuristic, I associate the perception of rhyme with the last accented syllable of the rhyme instance. By an "accented syllable," I mean any syllable within a rhyme class that has an accent in at least one instance. Because all the instances of the rhymes in "Whatta Man" have the same rhythmic structure, this last criterion is inconsequential in this case.

Having formalized the representation of two derived constituents of flow, accent and rhyme, we are now on much firmer footing to represent the flow of verses. Recall that flow is not exactly the accents and rhymes in a verse; it is the way these interact with meter in order to create vocal grooves. In the next chapter, I will introduce a method that incorporates these derived constituents into a compact representation of the interaction of accent, rhyme, and beat. This representation will enable both the stylistic analysis of rap music (by exploring features shared by the verses in the corpus) found in Chapter 5, as well as critical analysis of verses of the three artists found in Part II.

${\rm F}our$

From Accent to Vocal Groove

4.1 Comparing the Demo and Released Versions of Eminem's "Lose Yourself"

This chapter integrates the derived constituents of flow, accent and rhyme, into a model of vocal groove, the feature I consider most emblematic of flow. One way into vocal groove is to consider a case in which an emcee has released a fully worked-out demo for a major hit, affording an opportunity for comparison between an initial and improved version. The emcee is Eminem and the track is "Lose Yourself" (2002), from the soundtrack to the film *8 Mile*, in which he stars. Though the song is only heard in the closing credits, it encapsulates in its verses the plot of the film and maybe that of Eminem's life: the triumph of the emcee after a devastating initial failure. The track was a critical and commercial success, reaching the top of the *Billboard Hot 100* list and garnering an Academy Award and a Grammy. In 2014, twelve years after the film was released, a demo version of "Lose Yourself" appeared on Eminem's compilation album *Shady XV*. Eminem has distanced himself from this version, claiming not to remember writing or recording it (Eminem 2014). Likewise, the release of the demo drew scant attention. But the demo offers a rare analytical opportunity: here, we have two versions of an acclaimed track with very different appraisals by both the artist and the critical community. A comparison of the two versions of "Lose Yourself," especially with respect to rhythm, is instructive both in identifying a key trait of Eminem's flow (which I will pursue further in Chapter 6) and in defining a foundational aspect of flow itself, vocal groove.

Example 4.1 🌑 prints the texts of the first verse of the demo (a) and the first verse of the released track (b) side by side. Both versions deal with the problem of summoning creativity, but the creative virility of the protagonist differs between them. In the first half of the demo version, the protagonist seeks to prolong the creative openness that enables an effective verse. The second half of the demo's verse depicts an adoring, energized crowd, suggesting the surmounting of any impediments to flowing. In the released version, the protagonist's challenge in the first half is starker. He has already written an effective verse; that was supposed to be the hard part. But even with verse in hand, the protagonist—broke, sick, and weak—is unable to perform and unworthy of respect. As in the demo,

Example 4.1 (a) Eminem, "Lose Yourself" (2002, 0:54–1:40), lyrics of the first verse in released version. (b) Eminem, "Lose Yourself" [demo] (2014, 0:21–1:04), lyrics of the first verse in the demo version.

(a)	(b)
His palms are sweaty, knees weak, arms are heavy	If I was frozen inside of a moment
There's vomit on his sweater already, mom's	If I could capture time inside a capsule
spaghetti, he's nervous,	An hourglass full of sand in the palm of my hand, it
but on the surface he looks calm and ready to drop bombs,	passes through it
But he keeps on forgetting what he wrote down,	If I can grasp it, and just control what happens to it
The whole crowd goes so loud He opens his mouth,	Then I can trap it, so no more time elapses through it
but the words won't come out He's choking how,	If raps could do it, maybe I could tap into it
everybody's joking now The clock's run out,	Then I could try to channel it through Cadillacs and Buicks
time's up, over, bloah!	To transmit through 'em, to make you put your ass into it
Snap back to reality, Oh there goes gravity	And that's when you hit the roof because you can't sit
Oh, there goes Rabbit, he choked He's so mad,	through it
but he won't give up that Easy, no He won't have it,	Your passions too much for you to not be dancing to it
he knows his whole back's to these ropes It don't matter,	And as you do it, your movements become fast and fluent
he's dope	You're mashin' to it, moshing until you're black and bluish
He knows that but he's broke He's so stagnant, he knows	You're acting foolish, this music it has influenced you
When he goes back to his mobile home, that's when it's	to be rowdy but in an orderly fashion
Back to the lab again, yo This whole rhapsody	True it's chaotic, but it's got your body moving as a unit
He better go capture this moment and hope it don't pass him	Uniting together tonight, so make it last and you better just

there is a dramatic shift in the second half. Yet in the released version there are no adoring crowds, only the continuation of the first half's existential crisis. Because the released version delays the eventual triumph into later verses, it serves as a more effective rallying cry for the underdog. But, in my view, the released version is more effective for purely rhythmic reasons as well, and this pertains to vocal groove.

Provisionally, consider vocal groove to be the consistency with which an emcee does or does not accent each position within the cycle from measure to measure. When a verse always accents the same positions, confidence of prediction on the part of the listener grows as each correct prediction etches the rhythmic structure of the verse deeper into the grooves of memory. Example 4.2 🔊 prints a transcription of the demo version's first verse. Here, a single rhyme class carries much of the content from its introduction with *passes through it* on position **8** of m. 8, through that same position in every measure all the way to the end. This repeated rhyme endows an accent to **8** and **11** and thereby precludes accents on **9** and **10**. But accent in other positions is more variable; for example, precisely half of the measures accent position **0**. Example 4.3a visualizes this sense of variability by plotting how often each metric position is accented on the left. (The solid bars are 0_{mod4} positions.) The verse is somewhat groovy, in that it frequently accents positions **4**, **8**, **11**, and **14** while never accenting **3**, **9**, or **13**. But the other metric positions are sometimes accented, sometimes not. Example 4.3b captures this sense of grooviness by tabulating how many positions are accented once, twice, etc. As I have provisionally defined it, a maximally groovy verse would have tall bars on **0** and **16** and no bars elsewhere, that is, all the positions would be always accented or always not accented. In this verse, five positions are never or only once accented and two positions are all-but-once accented, but the others are more variable.

Example 4.3 Eminem, "Lose Yourself," first verse, demo version (2014 [2002]). (a) Instances of accent on each position. (b) Tabulation of instances of accent on each position. Note that "0" accents occur in three positions, i.e., 3, 9, and 13.

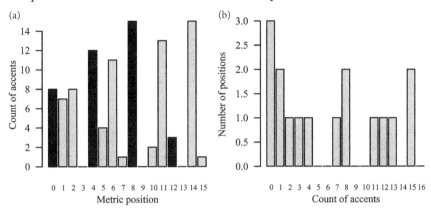

Example 4.4 🖲 transcribes the released verse, and Example 4.5 🌀 plots aspects of its grooviness analogously to Example 4.3. Here, I have divided the verse into two halves because these aspects of grooviness are quite different between them.[1] In the released version, the first half is similarly unpatterned. Positions 8 and 11 are accented through the rhymes of *arms are heavy, mom's spaghetti*, etc., and later *goes so loud, won't come out*, etc., but anticipations and echoes of these rhymes prevent a groove from fully developing. For instance, *sweater already* gives position 5 a rare accent, while *whát he wróte dówn* does the same for 13 and 15.

The rhythm of the verse changes abruptly at m. 9 in two ways. First, Eminem changes the positions that receive accents, from predominantly (4, 6, 8, 11, 14) in the first half to predominantly (2, 4, 7, 10, 12, 15) in the second half. Second, the patterning of accent becomes more rigid in the second half, where Eminem accents 13 of the 16 positions always, never, all-but-once, or only-once. The other three are accented either twice (0) or all-but-twice (2 and 14). Looking closer, three moments preclude absolute consistency. The first and last measure of the segment differ slightly from the others; *back* at the beginning of the excerpt creates an accent on 0 that other measures do not adopt, and *capture this moment* at the end creates the only accents on 5 or 8. Between these bookends are six measures entirely consistent in accent.

In my view, the released version improves on the demo by supporting its narrative through rhythm. In the released version, the protagonist fails to perform in the first half and seems to wallow in that failure in the second half. The lyrics allow only a single suggestion of confidence, just five words: *he's dope, he knows that*. But the groovy rhythm of the second half belies the protagonist's despair.

---

1. For the demo version, dividing the verse in half does not affect which positions are accented, nor the consistency with which they are accented.

Example 4.5 Eminem, "Lose Yourself," first verse, released version (2002). Compare to Example 4.3.

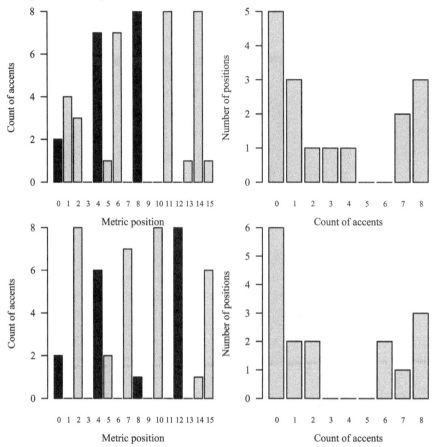

He may say that he choked and he's stagnant, but the rhythmic groove is that of an emcee in full command of his flow, foreshadowing his later triumph. In calling this patterning of accent "groove," I employ a term already laden with meaning in popular music discourse, especially in connection with jazz and funk. At this stage, having encountered "flow" and "accent," the reader should be comfortable with musical terms with multiple meanings. But my use of "groove" demands greater consideration. The term already has several book-length treatments (e.g., Danielsen 2006, Abel 2014, Roholt 2014). Like some of those writers, I will link groove to syncopation and repetition. Following Anne Danielsen, I also locate groove in a kind of abstraction of what we hear. But there are also considerable differences between these authors' and my own construal of groove. For some, groove exists between music and a moving or dancing listener; I find groove in the rhythms of the rapping voice. For some, groove exists in the rhythmic nuances, discarded in quantization, of the kind I explore in Chapter 8; I find groove in transcriptions of rap verses I have interpretively quantized. For some, groove exists in the interaction of multiple rhythmic streams; I find groove in the lone rapping voice. Finally, for some, the repetition of groove in artists like James Brown extends over many minutes; I find groove in rap verses that rarely last a minute and whose sounds (i.e., lyrics) are always changing. In Section 4.2, I will highlight divergences and correspondences between groove as presented in the last few decades of scholarship and the model of vocal groove I will present later. In Section 4.3, I will formalize my meaning of groove as patterning of accent and describe various mathematical properties of rap's stock of vocal grooves. One of the key differences between the rap music versus funk and jazz is rap's rhythmic variety, necessitated by the inherent limitations of rhyming and narrative demands. Because of this variety, I argue that vocal grooves in rap music are often presented with slight alterations, and I will detail in Section 4.4 a fuzzy model of groovy listening that is attuned to these alterations. The chapter closes by characterizing the grooviness of rap music generally, though much of that discussion spills over into Chapter 5. In short, my aim in this chapter is to present a method for aligning bars of rapping with one of a small number of possible grooves and, further, of segmenting a verse of rapping into a succession of such grooves. Later on, I will explore how the use of those grooves can characterize artists and eras (see Chapter 5), as well as underlie the unique expressive practice of emcees (see, in particular, Chapters 6 and 7).

4.2 Comparing Groove and Vocal Groove

Many discussions of groove cast the phenomenon not so much as a particular kind of music but rather as a way of being musical, and these construals often emphasize the connection between groove and movement. Studies support the commonplace observation that music spontaneously induces bodily movement, whether the slight nodding of the head or a full-bodied inclination toward dance (Toiviainen, Luck, & Thompson 2009; Demos et al. 2012). Some writers term this very inclination "groove," an association facilitated by the rhyming of "groove" and "move." Guy Madison (2006, p. 201), for example, defines groove as "the experience that motivates or induces such movement." Petr Janata, Stefan Tomic, and Jason Haberman (2012, p. 54) also emphasize movement, defining groove as "the urge to move in response to music." Other definitions are less explicit about movement, but their word choice is telling. For Jeff Pressing (2002, p. 308), groove is "a *kinetic* framework for the reliable prediction of events," while for Iyer (1998, p. 27), it is "the continual, *embodied* awareness of the relationship of the pulse to the generated musical material" [emphases added].

Tiger Roholt (2014, p. 105) goes much further, arguing that the "feel of a groove is a central element of the body's motor-intentional engagement with rhythmic elements of music." Roholt takes this "motor-intentional engagement" from Maurice Merleau-Ponty's idea of motor intentionality (2012 [1945],

p. 141). For Merleau-Ponty, to "know something" is to affirm its feeling of rightness, as determined by the history of the body. As Taylor Carman (2008, p. 110) writes, referring to Merleau-Ponty, "The intentionality of perception thus depends crucially on the normativity of the body schema. . . . [W]e have a *feel* for the kinds of balance and posture that afford us a correct and proper view of the world."[2] Thus in Merleau-Ponty and Roholt's view, groove begins with a body that recognizes the rightness of the music through motion. If groove is necessarily embodied, it would seem out of reach (to use a bodily metaphor) for a computational approach. But computational analysis, at least at the scale pursued in this book, coexists with the embodied awareness that Roholt prizes. This is because the findings of the analysis must pass the "smell test" of the author. In my experience, a computational process that delivers a surprising result, one that does not "feel right," more often than not is the result of an error or a problem in reasoning. And I, like anyone else, assess what "feels right" by referencing the history of my own body. Furthermore, insisting on an embodied account of groove privileges one sort of engagement with rap music—namely, dancing to it in a club. But many people experience and use rap music in all sorts of contexts: while transiting, working, exercising, or shopping. The effects of groove would be limited if they required the kind of spontaneous motion envisioned by Roholt, Madison, or Janata, Tomic, and Haberman.

One can hold the view that groove is the inclination to spontaneous motion without specifying what "in the music" induces that motion. Charles Keil is chief among earlier scholars proposing a "source" for groove, and he locates it in what he calls "participatory discrepancies." Keil writes, in the second sentence of his most cited article, that "music, to be personally involving and socially valuable, must be 'out of time' and 'out of tune.'" He then equates "participatory discrepancies" with "semiconscious or unconscious slightly out of syncnesses" (1987, p. 275). While these discrepancies could apply to pitch or melodic fragments, Keil focuses on rhythmic differentiation: "It is the little discrepancies within a jazz drummer's beat, between bass and drums, between rhythm section and soloists, that create 'swing' and invite us to participate" (p. 277). If groove is the result of these micro-rhythmic discrepancies, then an analytical approach like the one adopted here, which proceeds from quantized rhythm, would be unable to describe groove.

Keil's influence is not the only thing drawing together "groove" and "swing." As Madison and colleagues note, both groove and swing "are known to differ between performances of the same piece" (2011, p. 1579). Here, groove and swing are conflated because of the persistence of a "work concept" from classical music that emphasizes similarity in melody or chord progressions between two "versions" of a song that might sound quite different. Since groove and swing are both outside the bounds of this work concept (e.g., not represented in music notation), they are presumed equivalent. There are also linguistic motivations, at least in some languages, that

---

2. Middleton (1999, p. 269) also associates groove with "feel," defining it as "a feel created by a repeated framework within which variation can then take place."

conflate groove and swing. As Madison (2006, p. 201) writes, "The closest synonym for groove in Swedish is *svängig*, which is equivalent to 'having swing.'"

Keil's work on participatory discrepancies and groove makes two separate claims that are easily conflated. The first is that musicians use discrepancies like swing differently, and that different circumstances of genre or tempo call for different types of discrepancies. The second claim is that these discrepancies, these micro-rhythmic differences between musicians, are the source of groove. The first claim has been supported as well as one could expect considering the difficulty entailed in verifying it. (Chapter 8, on Talib Kweli, focuses on his use of swing, and this literature is reviewed there.) The second claim, however, appears untrue. Madison et al. (2011) seek to correlate aspects of sound with listeners' ratings of grooviness. While the salience of the beat (e.g., beat 1, beat 2, etc.) was correlated with high ratings of grooviness, swing was generally uncorrelated with listeners' ratings. This noncorrelation does not mean that groove is not dependent on swing—perhaps another method of measuring groove would reveal the correlation. But the ways musicians talk about grooving, even the word itself and connotations of being "in the groove," emphasize synchronicity rather than asynchronicity. Keil himself (1995, p. 6) was eventually won over, after the drummer and theorist John Chernoff suggested that "maybe most or all grooves get better the more precisely people played together." In rap music, which, at least since the mid-2000s, has relied ever more on sequencing and digital production, this emphasis on precision is particularly acute. Because of the repertoire I study, and given the lack of evidence that micro-timing variation is at the core of groove, I do not consider microtiming to be a constituent of groove. Instead, I maintain that groove and swing are distinct though possibly related concepts.

The writers discussed thus far tend to emphasize two genres of music, jazz and funk. In both these genres, songs are substantially longer than rap tracks, let alone rap verses. For Danielsen (2006, p. 161), this length is the result of extensive repetition and is itself a feature of groove. In considering the repetitive nature of funk music, Danielsen draws extensively on David Lidov's typology of musical repetition (1979). Lidov distinguishes between three kinds of repetition: formative, focal, and textural. These differ not only in their lengths, but also in their claims for attention. Formative repetition is the kind of repetition that is a formal requirement and therefore passes unnoticed. Lidov gives the example of the "parallel period" in classical music, in which a melody is repeated twice, but the composer changes the end of the second instance to give a more definitive sense of closure. (An example of this may be heard in Excerpt 4a ♠.) Formative repetition is relevant to rap music as well, specifically in hooks, where (often) segments of one or two measures repeat to fill out a four- or eight-measure span. Verses also often tend to evince formative repetition in the form of rhyming couplets.[3] Focal repetition occurs when repetitions accrue beyond the expectations of the genre,

---

3. About half of the rhyme classes in the genre-wide corpus exist as couplets (rather than longer chains of rhymes). The three emcees examined in Part II tend to use far fewer couplets (see the analysis script).

drawing attention to themselves and extending the sense of the present—what Danielsen (2006, p. 158) calls "an accumulation of time"—by dwelling on material that should have given way to something new. In Lidov's words, "The usual single repetition is neutralized by fulfilling a grammatical role; the extra repetition . . . is an immediate signal for a change of attention. Instead of focusing on the repeated material only, we focus on the repetition as an activity per se, and seek a symbolic interpretation of it" (1979, p. 15). In the rhymes of rap music, focal repetition can occur in rhyme chains whose very repetitiveness calls attention to the act of rhyming. If a listener asks how long the chain can continue, the rhyme has shed its transparency as a formal requirement.

But for Danielsen, groove applies to Lidov's third kind of repetition, textural repetition, where material is restated so many times that the listener begins to assume it will repeat indefinitely. As repetition becomes textural, it is no longer focal; instead, attention moves elsewhere, to "another voice" or alterations in the repeated material.[4] Danielsen aligns this kind of repetition with groove in funk music, though with an insistence that the repetition never fades entirely from view because in funk music repetition is always repetition-with-a-difference (2006, p. 161), in which each iteration strays from the previous iteration but is still recognized as a version of "the same thing" (p. 159).[5] In ascribing to groove a specific extent of repetitiveness, Lidov, and Danielsen by association, may have excised the vocal flow of a rap track from the concept of groove. While recurring instrumental streams are no doubt an instance of textural repetition, the vocal flow, by default, *is* the other voice to which attention turns. For the flow to merge into the instrumental streams' textural repetition, the sounds of the flow would need to be constantly repeated, and thus the words themselves would need to be constantly repeated. This kind of repetition both precludes narrative and undermines rap's priority on creativity and variety in lyrics.[6]

One way of reconciling my view of vocal groove and Danielsen's view of groove-as-repetition is to claim that vocal groove is focal repetition, not textural repetition. Indeed, Danielsen's claim of repetition as repetition-with-a-difference substantially undercuts

---

4. For Lidov, textural repetition arises after about 5 reiterations (p. 5) and "voice" refers to any line of music, including those played on instruments.

5. Danielsen also cites Henry Louis Gates's concept of "signifyin(g)" in her discussion of repetition-with-a-difference (Gates 1988, pp. xxii–xxiii, cited in Danielsen 2006, p. 58). Gates's signifyin(g) refers to the creation of meaning through the instantiation of tropes in African American literature, namely, tropes of conventional phrases, narrative forms, and gestures. In contrast to similar theories of meaning making (e.g., Barthes, Kristeva, etc.), Gates views this repetition as a means of reanimating traditions rather than creating something new.

6. Only one example of texturally repetitive lyrics comes to mind, though I am sure others exist: Das Racist's "Combination Pizza Hut and Taco Bell." In the track, two friends talking on cell phones claim to be at the same restaurant, when, in fact, there are multiple such franchises on the same avenue. The text is repetitive enough that textural repetition is obtained, as described by Lidov: attention is drawn to subtle differences in inflection and rhyme ("pizza gut," "taco smell," etc.), while each iteration is simultaneously heard as categorically equivalent. But it is not coincidental that the track is knowingly comedic: the idea that a rap verse would repeat lyrics unendingly and the idea that specifying the name and street of a restaurant would be insufficient to locate a friend are equally and mutually absurd.

the connection between groove and textural repetition. If there is a difference in repetition, and if that difference is noted by listeners, then the repetition is still present in attention, if not the focus of attention. More so, it seems to me that what unites both these kinds of repetition is the way they exceed expectation. In focal repetition, one is surprised that the repetition did not conclude after having met stylistic demands. In textural repetition, one is surprised that the repeated material has gone on long enough to become part of the texture. Vocal groove in rap music shares this element of surprise, that an emcee has managed to maintain a patterning of accent for a substantial portion of the verse, despite changes in narrative situation or rhyme patterning.

There is one more significant divergence between my concept of vocal groove and groove as encountered in recent scholarship. All the accounts of groove discussed so far are fundamentally social: you cannot groove by yourself (Zbikowski 2004). This sociality is inherent in the writing of Ingrid Monson, one of whose informants describes groove as a euphoria "that comes [from] playing good time *with* somebody" (1996, p. 68, emphasis in the original). While Roholt, Madison, and Janata, Tomic, and Haberman all focus on the sociality between the musician and the audience, other construals of groove emphasize rhythmic relationships between musicians. In his influential studies of African rhythm, Nketia (1974, p. 126) emphasizes what he calls "multilinear rhythm," meaning that the total rhythmic affect (i.e., the groove) results from the concatenation of many distinct rhythmic lines. Within this mixture of instruments, Nketia distinguishes between "divisive" rhythms, those that group equal numbers of units, and "additive" rhythms, that group unequal numbers of units. One can translate Nketia's divisive and additive rhythm to rap without too much trouble: generally, the steady boom-bap is divisive and the more varied rhythms of other streams (including the voice) are additive.[7] Viewing groove as multilinear rhythm also connects to other concepts addressed previously. Specifically, if the essential rhythmic character of a groove arises through the interaction and balance of distinct voices, then repetition is absolutely necessary. As Chernoff notes, "Changing the part of one drum in a composition . . . would alter the affect of the total rhythmic fabric" (1979, p. 58).

My construal of vocal groove is thus a significant departure from these approaches because I locate groove in a single voice, namely, that of the emcee. While I will examine the relationship between this vocal groove and other instrumental streams, especially in Chapter 7, I maintain that rap verses with similar patterns of accentuation share the same vocal groove even if the instrumental streams they flow over sound dissimilar. I have found in Rowan Oliver (2016) a precedent for this admittedly unusual conception of groove. Oliver discusses the "drop one" groove of reggae music, citing Bob Marley and the Wailers's "Crazy

---

7. Like all translations, this one is imperfect. Joseph Nketia and other later scholars of African rhythm insist that African rhythm (often, more specifically West African rhythm) has a "flat" metric hierarchy, where each position at the tactus level is equally weighted (e.g., Koetting 1970). This is not the case in rap music, where the relative weights of beats 1 and 3 vs. 2 and 4 are acknowledged. Furthermore, much of the music that draws the attention of Nketia falls in a 12-unit cycle rather than rap's 16-unit cycle. The rhythmic possibilities of a 12-unit cycle are in some ways richer because durations of both 3 and 4 units are divisive.

Baldhead" as an example. Here, both the drum and bass avoid the downbeat, but Oliver argues they do so not out of an interaction with each other but out of an interaction with stylistic conventions:

> Of course they are grooving together (rather than operating in some artificial, anti-musical isolation), but the point here is that, at the same time as grooving with one another, they are also each grooving individually with the contextual sense of time that is derived from prior knowledge of the drop-one idiom. (2016, p. 244)

I will revisit this idea in the conclusion that follows.

Despite all the dissimilarities described here, in many ways, my discussion of groove is rather conventional, although formalized to enable computational analysis. Like Mark Abel (2014, p. 31), Maria Witek (2017, p. 138), and Richard Ashley (2014, p. 157), I consider syncopation an essential feature of the rhythm of groove. Syncopation is another term that can take on many meanings. Godfried Toussaint writes, and I concur, that "syncopation is very much a Western concept, and for some types of music, new mathematical substitutes for syncopation, which are not culturally dependent, may be more appropriate and useful" (2013, p. 68). I will address these "new mathematical substitutes" in the next section, but here I would like to demonstrate two distinct phenomena (both called "syncopation") that writers like Abel, Witek, and Ashley have in mind. The first phenomenon is addressed by the definition given in the *Oxford Companion of Music* as "the displacement of the normal musical accent from a strong beat to a weak one" (Scholes & Jagley 2017). Example 4.6, reprinted from David Temperley (1999, p. 28), shows the syncopated melody of The Beatles's "Here Comes the Sun" (1969), in which every event from the second measure forward falls on the weak part of the beat. (The lowest level of dots in the metric grid are eighth notes, twice as long as the sixteenth notes normally relevant to rap music.) The lines connecting weak-position events to the following strong-position events represent a systematic displacement of the squarer "deep structure" of the melody. As Temperley points out, syncopation is more than the appearance of accents on a weak beat or a weak part of a beat; it is also the perception that those accents conceptually align with the strong beats they precede (1999, p. 20).

Another phenomenon that falls under the banner of syncopation is what is sometimes called "polyrhythm" or "cross-rhythms." Here, for example, five roughly equal durations are presented within a four-beat measure. In the 16-unit meter of rap music, this might occur as $3 + 3 + 3 + 3 + 4 = 16$, rather than $4 + 4 + 4 + 4 = 16$. These five dispersed events cannot map 1-to-1 onto the four beats of the measure, so they are not considered displacements of those beats, but rather part of a competing metric framework. The three-beat inter-rhyme intervals of The Flobot's "Airplane Mode" (see Example 1.11) are an instance of cross-rhythms in rap music, where several durations of three beats coexist with a metric framework of four beats.

Why should syncopation be so prominent in music that grooves? One answer is that it further encourages the embodied engagement just described. While not addressing groove specifically, Petri Toiviainen, Geoff Luck, and Marc Thompson

Example 4.6 The Beatles, "Here Comes the Sun," melodic transcription highlighting syncopation as displacement. Reprinted from Temperley (1999, p. 28), Example 5.

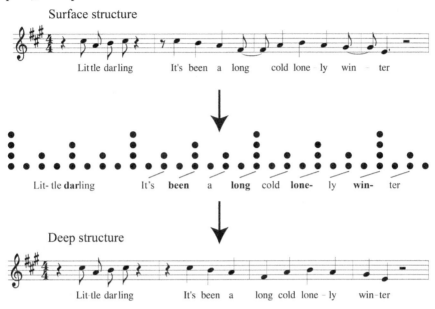

(2010) found that, when asked to spontaneously move to a performance of a 12-bar blues progression, participants aligned different parts of their bodies with different metrical levels, aligning their arms with the tactus level (i.e., the beat) and their torso with "higher" levels of two and/or four beats. Artists who aim to make their audience move are thus incentivized to articulate all these metrical levels. As Abel notes, (displacement) syncopation is a particularly effective means of clarifying the meter:

> Marking out off-beats is far more productive rhythmically than marking out on-beats as it is the most economical way of bringing into play an extra ["lower"] metrical level and thus provides more temporal information. (2014, p. 52)

For Temperley, the displacement of events to weaker parts of the beat not only clarifies metric structure, but also enables the syncopating performer to differentiate him- or herself from other non-syncopated layers of the texture, often the percussion (1999, p. 35).

More recently, Witek (2017) has presented an alternative view. She begins by noting that given enough syncopation, the listener hazards losing the main beat; this would suggest an optimal "level" of syncopation of zero. Why, then, is syncopation pleasurable? In their theories of emotion in music, Meyer (1954) and David Huron (2006) both argue that pleasure in music results from the playful denial of expectation; syncopation is surprising and therefore pleasurable. But

Afro-diasporic music combines this unexpectedness with pervasive repetition. At some point, the repeated denial of expectation is no longer surprising. Witek instead proposes that syncopation does not reveal the metric structure to us, but rather it presents gaps in the metric structure, moments that are silent because their events have been shifted elsewhere. These gaps—which are on strong beats—are the source of syncopation's pleasure:

> I propose that the gaps afforded by syncopations in groove are central to explaining our desire to move to music. Dancing to the beat is an active response to the music's invitation to add to the rhythmic fabric. The gaps revealed by syncopations . . . invite the body itself to fill in for the phenomenal accents: metric accents without phenomenal events open up spaces in the musical structure that the body desires to occupy. (2017, p. 146)

While I concur with Witek, I would also stress that this embodied pleasure need not require any particular kind of movement.

According to Ashley (2014, p. 156), syncopation also differentiates the beats in the measure. In the example of "polyrhythm" given earlier, 3 + 3 + 3 + 3 + 4 = 16, that final "4" will strongly emphasize whatever beat it falls on as the endpoint of the reiterated 3-durations. Perhaps it appears as 3 + 3 + 3 + 3 + 4, meaning the string of 3-durations terminates at 12. Or, perhaps it appears in the music as 4 + 3 + 3 + 3 + 3, meaning the string of 3-durations terminates at 0. For Ashley, emphasizing the downbeat through syncopation is a hallmark of funk music termed "The One" by funk practitioners. In contrast, emphasizing weak beats like beat four is a marker of an earlier style of R&B and soul. I will address this notion that syncopation changes the perceived quality of beats within a measure at greater length in the discussion that follows.

Another way in which my view of groove is conventional pertains to the "realness" of groove. Danielsen and others depict groove as endless repetition. But the music we hear seems messier, dependent on imperfect human performance, if not intentional variation. This duality between the ideal groove and the sounding music can take many forms: among those I will not pursue here include meter vs. rhythm (in the poetic sense), process vs. product, Ferdinand de Saussure's *langue* vs. *parole* (2013 [1916]), and Mikhail Bakhtin's sentence vs. utterance (1986 [1952]). In surveying these dualities, Oliver rightly states, "Whilst each iteration of the duality serves its own conceptual or analytical purpose, they can all be seen, in musical terms, to express a relationship between the abstract and the sounded aspects of the music" (2016, p. 243).

While not the only productive lens, Danielsen (2006, pp. 46–47) examines groove through the duality of the actual and virtual articulated by Gilles Deleuze, which together constitute the real. The actual and the virtual are different domains in which phenomena exist. Deleuze insists that the virtual is not abstract, nor is it the opposite of the real, but rather the real in another domain (Deleuze & Parnet 2002, p. 148). The groove we hear thus exists in both domains. Not only does the groove contain the actual sounds we hear, but it also contains virtual elements. Perhaps we imagine the same groove played by different instruments, or without one of its layers, or at a different tempo. These are virtual features of the groove, no less real just because they are not actual. For a more concrete example, the "boom-bap", of much rap music, with bass drums on 1 and 3, snare on 2 and 4, and perhaps hi-hats marking eighth notes, exists in the virtual domain. In the actual domain, the boom-bap might have a reverberant snare or a clipped one, or perhaps hand claps constitute the "bap." Similarly, a pattern of accentuation, such as the placement of accents on positions (2, 4, 7, 10, 12, 15) in the second half of "Lose Yourself," might align many verses with a shared "virtual" groove, even though they sound different in the actual realm. While each is the same in the virtual domain, each retains its actual particularity.

Out of this scholarship of groove several threads are vital for the formulation of vocal groove. First, groove is inherently repetitive. A sense of groove continues to gain prominence as material reiterates, and thus the duration of repetition is important. Second, groove is virtual: the mind and body of the listener can be quite forgiving of perturbations in the repetition of the musical surface. The groove as presented in performance is an approximation or representation of a more general, virtual groove articulated in many performances. Thus, the degree of similarity is also important. Finally, while microtiming is not necessary for groove, a syncopated groove is marked.

4.3 Seven Vocal Groove Classes

To begin formalizing vocal groove, Example 4.7 🔊 plots another snippet of Eminem's flow, from the last verse of "8 Mile" (2002), the title song of the film's soundtrack. (A more detailed analysis of "8 Mile" appears in Chapter 6.) Like the second half of "Lose Yourself," accent in the span is highly patterned, with every position either accented or not accented in all three measures.[8] Example 4.8 visualizes these two grooves as polygons inscribed in a circle through a position-class-set plot. The 16 positions around the circle are the positions of the measure; the sides of the polygon represent the inter-accent intervals (IAIs). "Lose Yourself" could be described as IAIs of [233233] starting at 2. "8 Mile" could be described as IAIs of [323323] starting at 0. Here, I have used the first accent of the measure as "the start." As seen on the clock face, these grooves are rotations of each other, with "8 Mile" starting one position after "Lose Yourself." In the mathematical field of combinatorics, these grooves are instances of the same "binary necklace," an arrangement of pearls (i.e., positions) that are either black or white (i.e., accented or unaccented).[9] We can thus represent both of them as the same IAI string, namely, <332_332>, starting at positions 4 ("Lose Yourself") and 5 ("8 Mile").[10] Since they are rotations, I call them members of the same **groove class**. The angled brackets

---

8. *My* on **14** of m. 22 does not conform to the pattern, but this does not affect the foregoing argument.

9. Regarding binary necklaces, "Two necklaces are considered to be the same if one can be *rotated* so that the color of its beads correspond, one-to-one, with the color of the beads of the other necklace" (Toussaint 2013, p. 74).

10. Because the IAI pattern <332_332> has an internal repetition, these two grooves could also be labeled starting at **12** and **13**.

Example 4.7 Eminem, "8 Mile" (2002, 4:05–4:13).

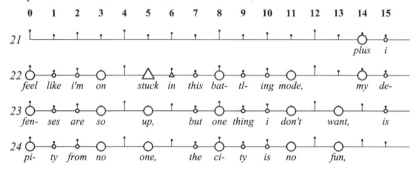

Example 4.8 The grooves of Eminem's "Lose Yourself," released version, first verse, mm. 10–13 (from Example 4.4, left), and "8 Mile," third verse, mm. 22–24 (from Example 4.7, right). Sixteen positions on the clock face represent 16 positions of the measure; filled dots represent accented positions; lines represent inter-accent durations.

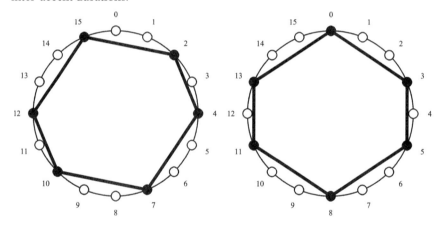

indicate that this groove class is a duration segment independent of rotation, and the underscore indicates that it is a groove class that bisects the measure into two spans of 8.

If these two excerpts both belong to the same groove class, how many groove classes are there? The range of grooves possible in rap music is limited by two factors: rap's pervasive meter of 16 positions and the prohibition on consecutive accents. Furthermore, in my view of groove, the IAIs of grooves are "well formed" in the sense that no such durations are twice as long as others.[11] Thus, all the IAIs of

---

11. This mirrors Lerdahl and Jackendoff's "metric well-formedness rule 3: At each metrical level, strong beats are spaced either two or three beats apart" (1983, p. 69), the same well-formedness rule that prevents consecutive accents (see Chapter 3). See also London (2004, pp. 100–109).

rap's vocal grooves span either 2 or 3 metric positions. In discussing what he calls "funky rhythms," Richard Cohn (2012) also limits durations to 2 or 3 units. Cohn calls the resulting rhythms "Platonic" because they consist entirely of durations of small, prime integers. In discussing musical intervals between pitches, Plato understands consonance as the extent to which one can describe an interval as the ratio between two small primes. Thus, the most consonant pitch interval is the unison, expressible as the ratio 1:1, followed by the octave (2:1) and the perfect fifth (3:2). For Plato, the integers of 2 and 3 represent unity and conflict, respectively. Following this perspective, Cohn sees durations of 3 as disordering. Powers of 2 generate the metric structure of rap and most other popular music, but no power of 3 is also a power of 2. Cohn thus maps 3-generation, which he calls a "centrifugal" impulse, to musical qualities of "conflict, instability, release, subversion, and tension." Generation by powers of 2 is, conversely, characterized as "centripetal," representing "resolution, stability, relocking, authority, and relaxation"[12] (para. 2.2). Translating Plato's conception from pitch to time, 3-durations are destabilizing because they rarely coincide with salient 2-durations. For example, in reiterated 3-durations in a 16-unit cycle, the origin of the cycle ("the downbeat") will coincide with the 3-derived rhythm only every three measures (i.e., after 48 units, but not 16 or 32).

In the Platonic tradition, the small-integer ratios explain the structure not only of music, but also of the cosmos, the human body, and nearly everything between. Of course, I am not asserting that this ancient Greek worldview is held by creators or listeners of rap music. And furthermore, I have no desire to be the "they" referred to by Talib Kweli when he raps,

> If I drop African thought they probably would lie and say it's Greek philosophy.
> —Talib Kweli, "Don't Let Up" (2000)

Other scholars have noted the necessity for 3-durations in groove without bringing Plato to the table. As Danielsen puts it,

> One has to avoid a basic pulse that is *too* authoritarian, or the fabric of the rhythm as a whole might end up too ordered or straightforward. (2006, p. 68)

The aim of my Platonic conception of groove is to focus on how emcees introduce and negotiate this disorder of 3-durations, not to coerce a broader Platonic worldview onto rap music. Cohn addresses this issue as well, and it is worth quoting him at some length:

> One can grant an innate psychological reality to these small numbers [Wynn 1992, Dehaene 2011]; one can hypothesize that they are susceptible to mobilization in opposition to each other; one can conjecture further that those oppositions might

---

12. The inclusion of both "tension" and "release" in the qualities of the centrifugal impulse is odd and may be erroneous.

stand in for other sorts of opposition that are more palpable to our observed and embodied experience. None of this forces one to subscribe to the view that numbers map in a particular way onto qualities in the world. (para. 8.7)

4.3.1 Properties of Groove Classes

Because all grooves in rap music consist of inter-accent durations of 2 and/or 3 units, and because all grooves repeat with each measure, summing to 16 units, there are exactly seven groove classes in rap delivery. Thus, the groove classes are <2222_2222>, <332_332>, <332_2222>, <323_2222>, <333322>, <333232>, and <3223222>. The first of these, with only 2-durations, I call the **duple** groove class. All the other classes have some 3-durations in them, and I call them **nonduple** groove classes. (The underscore indicates a groove class that can be bisected into 8 + 8.) The stipulation that grooves repeat every 16 units is somewhat artificial, and there are segments of rap that can be understood as repeated grooves of other durations (e.g., 12-unit grooves), but I believe the 16-unit grooves are by far most common.

Unless they have an internal repetition, each of these seven groove classes might occur in any of 16 rotations.[13] While the rotations differ significantly in ways I will address here, the classes themselves exhibit some properties irrespective of rotation. The first property one might examine is what Toussaint (2013, p. 47) calls their **rhythmic contour**, which indexes whether successive durations are the same length, shorter, or longer.[14] In the groove class <333322>, the rhythmic contour would be {0, 0, 0, –1, 0, +1}.[15] The rhythmic contour of this groove class has two nonzero entries. In other words, the rate of accent in the groove changes twice, from reiterated 3-durations at the beginning, to reiterated 2-durations at the end, and back to reiterated 3-durations as the groove repeats. The groove class <332_2222> has a similar rhythmic contour, only switching the rate of accent twice. The other four nonduple groove classes have more dynamic rhythmic contours, switching rates 4 times. Related to rhythmic contour is what I call **inner periodicity**, the longest-duration segment within a groove that repeats the same duration. The non-duple groove class with the longest inner periodicity is <333322>, which maintains Cohn's "centrifugal impulse" for 12 units. The class <332_2222> maintains an opposing "centripetal impulse" nearly as long, for 10 units. In contrast, the inner periodicity of groove classes <332_332> and <3223222> never surpasses 6 units. Inner periodicity is an important feature of a groove because it captures how often durational expectations are frustrated. In <332_332>, the second duration creates an expectation of continuing 3-durations, which the

---

13. The internal repetition in <332_332> reduces the number of rotations to 8; that of <2222_2222> reduces the number of rotations to 2.
14. Toussaint credits the concept of rhythmic contour to Hutchison & Knopoff (1987, p. 281). A rhythmic contour is equivalent to the contour adjacency series described in Friedmann (1985).
15. The final "+1" refers to the difference between the last and first duration in a repeating groove.

Example 4.9 Durations between all pairs of accent onsets in the groove class <333322>.

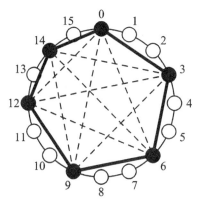

following 2-duration frustrates. In contrast, while the expectation for 3-durations must eventually recede in rap's pervasive duple meter, <333322> rewards that expectation considerably longer.

Rhythmic contour and inner periodicity, in essence, are properties of adjacent durations. Other properties of groove classes derive from the combination of durations. In the position-class-set plot of Example 4.9, solid lines visualize the successive durations of <333322>, while dashed lines connect every pair of onsets. Since these durations are distances around a circle, for any pair of onsets, there are two ways of measuring the distance, clockwise and counterclockwise. If one defines the interval as the shortest of those paths around the circle, a full account of durations between onsets in the <333322> groove class is (2, 2, 3, 3, 3, 3, 4, 5, 5, 6, 6, 6, 7, 7, 8). Example 4.10 tabulates these durations into an **interval content histogram**, while Table 4.1 represents such histograms of all seven groove classes.[16] The first three columns in the histograms are the same for grooves of the same accent-cardinality (i.e., number of IAIs), but the latter columns reveal important differences. Of particular note is the final column of the table, which counts how many intervals of 8 are in each groove class (i.e., how many ways a groove class bisects the measure). Toussaint calls rhythms that cannot bisect the measure "odd rhythms," and <3223222> is the only such rhythm among the groove classes.[17] In contrast, all the other grooves can place accents 8 units apart (i.e., every other

16. The interval content histogram is equivalent to the "interval class vectors" of (musical) set theory. In that usage, "interval class" refers to the equivalence of complementary integers in the modular space. For example, 9 and 7 are of the same interval class in *mod* 16 space because 16−9 = 7. I opt for Toussaint's "interval content histogram" both because I need not consider large intervals apart from their complements and because "histogram" captures what the object actually is—a tabulation of intervals. For computing interval content histograms, see the analysis script.

17. The groove class <3223222> has several other properties beyond rhythmic oddity that have drawn attention in mathematical music theory. Perhaps most significantly, the groove is maximally even (Clough & Douthett 1991), meaning it distributes 7 accents around a circle of 16 positions such that they are all as far apart from their neighbors as possible. <3223222> is also a

Example 4.10 Interval content histogram of groove class <333322>.

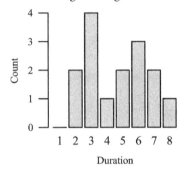

Table 4.1 Interval content of the seven vocal groove classes and the entropy of their IAIs

Groove class	Interval size								Entropy (scaled)
	1	*2*	*3*	*4*	*5*	*6*	*7*	*8*	
<2222_2222>	0	8	0	8	0	8	0	4	0.65
<332_332>	0	2	4	0	4	2	0	3	0.75
<333232>	0	2	4	0	4	2	1	2	0.81
<333322>	0	2	4	1	2	3	2	1	0.89
<332_2222>	0	5	2	4	2	4	2	2	0.90
<323_2222>	0	5	2	3	4	2	4	1	0.89
<3223222>	0	5	2	3	4	1	6	0	0.80

beat), corresponding to the boom-bap of rap music. Also of interest in Table 4.1 are the values in the fourth column, a count of the number of consecutive beats a groove class can accent. The classes <332_332> and <333232> never accent consecutive beats, while <332_2222> presents four opportunities for doing so.

Another feature of the histograms is the "evenness" of the distribution of durations between (possibly nonadjacent) accents. In this chapter and several that follow, this notion of the evenness of distributions—distributions of durations, of IAIs and IRIs, and the patterning of IAIs—will be critical. In general, the evenness of a distribution is important because it encapsulates the idea of predictability.

"deep rhythm," meaning that, as the interval content histogram shows, it employs each interval a unique number of times (Gamer 1967; Toussaint 2013, p. 183). In the existing literature, these properties are discussed for their inherent mathematical beauty as well as their prevalence in certain repertoires. To cite the most common examples, the major scale in the pitch domain is a "deep scale," as is the pentatonic scale. In the case of rap music, which relies on a driving, steady beat, <3223222> is rarely employed as a vocal groove despite its many interesting numeric properties.

Accent within the duple groove class is very predictable; accordingly, quantities in the first row of Table 4.1 are very unevenly distributed between 8 and 0.

Several studies of predictability in music use entropy as a measure of the flatness of a distribution (Toussaint 2013, p. 111). Frank Lambert gives an account of entropy from physics, where the term was first employed:

> The second law of thermodynamics says that energy of all kinds in our material world disperses or spreads out if it is not hindered from doing so. Entropy is the quantitative measure of that kind of spontaneous process: how much energy has flowed from being localized to becoming more widely spread out (at a specific temperature). (2002, p. 1241)

In statistics, entropy similarly refers to the evenness of a distribution, though without the implication that this evenness results from a process of dispersion. Entropy is affected by the number of bins or outcomes in the system; here, bins are represented by the different values of interval sizes. To account for this, Table 4.1 lists the "scaled entropy" of the durations, a value that is always between 0 and 1.[18] Entropy is low when the probability of one outcome is very high and that of other outcomes is very low, as is the case for IAIs in the duple groove class. Entropy is high when the probabilities of all outcomes are similar, as is the case in the class <333322>. I will later use scaled entropy to explore the predictability of IRIs and substrings and IAIs.

4.3.2 Properties of Rotations of Groove Classes

The properties discussed in the last section—rhythmic contour, rhythmic oddity, and entropy of IAIs—apply equally to all rotations of a groove class. But grooves of the same class starting at different points in the measure can be quite divergent, especially in the way their accents relate to the beats of the measure, that is, the 0_{mod4} positions. Example 4.11 shows a schematic representation of the two grooves just discussed, those of "Lose Yourself" and "8 Mile." Again, these are both of the <332_332> class. Each groove has two beats with accents depicted as |1001|, that is, accents on 0_{mod4} and 3_{mod4}. I call this arrangement of accents within the beat a **beat-accent type**.[19] The other beats have only one accent in them, but in "Lose Yourself" that accent falls on a 2_{mod4} position, whereas in "8 Mile" it falls on a 1_{mod4} position. Accents on 1_{mod4} positions account for only 6 percent of accents in the corpus, so the groove of "8 Mile" is more unexpected for an acculturated listener of

---

18. Scaled entropy may be found by dividing the entropy of a distribution by the log of the number of bins.

19. The beat-accent type is related to two other measures. The first is Toussaint's measure of "offbeatness" (2013, p. 282), which counts the number of onsets landing on a position that is not a multiple of a factor of the cardinality. For a cardinality of 16, all the 1_{mod2} positions would be "off-beat." The second is Stephen Handel's "metrical strength" (1992, p. 498), a count of accents on strong beats, that is, 0_{mod4} positions.

Example 4.11 Schematic outline of the grooves of "Lose Yourself" and "8 Mile." 1 indicates accent; 0 indicates non-accent or silence.

Lose Yourself: |0010|1001|0010|1001|
8 Mile: |1001|0100|1001|0100|

Example 4.12 Pressing's cognitive complexity of onset patterns within the beat.

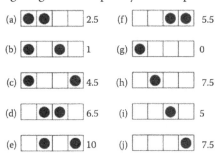

rap music.[20] In other words, the "8 Mile" groove, and its relationship to the meter, are more complex.

Jeff Pressing presents a more formal way calculating metric complexity. Example 4.12 shows ten beat-accent types, ten different ways one or two accents can be distributed in the four subdivisions of a beat. (The prohibition on consecutive accents means there cannot be more than two accents in a 4-unit beat.) Next to each, Pressing (1997, p. 6) assigns a value for what he calls the "cognitive complexity" of the type. This complexity measure is determined by, among other factors, whether the beat-accent type lacks accents in the 0_{mod4} and 2_{mod4} positions.[21] Half of the beat-accent types in Example 4.12 are not relevant to groove in rap music, either because they have consecutive accents [i.e., types (a), (d), and (f)], or because they imply inter-accent durations greater than 3 [i.e., types (g) and (j)]. Pressing's method of calculating cognitive accent is reasonable; still, a corpus enables an empirical estimation of cognitive complexity rather than a speculative one. The complexity of a beat-accent type is proportional to its prevalence in a corpus.[22] Table 4.2 shows the prevalence of the five beat-accent types involved in groove. Because we want the complexity of rarer beat-accent types to be higher, the example also presents the natural log of their prevalence, scaled between 0 and 1. For comparison, Pressing's complexity values are given as well (also scaled between 0 and 1). In deriving the cognitive complexity measure from the data, the ordering of the beat-accent types remains the same; however, the corpus suggests

20. See the analysis script.
21. The example is reprinted from Toussaint (2013, p. 119). Pressing himself lists complexity measures for six patterns (1997, p. 6); Toussaint calculates the measures for those Pressing omits. In Pressing (1997), the filled boxes refer to onsets, not accents.
22. See the analysis script.

Table 4.2 Prevalence of beat-accent types in the genre-wide corpus

Beat-accent type	Count in genre-wide corpus	Negative log of count	Pressing's, complexity, scaled	Estimated complexity, scaled
1010	3,176	0.37	0	0
0010	456	2.31	0.44	0.744
1001	554	2.11	0.39	0.721
0100	231	2.99	0.72	0.941
0101	161	3.35	1	1

a greater increase in complexity between |1010| and |1001| and, at the other end, a near equivalence between |0100| and |0101|. These differences do not seem to affect the relative complexity of different grooves. Using the value of complexity given in the final column of Table 4.2, we see that the groove of "8 Mile" is 3.32 out of a possible 4.00, greater than the groove of "Lose Yourself," at 2.93.[23] For perspective, the lowest-complexity value of a groove that includes at least one 3-duration is 0.94—this occurs in <332_2222> starting on 2_{mod4}.[24] The highest value is also found in <332_2222>, starting on 3_{mod4}. The rotations starting on 3_{mod4} place all the reiterated 2-durations in the groove on 1_{mod2} positions, resulting in a great deal of cognitive complexity.

As the comparison of "8 Mile" and "Lose Yourself" shows, the cognitive complexity of a groove pertains to a specific rotation—indeed, the three six-length groove classes have the same average complexity across their rotations, as do the three seven-length classes. Their average complexity "in the real world" is different, as many rotations of a groove class are seldom encountered in emcees' verses (see the discussion that follows). But one distinguishing feature of the classes is how the act of rotation changes their complexity. All the groove classes without internal repetition have four different complexity values in different *mod* 4 rotations. Example 4.13 shows the various complexity of different rotations of the groove classes. In the case of the class <332_2222>, as discussed previously, the most complex rotations of the class are more than 3 times as complex as the least. The class <323_2222> behaves similarly, eliciting either relatively high or relatively low rates of complexity. In practice, the high-complexity rotations of the class are avoided. The classes <3223222> and <333232>, on the other hand, have narrow ranges of possible complexity. The choice to groove to class <333232> means rather high complexity regardless of the chosen rotation.

Beyond their differing complexity, different rotations of the same groove class can, recalling the discussion of "The One" in funk music in Ashley and Danielsen, privilege or minimize different beats within the cycle. Consider the very common groove class <332_2222>. Example 4.14 🕭 plots three quatrains: (a) Rick Ross's "Aston Martin Music,"

---

23. See the analysis script.
24. See the analysis script.

Example 4.13 Complexity of different rotations of the seven groove classes. Each point represents four rotations in the case of classes without internal repetition. The number below each point refers to the onset of the rotation, *mod 4*.

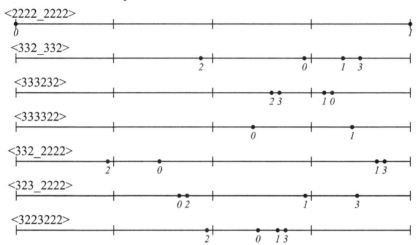

(b) Eminem's "Go to Sleep," and (c) Eminem's "The Way I Am." Each presents this groove class in different rotations, starting on **8, 10,** and **3,** respectively. These three grooves differ in their complexity: that of "Aston Martin" has the lowest complexity of all the Platonic grooves, and that of "Go to Sleep" is only slightly higher; the groove of "The Way I Am," on the other hand, has one of the highest complexities encountered in rap music.

But they also differ in the quality they impart to the four beats of the cycle. As just discussed, 3-durations are fundamentally at odds with the 16-unit cycle of rap music. A series of them might eventually connect one downbeat to another, later downbeat: (3 * 12) = 48 and 48_{mod16} = 0. But an individual 3-duration can, at best, begin or end on a beat, but not both. In looking at the 3-durations embedded in these three quatrains, notice that "Aston Martin" has a 3-duration starting on a 0_{mod4} position (i.e., 8), "Go to Sleep" has one ending on a 0_{mod4} position (i.e., 0), while "The Way I Am" neither starts nor ends a 3-duration on a 0_{mod4} position. In my hearing of "Aston Martin," the third beat is especially prominent for two reasons. First, it terminates the 10-length inner periodicity that begins on **14.** Second, it initializes the "centrifugal" motion of the 3-durations. Inversely, I hear the downbeat of "Go to Sleep" as especially prominent because it terminates the centrifugal 3-durations and initializes the series of 2-durations.[25]

25. My discussion of different beats' "quality" owes much to Victor Zuckerkandl's conception of meter as a cycle of energy in which consecutive beats lead to or away from each other (1973). As William Rothstein (1989, p. 43) points out, "Zuckerkandl's conception differs from the common one in that it focuses on the quality of motion between beats rather than on the beats themselves or on the absolute distance between them." While Abel (2014, p. 50) discusses Zuckerkandl in connection with groove, most accounts do not refer to Zuckerkandl, although his conception of beat quality has become widespread in descriptions of meter in popular music.

Example 4.14 Three quatrains exemplifying groove class <332_2222> in different rotations: (a) Rick Ross, "Aston Martin Music" (2010, 1:20–1:33); (b) Eminem, "Go to Sleep" (2013, 0:14–0:26); (c) Eminem, "The Way I Am" (2000, 2:43–2:54).

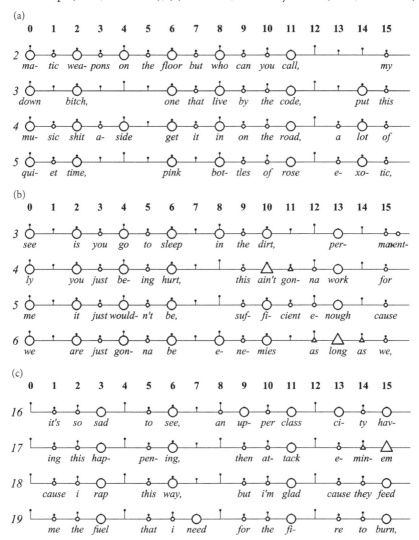

In my hearing of "The Way I Am," the rotation of the groove class also emphasizes one beat over the others, but through a different process. This verse is very unusual in the extent to which it accents 3_{mod4} positions, those just before the beat; in mm. 3–6, every such position is accented. The third beat of the measures shown in part (c) of Example 4.14 ◐ is emphasized precisely because the measures are not "preempted" by accents just before the beat. It is the use of <332_2222> in this rotation, rather than, say, <2222_2222> starting at **1**, that prevents the continuation of an accent on 3_{mod4} positions. Following m. 19, the groove returns to

<2222_2222> starting at **1** (the most complex groove possible) all the way to the end of the verse. In fact, the next beat that is not preempted by a 3_{mod4} accent is the first beat of the chorus. I will address this sort of phenomenon later, but it serves as an initial example of how groove can interact with the form of a verse and even a track. Put together, these three quatrains demonstrate the expressive range of different rotations of a groove class.

4.4 A Fuzzy Model of Groovy Listening

I can describe mm. 10–13 of "Lose Yourself" as belonging to groove class <332_ 332>, beginning on position **4**, because it presents accents every two or three positions. This is not true of many spans of flow. Example 4.15 🌑 shows the first four measures of Eminem's "Drug Ballad." This stretch of flow has IAIs of [2222352222334224223342233]. These IAIs are not of a groove class because they contain durations of 4 and 5. They also are not especially groovy in that they lack a single reiterated pattern of durations, though the substring [422233] does occur twice at the end. The unpatterned durations bely a consistent align-ment of accent and position: unless they are silent, Eminem always accents positions (**0, 2, 4, 6, 8, 11, 14**). What prevents this passage from articulating a groove class is the absence of (accented) syllables on **0** in mm. 3 and 4 and on **14** in m. 1.

In order to adopt a groovy mode of hearing, the duration of 5 units be-tween *Mark* and *this* across the downbeat of m. 2 must be divided into either [32] or [23]; in other words, one must assert an accent at either position **14** or **15** of m. 1. Asserting an accent at **14** both accords with the other measures, and privileges a 2_{mod4} position over a 3_{mod4} position. I call position **14** of m. 1 a **limit-3 accent**, a position that would be accented if one insists on hearing accents every 2 or 3 positions. All accents derived through the algorithm of Chapter 3 are also limit-3 accents; since there can be no consecutive accents, any adjacent position is not a limit-3 accent. Furthermore, all 0_{mod2} positions are limit-3 accents, unless they are already adjacent to an accent.[26] I realize that labeling a silent position as "accented" might seem strange. But silent limit-3 accents fall on strong parts of the beat, which in rap music means that it is very likely other aspects of the instrumental streams impart energy to those positions. In "Drug Ballad," for example, the bass drum hits every 0_{mod2} position.

Limit-3 accents address one challenge in finding vocal grooves in rap de-livery, but a more difficult challenge remains. Select any span of rapping at random, and it is unlikely that the IAIs will perfectly reiterate one of the vocal groove classes. While there are rap verses that maintain a groove for a long time—for example, the Eminem track "We Made You" reiterates <323_2222>

---

26. See `Scripts/DataScrubbingScripts/GetL3Durations.r`.

Example 4.15 Eminem, "Drug Ballad" (2000, 0:32–0:41).

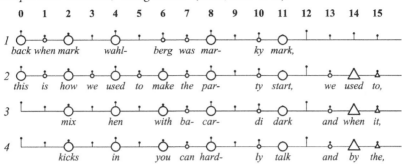

starting at **8** for nearly ten measures—most rap verses maintain a groove for only two or three measures at a time. This is the case for one of Eminem's most celebrated verses, his feature on "Renegade" from Jay-Z's *The Blueprint*, released in 2001. The verse has all the hallmarks of a great flow, with measures packed with rhyming syllables. In my hearing, the verse also grooves hard on <332_332> starting on **5** (i.e., [323323]). But in the first 12 measures, only 13 of the 24 half-measures have IAIs of [323], and only mm. 5, 8, and 9 actually articulate [323323]. Example 4.16 ◗ transcribes the second four-measure segment of the verse. This span, and indeed the rest of the verse, are pretty groovy: 12 of the 16 metric positions are always-or-never accented. But in order to assert that mm. 6 and 7 actually present the groove of mm. 5 and 8, one must hear the silence of position **5** in m. 6 as accented, rather than the rapped *put* of position **6**, which at any rate is metrically stronger. And one would need to hear *But* on position **13** of m. 7 as accented instead of *there's*, which is metrically stronger and, an examination of the wave form shows, is 6 times longer and a step higher than *But*.

I will not argue that a silence should be understood as more accented than a rapped syllable. Measures 6 and 7 do not reiterate [323323], but it is not very taxing *to hear them that way if one is so determined*—you just swap adjacent syllables' accents, twice. This swapping enables one to stay within the groove established in earlier measures, to hear each measure as a version of the same abstract (or virtual) scheme. If grooving is, as Don Byron described to Monson (1996, p. 68), "a euphoria that comes from playing good time *with* somebody," then excusing these "imperfections" enables that euphoria to continue. The ability to maintain a groove, even when a couple of accents do not line up, is reminiscent of Andrew Imbrie's distinction between "conservative" and "radical" listeners of classical music (1973). A composer like Beethoven might occasionally disrupt the meter, perhaps by presenting strong accents every three beats in a four-beat meter. A conservative listener will maintain in their mind the four-beat meter and hear the three-beat durations between accents within that framework. The radical listener seeks any chance to change the mental framework of meter, and so for her the meter *actually changes* during these disruptions. Hearing [323323] in

Example 4.16 Jay-Z featuring Eminem, "Renegade" (2001, 1:18–1:31).

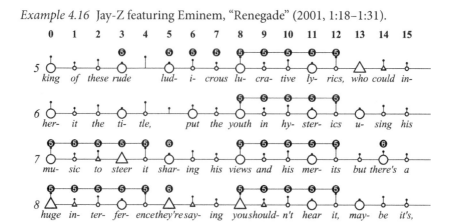

mm. 6–7 of "Renegade" is an act of conservative listening. Since these terms have unhelpful political connotations, I will instead contrast **persistent listening** and **adaptive listening**.

Persistent listening maintains an established groove even if some accents need to be swapped. The more swapping required, the less viable the hearing. In other words, a persistent listener *persists in hearing the same groove*. An adaptive listener *adapts to hearing many grooves*. Indeed, through some number of swaps and insertions, the span of "Renegade" could be heard as a purely duple <2222_2222> groove, though that hearing seems highly implausible. By implausible, I emphasize the effort involved in warping the accents actually presented into the virtual duple model. A method called dynamic time-warping provides a means for measuring this effort (Giorgino 2009). Measure 5 presents accents on (**0, 3, 5, 8, 11, 13**), sounding the [323323] groove. Measure 6 presents accents on (**0, 3, 6, 8, 11, 13**), or IAIs of [332323]. The time-warping algorithm infers a distance of 2 between these position sets, noting that one must subtract 1 from the positions of m. 6 to warp it into that of m. 5 (i.e., 6−1 = 5), and do the opposite to warp m. 5 into m. 6. I conceive of this distance as the **effort** a persistent listener exerts to hear m. 6 as [323323]. Trying to hear all four measures as reiterated instances of [323] requires an effort of four, two for each swap. For comparison, the implausible hearing of mm. 5–6 as the duple groove class <2222_2222> requires an effort of 36.[27]

In these measures, an adaptive listener, who accepts no swapped accents, never repeats the same groove twice. A persistent listener grooves on [323323] throughout, weathering four swaps overall, or one swap for every 16 units. Another persistent listener could hear the duple groove, but with a swap about every 2 units. And, given some amount of effort, there are five other groove classes

27. See the analysis script.

Example 4.17 Some plausible grooves beginning at m. 5 of the "Renegade" verse. The longer gray lines show the length of the groove; the black segment of that line shows the length adjusted for the rate of effort in hearing the groove. The line type indicates groove classes. The numbers in parentheses indicate length in position and number of swaps necessary to hear the full extent of the groove.

and many more rotations one could hear. How could a model of persistent listening choose from among them, arguing that one potential groove is more viable than another? As I have said, a persistent listener wants to hear grooves as operative for longer spans, but a very high rate of effort (i.e., effort divided by time in units) makes the hearing untenable. I reflect this in the model of groovy listening by scaling the length of a groove by the rate of effort, thereby penalizing effortful grooves and making them appear shorter than less effortful grooves. I make this adjustment through the following equation:

$$l' = l * 1 - \sqrt[4]{r},$$

Here, l is the length of the groove, l' is the adjusted length, and r is the rate of effort. I scale by $1 - \sqrt[4]{r}$ to penalize effortful grooves. When the effort is 0, the length l is scaled by $1 - \sqrt[4]{r} = 1 - 0 = 1$. Trying to hear the passage as <2222_2222> results in a rate of effort of 0.56 swaps per unit. In this case, the length of the groove is scaled by $1 - \sqrt[4]{.56} = 1 - .87 = .13$.[28] Example 4.17 shows the potential grooves that begin on the downbeat of m. 5 and have an adjusted length greater than or equal to 16 units.[29] In the first row, the four-measure [323323] groove, which translates to groove class <332332> starting on position 5, has the longest adjusted rate. This adjusted rate, for a persistent listener, is longer than the corresponding <333232>

28. The function for retrieving the grooves of a verse may be found in `Scripts/DataScrubbingScripts/GetVerseGrooves.r`. The function that builds the grooves' object appears in `Scripts/DataScrubbingScripts/BuildGroove.Object.r`.
29. To save space, some potential grooves with adjusted lengths equal to those in the example are not plotted. The longest adjusted length applies to only one groove. See the analysis script.

groove class starting on position 5 (i.e., [323332], row #6 in the example) because it requires half as many accent swaps.

There are more than 400 grooves at the start of m. 5; most of these are very effortful and thus have very low adjusted lengths. Returning to the idea that a persistent listener will try to hear as few grooves as possible within a verse, the last stage of the model of groovy listening goes through this very large collection of possible grooves in a verse and selects one groove at each position. The selected groove is the one that, among the grooves including that position, has the longest adjusted length, given a pre-set limit on rate of effort. I segment a verse at four different rates of effort: those corresponding to no swaps (i.e., an adaptive listener), one swap per measure, one swap per half-measure, and one swap per beat. This selection process segments the verse into a succession of operative grooves.[30]

Example 4.18 shows the result of this groove segmenter on the "Renegade" verse, with these four different limits on effort. The thicker lines in the first three plots show groove segments that are maintained in the next higher rate of effort. Segments are labeled by their groove class and starting position. In the first row, modeling the hearing of an adaptive listener with no tolerance for swapping accents, the groove of the verse changes very frequently. Yet with each increment of effort in maintaining a groove, a persistent listener hears fewer and longer grooves in the verse. Even with an effort of only one swap per measure, the seven short grooves of an adaptive listener in mm. 5–10 may collapse into a single, persistent [323323] (i.e., <332_332> starting on 5). In this case and in many others, much of this tidying of the segmentation occurs from the zero-swaps to one-swap-per-measure layers, and in the future I will not always plot the modeling of all four listeners.

To return to the beginning of this chapter, Example 4.19 segments both the demo version and the released version of "Lose Yourself," at rates of effort of 0 and 2 swaps per measure. Earlier, I noted that m. 9 in the released version was a moment of disjuncture, changing the narrative frame ("snap back to reality") and altering which positions in the measure tend to be accented (e.g., 8 vs. 7 and 11 vs. 12 from the first half to the second half). Furthermore, I argued that the second half adhered to the pattern of accentuation more closely. The groove segmentation plot highlights all of this. Adaptive listeners (never swapping accents) will experience a series of very short grooves in both versions. But that experience will apply to a fairly persistent listener of the second half of the demo version as well. (Some of these shorter grooves start to fall away at 1 swap per beat.) In contrast, the persistent listener of the released version hears the same groove throughout the second half, and the transition to that groove more clearly marks the midpoint of the verse, echoing the shifts in narrative tense.

30. See `Scripts/DataScrubbingScripts/GetVerseGrooveSegmentation.r`. The segments object is built through `Scripts/DataScrubbingScripts/BuildSegments.Object.r`.

Example 4.18 Jay-Z featuring Eminem, "Renegade," 2001, second verse groove segmentation. Diagonal text indicates groove class and rotation following the hyphen. Darker lines indicate grooves that are operative at the next level of persistent listening. Some brief grooves are unlabeled to prevent labels from overlapping.

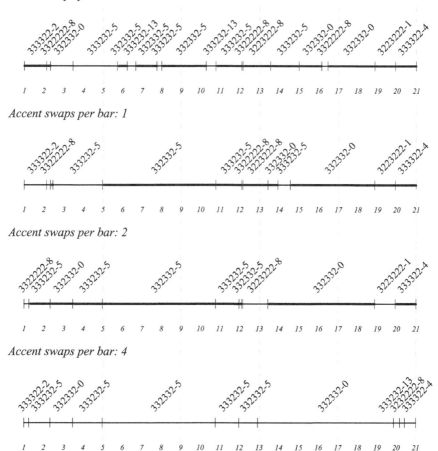

4.5 Groove-Class Usage in Rap's Flow

In the next chapter, I will present a portrait of flow in rap music informed by these models of accent, rhyme, and groove with the aim of demonstrating how the work of one emcee can be interpreted against the backdrop of the genre. The use of vocal groove is part of that portrait, and I will reserve many of my comments on vocal groove for that discussion, but here I will briefly detail how emcees deploy groove classes and their rotations. Earlier, I described features of the seven

Example 4.19 Eminem, "Lose Yourself," groove segmentation of the first verse of the demo version (left) and the released version (right) for adaptive (top) and persistent (below) listener.

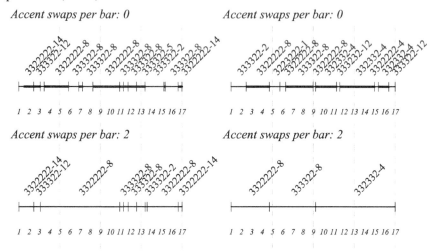

groove classes (e.g., their complexity) without qualifying their distribution in actual rap music. Like many musical features, this distribution is rather uneven (see Table 4.3).[31] Despite the closeness Abel and others depict between syncopation and groove, 44 percent of the measures in the genre-wide corpus present the duple <2222_2222> groove class, a rate that increases as tolerance for accent swapping increases.[32] This includes the entirety of 7 tracks with no swaps and 19 tracks at an effort rate of one swap per beat; this latter total amounts to a quarter of the corpus.[33] The next most common groove class is <332_2222>. As Example 4.13 showed, <332_2222> has the lowest complexity except for <2222_2222>, provided it is in a rotation that begins on 0_{mod2}. The other groove classes are all rare in the context of the corpus, accounting for 10 percent or less of the measures. But even so, they might support long spans of individual verses. For example, the groove class <333232>, which has the greatest minimal complexity (i.e., the lowest complexity of any rotation) and accounts for only 3 percent, nevertheless still supports nearly half of one track in the corpus, Blu's "Ambition." Similarly, the rhythmically odd groove class, <3223222>, accounting for only 4 percent of the corpus, supports half of The Treacherous Three's "Feel the New Heartbeat."

As the groove classes are unevenly distributed throughout the corpus, so, too, are the rotations of groove classes. In discussing rotations of the *tresillo* rhythm, [332] in an 8-unit cycle, Toussaint (2013, p. 75) introduces the notion of a robust rhythm, which he defines as "a rhythm necklace that has the property that all its

---

31. See the analysis script.
32. Again, here I refer to syncopation at the level of the 16-unit cycle. Some spans that I describe as duple may be considered syncopated at the level of the 8-unit cycle (i.e., the "eighth note level").
33. See the analysis script.

Table 4.3 Distribution of groove classes by rate of effort

Accent swaps per measure	0	1	2	4
<2222_2222>	0.44	0.49	0.54	0.54
<332_2222>	0.27	0.23	0.25	0.28
<323_2222>	0.10	0.10	0.07	0.06
<332_332>	0.07	0.07	0.06	0.07
<333322>	0.05	0.03	0.03	0.02
<3223222>	0.04	0.04	0.03	0.02
<333232>	0.03	0.03	0.02	0.01

onset rotations are used as timelines in practice." A robust rhythm, according to Toussaint, is special because its "effectiveness . . . does not depend crucially on the starting onset." To wit, the three rotations of [332] rhythm can be found in the music of people on every continent. Example 4.19 plots the distribution of different rotations for the seven groove classes. Here, lots of medium-sized bars (e.g., <3223222> and <333232>) indicate robust groove classes; a few tall bars and lots of zero entries (e.g., <2222_2222> and <332_2222>) indicate a lack of robustness. Why do some rotations of a groove class predominate? It seems that the groove classes with the least robustness are those that have the greatest variation in complexity among their rotations. For example, rotations of <2222_2222> will either have no metric complexity (because, in rotations starting on 0_{mod2}, all four beats have the accent-beat type $|1010|$) or maximal complexity (with four beats of $|0101|$ for rotations starting on 1_{mod2}). If Witek's suggestion that moderate syncopation is best, then one would expect the even-numbered rotations to outweigh the odd-numbered ones, which they do at a rate of 13 to 1. Similarly, the groove classes <332_2222> and <323_2222> both have a wide disparity between complexity in rotations starting on 0_{mod2} vs. 1_{mod2}. Nearly all instances of these classes start on 0_{mod2}. In contrast, classes <3223222> and <333232>, which result in substantial complexity regardless of rotation, are present in the corpus in nearly every rotation.

Metric complexity seems to explain why some groups of rotations predominate, but it does not explain variation among positions that are *mod* 4 equivalent and thus have the same metric complexity. Here, the most common rotation is usually the one that places an accent-beat type of $|1001|$ on beat three (i.e., places accents at 8 and 11). The class <333232> is fairly robust, but the most common rotations, those starting on 5, 2, and 13, account for about 80 percent of instances. These are three of the rotations that create an accent-beat type of $|1001|$ on beat three; rotations starting on 5 and 13 create an accent-beat type of $|1001|$ on beat one as well. Similarly, the two most common rotations of <333322>, those starting on 8 and 2, which together comprise about 75 percent of the total, create type $|1001|$ on beat three. They are also among the only rotations that place accents on 0 and 8 (in the case of starting on 2) or on consecutive beats (in the case of starting on 8).

In modeling rap's rhythms as reiterated, patterned durations between accents, the view of flow culminating in this chapter is in many ways closer to the rhythms of instrumental grooves, percussive grooves in particular, than to those typically associated with song or melody. This reflects the language of rappers themselves. The idea of the voice as a percussive instrument arises in many of Paul Edwards's interviews with emcees. When Shock G of the Digital Underground says, "I hear and remember the word positions like percussion parts in my head," I would argue that those "positions" are quite analogous to what I have called positions within the metric grid. Another emcee, Del the Funky Homosapien, speaks even more directly of vocal groove, stating that "I could write out my lyrics like a drum pattern, because I know how to write drum notation, basically" (both quoted in Edwards 2013, p. 3). I suspect the connection between rapping and vocal groove is becoming even more prominent with younger emcees, many of whom are adept with digital sequencers that make the metric grid visually explicit.

Tech N9ne is another of the half-dozen or so emcees whose method of composition, as described to Edwards, is reminiscent of vocal groove. He tells Edwards that "I come up with styles first sometimes. I might say I wanna sound like a ping-pong ball on this one, so I will [come up with the rhythm first and then] put words to it" (2010, p. 4). While this metaphor is somewhat opaque, his meaning is clearer in the audio of the interview that Edwards has posted online.[34] After saying he "comes up with styles first," Tech N9ne launches into four measures of vocal percussion on syllables like "digga dun, d'dun dun, d'dun dun." The end of these four measures produces the groove class <3223222>, starting on 4. After finishing the "scatting," he declares, "I wanna sound like a ping-pong ball." The source of the metaphor, in my view, is the unpredictable rhythm of a well-played ping-pong game, in which variably slow and fast shots might create a rhythm not unlike the groove class Tech N9ne articulates. While there may be other features that he associates with the "ping-pong" metaphor—perhaps higher pitches suggested by the small size of the ball?—his demonstration of his compositional process for Edwards shows that groove classes like those I have described can precede the creation of verses and have a sort of virtual, idealized existence that transcends the boundaries of individual flows.

The fuzzy model of groovy listening I have presented in this chapter opens up many avenues of analysis, some of which I will pursue in the case studies in Part II of this book. In Chapter 6, I will pursue further how Eminem, a particularly groovy emcee, uses grooves to support the narratives of his verses. With some minor adjustments, the method for detecting groove can be employed on the instrumental streams of rap music as well. How, then, does the groove of the voice interact with the groove of the instrumental streams? I will pursue this question in Chapter 7, focusing on the flow of Black Thought of The Roots. And while I have cordoned off the issue of microtiming and groove by my quantizing of rhythms, I will aim to recover what is lost in that process by examining the work of Talib Kweli in Chapter 8.

34. See https://www.youtube.com/watch?v=laLco_BrvjI or hear Excerpt 4b.

My construal of groove is, as I have demonstrated, particularly well suited for rap music, but could easily be extended to music analysis in other genres, such as sung popular music. I foresee two considerable challenges here. First, because of rap's particularities, I have gotten away with engaging pitch only minimally. My model of accent obliquely accounts for pitch in that pitch is present in the model because it is the primary determinant of word-level phonetic accentuation. A more thorough consideration of the sustained, quantized pitches of sung melody could result in a suitable accent-detection method for a wide variety of popular music. Were such a method developed, I believe that subsequently the groove detection method and segmentation method I have presented here could be used as is. The other issue is the relevant groove classes. Almost all rapping occurs within a 16-unit cycle, so the groove classes I have presented are most appropriate. For singing in other genres, it may be that an 8-unit or 12-unit cycle is more appropriate.[35] For the time being, I leave this work to others.

35. Don Traut (2005) treats what I have called vocal groove in the choruses of 1980s popular music, though his approach is to present a large number of exemplars rather than demonstrate the relative frequency of these grooves through a corpus approach. Though we differ in other ways as well (e.g., he admits IAIs greater than 3 and does not permit a "fuzzy" or persistent mode of hearing), that we each find the same durational patterns in rather different repertoires is testament to their pervasiveness throughout Anglo-American popular music.

CHAPTER Five

Features of Flow in the Genre and the Artist

Having represented and formalized flow through the model of accent, rhyme, and groove class, we are now ready to address questions raised in previous chapters in a more formal manner, questions such as:

- Is Jonny 5's reiteration of three-beat IRIs rare enough to support the significance I attribute to it?
- Is the regular alignment of particular sounds to particular metric positions encountered in Eminem's "Business" "flawless" in a way that other verses tend not to be?
- Are changes in rate of delivery (à la Outkast's "Flip Flop Rock") unusual enough to constitute a flipped flow?
- Is the fidelity with which Eminem hems to groove class <332_332> starting on position 4 in the second half of "Lose Yourself" commonplace or remarkable?

In the remainder of this chapter, I will explore questions like these in reference to the genre-wide corpus described in Chapter 2. I do so by introducing a series of what I call global features that measure characteristics of delivery, rhyming, rhythm, and groove in a collection of verses. I will also use this chapter to define several statistical and visualization tools that will be familiar to readers from the social sciences but perhaps unfamiliar to others. I will address these questions first through these global features of flow in the larger corpus. But at the end of this chapter, I will use the features to characterize the flow of one emcee, Black Thought of The Roots. I intend this characterization to demonstrate how computational methods can bring out elements of an emcee's flow in comparison to conventional rapping.

5.1 Stylistic Analysis: Global Features of Flow

5.1.1 Global Features of Delivery

In common parlance, the first feature of flow is speed: Is the flow fast or slow? This measurement of speed is more complex than one might assume. Measurements of

Example 5.1 Visual demonstration of the *t*-test of equal means. Samples *b* and *c* each have means greater than *a*, but the difference between the means *c* and *a* might have arisen by chance.

speed in the popular press count the words in the lyrics and divide by the duration of the track (e.g., Chalabi 2014). Yet varying proportions of tracks consist of hooks and breaks rather than verses. Furthermore, the relevant rate to measure is syllables over time, not words over time. The average number of syllables per word varies widely within the corpus, from a low of 1.10 in Kurtis Blow's "The Breaks" to a high of 1.54 in The Roots "What They Do." If the number of syllables in a word varies between verses, it would seem a poor choice for representing the speed of flow. The difference between average word per syllable in "The Breaks" and "What They Do" is, to use a technical term, **statistically significant** according to the *t*-test of equality of means familiar to readers in the social sciences. While syllables per word is not an especially notable feature of flow, it does provide an opportunity to demonstrate the meaning of the *t*-test, which will be more important later in this chapter and in subsequent chapters. Put simply, the *t*-test takes two samples, measures whether the difference in their means is significant given the **variance** (i.e., "spread") in the samples, and reflects the likelihood that the difference in means would arise if the second sample were randomly drawn from its distribution. Example 5.1 demonstrates the *t*-test graphically, plotting three samples: *a*, *b*, and *c*. The means of samples *b* and *c* are similar, and both means are greater than the mean of sample *a*. But sample *c* has fewer points as well as greater variance, that is, the average distance to the mean. So while the mean of *c* is greater than the mean of *a*, several points in *c* are less than several points in *a*. If we took a random pair, one from *a* and one from *c*, not infrequently the one from *a* would be greater; the difference in means between *a* and *c* is thus said not to be significant. The *p*-value of a *t*-test reflects this likelihood that the difference in means arises by chance; by convention, if the *p*-value is less than 0.05 (1 in 20), the difference in means is considered significant. In the case of the number of syllables per word of "The Breaks" vs. "What They Do," the *p*-value is less than 0.001.[1]

To more accurately measure delivery rate, one need account for the number of measures in the verse, the tempo of the track, and the average length of syllables in beats. I therefore define **syllable speed**, the rate of syllables per second, as

$$\frac{1}{\mu d' * t}$$

---

1. Here and in the future, I will report the details of a *t*-test in the footnotes. The length of the average word (in syllables) in "What They Do" ($M = 1.54$, $SD - 0.97$) is greater than in "The Breaks" ($M = 1.10$, $SD = 0.35$) by 0.44 syllables ($t(160) = -4.84$, $p < 0.001$). See the analysis script for this demonstration and the derivation of syllables per word.

Example 5.2 Plot of kernel density estimate of syllable speed in rap music. The area under the curve is equal to 1.

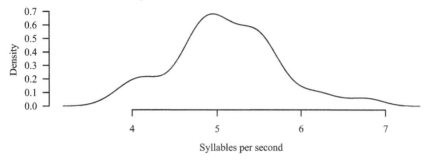

Example 5.3 Non-correlation between syllable speed and region (left) and delivery rate and year (right).

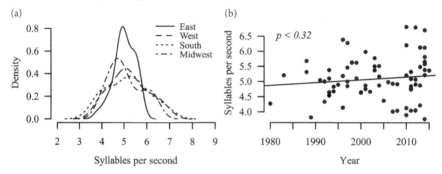

where $\mu d'$ is the average duration, in positions, of syllables that do not end lines or phrases of rapping, and t is the duration of a position in seconds.[2]

Example 5.2 shows syllable speed in the corpus through a probability density estimation, a common way of showing the distribution of a random variable. In a **density estimate plot**, the area of space under any segment of the curve expresses the likelihood that a variable (e.g., syllable speed) will fall within that interval; therefore, the area under the entire curve is 1. Density estimate plots are useful in showing the distribution of continuous variables (like syllable speed) and are preferable to other visualizations (e.g., histograms) because they appear smooth even if the data are sparse (Devore 2000, pp. 144–146). In the genre-wide corpus, syllables occur around a rate of 5.09 syllables per second.[3] But as Example 5.3

2. Recall that lines of rapping are segments that are grammatically closed and result in as many segments in a verse as there are measures; phrases of rapping are the syllables rapped in one breath. Excluding syllables that end lines or phrases is important in a case like "The Breaks," where every other measure is the crowd's response—"that's the breaks, that's the breaks." The duration of the last syllable of rapping before the response is very long because it includes the entire measure of audience response, but that should not affect the measure of Kurtis Blow's rate of delivery. See the analysis script for the derivation of syllables per second.

3. See the analysis script.

Example 5.4 (a) Tempo of rap tracks in the corpus over time; (b) metric saturation of rap verses over time.

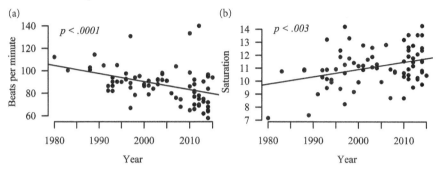

shows, there is no significant difference between syllable speed and region,[4] nor does syllable speed change over time.

This lack of an upward trajectory in syllable speed contradicts the widespread idea that "New School" rap is faster than "Old School" rap. Robert Marriott (2004, p. 193) speaks of the "faster cadences" of so-called "Golden Age" hip hop of the early 1990s in comparison to rapping of the 1980s. This distinction also underlies Krims's differentiation between the "sung style" of early rap and the "speech-effusive" and "percussion-effusive" styles of later rap (2000, p. 50). I do not dispute Krims's genre system; perhaps the corpus paints a more static picture of rap development due to small sample sizes. Furthermore, these differing styles of rapping have probably always coexisted.[5] Perhaps emcees of one style or another gained greater prominence in different eras as listener tastes and industry offerings changed. But the selection of artists in the corpus, including commercially successful as well as "slept-on" artists, ought to be unaffected by such shifts.

This constancy in syllable speed belies two real changes in rap music over the course of the corpus. The first, seen in Example 5.4a, is that rap music in all regions is getting slower. How can syllable speed stay constant while tempo decreases? Emcees are packing in more syllables per measure. I capture this shift with a feature termed **saturation** of a rap verse, the average percentage of positions within the measure that are occupied by a syllable.[6] As tempo decreases, saturation increases (Example 5.4b). Calculating saturation at the level of the measure rather than verse helps identify instances of "flipped flows" that change from slow to fast or vice versa, à la Outkast's "Flip Flop Rock" (see Example 1.5 🌑).

4. See the analysis script.
5. Krims acknowledges that his genre system of music does not sort emcees by era or geography and that multiple genres of rapping coexist even within a single verse. "Rhythmic styles of many commercially successful emcees . . . have progressively become faster and, as it is often put, more 'complex' . . . at the same time, older styles persist (and new *kinds* of complexity develop) [emphasis original], thus affording an opportunity for rhythmic-stylistic contrasts to open up into historical, geographic, political, and other kinds of signification" (2000, p. 49).
6. In measuring saturation, I handle syllables in metric spaces larger than C_{16} by quantizing them into C_{16} space and discarding any resultant simultaneous syllables. See the analysis script.

Example 5.5 Density plot of change in measure-to-measure saturation in the corpus.

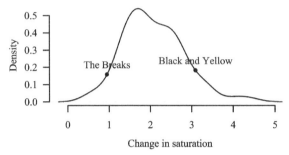

Saturation in a verse, the mean number of occupied positions in each measure, indicates how active an emcee is in the texture; the **change in saturation** in a verse, defined as the average absolute difference in occupied positions from measure to measure, indicates how much that activity changes from line to line.[7] Example 5.5 documents the stability of saturation in most verses; emcees usually add or subtract only one or two syllables from line to line. Those verses on the long tail of the example represent verses with frequent shifts in saturation. Wiz Khalifa's "Black and Yellow" is one such verse, with a change in saturation of nearly 3; Example 5.6a and Example 5.6b ◐ contrast the second quatrain of that verse with the second quatrain of Kurtis Blow's "The Breaks," which has a change in saturation of less than 1. This means that while Kurtis Blow tends to have the same number of occupied positions in each measure, Wiz Khalifa adds or subtracts more than three positions per measure.

Another global feature of a verse's flow is how its segmentation aligns with the meter. Example 5.7 shows the density estimates of phrase beginnings and endings within the metric cycle in the corpus. Recall that "phrase endings" are defined as the last syllable before the emcee breathes.[8] Because meter is a cycle, these densities rely on "circular" or "directional" statistics (Mardia & Jupp 2000). For example, consider two lines, ending, respectively, on position **14** and position **2**; one ends just before the downbeat and the other just after it, while the average of 14 and 2 is $(14 + 2) \div 2 = 8$. A better interpretation of "average" in this case is **0**, the circular average within a *mod* 16 cycle.[9] Under both models of segmentation, most segments begin near the downbeat and end near the fourth beat. Notice also that the density estimate of phrase endings is more concentrated at beat four compared to the beginning. This means that although the length of phrases in

---

7. See the analysis script.
8. Here, I focus on phrase endings rather than line endings because of how line endings are annotated. There are as many lines in a verse as there are measures, a stipulation that builds in a bias for lines to begin near the downbeat. Phrases, defined by where the emcee breathes, have no such bias.
9. The plot of Example 5.7 calculates circular densities using functions included in Tsagris, Athineou, & Sajib (2017) and Agostinelli & Lund (2017).

Example 5.6a Kurtis Blow, "The Breaks" (1980, 0:46–0:56).

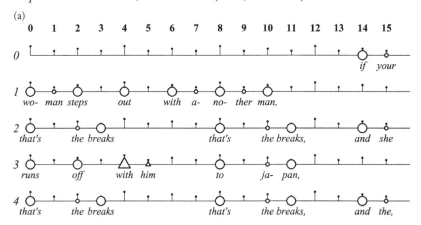

Example 5.6b Wiz Khalifa, "Black and Yellow" (2011, 0:48–1:00).

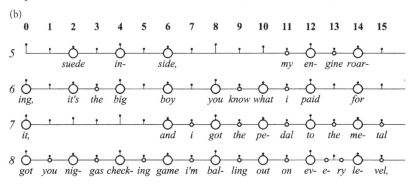

Example 5.7 Density of phrase beginnings (dashed line) and phrase endings (solid line) by metric position.

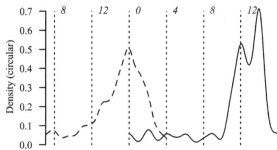

Example 5.8 Kanye West, "Stronger" (2007, 0:50–0:61).

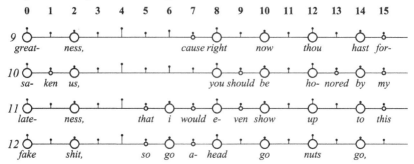

rapping is variable, differences in length are accommodated by starting later, not ending earlier.

The peak of the density estimate of phrase endings, either within a verse or within the corpus, is analogous to the **central pillar**, a term coined by Griffiths (2003, p. 43) as "the point at which a line begins and ends, the division of the musical phrase, [which] can be imagined as being like a pillar in architecture, or as posts on a fence alongside the song's ongoing road: the return of the pillar or post can be a moment of some drama." The verses of the genre overwhelmingly place phrase endings near the fourth beat. Consider a verse's central pillar the point in the measure that coincides with the maximum of the density estimate of phrase endings. Only nine of the seventy-five verses have central pillars in the first half of the measure, while two thirds have central pillars on or after position **12**.[10] Why are so many phrases directed toward the last beat of the measure? Ends of phrases are important: they often clarify meaning or introduce wordplay and, further, they are the most common site of rhyme. In most tracks, cutting through the instrumental streams will be easier on beat four than on beat one, as beat one is often the site of chord changes in rhythm section instruments (e.g., keyboard, bass, etc.). There is thus an individualizing effect to placing line endings on beat four, where the emcee is in competition with the snare drum and frequently little else.

In contrast, aligning phrase endings with the beginning of the measure suggests an emcee merged with the instrumental streams, rather than flowing over them. Kanye West, in the first verse of "Stronger," places the pillar just after position 2 (Example 5.8 ◆). This places him in competition with the bass drum and, in the second half of the verse, with the synthesizer. West's phrasing also seems to be a response to the sampling of Daft Punk's "Harder, Better, Faster, Stronger," a track with heavily processed vocals performed by a duo rarely seen without their robotic helmets. Using a persistent sample with its own words is a rarity in rap music, and each line of the sample places its own ending at the end of measure, which West has to avoid. In addition, ending a phrase at the beginning of the measure adds

10. See the analysis script.

a kind of seamlessness and almost motoric quality to this verse that supports the dehumanized aesthetic of Daft Punk.

5.1.2 Global Features of Rhyme

In this section, I will discuss three features of rhyming in the corpus. The first of these details what scholars of lyric poetry call "internal rhyme." In printed verse, any rhymes not at a line ending are internal. But rap lyrics are not printed; line endings are often ambiguous, making internal rhyme hard to define. The coding of rhyme undertaken in Chapter 3 offers a new way of recognizing internal rhymes. Example 5.9 🌑 transcribes quatrains from four measures of two verses from the corpus and encodes their rhyme scheme with letters.

In (a) "Feel the New Heartbeat," the rhyme scheme can be described as AABB, all end rhymes. In (b) "Y'all Ready Know," the scheme is ABABCCDDC, where A is <come, from>, B is <go, O>, C is <pimpin', different, limpin'> and D is <pops, bop>. Defining which rhymes are end rhymes is futile, especially since others might disagree with my segmentation of lines. Therefore, a better question to ask is this: How would the rhymes of the verse need to be rearranged such that every instance of a class was uttered before another class was heard? In other words, how difficult would it be to transform a rhyme scheme of ABABCCDDC into one of AABBCCCDD? This is, in essence, a sorting problem. One sorting algorithm, the insertion sort, moves through an input vector from left to right. Each new element is compared to the element to the left and moves leftward if it is lesser. In the rhyme scheme ABABCCDDC, the second A would be moved to the left of the first B and, much later on, the last C would be moved to the left of the two Ds. Rhyme schemes that require more insertions in sorting have what I call a greater degree of **rhyme mixture**. We can measure mixture by noting the number of insertions necessary to sort the scheme—this count of insertions is a proxy for the amount of effort the algorithm exerts.[11]

In this case, three moves are necessary, one to get the second A in place and two to get the last C in place. Notice that the distance these two unsorted elements move differs. In my view, this is not significant in the experience of hearing rhyme. It is surprising that Joell Ortiz returns to the <pimpin', different> rhyme class with limpin', and I believe it would have been equally surprising even if several other instances of the <pops, bop> rhyme class had occurred. What matters is how many rhyme instances have to move in order to sort the scheme, not the distance that they move. So I measure the mixture of the "Y'all Ready Know" quatrain as 2. And because verses in the corpus can be of different lengths, I also scale the mixture by the number of measures. While there is little of significance in the distribution of mixture in the corpus—almost half the verses have no mixture at all—the concept

---

11. The insertion sort is reminiscent of the dynamic time warping employed in Chapter 4, but insertion sort assumes that the final vector contains the same elements as the initial vector. See the analysis script.

Example 5.9 (a) The Treacherous Three, "Feel the Heartbeat" (1981, 0:34–0:43); (b) Slaughterhouse, "Y'all Ready Know" (2015, 0:30–0:41).

> Party people got a brand new treat (A),
> On the well-known tune we call heart-beat (A).
> But we jazzed it up and we broke it down (B),
> And came out with a brand new funky sound (B).
>
> I seen a lot of come (A), I seen a lot of go (B),
> But ya'll know where I'm from (A), B.R. double O (B), you know the rest,
> Pimpin' (C), yeah I was bred different (C).
> Here come the pops (D) with the N.Y. bop (D), you know, the leg limpin' (C).

will be important in the case studies of the coming chapters in identifying verses of individual emcees with a greater concern for complexity of rhyme.

The other global features of rhyme involve the patterning of inter-rhyme intervals (IRIs). Example 5.10 ◐ shows two quatrains from the corpus: (a) one from the beginning of Kanye West's "Stronger" and (b) the other from the end of Jean Grae's "My Crew." The difference in patterning is stark. In "Stronger," rhymes (and the phrase endings they precede) all fall on position 3, just after the down-beat.[12] Thus, all these rhymes have IRIs of 4 beats. In "My Crew," IRIs range from 0.5 beats (*just / begun*, m. 14) to 5.5 beats (*picture / with ya*, mm. 15–16). Example 5.11a captures the difference in these flows by tabulating their IRIs, discarding any IRI greater than 8. (This reflects a window of perception of two measures and asserts that rhymes at a greater distance will not be heard as such.[13]) Already, "My Crew" looks different in that it has many more values of IRIs than "Stronger." But the IRIs themselves do not capture the complete picture. In "My Crew," an IRI of 3 occurs twice, more than any other IRI longer than a beat. These three-beat IRIs occur be-tween *realize* and *reasons* in m. 13 and *done* and *us* in mm. 13–14. There is, however, another three-beat IRI, between repetitions of *us* in m. 15. The table omits this be-cause other instances of the same rhyme class (*just* and *begun*) intervene. Example 5.11b tabulates the IRIs of the two spans again, counting not just the durations be-tween successive instances of a rhyme class, but the durations between all pairs of instances of a rhyme class. Those more than eight beats are still discarded.

A key difference between these two flows is the difficulty of predicting when rhyme will occur. In "Stronger," "four beats" is always a good guess. In "My Crew," there are ten different IRI values, though some are more likely than others. In other words, the distribution of IRIs in "My Crew" is "flatter" than in "Stronger." In Chapter 4, I employed entropy as a tool for documenting the flatness of a distri-bution (see the discussion of Table 4.1); recall that entropy is low when the prob-ability of one outcome is very high and that of other outcomes is very low, as is

---

12. Recall that the time point of a polysyllabic rhyme is defined as the position of the final syllable that carries an accent in at least one instance; thus, the rhymes in "Stronger" fall on position 3, not position 0.
13. See the discussion surrounding Table 3.1 ◐ in Chapter 3 for a more thorough treatment of this issue.

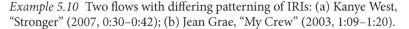

Example 5.10 Two flows with differing patterning of IRIs: (a) Kanye West, "Stronger" (2007, 0:30–0:42); (b) Jean Grae, "My Crew" (2003, 1:09–1:20).

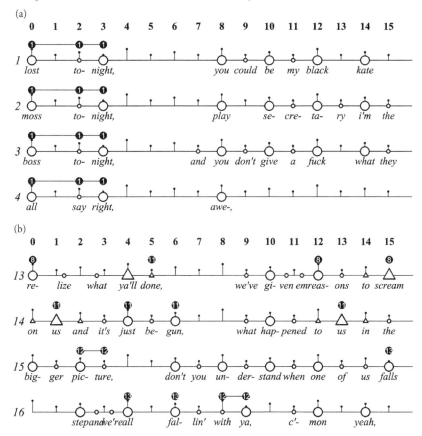

the case of IRIs in "Stronger," and that entropy is high when the probabilities of all outcomes are similar, as is the case in "My Crew." Example 5.12 plots the density estimate of IRI entropy in the corpus and locates these two verses on the curve. (Lil Kim's "Lighters Up" is on the curve as well, for reasons that will become clear in a moment.) Several emcees with reputations for complex flows, such as Jean Grae, Bizzie Bone of Bone Thugs-n-Harmony, and Big K.R.I.T., have among the highest entropy of IRIs in the corpus, suggesting that complexity in flow is related to the unpredictability of durations between rhymes.[14]

14. IRI entropy captures how unpredictable rhyme is within a verse, but does not address one of the questions I raised in the beginning of Chapter 2 and again in this chapter: Is The Flobot's use of four rhymes of the same class, each separated by three beats, uncommon in the genre? The answer is yes: none of the seventy tracks in the genre-wide corpus do this, and only three of them (Action Bronson's "Easy Rider," Lil' Kim's "Lighters Up," and Phonte's "The Good Fight") have three rhymes of the same class, each separated by three beats. See the analysis script.

Example 5.11 Inter-rhyme intervals in "Stronger" and "My Crew": (a) IRIs among successive instances of rhyme classes; (b) IRIs among all pairs of instances within a rhyme class.

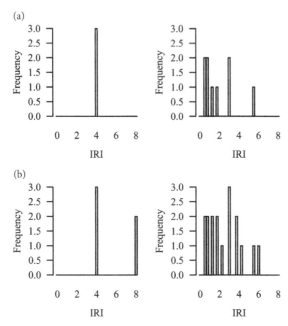

Example 5.12 Density of IRI entropy in the genre-wide corpus.

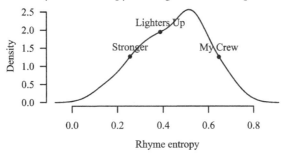

Example 5.13 🖳 🜂 transcribes the first half of Lil Kim's "Lighters Up," and Example 5.14 tabulates its IRIs analogously to Example 5.11b. In its first 12 measures, this verse has a remarkable patterning of rhythm, a version of the <332_332> groove class at the level of the beat (i.e., C_4), not the metric position (i.e., C_{16}). Rhyme usually aligns with this groove, as in mm. 1–2, where there are three rhyme instances three beats apart (*sty* to *die* to *by*, the [33] substring of [332]), with another two beats of rapping before the next rhyme class begins (the [2] substring of [332]). Example 5.14 shows the histogram of IRIs in the verse. There are many three- and six-beat IRIs, and because the rhyme scheme sometimes spills over

Example 5.14 IRIs (among all pairs of instances) in "Lighters Up" (entire verse).

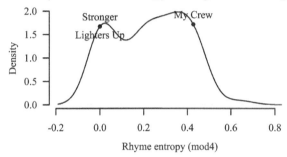

Example 5.15 Density of *mod* 4 IRI entropy in the genre-wide corpus.

into a new instance of the <332_332> groove, there are some other values as well. Those other values push the entropy of IRIs in the verse higher than "Stronger," though not as high as "My Crew."

In both "Lighters Up" and "My Crew," IRIs are difficult to predict because, unlike "Stronger," there are many possible IRI values. But where the two differ is this: all the IRIs in "Lighters Up" are whole numbers. Lil' Kim's placement of rhyme is difficult to predict at the *mod* 16 level (i.e., position within the measure) but not at the *mod* 4 level (i.e., position within the beat); Jean Grae's placement of rhyme is difficult to predict at both. It is thus important to distinguish between entropy at these two levels by taking the *mod* 4 value of the position of onset. Example 5.15 plots the density estimate of the *mod* 4 IRI entropy in the corpus, where the entropy of "Lighters Up" is the same as that of "Stronger" because both place all rhymes on the same part of the beat.[15]

5.1.3 Global Features of Rhythm and Groove

The final set of global features of flow relate to the deployment of the rhythm and groove classes described in Chapter 4. Recall from Chapter 4 the idea of

15. See the analysis script.

Example 5.16 Groove segmentation for a persistent listener in two verses: (a) Rick Ross, "Aston Martin Music" (2010, 1:18–1:40); (b) Wiz Khalifa, "Black and Yellow" (2011, 0:36–1:00).

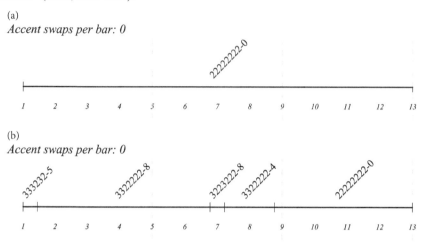

(a)
Accent swaps per bar: 0

(b)
Accent swaps per bar: 0

syncopation as two different phenomena, both the displacement of a regular rhythm off the beat, and as the use of consistent durations that do not equally divide the cardinality of the metric cycle (e.g., 3-durations). The former notion of displacement is captured in the data by the use of the duple groove class starting on position **1**, a groove articulated in 2 percent of the corpus. The latter notion of non-alignment with the meter is captured in the data by IAIs of 3. A gross measure of this sort of syncopation is the average of the limit-3 IAIs in a verse, a number that by definition will fall between 2 and 3. For twelve of the verses in the corpus, this value is 2 (i.e., those verses are entirely duple). In another fifteen verses, only 1 in 10 IAIs is a 3-duration. At the other end of the spectrum are verses that balance 2- and 3-durations, usually by grooving to classes such as <333322> (in the case of Jay Rock's "Pay for It") or <332_332> (in the case of ScHoolboy Q's "Studio").

While average IAI captures how often an emcee resists rap's persistent duple meter by inserting a 3-duration, it does not capture how patterned those 3-durations are. The patterning of 3-durations is captured by the concept of vocal grooves presented in Chapter 4. There, I described a method that segments a verse into a succession of grooves. The general **grooviness** of a verse is a measure of how rapidly these grooves change. I also described a method of calculating the effort required of an adaptive listener to hear longer grooves, as opposed to shorter ones. **Groove adherence** is a measure of this effort. Finally, some grooves are more common in the genre than others, and **groove typicality** is a measure of how unique an emcee's choice of grooves is.

Example 5.16 ◑ shows groove segmentations for a persistent listener in two verses: (a) Wiz Khalifa's "Black and Yellow" and (b) Rick Ross's "Aston Martin Music." The former is exclusively duple. The latter is duple in the last four measures and includes a long groove in the class <332_2222> starting on position **8** in the first half,

Example 5.17 Density of grooviness in the corpus, with two verses highlighted.

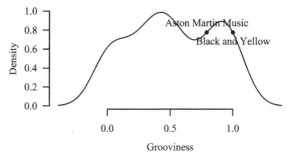

placing the syncopation in the second half of the measure. In a sense, "Black and Yellow" is groovier, maintaining the same groove throughout. But consider the in-time experience of hearing "Aston Martin Music." In much of the verse, the memory of the recent past (say, the past two measures, or roughly six seconds) includes only one groove; this is true in both the beginning and end while untrue around mm. 7–10. A listener of "Aston Martin Music," in other words, spends most of the verse grooving to something locally familiar. To capture this sense of familiarity, I define grooviness as the proportion of the verse occupied by grooves that last at least two measures for an adaptive listener (e.g., one who does not swap accents to maintain a groove).[16] Example 5.17 plots the density estimate of grooviness in the corpus, showing Wiz Khalifa with a grooviness of 1 and Rick Ross with a grooviness of 0.8.

Grooviness measures how much of a verse stays within long grooves for an adaptive listener, one unwilling to swap accents in order to hear longer grooves. It can thus obscure the relationship between verses that, for a persistent listener, have a lot in common. Example 5.18 ◉ plots groove segmentations of the first eight measures of two verses: (a) Boots Riley's verse on The Coup's "The Magic Clap" and (b) The Treacherous Three's "Feel the New Heartbeat." The thicker lines in the segmentation plot indicate grooves that are available even for persistent listeners swapping two accents per measure. For an adaptive listener, with an allowable swap rate of zero, "The Magic Clap" is groovy and "Feel the New Heartbeat" is not. But for a persistent listener, swapping accents once per half measure, both these verses groove on the same class and rotation, <332_2222> starting on position **8**. Groove adherence reflects the fact that the shared groove is immediately apparent in "The Magic Clap," while only available to a persistent listener of "Feel the New Heartbeat." Groove adherence takes groove segments of verses at an effort rate of one swap per half measure that are longer than two measures and calculates what portion of those segments is in the same groove class and rotation without any accent swaps.[17] "The Magic Clap," with no accent swaps, adheres to the groove that dominates at an effort rate of one swap per half measure for nearly the full

16. The choice of two measures as a threshold for grooviness reflects the fact that the groove classes are all one measure long and must repeat at least once. See the analysis script.
17. See the analysis script.

Example 5.18 Two verses with similar grooves and different levels of adherence: (a) The Coup, "The Magic Clap" (2012, 0:37–1:06); (b) The Treacherous Three, "Feel the Heartbeat" (1981, 0:34–0:52).

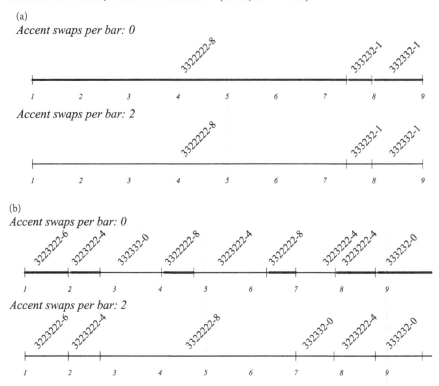

extent of that groove, breaking off in m. 6. In contrast, "Feel the New Heartbeat" articulates the <332_2222> groove beginning on position **8** only in mm. 4 and 6, yielding an adherence of about 0.25 in these measures. (The figure is slightly higher for the verse as a whole.) Example 5.19 plots the density estimate of groove adherence in the corpus, showing "The Magic Clap" as much higher than "Feel the New Heartbeat," despite their shared grooves.[18]

These first two measures related to groove, grooviness and groove adherence, are independent of the chosen groove classes. But judging by their paucity in the corpus, some groove classes are harder to execute than others because, for example, they rarely place accents on strong beats. Groove typicality is a measure of the prevalence of the grooves of a verse taken as a whole. Example 5.20 🌑 shows groove segmentations of two earlier flows, as heard at a rate of effort of 0 and one

---

18. In my view, "groove adherence" is what Eminem refers to in the first verse of "Business" when he claims his flow is "almost flawless." Indeed, in the segmentation of the verse, the first four measures (plotted as Example 1.4 🌑) articulate a <323_2222> groove starting on position **2** for a persistent listener, and this groove accounts for all but one beat of the experience of an adaptive listener.

Example 5.19 Density of groove adherence in the corpus, with two verses highlighted.

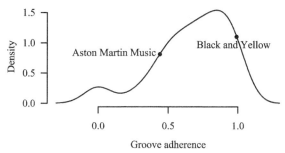

Example 5.20 (a) Big Daddy Kane, "Ain't No Half Steppin'" (1988, 0:21–1:28); (b) Kurtis Blow, "The Breaks" (1980, 0:47–1:26).

(a)

(b)

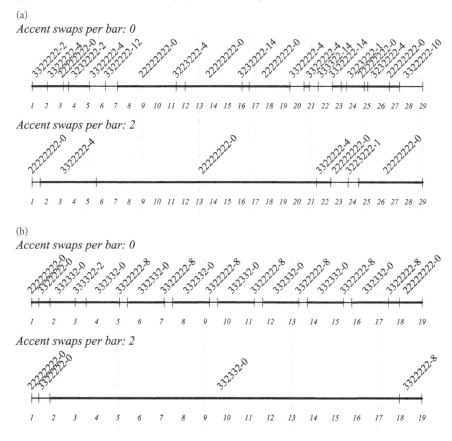

swap per half measure, from Big Daddy Kane's "Ain't No Half Steppin'" and Kurtis Blow's "The Breaks." Visually, these segmentations look similar: both change grooves frequently for a persistent listener, but at a rate of effort of one swap per half measure, an adaptive listener hears the same groove through much of the verse. In other words, the grooviness and groove adherence of the two verses are similar. But, of course, the groove informing the verse is different. "Ain't No Half Steppin'" employs the very typical <2222_2222> groove class, while "The Breaks" employs the much less typical <332_332> groove class.

Because the duple groove class is much more prevalent in the corpus than the <332_332> groove class (see Table 4.3), it would seem that Kurtis Blow's flow is closer to the typical mixture found in the genre than Big Daddy Kane's. Were this typicality just the extent of the duple groove, we could measure it with a single number. Were it the interaction of two groove classes, we could plot the mixture in a two-dimensional plane. But this measure of typicality depends on the use of all seven groove classes—it is a description of where a verse lies in a seven-dimensional space. We can simplify that space into something we conceptualize through the technique of principal components analysis (PCA).

Suppose for the moment there are only two groove classes: a duple class and a nonduple class. Example 5.21 plots the distributions of groove classes in five imagined verses in these two classes.[19] In the upper-left plot of the example, the verses have incrementally more duple grooves and fewer nonduple grooves. I have drawn a wide-dashed line that reflects this tendency and another narrow-dashed line perpendicular to the first. The upper-right plot shows the PCA of these imagined verses. In essence, it has rotated the upper-left plot and created two different axes or dimensions. The rotation the analysis selects maximizes the variance in Component #1.

We can name these dimensions, calling the new horizontal dimension the "duple is the complement of nonduple" dimension. The new vertical dimension could be called the "duple is the same as nonduple dimension." The five verses can now be viewed as a mixture of these two dimensions rather than a mixture of duple and nonduple groove classes. Though the ratio of duple to nonduple varies in Component #1, they are all alike in having no equivalence between the two, so they all have the same value (0) in Component #2. And since all five have a value of 0 in Component #2, there is no reason to represent that component: the PCA has reduced the dimensionality of the data from 2 to 1. In addition to reducing dimensionality, PCA can also describe the typicality of each point in the plot. The most typical point (verse) is the one with the least distance from the origin in the components. In the upper-right plot, Verses 1 and 5 are least typical, with a distance of approximately 1.8 from the origin in Component #1. The lower plots of Example 5.21 revise the data, such that one verse has much less duple groove than before. (That verse's combination of duple and nonduple no longer sums to

---

19. My approach to demonstrating and visualizing PCA is indebted to Powell & Lehe (2015).

Example 5.21 Visual demonstration of principal component analysis (PCA).

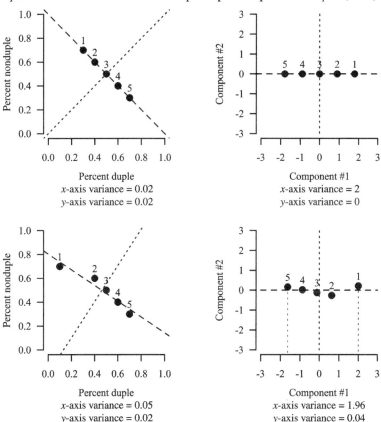

1, but this is not relevant to our discussion.) This revision changes the rotation of the original axes but still maximizes the variance in Component #1. The revision, which pushed Verse 1 further from the tendencies of the others, also breaks the tie in typicality in the upper plots since Verse 1 is now further from the origin in Component #1.

PCA can be extended to arbitrarily many dimensions, so it is equipped to describe typicality in the seven-dimensional space of groove class usage. But an issue arises with the nature of the groove classes. The PCA technique applies to continuous data in which different variables can be related to each other numerically. The groove classes are categorical—one cannot say that a measure of <2222_2222> equates to some number of measures of <332_2222>. A different technique, called correspondence analysis (CA), performs similar work to PCA but with categorical data. The archeologist Gianmarco Alberti (2013) describes CA this way: say you are studying the distribution of different types of pottery shards across a number of dig sites. Are the types of pottery evenly distributed among the sites, or do some sites have more examples of one type than should be expected? Like PCA, CA

Example 5.22 Correlation between the seven groove classes and the first two dimensions of the correspondence analysis (CA) of groove class distribution.

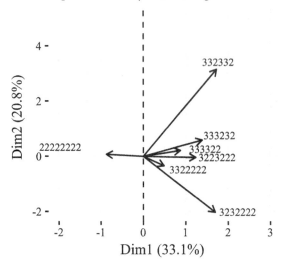

takes *n*-dimensional data (here, *n* = 7, one for each groove class) and transforms them into *n* new dimensions, ranked by the proportion of variance in the data explained by each dimension. The first dimension in CA, like PCA, thus tries to isolate what makes the verses different from each other.

Example 5.22 plots the correlation between the seven groove classes and the first two dimensions of the CA; these correlations give a sense of what mixture of classes creates the dimensions. All classes except <2222_2222> correlate with the first dimension; in other words, using any groove class except the duple class already places a verse at a distance from typical ways of flowing. The correlation of all the groove classes with the second dimension, except <332_332> and <323_2222>, is roughly 0. This means that the mixture of grooves for verses that employ <332_332> are more different from those that employ <323_2222> than they are for the other nonduple classes.

Like PCA, CA provides a way of characterizing the typicality of a verse's mixture of groove classes. Recall that the first dimension in the CA will account for the most variance in groove mixture. One can determine the contribution each verse makes to this dimension. If a verse makes a large contribution to the first dimension, then we understand that verse to be less typical since it makes a large contribution to a dimension that itself captures the most variance. By summing the contributions verses make to the first several dimensions, we can describe the most typical verses as those that make the least contributions to those dimensions.[20] Table 5.1 shows the contributions to the first four dimensions by the five verses making the least and most contributions, along with the proportion of

---

20. More accurately, the contribution a verse makes to a dimension is scaled by the amount of variance captured in that dimension (i.e., the eigenvalue).

Table 5.1 The most atypical and typical verses in the corpus, determined by the contribution made to the first four dimensions of the correspondence analysis

Verse	Atypicality	Proportion of verse in groove class						
		22222222	3322222	3232222	3223222	333322	333232	332332
Kurtis Blow, "The Breaks"	22.95	0.02	0.06	0.00	0.00	0.00	0.00	0.92
Grandmaster Flash, "The Message"	20.75	0.00	0.00	1.00	0.00	0.00	0.00	0.00
Blu, "Ambition"	15.68	0.36	0.04	0.00	0.00	0.00	0.61	0.00
Lil' Kim, "Lighters Up"	5.50	0.08	0.09	0.44	0.00	0.00	0.14	0.25
50Cent, "Candy Shop"	4.90	0.00	0.54	0.45	0.01	0.00	0.00	0.00
...								
Jean Grae, "My Crew"	0.17	0.53	0.28	0.11	0.00	0.09	0.00	0.00
Slaughterhouse, "Y'all Ready Know"	0.14	0.70	0.00	0.08	0.03	0.19	0.00	0.00
Ca$his, "Water Whippin'"	0.13	0.70	0.18	0.05	0.00	0.07	0.00	0.00
KRS-One, "MCs Act Like . . ."	0.10	0.69	0.17	0.05	0.00	0.03	0.00	0.06

the verse spent in each groove class.[21] The most atypical verses are those that dwell in groove classes rarely encountered, such as "The Breaks," largely in class <332_332> or Blu's "Ambition," almost half of which is in class <333232>. Notice that the most typical flows are not necessarily those that are entirely duple. Since the genre is largely but not exclusively duple, the most typical verses are those that mirror the distribution among the groove classes within the genre.

5.2 Critical Analysis: Situating Black Thought of The Roots within the Genre as a Whole

The foregoing stylistic analysis of the rap corpus details a diverse genre. The global features introduced in the previous sections would likely distinguish rap music from vocal delivery, rhyme, and rhythm in competing genres like pop, country, or rock-and-roll. Yet it also enables the kind of critical analysis Meyer (1973) describes because it allows the analyst to view an artist against a representative sample of the genre. As an initial demonstration of how this comparison and contextualization might work, I will devote the rest of this chapter to an emcee already familiar in this study: Black Thought of The Roots. Black Thought enjoys widespread critical and popular esteem, and I will use the corpus and features defined previously to examine what about his flow contributes to this reputation.

Black Thought was born Tariq Trotter in Philadelphia in 1971.[22] His birth year makes him about a decade younger than the first generation of emcees (e.g., Mellie Mel, Kool Moe Dee, Kurtis Blow, etc.). While that generation was concentrated in New York City in the late 1970s, Angela Carter (2005) describes a fully formed hip-hop scene in Philadelphia as early as 1985 when Black Thought was a middle schooler. His musical training as an emcee began in childhood when he formed his first rap duo with Beanie Sigel (born Dwight Grant), another noted Philadelphia emcee (DeLuca 2012). He further developed his skills at the Philadelphia High School for the Creative and Performing Arts. The School in the mid-1980s enrolled several young men who would represent Philadelphia musically in the following decades in

21. As with principle component analysis and other clustering methods, the analysis I undertake here is sensitive to the number of components (k) whose contribution is summed. The most typical ways of validating a value for k do not present obvious choices in this regard. Usually, one looks for a big drop-off in the cumulative variance explained with the addition of each new component. For example, perhaps the first component explains 45 percent of the variance, the second explains 35 percent, and the remaining 10 percent is distributed among the other components. In this example, the first two components account for almost all the variance, so retaining only those two components provides a reasonably faithful account of variety in the data. Another approach to choosing a value for k argues that if data of n dimensions were random, each component would explain $1/n$ of the data's variance, and therefore components explaining more variance are necessary for describing the data. That approach applied to the correspondence analysis of flow suggests four components, my choice here.

22. In his current public appearances on *The Tonight Show with Jimmy Fallon*, the host addresses him as Tariq. Since I am examining his output as an emcee, I will use the name "Black Thought."

many genres, including the future members of the R&B quartet Boyz II Men (Nagle 2014) and the jazz organist Joey DeFrancesco (Wyckoff 2003). Black Thought's most significant introduction at the school was to the drummer ?uestlove (born Ahmir Thompson), a child of Philadelphian doo-wop and soul musicians. He and ?uestlove together formed The Roots while in high school in 1987 (Hess 2010). With a frequently changing line-up of other instrumentalists, emcees, and turntablists, The Roots have released fourteen studio albums since 1993. Black Thought's output as an emcee consists of those recordings and dozens of featured verses.

While Black Thought's reputation as an emcee is unassailable, he nevertheless occupies a somewhat peculiar position within the genre. His critical success exceeds his commercial success—although he has been a highly visible emcee for more than twenty years, the "slept-on" descriptor is often applied to him (Syron 2013).[23] Aspects of his reputation would seem to reflect a greater esteem among the overlapping circles of academic listeners, music critics, and fans of the nebulous Underground.[24] Music journalists' descriptions of Black Thought attest to complex rhyme schemes and virtuosic performance, hailing his "vocal gymnastics" (Abdul-Lateef 1999, p. 162), "powerful rhyme scheme" (Frosch 2004, p. 141), "motor-mouthed [delivery]" (Paréles 1996), and "head spinning rhymes" (Chinen 2008). His fans' comments, on the other hand, emphasize consistency and workmanship over superior performance abilities. In their view, Black Thought has never written a bad verse. The following comments on YouTube videos and discussion lists are emblematic:

> "His lyrical content, consistency, and versatility separates him from the rest." (divine12th 2014)
> "The most consistent Emcee in terms of bars!!" (DG 2015)
> "Is there such thing as a bad Black Thought verse? I ain't holding my breath." (ImTheFxckingPoop 2015)
>
> "Has he ever done a bad verse? The guy is so fucking consistent!" (Twrocks 2014)

Part of Black Thought's critical and popular appeal is his ability to work in both of the major modes of rap performance: improvisation and composition. The value of improvisation (or "freestyle") in rap communities varies across time and place. Many old-school emcees—who understood "freestyle" to mean a composed rhyme without specific subject material—consider "rhyming off the dome" the refuge of emcees that could not write.[25] As Kool Moe Dee says, "The coming

23. Black Thought himself does not shy away from the "slept-on" label, rapping in "Water" (*Phrenology* 2002) of how he and his band mates "slept on floors / tryna figure what the fuck we gettin' slept on for," and describing himself in "Doin' It Again" (*How I Got Over* 2010) as "This unsung, underrated, underappreciate, the one / them underachievers had underestimated."

24. Cornel West is but one academic to spotlight Black Thought in his curated album *Never Forget: A Journey of Revelation*, where he is singled out as a worthy voice to relate 400 years of black experience in America.

25. According to Big Daddy Kane, "That term, freestyle, is like a new term, because in the '80s when we said we wrote a freestyle rap, that meant that it was a rhyme that you wrote that was free of style, meaning that it's not on a particular subject matter—it's not a story about a woman, it's not a

off the top of the head rhymer had a built-in excuse not to be critiqued as hard" (Edwards 2015, p. 59). Kool Moe Dee (2003, p. 10) also voices the sentiment that improvisation is unserious, that it is "free" in the sense that no one will pay you for it. Speaking of Mach 10, he says, "I think I heard Mach 10 say once there is no such thing as freestyle; everything for him is about being paid. I don't think he's even interested in freestyling."

The value of improvisation has risen since rap's first decade. Several of the emcees Edwards interviews in *How to Rap* highlight improvisation's ability to encourage creativity and heighten the experience of both the emcee and the audience. Evidence of the trio Dilated Peoples attests to a greater sense of creativity in improvised rapping, noting that improvisation can elicit unexpected words that instigate new rhyme classes (Edwards 2009, p. 150). Similarly, K-O argues that improvisation enables an emcee to expand his or her phonetic abilities in creating rhymes from words that do not rhyme in everyday speech:

> I think [bending the pronunciation of words to make rhymes] comes from freestyling a lot, because when you freestyle, you're in survival mode, so you're looking for the next word that's gonna fit, and it just ends up fitting. (Edwards 2009, p. 86)

Many emcees excel at either improvisation or composition. Battle emcees generally do not compose verses for recording, and many successful recording artists seem not to improvise. But Black Thought is in the smaller circle of emcees equally skilled at both modes of performance. Since a young age, he has been an able improviser. The oldest recorded freestyle I have located is in the film *Freestyle: The Art of Rhyme*, in which he would appear to be in his early twenties (Fitzgerald 2000). In the clip, he spits nearly three minutes worth of rhymes with ?uestlove providing a beat box pattern. Toward the end of the clip, ?uestlove begins announcing colors of the graffiti on the wall in the background on the downbeat of every other measure. Black Thought then packs as many as eight rhyming words into the two measures, instigating a new rhyme class literally without missing a beat.

Black Thought's abilities as a freestylist remain evident. In his collaboration with ?uestlove, a topic explored more deeply in Chapter 7, he is able to bring a spirit of improvisation to live hip-hop performance that is often absent among "studio emcees." Reviewing a Radio City Music Hall performance from 2006, Kelefa Sanneh (2006) relates how ?uestlove attempted to disorient Black Thought by "adding a pause at the end of every bar; Black Thought stumbled for a second, then adapted and recovered." This sort of in-the-moment adjustment would pose severe challenges for most emcees. More recently, after The Roots became the house band of first *Late Night with Jimmy Fallon* and subsequently *The Tonight Show with Jimmy Fallon*, Black Thought frequently improvises freestyles on comedic topics.

story about poverty, it's basically a rhyme just bragging about yourself, so it's basically free of style" (Edwards 2015, p. 57).

At the same time, Black Thought is also a masterful composer of verses. His recorded verses are imbued with a sense of craftsmanship that his public statements reflect. Asked by an interviewer to list the favorite of his own verses, he responded that

> It's easy to write a song that's dope, that's gonna be catchy, but something that's gonna tug at your heart strings, something that's gonna hold more weight, that's gonna sit heavier, sometimes it takes two, three, four, five drafts. Those are the songs that stick with me over time. (Heights & Charles 2011, 1:00–1:38)

Perhaps reflecting the relative value of composition in comparison to improvisation, the discourse on Black Thought focuses on his composerly aspects. Wayne Marshall, writing primarily about The Roots's avoidance of sampling in preference for live performance, draws on Adam Krims's analytical work to identify aspects of complexity in Black Thought's verse on "Concerto of the Desperado." Marshall cites his increase in syllable length of rhymes, diminished insistence on end rhyme, reduced number of rhyme classes per verse, and coercive pronunciation as evidence of his virtuosity. But these features are the result of his compositional (not improvisational) approach:

> [Black Thought's] manipulation and syncopation of rhyme placement can be heard as a kind of hypermetrical, polyrhythmic approach to composition. In this virtuosic style of rapping, the rhyme serves as the MC's point of accent—as a kind of temporally salient motive, if you will, with which one can create flexible, large-scale rhythmic structures. (2006, p. 881)

The praise Marshall devotes to Black Thought would hold for many other emcees who have not received scholarly attention. But is the "Concerto of the Desperado" an anomaly? What is the relationship between Black Thought's expressive practice and his critical reputation? The first possibility to consider—a kind of null hypothesis—is that the two are wholly separate. Critics and, especially, academics might have entirely nonmusical reasons for admiring Black Thought.

Through collaboration and mutual admiration, Black Thought associates with a circle of emcees (e.g., Mos Def/Yasiin Bey, Talib Kweli, Common, Lauryn Hill, etc.) who attract the label of "conscious emcees." Conscious rap arose in the late 1980s with a wave of artists such as the Native Tongues collective, Public Enemy, De La Soul, and Queen Latifah. This first cohort drew from the philosophies and ideologies of the Nation of Islam and the Five Percent Nation, as mediated by the earlier Universal Zulu Nation of Afrika Bambaataa (Swedenburg 2004, p. 586). Black Thought and his cohort thus embody a second wave of conscious rap. The original "conscious moment" lasted for roughly a decade before giving way in the 1990s to the "keeping it real" perspective of the contemporaneous West Coast gangsta rap. Felicia Miyakawa (2005, p. 140) also cites the anti-Islamic sentiment of the 1990s and, especially, the war on terror of the 2000s in conscious rap's decline.

Conscious rap lends itself to critical and academic admiration both because of its association with the black middle class (as opposed to the black working class) and because of its contrast with gangsta rap. Davarian Baldwin details the connection between conscious rap and the upwardly mobile black middle class. In the late 1980s, a new generation of black university students enlisted the Afrocentricism of conscious rap in their interactions with both the white educational establishment and the black working class. Directed toward their professors, conscious rap became a tool in debates over the importance of multicultural education and African American Studies programs. Directed toward the black working class,

> the study and consumption of Afrocentric goods and literature could justify a class distinction without raising issues of black authenticity. Designer wear and bourgeois habits were legitimized with, respectively, kente cloth and reconstructed Yoruba origins. (Baldwin 2004, pp. 162–163)

Those who continue to support multicultural education as I do are therefore inclined to admire an artist like Black Thought. The supposed contrast between conscious and gangsta rap strengthens this inclination. Gangsta rap, with its hyper-masculinity, profanity, and preoccupation with violence, appeals, in Stuart Alan Clarke's words, to white America's "enormous appetite for images of black men misbehaving" (1991, p. 40). As the conservative political establishment of the early 1990s excoriated gangsta rap, the academic establishment celebrated its supposed opposite. Julius Bailey, writing twenty-five years after the origins of conscious and gangsta rap, affirms the academy's attraction to the style:

> The works of conscious hip hop artists make it possible for me as a philosopher to engage with the culture of hip hop in a meaningful way. . . . [It eschews] the superficial in favor of the substantive, the material in favor of the spiritual, the commercial in favor of the communal. . . . It has brought hip hop into the academy as a respectable field of knowledge and study. (2014, p. 62)

It must be said that writers have challenged these distinctions between conscious rap and gangsta rap for nearly as long as the styles have coexisted. First, most of the artists labeled as conscious emcees reject the term. Talib Kweli, for example, sees the label as a ploy by industry to attract educated white consumers.[26] Furthermore, distinctions between the political and ideological stances of the two styles are often unclear. For example, misogyny, while explicit in the gangsta rap of artists like The Notorious B.I.G. and P. Diddy, lurks close to the surface in the patriarchy of conscious rap. As Ted Swedenburg (2004, p. 587) argues, "Nationalist rap tends to relegate women to second place, to supporting roles, and at best 'respects' them as 'mothers' and 'queens.'"[27] Because Black Thought is associated with conscious

---

26. As Kweli relates to Jeff Chang (2005), "'Party' or 'gangsta rap' is marketed to mass audiences— crucially through black and brown urban audiences first . . . but 'conscious rap' is seen as a rap submarket and is often pushed first to educated, middle-class, multicultural—often white—audiences. Some black audiences then tend to reject such music as 'white music.'"

27. For Baldwin, the difference between conscious and gangsta rap is not ideological but pragmatic. "Gangsta rappers aren't anti-nationalist or apolitical, but they do oppose a political correctness which obscures the historical realities of class, gender, and locational difference within the representation of black communities" (2004, p. 165).

rap, it is possible that his academic and critical esteem, even when couched in musical terms, derives from the esteem of his personal and lyrical style rather than specific musical features. And his famous aloofness—"cold and uncharismatic" in the words of Tom Breihan (2006)—might also play into critics' admiration. An introvert by nature, he happily cedes the spotlight to the more gregarious ?uestlove. This reticence allows his fans (myself included) to assume a deepness underneath the silent surface.

So we are left with two related questions: First, does Black Thought's musical practice distinguish him from other emcees and, if so, how? And second, if he can serve as a model for a "virtuosic" and "powerful" rhymer, what markers of complexity do critics, scholars, and listeners associate with these traits? The stylistic analysis undertaken earlier in this chapter, combined with the transcription of Black Thought verses compiled for Chapter 7, affords us a unique opportunity to evaluate this relationship between complexity, virtuosity, and status.

Many of the global features of rapping defined heretofore intuitively correspond with virtuosity and complexity. Some of these features overlap with the critical discourse on Black Thought as well. If, in Pareles's words, he is "motor mouthed," we should expect a high syllable rate. If his rhymes are "head spinning," we might anticipate a high degree of rhyme mixture. More generally, an idealized "virtuosic" emcee would have a high syllable rate, reflective of high saturation. Her varying saturation and low entropy of IRIs would reflect a value placed on "playing" with the recurrent instrumental streams. Her low levels of change in cardinality, high entropy in $mod\,4$ IRIs, high grooviness and groove adherence would reflect an accordance with the "law of flow." Her longer rhyme class lengths, longer rhyme instance lengths, and greater rhyme mixture would confirm her as a complex wordsmith.[28]

In order to uncover what distinguishes Black Thought, we can compare the averages of the features defined in the thirty verses compiled for the corpus examined in Chapter 7 with the seventy-five verses in the genre-wide corpus. Table 5.2 shows the results of t-tests between Black Thought and the corpus for the features defined in this chapter, and a few others I have not yet explicitly defined because they are meaningful only in comparing two sets of verses, as I will do here.[29] (The p-values in Table 5.2 are corrected using the Bonferroni method.[30]) For each feature, the table gives the mean (M) and standard deviation (i.e., the square of the variance, SD) for both Black Thought and the genre-wide corpus ("Rap Music"), the difference in the two means, and the results of the t-test and corrected p-value. What

---

28. Some features I've defined, especially syllables per word and central pillar, do not intuitively correspond to virtuosity.

29. These features are the average lengths of phrases (in seconds), the variance of the same, the average number of instances in a verse's rhyme classes, the average number of syllables in each instance, and the percentage of the verse that is in the duple rhyme class for a persistent listener. See the analysis script for feature generation and t-tests.

30. Recall that the p-value calculates the change a difference in means might arise by chance, and less than 1 in 20 is considered significant. If one ran twenty t-tests, one would probably obtain a "significant" result that is not actually significant. The Bonferroni method adjusts the p-values of Table 5.2 given that I conducted fifteen t-tests.

Table 5.2 Difference in means among features of flow, Black Thought compared with the genre-wide corpus ("rap music")

		Black Thought		Rap music		Different in means		
		M	SD	M	SD		t	p
1.	Saturation (positions)	11.79	0.97	11.1	1.45	0.69	2.85	0
2.	Change in saturation	1.7	0.53	2.07	0.73	−0.37	−2.9	0
3.	Phrase length (seconds)	2.13	0.31	2.37	0.43	−0.24	−3.23	0.03
4.	Phrase length variance	1.77	1.16	2.87	4.07	−1.1	−2.14	0.04
5.	Instances per class	5.07	2	3.62	2.47	1.45	3.14	0.05
6.	Syllables per instance	2.31	0.68	1.65	0.44	0.66	4.93	0.07
7.	Rhyme mixture	0.27	0.39	0.15	0.21	0.12	1.6	0.08
8.	Percent duple (effort = 0)	0.27	0.23	0.45	0.34	−0.18	−3.04	0.35
9.	Syllables per second	5.14	0.38	5.09	0.71	0.05	0.44	0.52
10.	IRI entropy	0.51	0.12	0.44	0.15	0.07	2.32	1
11.	IRI *mod* 4 entropy	0.25	0.13	0.23	0.16	0.02	0.76	1
12.	Grooviness	0.4	0.23	0.51	0.34	−0.11	−2.01	1
13.	Groove adherence	0.63	0.15	0.67	0.27	−0.04	−1.06	1
14.	Tempo	90.59	9.27	87.69	15.56	2.9	1.18	1

emerges from a close look at these features is indeed the portrait of an artist simultaneously concerned with complexity and comprehensibility. Chinen's observation of "head-spinning rhymes" is supported by the difference in mean rhyme instances per class (Feature #5), syllables per rhyme instance (Feature #6), and entropy of inter-rhyme interval (Feature #7). Black Thought has two more instances per rhyme class than his peers, and his rhymes are a syllable longer. Black Thought also dominates his music texture to a greater extent (Feature #1), saturating the measure by occupying more positions than his peers and maintaining that saturation from measure to measure more faithfully.

Other features of Black Thought's flow emphasize consistency and comprehensibility rather than virtuosity. Similar to his lower change in saturation, his verses have a lower variance in the lengths of phrases (in seconds, Feature #4), evocative of one who stands at the mic and flows unendingly until the verse is finished. The fact that he is not significantly different from the genre in terms of $mod\,4$ IRI entropy highlights his comprehensibility in that predicting where his rhymes will fall within the beat is not particularly difficult. This comprehensibility is also evident in his speed of delivery. Despite Pareles's comment that he is "motor-mouthed," Black Thought is not an especially fast rapper but rather one who wants his words understood. In fact, seven verses in the corpus of seventy-five are faster than his fastest verse. A final aspect of his consistency as an emcee concerns not the difference between him and the corpus, but the variation within the thirty verses of his corpus vs. those of the genre. While he is not groovier than the genre, and he does not adhere grooves more faithfully, the standard deviation of these features is substantially lower in Black Thought.[31] Indeed, this reduced variability is evident in all features in which the means are not significantly different.

This combination of features indicates a particular kind of virtuosity: complex rhyme schemes and avoidance of dupleness indicating a composerly craft, coupled with a consistency of delivery and grooviness indicating an assuredness that speaks to deep experience. Furthermore, the features by which Black Thought is indistinguishable from the genre—especially, syllable delivery rate and IRI entropy—are features in which exceptional values might detract from an emcee's comprehensibility. In my experience, the fastest emcees require printed lyrics in order to be understood. Black Thought delivers syllables fast enough to impress listeners but slow enough so that their meaning might be conveyed. His moderate entropy of $mod\,4$ IRIs ensures that rhymes engender meaningful expectations for the arrival of rhyming syllables without being overly predictable. And if we consider a subset of this corpus, then Black Thought's virtuosity is more apparent. I consider the following eight features indicative of virtuosity: syllables per word, syllables per second, metric saturation, change in saturation, rhyme class length in instances and syllables, rhyme mixture, and aversion to the duple groove. A verse by Black Thought is two-and-a-half times as likely to surpass the corpus average in at least five of these features, as compared to the typical artist in the corpus.[32]

In Meyer's distinction between stylistic and critical analysis, style analysis aims to document "the rules of the game" operating in any particular genre. In doing so, it identifies the various options available to artists, affixes probabilities to these options, and suggests the consequences of wandering down one path or another. Critical analysis, on the other hand, details how a particular composition interacts with its genre, how the choice of rare alternatives can lead to surprising ends, and how a listener might understand the consequences of those choices. The stylistic analysis undertaken in the first half of this chapter documents some of the

31. This is not merely an artifact of the smaller sample for Black Thought; the average standard deviation of grooviness and adherence in 100 thirty-verse samples of the genre-wide corpus does not differ from that of the corpus as a whole. One feature discussed in the previous section not discussed here is groove typicality. Recall that typicality was characterized by the contribution of a verse to the first several components of a correspondence analysis. I augmented that analysis by iteratively adding one Black Thought verse in the rest, and his verses are typical in this respect, usually falling in the middle of the ranking of contributions to factors. Furthermore, his deployment of rotations of groove classes mirrors that of the genre as a whole as well.
32. See the analysis script.

constraints under which emcees operate. For example, there are upper and lower limits of syllable delivery rate, and the tempo of a track modulates metric saturation. There are similar constraints on variation in rapping, evidenced by global rates of grooviness and IRI entropy. Identifying these constraints invites critical interpretation when we identify verses that defy them.

In essence, stylistic and critical analysis employ the same methods on groups of pieces of different sizes. Meyer is agnostic about which methods to employ in analyzing music, writing that "all the methods, theories, and techniques which are relevant to and will illuminate the composition being considered should be brought to bear" (1973, p. 24). It is the size of the groups that matters. One piece comprises the group for critical analysis; some undefined but large number of pieces comprise the group for style analysis. Meyer, like most music theorists, construed this larger group selectively, defining stylistic traits through a combination of his own experience, the writings of previous theorists, and conventional views of a genre's rules.

The data-driven approach adopted here, unavailable to Meyer, enables a third path into analysis. The contextualizing of Black Thought as an emcee undertaken in this chapter is an analysis of his style, insofar as I have abstracted the features of many of his creations. But it is also a critical analysis with respect to the larger corpus of rap music as a whole. This, in my view, is one of the prizes earned in computer-aided music analysis. We are still working with differently sized groups of pieces, but the group of pieces that constitute style analysis are clearly defined and carefully constructed. And the group of pieces that constitute critical analysis need not be restricted in size to one piece.

This flexibility enables the case studies of Part II. Each chapter will explore a particular aspect of flow—the relationship of groove to meter, the relationship of the flow to the beat, and the relationship of the rhythm of speech to the rhythm of music—by comparing an artist to the genre and also situating individual verses within an artist's practice. In the course of these studies, I hope to document what it means to flow, both in a particular moment and for a particular artist.

PART II

Three Flows

CHAPTER Six

Flow, Metric Complexity, and Text in Eminem

At the beginning of Chapter 4, I introduced the concept of vocal groove by contrasting two versions of Eminem's landmark first verse on "Lose Yourself," from the soundtrack of the film *8 Mile*. Briefly, I showed that the released version features an abrupt shift in groove in the middle of the verse, toward a groove with greater metric complexity. (A refresher on groove class and metric complexity follows here.) Noting this increase in grooviness and complexity, I argued that these rhythmic features foreshadow the protagonist's eventual triumph as an emcee, even when self-doubt permeates the lyrics. That grooviness, in my hearing, enhances the released version in comparison to the demo. In this chapter, I will further address the association between metric complexity and assured rapping in Eminem's flow. Not only does Eminem articulate this association across several verses and even entire tracks, but he also uses it as a narrative device in the rhythm itself. I focus on Eminem because I believe he is particularly noteworthy in his deployment of the association between metric complexity and rapping virtuosity.

Still, writing about music is an act of advocacy, as the oceans of music require selectivity. In selecting Eminem, I imply that one should listen to more of his music than one would otherwise. This implication should raise concern. Eminem cemented his status as an emcee through a run of success in the early 2000s, with three chart-topping albums released at the apex of compact disc sales. His prominence in rap music and pop culture generally has spawned considerable scholarship and criticism. While a search on YouTube for "Eminem rhyme analysis" unearths a cottage industry, very little of this content relates to the rhythm of his voice. Instead, in both scholarly and popular literature, Eminem is often considered from three angles. The first is through the lens of cultural appropriation, casting him as another link in a long chain of white artists to profit, disproportionately, from Afro-diasporic music (Armstrong 2004, Hess 2005, Rodman 2006, Grealy 2008, Harrison 2008). Even without declaring him appropriative, one can still note, as Harry Allen (2003) does, the ways in which Eminem accrues privilege as a white emcee:

> It always seemed that the amount and quality of coverage Eminem received, even before he had done anything significant, was unusually high. The prominent

magazine covers he received, the significant interviews he did, seemed to come unusually early and stay unusually late. . . . Compared to black artists, Eminem, like Vanilla Ice, Beastie Boys, 3rd Bass and a number of white rappers before him, got more by doing less; an almost sure way to mark someone as white under the system of race.

It is possible to see this chapter's emphasis on Eminem as another instance of him "getting more by doing less." The two other lines of typical critique against Eminem concern his lyrics. Several of his songs contain extreme depictions of violence against women and encourage listeners to commit similar violence. Other lyrics are rampantly homophobic (Keller 2003, Stephens 2005, Enck & McDaniel 2012). While rap music generally has curtailed homophobic language in the past decade, Eminem continues to use gender- and orientation-based slurs, earning him widespread condemnation even in his recent work (such as 2013's *The Marshall Mathers LP 2*). For his part, he claims that such terms are divorced from their original context of sexual orientation (Hiatt 2013). My concern is that silence regarding these issues, even in an analysis of the rhythm of voice, perpetuates the silence of victims of gender-based violence and hazards obscuring and excusing Eminem's appropriation.

These are important issues, and I am grateful for the nuanced approach to them encountered in the literature just cited. Still, I believe part of Eminem's success is separate from his notoriety, and even separate from his attested skills with rhyme and wordplay. More than any artist whose work I know well, Eminem cannot only maintain a groove class, but often uses groove classes to create narratives of rhythm in his verses that support the narratives of his lyrics. In what follows, I will trace several of these narratives. Two brief discussions precede my analysis of groove narratives. First, I will rehearse several of the concepts and tools introduced in Part I for readers joining the argument. Second, I will detail general aspects of Eminem's use of groove.

6.1 Vocal Groove: A Refresher

My model of vocal groove in rap flows, defined in Chapter 4, primarily addresses the durations between accented syllables (the "inter-accent intervals" or IAIs of flow) and further stipulates that rap flows are usually a combination of IAIs of 2 or 3 units in length. I call these accented syllables "limit-3 accents" and the durations between them either 2-durations or 3-durations. These IAIs combine into grooves that repeat every measure, or sixteen positions. Because the grooves are combinations of 2 and 3 that sum to 16, there are seven possible "groove classes": <2222_2222>, <332_2222>, <323_2222>, <3223222>, <333322>, <333232>, and <333322>. (The underscore indicates a groove class that divides the measure evenly in half.) Groove classes assume rotational equivalence, so [3322222] and [2332222] are both members of the class <332_2222>; the latter is expressed as <332_2222> starting on position 2. The first groove class listed here, <2222_2222> is termed the "duple" class and is the most common; the others are termed "nonduple."

Among many features one might note about vocal grooves is their metric complexity, by which I mean the extent to which a groove places accents on positions that do not usually carry accents in rap music. My means for expressing this is the beat-accent type, a length-four string of ones and zeros that represents accents within a beat. For example, the duple class starting on position 0 places accents on all 0_{mod4} and 2_{mod4} positions, and thus has four instances of the |1010| beat-accent type. The metric complexity of a groove is derived from the uncommonness of the groove's four beat-accent types, ranging from 0 in the case of the duple class starting on position 0_{mod2} to 4 in the case of the duple class starting on position 1_{mod2}. This latter groove would have four instances of the beat-accent type |0101|, a beat-accent type that occurs in only 5 percent of the beats in the genre-wide corpus. In addition to metric complexity, I also quantify a flow's syncopation through the "mean IAI." Because all IAIs are either 2-durations or 3-durations, and because 3-durations are fundamentally at odds with rap's persistent duple meter, an average IAI closer to 3 indicates greater syncopation.

In practice, emcees usually alter the groove classes slightly to accommodate specific words or insert moments of surprise. I maintain, however, that some listeners will continue to hear a vocal groove through these moments of disruption, and Chapter 4 presents a model of such groovy listening. The model contrasts listeners willing to swap accents around in order to maintain a groove (termed "persistent listeners") with those who change grooves as often as necessary (termed "adaptive listeners"). In addition, the model segments verses into grooves at different rates of persistence. "Grooviness," then, refers the proportion of a verse made up of relatively long grooves, and "groove adherence" refers to the proportion of a verse in which persistent listeners and adaptive listeners hear the same groove.

6.2 Groove and Metric Complexity in Eminem's Flow

Before considering how metric complexity relates to narrative in Eminem's work, I will detail general characteristics of Eminem's grooviness. First, a sustained consideration of metric complexity in Eminem is warranted because Eminem, to a large degree, avoids the duple groove class. For an adaptive listener, never swapping perceived accents in order to maintain a groove, a fifth of the measures of a typical Eminem verse support the duple class, in comparison to nearly half of those of the genre as a whole.[1] Considered from the perspective of an adaptive listener, two fifths of Eminem's verses are entirely nonduple, compared with only 11 percent of those in the genre as a whole.[2] Eminem also excels at groove adherence, at least

1. The percent of measures in a verse in the duple class in Eminem ($M = 0.20$, $SD = 0.22$) differs from the genre at large ($M = 0.45$, $SD = 0.34$) by 25 percent [$t(81) = -4.4$, $p < 0.001$]. See the analysis script.
2. The percent of verses at an effort rate of one swap per beat with no measures in the duple groove class in Eminem ($M = 0.40$, $SD = 0.50$) differs from the genre at large ($M = 0.11$, $SD = 0.31$) by 0.29 [$t(38) - 3.0$, $p < 0.01$]. See the analysis script.

Example 6.1 Distribution of groove classes in Eminem and the genre as a whole.

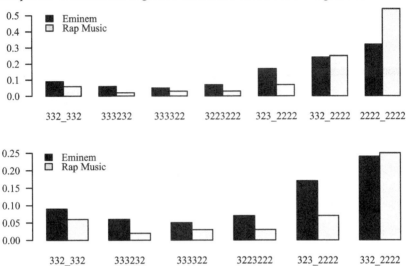

when flowing to a nonduple groove class. Eminem does not differ from the genre as a whole in terms of groove adherence, but a difference (though not a statistically significant one) does emerge when grooves of the duple class are discarded.[3] In other words, Eminem not only uses the nonduple classes more often, but he also uses them with greater fidelity than other emcees.

Eminem's distribution of nonduple groove classes also differs from that of others. Example 6.1 shows the proportion of his music occupied by various groove classes. (The lower plot omits the duple groove, so the others can be examined in finer detail.) There are several consequential differences in Eminem's treatment of groove. First, as previously discussed, Eminem uses the duple groove about half as frequently as others. Second, although both Eminem and the genre as a whole use <332_2222> extensively, Eminem also uses <323_2222> frequently as well, 3 times as often as others. Finally, Eminem uses the remaining groove classes at least 5 percent of the time, a rate never reached by the genre as whole for classes <333232>, <333322>, or <3223222>. The increased use of these classes means that Eminem tends toward greater metric complexity. Example 6.2 reprints Example 4.13, showing the metric complexity of rotations of the groove classes, depending on which *mod* 4 position the rotation begins at. The classes that Eminem employs relatively frequently compared to the genre (i.e., <323_2222>, <333232>, <333322>, and <3223222>) are those that are most likely to result in higher levels of metric complexity. Furthermore, two of these, <333232>

---

3. Eminem's groove adherence disregarding the duple class ($M = 0.49$, $SD = 0.31$) is greater than the genre as a whole ($M = 0.38$, $SD = 0.37$) by 11 percent [$t(63) = 1.43$, $p < 0.16$]. See the analysis script.

Example 6.2 Complexity of different rotations of the seven groove classes. Each point represents four rotations in the case of classes without internal repetition. The number below each point refers to the onset of the rotation, *mod 4*.

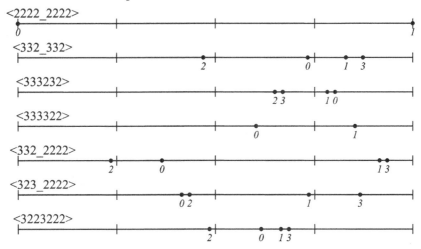

Example 6.3 Distribution of rotations of the groove class <323_2222> in Eminem vs. the genre as a whole.

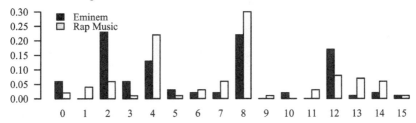

and <333322>, are the groove classes with the longest inner periodicities of 3-durations.

Eminem's tendency toward metric complexity affects his choice of not only groove class but also rotation. This difference in rotation is most noticeable in his treatment of the class <323_2222>. Example 6.3 shows the distribution of different rotations of the class in Eminem and other emcees. Most of the rotations are rare, and the signal difference between Eminem and his peers is his preference for starting the groove on position 2, which he does more than a quarter of the time, compared to 5 percent of the time in the genre as a whole. In compensation, he is less likely than his peers to start on either position 4 or 8. Example 6.4 shows position-class set plots of his preferred rotation against the one starting on position 4. Rotation 2 has a slightly higher metric complexity than rotation 4 because the former has two 0_{mod4} accents, while the latter has three of them. But rotation 2 undermines the meter in several other ways. Both rotations will bisect the measure exactly once. In the case of rotation 4 (the one preferred by other emcees), this

Example 6.4 Groove <323_2222> in rotation 2 (preferred by Eminem) and rotation 4 (preferred by the genre as a whole).

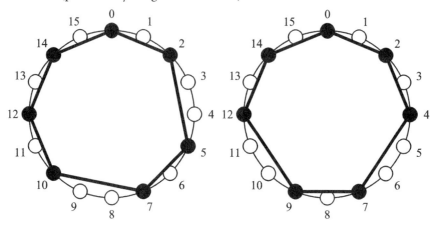

bisection highlights 0_{mod4} positions, placing accents on beats 2 and 4 (i.e., positions 4 and 12). The bisection in rotation 2 lands on positions 2 and 10, undercutting the meter. A corollary of this bisection is that in rotation 4, an inner periodicity of consecutive 2-durations spans two entire beats (i.e., from beat 4 to beat 2 of the next measure). The rotations also place their 1_{mod2} accents in a different relationship to the beat. Each of the rotations also has two such accents. Where these accents fall adjacent to a beat, the prominence of that beat will be obscured. In rotation 4, both 1_{mod2} accents (i.e., positions 7 and 9) obscure a single beat (i.e., position 8), while in rotation 2, accents on positions 5 and 7 obscure both beats 2 and 3 (i.e., positions 4 and 8).

The aural difference between these two grooves can be heard in the two excerpts of Example 6.5 🔊, which plots one of the longer rotation-4 grooves of the genre as a whole (from Phonte's "The Good Fight") and one of the longer rotation-2 grooves of Eminem (from the first verse of "Till I Collapse").[4] Though they articulate the same groove class, these excerpts relate to the meter very differently in my hearing. The Phonte excerpt, to my ears, sounds groovy in the sense that the accents on positions 7 and 9 seem early. I can imagine a duple (and very square) version of the lines that place the rhymes *one day* and *once they* on positions 8 and 10. No similarly simple transformation of the Eminem excerpt can align it to the meter. Indeed, like the first lines of "Business" discussed in Chapter 1 (see Example 1.4 🔊), which is also an example of <323_2222> in rotation 2, the lines seem to create a meter all their own. The accents on positions 2, 5, 7, 10, 12, and 14 sound in pairs, suggesting an uneven three-beat meter with "beats" on positions 2, 7, and 12 (i.e., duration segments of [556]).

---

4. These excerpts have effort rates of 0; the model of adaptive groovy listening finds much longer grooves.

Example 6.5 Grooves of class <323_2222> in rotations 4 and 2: (a) Phonte, "The Good Fight" (2011, 0:43–0:52) and (b) Eminem, "Till I Collapse" (1:24–1:42).

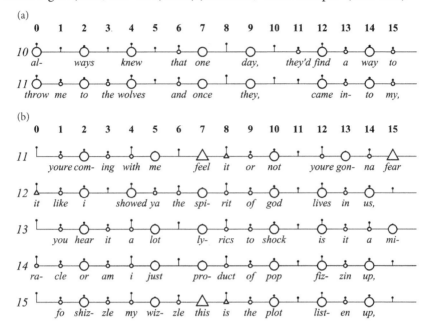

I believe it is this suggestion of a three-beat cycle countering the meter that explains the appeal to Eminem of <323_2222> starting on position **2**. To create this counter-meter, a groove class must have consecutive durations that sum to 5, 5, and 6. All the nonduple groove classes meet this requirement, but most of the time the subdivisions of the two 5-durations differ. For example, the groove class <332_2222> might be grouped in three parts as <23|32|222>, but the two implied 5-durations contrast 2-3 vs. 3-2. The only classes that avoid this contrast (i.e., contains the inner duration segment [3232]) are <323_2222> and <333232>. Eminem does employ <333232> more than others, but any rotation of that class is extremely metrically complex. In other words, Eminem's preferred groove of <323_2222> starting on position **2** allows him to undermine the meter by suggesting a different cycle, but in a way that also avoids the greatest extent of metric complexity.

6.3 The Complexity–Competency Nexus in Selected Verses and Tracks

The previous section detailed Eminem's heightened use of metrically complex groove classes, those that mix 3-durations and 2-durations. In addition to their prevalence, many Eminem tracks sequence these grooves in ways that support the narrative of the verse. Specifically, many of Eminem's verses (and many verses in rap music generally) are about his own development as an emcee. To support this narrative of accruing competency, Eminem often sequences grooves such that they accrue metric complexity.[5] This nexus of complexity and competency can play out within a verse or across the many verses of a track. In what follows, I will show how Eminem establishes this association between complexity and competency in some verses and plays with it in others to support more complex narratives.

6.3.1 "Go to Sleep"

An initial example of accruing metric complexity, and one of the clearest, is heard in Eminem's verse on "Go to Sleep," a track featured in the 2003 film *Cradle 2 the Grave*. The track fulfills the generic expectations of a "diss track," a combination of argument and threat against another rapper. (The verse can be heard in Excerpt 6a ◐.) The first two thirds of the verse visualize victory (mm. 1–4 and 10–16) and detail the reasons for the feud (mm. 4–10). The last third of the verse depicts a hypothetical fight that the enemy eventually forfeits, leaving him victorious. Throughout, verb tense delineates these sections; most of the beginning of the verse is in the future continuous tense (e.g., "I ain't gonna"), but a pivotal shift to the present tense in m. 15 ("I see you, D-12") brings about the depiction of the (averted) fight.

The plot of the verse, such as it is, could be summarized very briefly. Although some of Eminem's most well-known tracks have sustained narratives over the course of several verses (e.g., "Stan," "Kim," "97 Bonnie and Clyde," etc.), many others, like the "Go to Sleep" verse, are relatively sparse in terms of action. This sparseness presents a challenge in crafting a flow: because so little happens, each stage of the narrative must expand across many measures. But the anticipatory nature of the narrative also demands that the prolonged preparation remains vital, even accruing in energy. How does one continually ratchet up energy over the long process of preparing for the fight? One way is through the pitch of the voice. As Example 6.6 shows, pitch increases steadily through most of the verse, plateauing as the confrontation begins. Each point in the plot represents a line of flow and reflects the median pitch of syllables in the line.[6] From the beginning of the verse, Eminem gradually raises the pitch of his voice, stabilizing around Line 15 ("And you're gonna see this gangster . . . "). Pitch reaches an apex with the final dare to engage in Line 21 ("Pick me up, throw me . . . ") before receding once the invitation to fight is declined. This trajectory of pitch is an effective way to increase energy in the verse; a listener, especially one embodying the music and imagining producing it by oneself (Overy & Molnar-Szakacs 2009), will understand that the higher pitches require more energy to create.

---

5. I mean "competency" in its literal sense, as the ability to do something successfully. I do not intend the connotation of "mere competency," as in acceptable but not exceptional.

6. More technically, the "pitch" of each syllable is the median pitch detected during the syllable's vowel by the pitch detection algorithm of the PRAAT software package. Each point in the plot is then the median of those medians for each line.

Example 6.6 Median pitch of syllables, by line, in Eminem, "Go to Sleep."

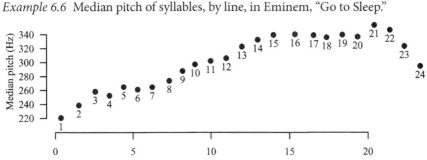

Example 6.7 Groove segmentation of "Go to Sleep" at two rates of effort.

Accent swaps per bar: 0

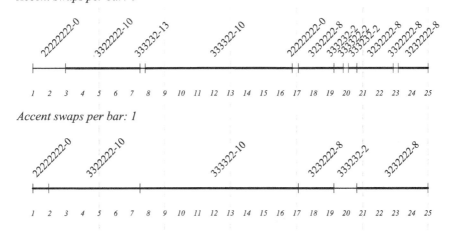

Accent swaps per bar: 1

Less obvious is the way groove supports the narrative of the verse. Example 6.7 segments the predominant grooves of the verse for an adaptive listener (effort rate of 0) and a slightly persistent listener (effort rate of one swap per measure).[7] For a persistent listener, the verse is in six sections. The beginning is entirely duple; the first 3-duration coincides the word *permanently* in m. 3. In the same bar, on position **10**, the groove flips to <332_2222>. This groove contrasts a duple first half of the bar with an inner periodicity of 3-durations leading back to the downbeat. The dupleness of the first half of the bar disappears at m. 8 with *terms where we can agree*, creating a groove of <333322>, also beginning on position **10**, in mm. 7–17. The downbeat of m. 17 creates a moment of disruption, in both the flow and the

7. The choice of effort rate (other than 0) does not change the segmentation. At other rates, the short groove around m. 19 may be slightly shorter.

Example 6.8 Position-class set plots of successive grooves in "Go to Sleep." Duple groove of m. 1 not shown. Groove <323_222> starting on position 8 returns to end the verse.

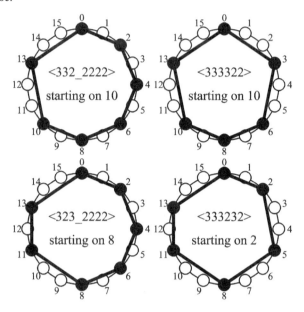

instrumental streams. In the latter, a gunshot sound on the downbeat signals the start of a new section, one that includes the snare and hi-hat that have been absent heretofore. In the flow, the groove <323_2222> starting on position **8** emerges, introducing accents on positions **2**, **4**, **8**, and **11** while removing previous accents on positions **3** and **10**. Another shift, to <333232> in mm. 19–20, introduces the first accents on position **5** of the verse. In the final measures, the groove of m. 17 returns. The position-class set plots for the four nonduple grooves in the verse are given in Example 6.8.

Table 6.1 shows these six groove patterns and counts the number of accents they attach to each part of the beat (i.e., each *mod* 4 position). In the last two columns, I have summed the number of accents on strong and weak parts of the beat (i.e., each *mod* 2 position). With each change of groove until m. 21, Eminem gradually places more accents on weak parts of the beat and fewer accents on strong parts of the beat; in other words, metric complexity increases through the verse. The predominance of accents placed on the beat in rap music confers greater status to emcees who place them off the beat. In preparing for the confrontation that coincides with the change of tense in m. 15, Eminem shows himself not only to be an emcee who can maintain a groove for many measures, but he also seemingly accrues power as an emcee through his choice of groove. After presenting the most metrically complex groove of the verse in mm. 19–21, his opponent walks away from a battle with such an emcee. Subsequently, Eminem returns to a less complex groove. By incrementally increasing metric complexity through a succession of

Table 6.1 Count of accents by metric position, *mod* 2 and *mod* 4, as well as metric complexity, for grooves in Eminem's "Go to Sleep"

		Accents		*mod* 4				*mod* 2		
Groove	Measures	0	1	2	3	0	1			Complexity
<2222_2222>, 0	1–2	4	0	4	0	8	0			0
<332_2222>, 10	3–7	3	1	3	0	6	1			0.94
<333322>, 10	7–17	2	1	2	1	4	2			2.41
<323_2222>, 8	17–19	3	1	2	1	5	2			1.66
<333232>, 2	19–21	2	2	1	1	3	3			2.6
<323_2222>, 8	21–24	3	1	2	1	5	2			1.66

grooves, Eminem creates a rhythmic narrative to the verse that tracks the narrative of his voice and lyric.[8]

6.3.2 "The Re-Up"

If "Go to Sleep" shows how an emcee derives power through metric complexity, then "The Re-Up" shows the limits of this association. The track appears on a 2006 compilation album of the same name that Eminem released to highlight artists on his Shady Records label such as 50 Cent, Obie Trice, and Ca$his. The first eight measures are transcribed in Example 6.9 🔊 ▶, and groove is segmented in Example 6.10. These measures are among the least groovy in Eminem's output. Of particular note are mm. 4–5, which contrast half a measure of exclusively 1_{mod2} accents (*víllainóus Dré prótegé, Shá-*) with a string of five 3-durations (*Shády appréntice, dróp them zéros and gét with the héroes*). The mean IAI of the verse is 2.34, higher than all but 8 of the 75 verses in the genre-wide corpus. Thus, the use of all these 3-durations is itself rare, and rarer still that they do not combine to form some kind of patterning of 3-durations like <332_332>.

For an adaptive listener, a groove never emerges from the free mixture of 2- and 3-durations until mm. 19–23 clearly articulate groove <323_2222> starting on position 12 (see Example 6.11 ▶). Otherwise, all the grooves found in the segmentation are shorter than two measures, and many of them are of classes and rotations rarely encountered. (This is most evident in the fact that many of the rotations are odd-numbered.) Even for the most persistent listener, the verse offers few spans of sustained groove. But those that it does offer plot a trajectory away

---

8. One could substitute "teleology" for "narrative" in this "rhythmic narrative." Most studies of popular music resist teleological arguments that depict a track as having continuous progress toward a goal reached at the end. In contrast, teleological arguments permeate analyses of classical music. To posit a verse- or track-spanning rhythmic narrative here should not suggest that such arguments are always appropriate. For a historical overview of teleology in music analysis, and for an example of a goal-directed analysis of Afro-diasporic popular music, see Fink (2011).

Example 6.10 Groove segmentation of "The Re-Up" at two rates of effort.

Accent swaps per bar: 0

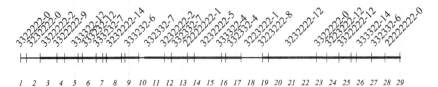

Accent swaps per bar: 4

Example 6.11 Eminem, "The Re-Up" (2006, mm. 19–24,1:11–1:28).

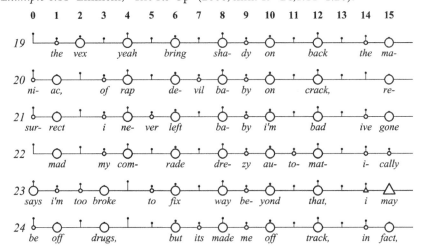

from metric complexity. This is most telling in comparing the grooves of mm. 2–6 (<333322> starting on position **12**), 17–23 (<323_2222> also starting on **12**), and 26–28 (<332_2222> starting on position **14**). These three grooves incrementally lose complexity, from 2.41 to 1.66, to 0.94.[9]

The lyrics of the verse consist almost entirely of boasts of sexual and lyrical prowess, but they end with a common theme in Eminem: that the success of other

9. This trajectory does not include measures 7–16, which do not articulate a sustained groove, and even briefly state one (<332_332> starting on position 7) with an even higher complexity than the beginning.

rappers he views as unskilled means he should quit rapping himself. Although he only raises this topic in the last three measures, the rhythmic narrative of the verse foreshadows this idea by inverting the trajectory of accruing metric complexity seen in "Go to Sleep." By the time he quits in the last line, he has shed the unpredictable 3-durations and joined the exclusively duple emcees he alludes to as "wack ass" rappers.

6.3.3 "Soldier"

While the association of complexity and competency plays out within the verses of "Go to Sleep" and "The Re-Up," Eminem also uses the association to structure metric complexity both within and between verses. "Soldier," from the 2002 release *The Eminem Show*, is an example of this technique. Like "The Re-Up," the song has little by way of a plot in the lyrics—it is more or less a constant stream of boasts, each verse narratively independent. If there is to be an overarching narrative to the verse, it is left to the rhythm to establish it.

In "Soldier," the association of metric complexity and lyric virtuosity plays out in two ways. The first is how each verse begins. Example 6.12 🔵 ⬤ plots the first four measures of each verse (a–c). Each of these four-bar segments has the same number of accented syllables (28), but the number of those accents falling on 1_{mod2} positions increases from 2 in the first verse to 5 in the second verse and 9 in the third. Furthermore, as a means of kick-starting metric complexity, the first two verses begin with greater syncopation than the predominant grooves that later emerge. For example, although much of the first verse is duple, the first two lines have accents on position 11. Similarly, much of the second verse settles into a groove of <332_2222> starting on position 8, but the first line includes an additional bit of syncopation with an accent on position 5 instead of 4. This habit does not continue into the third verse, perhaps because it is already complex, articulating the groove class <333232>, one that accounts for only 3 percent of the genre as a whole.[10]

The association of complexity and virtuosity extends between the verses as well. Example 6.13 plots the groove segmentations of all three verses for an adaptive listener (no swaps) and a persistent listener (one swap per beat). Two things are evident from Eminem's use of groove throughout the track, even with no tolerance for accent swapping. The first is the decreasing use of the duple groove class. The first verse articulates that class literally in mm. 3–4 and 9–13; a persistent listener will hear the groove even longer. In contrast, the duple groove never appears in Verses 2 or 3, even for a persistent listener. The second is that more complex groove classes predominate in later verses. The most frequent groove of each verse is <2222_2222>, <332_2222>, and <333232>, respectively, and each of these is incrementally more complex.[11] Furthermore, the second and third verses create

10. See Table 4.3.
11. See the analysis script.

Example 6.13 Groove segmentation of the three verses of "Soldier" at two rates of effort.

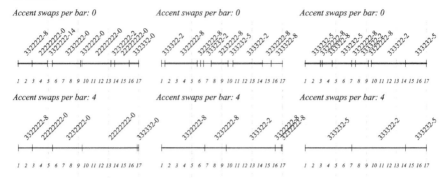

greater coherence across the track by reiterating and prolonging the most complex groove of the previous verse. While <332_2222> makes a two-measure appearance in the first verse, it makes a six-measure appearance in the second. Similarly, while <333322> makes a five-measure appearance in the second, it makes a seven-measure appearance in the third. What I find especially remarkable is that even while Eminem is increasing metric complexity across the verses, he also increases grooviness, defined in Chapter 4 as the proportion of the verse, for an adaptive listener who does not swap accents, that contains grooves lasting at least two measures. Each verse in "Soldier" incrementally raises this proportion, from 60 percent in the first verse to 75 percent in the third.[12]

6.3.4 *"Till I Collapse"*

Like "Soldier," "Till I Collapse," also from *The Eminem Show*, spins out an association between complexity and competency across the entire track. And like "Soldier," this track is lyrically homogenous; all three verses essentially reiterate the first seven words of the first verse: "Till I collapse I'm spillin' these raps." With so little narrative in the text, it is the rhythm's responsibility to give shape to the song, and Eminem does this through his selection and sequencing of grooves, both within verses and between them. Example 6.14 plots the groove segmentation of the first verse at effort rates of zero swaps per measure and one swap per half measure. The beginning of the verse, for an adaptive listener, articulates <332_2222> starting on position 2 from mm. 2–5; a persistent listener will hear this groove a bit longer. The second half is more disjointed for an adaptive listener, but a persistent listener will piece together a <323_2222> groove starting on 2 for most of the measures. Example 6.15 🌀 (a and b) transcribes the flow of mm. 3–4 and 15–16, exemplifying the main grooves of the first and second halves. The only difference between the two grooves is that the groove of the second half places

12. See the analysis script.

Example 6.14 Groove segmentation of the first verse of "Till I Collapse" at two rates of effort.

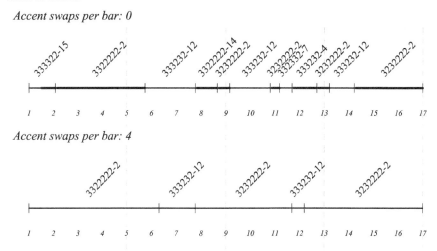

accents on position **7** instead of position **8**. Yet this minor shift makes the second half more metrically complex, substituting a 1_{mod2} accent for a 0_{mod2} one.

The end of the first half—among the most syncopated of any artist measured through average IAI—instigates the increase in metric complexity. Example 6.16 🌓 plots measures 5–8, a passage that suggests the uncommon <333232> groove with accents on positions (**2, 5, 7, 10, 12, 15**). Note that this groove has as many accents on 1_{mod2} positions (i.e., **7, 5,** and **15**) as 0_{mod2} positions (i.e., **2, 10,** and **12**). In contrast, the groove of the opening has only a single 1_{mod2} accent. The metric complexity of the passage echoes its syntactic complexity. The first line (*Subliminal thoughts, when I'm a' stop sendin' 'em?*) is a question whose end on position **14** leads immediately in the next line. That line (*Women are caught in webs, spin 'em and hock venom*) also ends without a musical pause. The end of the verse, some of which is plotted in Example 6.15a 🌓, slightly retreats from this complexity, swapping the accent on position **15** for one on **0**. The narrative of groove in the verse, then, is the presentation of a groove with little metric complexity, an abrupt turn to a very complex groove, and a retreat back toward metricity, though not a return to the beginning's simplicity. As will be seen next, this narrative informs the other verses in microcosm, as well as the track as a whole.

Example 6.17 🌑 shows the groove segmentation of the second verse. Like the first, there are two predominant grooves, <332_2222> starting on position **8**, operative in mm. 5–10, and <333322>, also starting on position **8**, operative from m. 12 to the end. Also like the first verse, these two grooves overlap extensively in the positions they accent; essentially, the end of the verse replaces accents on positions **0** and **2** with a single accent on position **1**. This substantially increases metric complexity by removing two 0_{mod2} accents and inserting a 1_{mod2} accent. And again, a section in the middle of the verse (here, mm. 10–12) presents a highly

Example 6.15 Representative measures of flow in "Till I Collapse," Verse 1: (a) mm. 3–4 and (b) mm. 15–16.

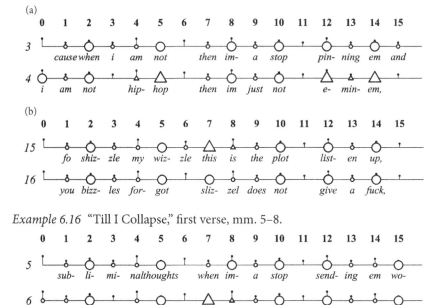

Example 6.16 "Till I Collapse," first verse, mm. 5–8.

Example 6.17 Groove segmentation of "Till I Collapse," second verse, for a persistent listener.

Accent swaps per bar: 2

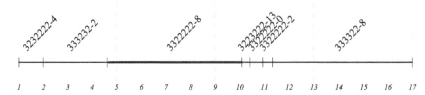

syncopated flow that seems to heighten the syncopation of the rest of the verse. While the second verse reiterates the groove narrative of the first verse—less complex, then very complex, then moderately complex—it does so with a selection of grooves that are uniformly more complex than their corresponding grooves in the first verse.

Example 6.18 Groove segmentation of "Till I Collapse," third verse, for a persistent listener.

Accent swaps per bar: 2

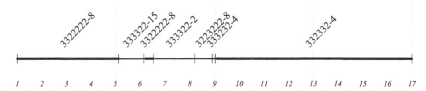

A similar groove narrative can be traced in the third verse, though less convincingly (see Example 6.18 ⬤). Here again, the groove that dominates the second half (<332_332> beginning at position 4 in mm. 9–17) is more complex than that of the opening (<332_2222> beginning at position 8 in mm. 2–4). And the middle includes some very complex grooves (e.g., <333322> beginning at position 15 in mm. 6–7). I find this narrative less convincing only because what I have called "the groove of the opening" lasts only four measures. Yet if one hears the groove narrative I have described in the third verse, then not only has Eminem created three verses that trace the same impulse toward complexity, but that narrative also extends to the relationships between the verses as well. As within each verse, the track consists of an opening verse with relatively little metric complexity, a markedly more complex second verse, and a third verse that maintains some but not all of the complexity of the second.

Though some readers will find this analysis to be a stretch, I hear echoes of Eminem's sentiments, as expressed in the lyrics, in this nested trajectory toward complexity. Beginning with the association between complex grooves and lyrical prowess, the second verse features the greatest virtuosic display. This coincides with Eminem's practice of an activity usually reserved for fandom: the creation of a list of the greatest rappers, in which he places himself ninth. It is an uncharacteristic piece of humility, but corresponds with the narrative of groove in the track. While he shows himself in the second verse capable of the highest levels of metric complexity, his moderation in the third verse is the stance of a work-a-day emcee who emphasizes consistency in every verse.

6.3.5 "8 Mile"

In tracks like "Go to Sleep," "Soldier," and "Till I Collapse," Eminem associates complexity and competency to assert his dominance as an emcee. Metric complexity means resisting placing accents on the beat and shifting them away from the beat. Yet this description hinges on intentionality: if an emcee lacks the skills necessary to place accents on the beat, then the result of his or her incompetence may sound like complexity. This hazard gives rise to the "law of flow" discussed in Chapter 1, the idea articulated by Chuck D (Alim 2006, p. 96) that "the rhythm of the lyrics must fit with the basic rhythm of the music." So while metric complexity is often associated with outstanding rapping, it can also be a sign of its opposite. This duality of complexity plays a significant role in one of Eminem's longest tracks, the song "8 Mile," from the soundtrack of the film of the same name. The track plays a vital role in the film as its first diegetic music (i.e., music that can be heard by characters in the narrative world of the film).[13] Sixteen minutes into the film, an excerpt of the first verse plays through the headphones of B-Rabbit, Eminem's character, while he sits on the bus writing lyrics. The audio of the track is altered in this introduction, as all but the rhyming words of the first verse are removed. The scribbled lyrics and fragmented audio suggest a character in the process of writing, marking an important moment of artistic growth. This path toward becoming an emcee plays out in the finished track as well.

This narrative of artistic growth dominates the track in successively longer verses, increasing in duration from 16 to 28 to 45 measures. The last verse's length is on par with some of hip hop's longest verses. With so many measures to fill, Eminem presents a host of recurring themes, namely, the challenges of overcoming self-doubt, family conflict, and performance anxiety in order to "make it" as a rapper. Example 6.19 summarizes the narrative content of the track, highlighting key lyrics in each section. Although the text could be read through many lenses, the most pertinent to this discussion is the ongoing question of the protagonist's outlook on his likelihood of and worthiness for success. In the first verse, this outlook begins bleakly and then deteriorates as he wallows in insecurities, depictions of failure, and resignation. Those themes continue into the second verse, which also addresses family conflict and begins to suggest a brighter future. The third verse includes the protagonist's only positive assessment of his own skills, as well as the frustration and determination encountered in the second verse. Though the second and third verses address similar topics, their scope changes, with the protagonist's determination in the third verse filling twice as many measures as in the second verse.

Looking more closely at the lyrics of the first verse reveals three shifts in narrative. The protagonist states his ambitions in mm. 4–5 (to "jump on stage" and "show these people . . . my skills"), but those ambitions are dashed through a depiction of a rap-battle loss in mm. 7–11 (see Example 6.20 🔊). The character does not just perform badly in this battle, but actually stops rapping words (i.e., the "uh, b'nuh nuh nuh" of m. 9). Even when he regains his language, he continues matching the pitch of the piano through the remainder of mm. 9 and 10, simulating an instrumental rather than vocal performance. The emotional drain of this failure dominates mm. 10–14; never recovering, the verse ends in abject resignation ("I'm going the fuck home"). The rhythm of the flow reflects the dynamics of the protagonist's outlook, but in a way that contrasts with the complexity/competency association discussed previously. Table 6.2 captures

13. In the opening scene, the protagonist is holed up in a bathroom preparing for a rap battle while Mobb Deep's "Shook Ones, Part II" plays as non-diegetic music, though the character seems to be imagining the music and moving along to it.

Example 6.19 Narrative themes in the lyrics of "8 Mile."

Verse One:

   mm. 1–5: aspirations
      Sometimes I wanna jump on stage and just kill mics,
      And show these people what my level of skills like.
   mm. 6–8: insecurities
      But I'm still white, sometimes I just hate life.
   mm. 9–14: present failure
      And I clam up, I just slam shut, I just can't do it.
   mm. 15–16: resignation
      I'm going the fuck home, world on my shoulders as I run back to this 8 Mile Road.

Verse Two:

   mm. 1–4: resignation
      Tryna regain back the spirit I had 'fore I go back to the same crap, to the same plant, and the
      same pants.
   mm. 5–10: family conflict
      Momma's got a new man, poor little baby sister, she don't understand.
   mm. 11–17: frustration
      Sometimes I get upset 'cause I ain't blew up yet.
   mm. 18–21: prayer
      Please, I'm begging you God, please don't let me be pigeonholed in no regular job.
   mm. 22–26: determination (familial)
      Tell my mother I love her kiss baby sister good-bye,…I'm 'a be back for you the second that
      I blow.
   mm. 27–28: determination
      On everything I own, I'll make it on my own.

Verse Three

   mm. 1–8: affirmation
      You never seen, heard, smelled, or met a real emcee who's incredible upon the same pedestal
      as me.
   mm. 9–14: frustration
      But yet I'm still unsigned, …go to work and serve emcee's in the lunch line.
   mm. 15–18: insecurity
      I'm starting to doubt shit, I'm feeling a little skeptical who I hang out with.
   mm. 19–25: poverty
      At the salvation army tryna salvage an outfit.
   mm. 26–32: frustration
      Sometimes I feel like a robot, …sometimes my mouth just overloads the acid I don't got.
   mm. 33–44: determination
      I got every ingredient, all I need is the courage…I am no longer scared, now I'm free as a bird.

metric complexity in the three main grooves encountered by a persistent listener of the verse, both in terms of *mod* 4 and *mod* 2 accents, and in terms of
the measure of metric complexity defined in Chapter 4. Not only does the verse
monotonically increase metric complexity, but it also does so through the whole
range of complexity encountered in the track, beginning with the song's least
complex groove and ending with its most complex. That final groove, <2222_
2222> starting on position **1**, is maximally complex because it places accents
only on 1_{mod2} positions. And mm. 9–16 of this verse contain a longer segment of

Example 6.20 Eminem, "8 Mile," first verse, mm. 7–11.

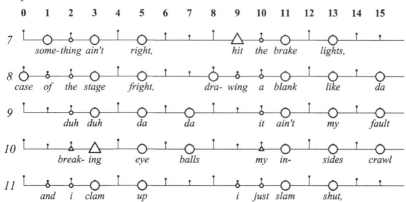

Table 6.2 Metric complexity in grooves of Eminem's "8 Mile," first verse

		Accents				mod 4		mod 2		
Groove	Measures	0	1	2	3	0	1			Complexity
<323_2222>, 8	2–6	3	1	2	1	5	2			1.66
<332_2222>, 5	7–8	1	3	0	3	1	6			3.66
<2222_2222>, 1	9–16	0	4	0	3	0	8			4.00

that groove than any encountered in the genre-wide corpus save that heard in Ca$his's "Water Whippin.'"[14] Because the moments in which groove changes coincide with changes of lyrical topic, a different association emerges in the verse, that of metric complexity and incompetence. This association inverts the more common one, and it is the task of the rest of the verse to "earn back" metric complexity as a sign of lyrical dominance.

The second verse also maps groove onto lyrical topics, but without the trajectory of the first verse. The grooves of the verse form a palindrome (see Example 6.21 🔊), starting and ending with <332_332> in rotation 5; this palindrome prevents any sense of accruing metric complexity in the verse. Instead, the contrast between complexity and noncomplexity plays out in the treatment of the topic of family. A theme in this track and others of Eminem's is that of older siblings forced into parental roles by absent or negligent parents.[15] Here, in one passage depicting a younger sister observing adults fighting, and in another in which the protagonist

---

14. Eminem himself employs this maximally complex groove for longer spans in other tracks, namely, "Mosh," where the groove lasts 16 measures, and "The Way I Am," where it lasts 11 measures. That the other long instance of this groove is rapped by Ca$his, an artist who has collaborated extensively with Eminem and was signed to his Shady Music label, is suggestive though likely coincidental.

15. Eminem also addresses this topic in "Headlights."

Example 6.21 Groove segmentation of "8 Mile," second verse, for a persistent listener.

Accent swaps per bar: 2

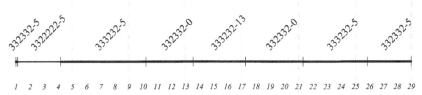

Example 6.22 Groove segmentation of "8 Mile," third verse, for a persistent listener.

Accent swaps per bar: 2

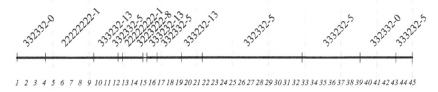

vows to rescue her himself, the groove turns to <332_332> starting on position 0, the least complex groove of the verse. Without a trajectory toward less or more metric complexity, the rhythmic narrative of the track is unchanged.

It is in the third verse (segmented in Example 6.22 🌑) where the dynamics of the protagonist's outlook change decisively, first by affirming his own skills in mm. 1–8 and later by affirming his determination to change in mm. 33–44. The first eight measures also advance the rhythmic narrative by "re-earning" the association between metric complexity and lyrical virtuosity. Both of the grooves in mm. 1–8 have appeared before. The first, <332_332> starting on position 0, occurs in Verse 2, underlying the expression of frustration in mm. 10–13 and the prayer of mm. 17–20. The second, <2222_2222> beginning on position 1, underlies the failure and resignation of the second half of the first verse. The beginning of the third verse is the first passage in which the protagonist asserts that his potential as an emcee is not something he desires but something already within him. By returning to grooves he has already employed, first a less complex one and then a maximally complex one, he attains the vital association between complexity and rapping competence, associating the supposed simplicity of a child with metric noncomplexity.

Although the topics of frustration and poverty continue before the protagonists's outlook improves for good in mm. 33, the rhythmic victory of the beginning of the verse establishes a more confident flow for its remainder.

The end of the verse, from m. 22 forward—a passage by itself longer than a typical verse of rap music—features longer groove segments than those yet encountered, including a 10-measure groove in mm. 22–32. Metric complexity remains high, though the maximally complex groove of mm. 4–9 does not return. Having found his voice, the protagonist also returns to groove <333232> starting on 5, associated with the younger sister in Verse 2. He ends the verse (and the track) with a <332_332> groove. As a groove class with an internal repetition, this groove demonstrates a different kind of rapping virtuosity, one in which accent patterns (and likely rhyme) must be repeated twice as often. In summarizing the whole track, "8 Mile" not only rearticulates the complexity/ competency nexus heard in other songs, but also suggests that the process of becoming a great emcee is the process of associating complexity with competency and not insecurity.

6.4 The Complexities of Complexity

In this chapter, I have attempted to show how Eminem uses metric complexity to create narratives of rhythm that align with the narratives already unfolding in his lyrics. Perhaps more significantly, the rhythmic narrative often foreshadows developments in the lyrics' narrative. I now must address what might be an elephant in the room: the problematic status and history of complexity as an analytical category. Writing about rap music, even writing about flow, Oliver Kautny (2015, p. 104) cautions that "we always run the risk of choosing musical examples which fit well into our scholarly tools and concepts (e.g., of complexity, unity, etc.)" and asks if these concepts are significant to fans and artists. Kautny, like myself, does not take an informant-based or fieldwork-based approach to the study of flow, and thus he does little to answer the question. But he does raise the issue of a disconnect between the hip-hop community and scholars, and he concludes with a more pointed observation along the same lines: "It is easy to fall into the 'trap of complexity,' overlooking the fact that complex flows are not appreciated by all members of the hip-hop community" (p. 115).

There are two sides to Kautny's warning. The first is that complexity as an analytical category should be avoided because it is not valued in the culture surrounding rap music. This is an important concern, though my own suspicion (and my experience as a listener) is that the way in which one values complexity varies both within and between individuals. There are listening contexts in which complexity might be highly valued (e.g., introspective listening) and those in which it might be distracting (e.g., as a soundtrack for social events). I also suspect that the kind of complexity I have emphasized here—essentially the rate at which accented syllables align with stronger positions within the beat—may not be the most typical marker of complexity in rap music. Kautny's comment suggests that the kinds of rap music valued by analysts differ from the "most popular" music in the genre.

This seems true, and the next two chapters address artists with four songs between them that charted on the Billboard Hot 100 and several hundred that did not. But in the somewhat small sample of the corpus compiled for this book, one cannot distinguish the songs that chart on that list from those that do not by their rate of metric complexity or mean IAI.[16]

The other side of Kautny's claim is that complexity is an "aspect [that] fits [academics'] values best." This is, in my view, a more urgent concern. The value academic music analysis places in complexity is not arbitrary: emphasizing the complexity of music remains a key plank in the argument that universities should employ specialists in music theory. Complexity is still at the center of most analytical methods as well, and it may be that music theory's viability as a field is dependent on the viability of analytical methods that highlight complexity. If that is what motivates one to emphasize complexity in the study of flow, then one must ask for whom the analysis is undertaken, and whom it benefits.

An emphasis on complexity also plays into previous discourses dismissive of many Afro-diasporic styles. Many such styles of music have been dismissed on the grounds that they are "less complex" than (usually) European classical music in certain parameters (e.g., harmonic organization). A frequent rejoinder is that these forms are complex if one examines other parameters (e.g., rhythm). Wynton Marsalis (1988) has long made this sort of argument, painstakingly demonstrating jazz's complexity. He does this to refute critics who, having ignored the knowledge and training jazz artists acquire in their communities, marvel that they could produce such art from a supposed state of ignorance. Such a "noble savage" narrative erases black traditions of transmission and education, and complexity as an analytical category may be tainted through its association with this narrative. Furthermore, there is a danger that emphasizing complexity replicates the same analytical prism that undergirds racist commentary of the past, even if one sees the music differently through that prism.

Finally, emphasizing complexity, particularly rhythmic and metric complexity, in the study of rap music brings another hazard, that of playing into a racist association between black people and rhythm, even if this chapter addresses a white rapper. Kofi Agawu (1995, p. 380) traces this association back a thousand years:

> The eleventh-century Christian physician and theologian Ibn Butlan, in a tract entitled "On How to Buy Slaves and How to Detect Bodily Defects," claimed that "if a black were to fall from the sky to the earth, he would fall in rhythm." In other

16. The Billboard Hot 100 is an imperfect proxy for the value a fan community places in its music. This is perhaps especially true for rap music. As Chris Molanphy (2014) points out, through much of the late twentieth century, Billboard charted the success of songs in genres like R&B and Soul through charts like the "Hot Black Singles" and "Hot Soul Singles" charts. These were calculated by polling "retailers, many black-owned, in cities that sold primarily R&B records to a largely, though not exclusively, black clientele." With the advent of digital sales tracking, first through SoundScan and then through outlets like the iTunes music store and Spotify, modern charts are unaware of community affiliation and thus the highest-charting rap tracks on the Hot 100 may be more popular among listeners with relatively little invested in hip hop, rap music, or the people who make it.

words, even while facing certain death—speaking as metaphorically as Butlan did—blacks (especially black women) continued to exhibit an essential and irreducible rhythmic disposition.

Through hundreds of years of music theory, an emphasis on rhythm was evidence of "animalistic inferiority," something Europeans had "evolved beyond" with the invention of their system of tonality (Perchard 2015, p. 326). For Perchard, the effort to distinguish the rhythmic values and abilities of black people follows the script of a suite of "race sciences," including phrenology and eugenics, that "attempted to map individual and group genetic makeup onto cultural potential" (p. 325). Perchard hears echoes of "race science" in a wide swath of twenty-first-century studies of rhythm in many Afro-diasporic genres, even when authors like Jeff Pressing construe rhythmic complexity as the product of complex cognitive processes, not an unconscious and ineffable rhythmic practice. Yet it seems to me that Perchard downplays this aspect of the work of Pressing and others (including myself). The emphasis on rhythm in the "race science" literature Perchard and Agawu highlight is not what is odious. What is contemptable is that the practitioners of the music allegedly could not comprehend its complexity, that it emerged fully formed without any conscious effort or understanding. For "race scientists," this could not be otherwise: these scientists assumed that which they did not understand to be unintelligible to others. But all the talk of rapping "in the pocket" and "on the beat" and "with the snare" demonstrates that rhythmic complexity is by no means incomprehensible to artists or listeners. And the trajectories of complexity discussed in this chapter are further evidence to me that metric complexity is not something emcees mindlessly produce.

Still, given a terrain as fraught with hazards as this, one might wonder if annotating trajectories of metric complexity as I have is worth potentially repeating racist scholarship of past centuries or the dismissal of some segment of rap listeners. The payoff as I see it is this: in the analysis of rap music, it is very difficult to associate the rhythm of lyrics with the meanings of those lyrics. In Western classical music, this association is often annotated through "text painting," in which, for example, lyrics about ascendance are paired with ascending melodies. But this sort of signification is rare in rap music. The difficulty of mapping semantic meaning onto musical meaning has implications both within and beyond music studies. Because lyrics are so important to artists and fans, and because they are not easily mapped onto musical features, much of the discourse on rap music proceeds as though it were poetry or spoken-word performance, erasing the musical contributions of artists. But within music discourse, analysts of flow—and I am no exception—avoid engaging with the meanings of lyrics. Adams (2008), for example, argues that meaning in rap music maps from music to lyrics, rather than the other way around. Rhythmic features in the music suggest rhythmic features of the lyrics and the semantic meaning of the selected lyrics is often beside the point: "The best way to analyze many rap songs is to examine not how the music supports the text, but how the text supports the music" (para. 1).

Attending to metric complexity and its dynamics in Eminem's output in this chapter, I hope, shows a path toward relating the lyrics of rap music to its rhythms.

This is important not because the text should be primary. Adams is certainly correct that many rap verses are constructed in response to a musical beat that "comes both logically and chronologically before the text" (para. 43), and the next chapter will show how an emcee might relate to a preexisting beat. But without a means to connect text to music when appropriate, flow's status *as music* is all too easily devalued.

CHAPTER $\mathcal{S}$even

Flow, Groove, and Beat in Black Thought

7.1 Beat to Flow and Back Again

This chapter extends the model of groove presented in Part I to encompass not only the vocal flow but also the instrumental streams (i.e., "the beat," not to be confused with an abstract time point within a measure such as "beat one"). From the perspective of groove, how do flow and beat complement each other? Which is conceptually prior? How might one change in response to the other? To probe these questions, I will examine more fully the work of Black Thought, an artist who exemplifies an especially wide variety of flow–beat relationships. Many artists, music critics, and scholars describe this relationship as a mapping from the beat to the flow. MC Kylea, of the Seattle-based group Beyond Reality, describes this congruence in conversation with Joseph Schloss as follows:

> The drum pattern could be one thing, and then there's a bass line that's happening that could just be real funky. . . . And it's like, "Well I wanna rhyme to the bass line when it does that". . . . I know there's a lot of artists that do that, though. You can listen to their cadence and see that, "Oh, OK, I can hear what they're flowing off of," you know? What part that they're following in the song. (2014, p. 173)

Other artists interviewed by Paul Edwards (2013) express similar sentiments. Masta Ace, for example, says he starts by "mumbling words, a flow to that beat . . . what I'm trying to formulate is how the rhymes that I'm gonna create are gonna flow into that beat." Similarly, Thes One of People Under the Stairs describes "flow[ing] some nonsense over [a beat] until I find some pattern or groove that I really like. . . . I'm getting a syllabic count and I'm getting the pauses and I'm getting all that together in my head and then I actually fit words to it" (p. 5). Like MC Kylea, some artists interviewed by Edwards attend to specific parts of the instrumental stream in formulating flows. Big Pooh of Little Brother describes "picking out certain things in the beat, whether it's the bass line or its drums or a piano." Gift of Gab, of Blackalicious, describes trying to "ride [the beat] like the bass line is riding it, only with words" (both quotes appear in Edwards 2009, p. 115).

Although most artists point to the advantages of writing in response to the instrumental streams, stic.man frames the issue as a defense against wackness:

> When you don't have the beat first, you are not writing to a known speed or pattern. This means that your choice of words and your breathing needs may not fit the beat that you end up choosing for your song. . . . When people hear the record nobody knows all that. . . . All they say is, it's either "hot" or it is wack! (stic.man 2005, p. 32)

MC Kylea and these other artists point to two features of the relationship between flow and beat explored further in this chapter. First, as so many describe it, the beat generates the flow. Second, the beat and the flow share features, in this case aligned moments of rhythmic emphasis. These two features suggest a relatively straightforward method of analysis for flow–beat relationships. An analysis would specify which features of the beat the emcee has selected and describe the congruence between the relevant portions of the flow and the beat. I suspect some (and perhaps many) rap tracks could be analyzed in this manner.

But what we know of rap music production suggests that neither of these features holds true all the time. The beat does not always generate the flow, and congruence is not the only viable relationship between them. MC Kylea's mode of writing might be thought of as *Beat to Lyrics*, implying that the beat generates the lyrics. But some tracks are written as *Lyrics to Beat*. In the Tupac Amaru Shakur Collection at Atlanta University Center resides a scrapbook put together by his family in 1995. The scrapbook contains many handwritten lyrics. Some were recorded and released in his lifetime, some were recorded and released posthumously, and some were never recorded to a beat. Among those never recorded are lyrics written during his time in the Clinton Correctional Facility (Williams 2009). It is doubtful those were written with a particular beat in mind: sometimes no mapping connects *Beat* and *Lyrics*.

Furthermore, the notion that lyrics logically follow the beat deserves scrutiny. It is certainly true that many beat makers work without knowing who, if anyone, will eventually release a rhyme over the beat. But some beat makers describe thinking explicitly about characteristics of particular emcees in the construction of the beat. Q-Tip, of the group A Tribe Called Quest, describes making beats for the album *The Low End Theory* this way:

> Back then and still today, when I make a beat I always envision how Phife [Dawg] is going to sound on it. His tone over my beats is always such a great contrast. (Coleman 2005, p. 441)

This suggests a kind of *Lyrics to Beat* process as well, though the lyrics here are not specific words but rather a personal emceeing style. And note that Q-Tip does not admire Phife Dawg's flow for its congruency with the beat but rather for its complementarity.

The mapping from beats to lyrics can also run in both directions and, like the beat, loop back upon itself. Consider The Notorious B.I.G.'s "Dead Wrong," a hit single from the 1999 posthumous album *Born Again*. An original version, not released, features a beat produced by Easy Mo Bee (Bark 2009).[1] The Bad Boys production team of Chucky Thompson, Mario Winans, and Sean Combs produced the *Born Again* version. Whatever congruence one hears in Biggie's verse on the 1999 version arises through a path represented as *Beat to Lyrics to Beat*. What sounds like congruence in the 1999 version may have been engineered by the Bad Boys team in an absence of congruence in an earlier version. And then there is an Eminem-featured verse in the posthumous version. To which beat should this be compared? Justin Williams describes how this process can occur even within a single release. Williams (2009), drawing on Krims's analysis of Ice Cube's "The N*gga Ya Love to Hate" (Krims 2000, Chapter 3), holds that the instrumental streams in a rap track consist of a "basic beat" and a host of added sounds, "sonic additions and subtractions, manipulations of digital samples, and even sharp changes in aspects of the 'basic beat'" (para. 6). These amendments to the instrumental stream may be a response to the flow and may further affect subsequent takes of the flow or subsequent performances of the song.

In this chapter, I focus on Black Thought, an emcee who works with live instruments, further complicating the flow–beat relationship. In the usual scenario, the emcee creates the flow and the DJ or producer creates the beat: authorship of the beat and authorship of the flow are mutually exclusive. Not so in the case of Black Thought, as his bandmate ?uestlove describes:

> By week number three of the sessions [for the album *Do You Want More?!!!??!*], we were having some tension in the studio. I think Tariq [Trotter, a.k.a. Black Thought] was feeling like he wasn't contributing enough to the music, like he was at the mercy of whatever we created. So that [the song "Mellow My Man"] was one of three songs that were his brainchild. His method was to basically go up to [bassist Leonard Hubbard] and hum the bass line he wanted, and then we'd spice it up. (Coleman 2009, p. 387)

This bass line might be unrelated to the lyrics that would be added to the beat. But it is equally plausible that Black Thought had some musical feature of his verses in mind when creating the bass line, which become the beat, which may well have had an impact on the verses. *Beat to Lyrics* becomes *Lyrics to Beat to Lyrics*.

And the chain can continue. In one instance I will discuss later, I am confident that ?uestlove configured aspects of the beat (or at least his contribution to it as the drummer) in response to Black Thought's lyrics, stretching what might have simply been *Beat to Lyrics* to *Beat to Lyrics to Beat*. And in many cases, The Roots songs will be performed live repeatedly over many years (see the upcoming discussion of "You Got Me"). On the one hand, there is pressure on an emcee to reiterate a recorded verse with as little variation as possible. After all, many audience members want to rap along with the lyrics and emcees elicit this kind of audience interaction. On the other hand, depending on who is onstage, the "beat" of a verse might change substantially, instigating revisions from the emcee. What started as

---

1. The Easy Mo Bee version can be heard on the unreleased Mister Cee mixtape, "The Best of Biggie 10th Anniversary Mixtape," made available for download in 2008.

a simple *Beat to Lyrics* construction might become *Beat to Lyrics to Beat to Lyrics*. These cycles of interaction might continue further still.

If the directionality MC Kylea describes is subject to change, so, too, is the congruence she ascribes to the beat and flow. While an emcee might do as MC Kylea maintains and try to "match" her flow to the beat, she might just as easily decide to do the exact opposite of the beat, creating contrast rather than congruence as Q-Tip describes. Garrett Michaelsen (2013) presents a rich methodology for describing these different kinds of interactions between musical agents. Michaelsen deals primarily with jazz, where such interaction occurs in the course of improvisation. In Michaelsen's view of jazz, one player configures her performance to suggest (or "project") possible continuations to others. The responding performer must either choose from among the continuations proffered or offer material at odds with them. In this way, the two performers can interactively converge if possible continuations are chosen or diverge if there is a sustained rejection of these continuations. Rap music contains a similar dialogue to the one Michaelsen describes in jazz, although often this dialogue takes the form of exchanges of recorded material between emcees and producers rather than spontaneous improvisation.

Two other features of Michaelsen's view of interaction are relevant to interaction in rap music. First, projections and continuations need not be temporally adjacent. In other words, a performer may delay presenting a suggested continuation. Therefore, the analyst of interaction must consider all the material of one agent as the possible continuation of the actions of another. And second, a jazz musician interacts not only with the other musicians sharing the performance, but also with the continuations that are suggested by the musician's own personal style or by stylistic norms writ large within the genre.[2] In one instance, an artist may deliberately diverge from his or her own style, whether or not the result is convergent with the suggested continuations of the other players. Both of these features have clear analogues in rap music. If a feature of a beat—perhaps something from the introduction or hook—catches an emcee's attention, that person might mimic such a feature at some other point in their his or her verse. The features of flow can also be understood as a reaction to hip-hop norms or the emcee's personal style, and here the genre-wide corpus gathered in Part I will be especially useful when combined with a smaller corpus of Black Thought verses.[3]

In this chapter, then, I examine some of these more complex interactions between the flow and the beat in Black Thought's verses. I will argue that, in general, Black Thought avoids simple *Beat to Lyrics* flow–beat–convergent relationships. Instead, I will show examples where this relationship is characterized by divergence rather than congruence. In other examples where the flow does converge on the beat, it does so either with a temporal difference or with processes at work

---

2. This echoes Oliver's description (2016, p. 244) of "grooving individually with the contextual sense of time [of a genre]" discussed in Chapter 4.

3. This smaller corpus contains transcriptions of thirty Black Thought verses. Like the genre-wide corpus, the chronological distribution of tracks in the sample is the same as that of all verses Black Thought has recorded. Additionally, the distribution of the "type" of verse—whether a Roots

in the beat rather than any particular sonic feature. I will also examine two verses that exemplify cycles of interaction that go well beyond *Beat to Lyrics*.

As a case study, I do not intend to present an overarching theory for how Black Thought relates to his beats. Instead, I have two other aims. The first is to show how flows and beats might relate beyond the *Beat to Lyrics* process so many emcees and critics assume; the use of syncopation will be an important trace of this relationship. The second aim is to demonstrate how we can support and constrain claims for divergence or convergence between the flow and the beat. Because Black Thought's complex flow–beat interactions are not unique, I hope to provide a framework for describing the interaction between flows and beats in other artists and demonstrate the kinds of evidence that can support those descriptions.

7.2 Flow–Beat Divergence

No doubt, many emcees would recognize MC Kylea's description of congruence and configure their flow to support the particularities of the beat. However, several flows of Black Thought would seem to reject this strategy. Rather than placing significant events in the flow to coincide with significant events in the beat, Black Thought seems most likely to assert his flow at moments when the beat is relatively placid. In this way, he does more to complement the beat than conform to it. And while many emcees speak about conforming to the beat, the practice of complementing the beat is less often discussed in rap-music scholarship.

Yet rhythmic complementarity is pervasive in scholarship of other Afro-diasporic genres such as jazz, blues, rock, and gospel. In describing the rhythms of such genres, Pressing (2002, p. 300) draws on the idea of perceptual rivalry to explain why syncopation and other rhythmic complexities might permeate Afro-diasporic music. Perceptual rivalry arises when our perceptual systems confront ambiguity. In rap music and other related genres, this rivalry arises between events that align with the metric grid (e.g., the boom-bap) and those that do not. Events that do not align with the grid might signal syncopation, displacement, or what Krebs (1999, p. 31) calls "grouping dissonance," a reiteration of durations that do not typify the meter (e.g., a long string of 3-durations in rap music's persistent duple meter). Perceptual rivalry, in Pressing's view, accomplishes two aims. First, it increases engagement with the music. As discussed in Chapter 4, people spontaneously move to music and discover aspects of its structure in doing so. If more of the metric framework is active, there are more events to move to. Second, perceptual rivalry increases listeners' attention to the music by presenting a complex or ambiguous surface to tease apart.

album track, a Roots single, or a featured verse on the track of another artist—is the same in the sample and the population of Black Thought verses. Not all verses discussed in this chapter are part of this smaller corpus; I transcribed additional verses because their flow–beat relationship is compelling, but they are not included in descriptive statistics of Black Thought's flow.

An initial example of perceptual rivalry in Black Thought's flow may be seen in the first half of the first verse of "The OtherSide." Example 7.1a 🔊 transcribes the instrumental streams of keyboard, bass, and drums. Readers unfamiliar with music notation can safely disregard the pitches—I will have very few comments about this parameter. To aid in decoding the rhythm, my primary concern, I have plotted the position of each accented note above the note head. Here, I use a very simple algorithm for accent: 1_{mod2} positions coinciding with notes lasting longer than 1 unit are accented. Additionally, 0_{mod2} positions coinciding with events are accented, unless they precede long events on 1_{mod2} positions. I consider the drum set as a collection of instruments, not a single instrument. This algorithm is, in essence, the accent discovery algorithm detailed in Chapter 3, minus the consideration of "word accents." The instrumental streams of "The OtherSide" are among the most active and syncopated of any of The Roots's beats. The bass drum, typically heard only twice per bar, has seven hits in each measure, four of which are on accented 1_{mod2} positions. The keyboard is syncopated as well, supporting the bass drum on position 7 in the first two bars of each four-bar group, while emphasizing position 6 along with the bass in the last two bars of each group.

In contrast, Black Thought's flow in these 8 measures (transcribed in Example 7.1b 🔊) is less syncopated than all but one of the verses in his corpus in terms of mean IAI. Recall from Chapter 5 that completely non-syncopated verses will have a mean IAI of 2, since that will be the only IAI value.[4] There are only three 1_{mod2} accents in these measures—at the beginning of m. 7 (*soaking*) and at the ends of mm. 4 and 8 (*highness is* and *complements*). As a result, the groove segmentation of this half of the verse, even with an adaptability of one swap per measure, is exclusively the duple groove class (i.e., <2222_2222>) until the last beat; it is the fourth longest such span in the Black Thought corpus.[5] In listening to the excerpt, one is struck by the off-kilter groove of the instruments contrasted with the constancy of the rapping, as though the flow is needed to anchor the beat, not the other way around.

When the beat is highly syncopated, as in "The OtherSide," perceptual rivalry is easily attained by a duple flow. Unlike "The OtherSide," "Kool On" presents a beat that is texturally denser and at the same time less syncopated (see Example 7.2a 🔊). Of the five prominent streams, two are syncopated and three are not—the second guitar part, the bass, and the drums have only 0_{mod2} accents, while the vocals and first guitar part accent mostly 1_{mod2} positions. Black Thought's flow is transcribed in Example 7.2b 🔊. It is less patterned than many other verses: the groove organizing these measures for a persistent listener, <332_2222> beginning on 4, only fully emerges if one is willing to swap two pairs of accents per measure. Put another way, and recalling the distribution of accents within the

---

4. See the analysis script. The only verse with a lower mean IAI is "Birthday Girl," though the mean IAI of the entire "The OtherSide" verse is higher than that of the first 8 measures. I recognize that a verse could have only IAIs of 2 and still be quite syncopated, that is, the duple groove starting on position 1 might organize the verse, but this groove is sufficiently rare that mean IAI is still a good measure of relative syncopation.

5. See the analysis script.

measure in Eminem's "Lose Yourself" (Example 4.5 ◐), Example 7.2c ◓ counts the number of times the instrumentalists and Black Thought accent each position in the measure. The two plots are quite contrastive, showing the instrumentalists more concerned with articulating the strong beats (i.e., positions 0 and 8) and Black Thought emphasizing the weak beats (i.e., positions 4 and 12). Of particular note is his treatment of the middle of the measure, positions 5–11. Here, whereas the instrumentalists emphasize 8 and never accent 7, Black Thought does the reverse, accenting position 7 in five of the eight measures. In configuring a flow to a beat that has moderate syncopation, Black Thought could be said to converge by using moderate syncopation himself. But he deploys that syncopation in a way that creates perceptual rivalry and divergence by consistently emphasizing a position never accented in the beat.

A final example of perceptual rivalry is seen in the beginning of "Now or Never." The instrumental streams transcribed in Example 7.3a ◓ include a stationary keyboard part, an entirely duple snare and conga part, and a much more active and syncopated bass drum part. In response, Black Thought presents a flow that is both highly syncopated and unpatterned (see Example 7.3b ◓). In the first four measures, 40 percent of the accents are on 1_{mod2} positions—higher than any other verse in his 30-verse corpus save one. At the same time, at every rate of effort greater than zero, the first four measures have (or are tied for having) the most groove segments of any other opening in a transcribed Black Thought verse.[6] These two features are moderately correlated, but Black Thought can use lots of 1_{mod2} positions and a groovy flow (as in the beginning of "Radio Daze"), or use very few 1_{mod2} accents and present an unpatterned flow (as in the beginning of "Sleep").[7] There is an obvious perceptual rivalry between the syncopated flow and the duple keyboards, snare, and congas. But does the flow complement or support the syncopated bass drum part? And what sort of evidence would bear on this question?

As the beat transcription shows, the bass drum presents accents, in every measure, on positions 0, 2, 5, 8, and 11. In both of the first two measures, Black Thought accents positions 4, 7, 12, and 15. There are two other accents in the measure, varying between positions 1 or 2 and 9 or 10. Of the positions accented in both measures, none overlap with the bass drum, and only one of the positions accented in just one measure does (i.e., *sick* on 2 in m. 1). This suggests a high degree of rivalry and complementarity. This sense of rivalry is highlighted by considering the other ways in which this flow could relate to the meter. With some practice, and with varying degrees of credulity, one can imagine shifting the syllables of m. 1 (and measures like it, i.e., mm. 2, 5, 6, and 7) forward or backward a position or two. Shifted forward one position, the rhyme class (*vain, game, change, chains*) lands on positions 0 and 8, both of which are accented by the bass drum. Shifted backward one position, the rhyme class (*wait-, play-, mak-, fin-*) lands on positions 3 and 11, one of which is accented by the bass drum. Extending this analysis, Example 7.4 counts how

6. See the analysis script.
7. See the analysis script.

Example 7.4 The Roots, "Now or Never," first verse, mm. 1–2, percentage of accents aligned with bass drum given displacement of flow.

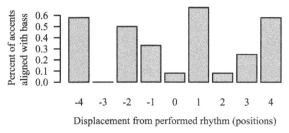

Displacement from performed rhythm (positions)

many of Black Thought's accents would coincide with the bass drum's accents, were he to shift the start of his verse by 0–4 positions in either direction. The rate of coincidence with the bass drum as he performed the verse (i.e., with a displacement of 0) is among the lowest possible (though not as low as shifting backward 3 positions). Furthermore, shifting forward or backward by 4 positions is perhaps the most viable; this retains all the existing relationships between syllables and *mod* 4 positions. But those displacements would produce among the most coincident accents. The flow of "Now or Never" is highly unpatterned, so later measures inevitably present some coincident accents with the bass drum. But when introducing the flow of the verse, Black Thought ensures that accents saturate the metric positions of the measure as much as possible.

These examples suggest that divergence with the beat is as viable a relationship as the convergence proffered by so many writers and emcees. When comparing a flow to a beat, it is easy to assume that the task of the analyst is to demonstrate their congruence. Indeed, this is reminiscent of the problematic "search for unity" undertaken by music theorists (Kerman 1980, p. 313), a search already at odds with the value hip hop and rap music specifically places on divergent sounds like scratching and juxtaposed samples (Adams 2015a, p. 120; Rose 1994, p. 39; Chang 2006, p. x).[8] In my view, one should be open to both convergence and divergence. Distinguishing the two, while not easy, is a matter of identifying the most salient features of the flow and the beat, *and also* comparing those features to what the artist has done in other circumstances or what the artist reasonably might have done in the verse.

7.3 Flow–Beat Convergence on a Formal Process

"The OtherSide," "Kool On," and "Now or Never" demonstrate Black Thought's tendencies toward divergence, as opposed to the convergence so often associated with rapping. This is not to say that Black Thought's flows are never congruent

8. In Chapter 8, I will return to this value of divergence in connection to Talib Kweli.

Example 7.5 The Roots, "I Remember" (2011, first verse, mm. 1–4, 0:22–0:34): (a) instrumental streams and (b) flow transcription.

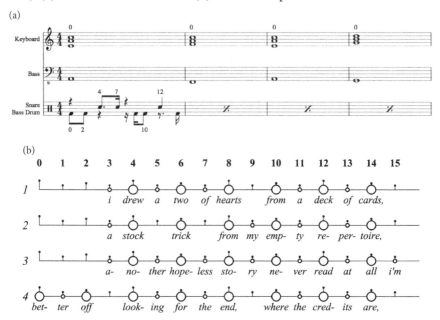

with his beats. Yet even when he does highlight a feature of a beat, he tends to do so at a remove. Perhaps the feature is a process that the beat undertakes rather than a specific sound. Or, he might imitate the sonic features of the song without configuring those features to coincide in the beat and the flow. These techniques are a kind of convergence at a distance, a distance that might be conceptual or temporal.

Consider the first verse of "I Remember," a rare eight-bar verse. Example 7.5a 🜄 transcribes the first four measures of the beat, and Example 7.5b 🜄 plots Black Thought's flow in those measures. Both the beat and the flow are extremely sparse—whole notes in keyboards and bass and a slightly more active drum set that accents position 7 in the snare, paired with four exclusively duple measures of rapping ending in rhyme. Indeed, relating them is difficult as neither present especially salient features. Perhaps the flow complements the beat by avoiding the downbeat, the only position most of the instruments play.

In m. 5, a synthesizer joins the beat, making it more rhythmically active by anticipating position 8 with a pair of sixteenth notes (see Example 7.6a). There is also a trajectory toward rising pitch, both in the sixteenth notes of mm. 5 and 6, and in the sustained eighth notes at the end of the measure between mm. 7 and 8. Black Thought does not converge on this new emphasis on position 8, nor does he rap faster or insert more syllables into each measure. But the flow, plotted in Example 7.6b, does change: specifically, inter-rhyme intervals (IRIs), which have been four beats up to this point, reduce to three beats for mm. 5–7, before reducing to two beats in m. 8. In this way, Black Thought echoes the acceleration of

Example 7.6 The Roots, "I Remember" (2011, first verse, mm. 5–8, 0:34–0:45): (a) instrumental streams with new synthesizer part and (b) flow transcription.

the new stream in the beat, not by rapping faster but by instigating his own process of acceleration in IRIs.[9]

A similar flow–beat relationship is obtained in Black Thought's verse on "Lighthouse." Like "I Remember," "Lighthouse" begins extremely sparsely, a standard boom-bap with the bass also accenting positions **3** and **11** (see Example 7.7a 🔊). Black Thought's flow in the first half (Example 7.7b 🔊) is similarly sparse, the kind of duple, end-rhyme flow reminiscent of Bubba Sparxxx's "Deliverance." In m. 9, a keyboard stream enters, increasing the activity of the beat, especially in the first half of the measure. Black Thought's flow shifts as well, accenting position 7 in every measure from 10–16 (Example 7.7c 🔊). This shift is convergent in two ways, but not in terms of sonic congruence. First, the segmentation of the flow shifts to begin lines on position **9** and end them on position 7, like the new keyboard line. Second, the accenting of position 7 can be seen as an analogy for the rhythm of the keyboard. Whereas the flow gains syncopation in the second beat where there was none before, the beat gains a new level of rhythmic activity.

For a final example of convergence through analogy, consider the shifts of rhythm in the second half of "How I Got Over." The first half of the verse is among

---

9. This congruence may not be attributable to Black Thought—perhaps the synthesizer part was added later. But if it was added to Black Thought's flow, the same reasoning applies: one process of acceleration invites another.

Example 7.8 The Roots, "How I Got Over" (2010, first verse, 1:09–1:43): (a) groove segmentation of the flow; (b) instrumental streams, from top to bottom: organ, congas, drum set; (c) new guitar heard in mm. 9–13; (d) more active organ part, heard in mm. 15–16.

(a)

Accent swaps per bar: 0

(b)

(c)

(d)

Black Thought's grooviest, projecting a single groove class, <323_2222> starting on 4 (see Example 7.8a). Only one other verse begins so securely in a groove.[10] This groove creates only moderate syncopation, with accents on positions 7, 9, and other 0_{mod2} positions. This predominantly unsyncopated groove (Example 7.8b) is befitting a beat that accents no 1_{mod2} positions. Yet two moments insert greater activity into the verse. The first occurs from m. 9–12 with the entrance of a new guitar part (see Example 7.8c); the second occurs from mm. 14–16 when the keyboard part switches to continuous eighth notes (see Example 7.8d). At each of these moments, Black Thought inserts another [323] inter-accent interval segment, with *too much lyin'* before m. 9 and *just like I am* at the end of m. 16. This is not convergence, strictly speaking, because the beat features an increase of activity, while the emcee features an increase of syncopation. But Black Thought could

---

10. See the analysis script.

not increase his activity (i.e., rate of syllables) beyond where he already was. This example, taken together with "I Remember," demonstrates that sometimes converging on the rhythm of the beat might mean finding an analogy between its rhythm and the rhythm of the flow.

In m. 9, a new guitar part enters, one that shares "eighth-note" syncopations with the keyboard but has many more of them. Black Thought could not converge on this new syncopation because he is rapping much too quickly, producing approximately fourteen syllables per measure in comparison to the guitar's four events. Instead, he increases his own use of syncopation by adding another pair of [323] inter-accent dsegs (i.e., *it's too much lyin'*). His approach to convergence is the same when a more active keyboard part heralds the end of the verse in m. 14, and Black Thought again increases syncopation (with *you just like I am*).

7.4 Flow–Beat Convergence with a Temporal Difference

MC Kylea articulates a common technique of convergence in emceeing: selecting a feature of the beat and mimicking that feature. This correspondence between the flow and the beat need not be temporally adjacent. Perhaps the feature the emcee selects comes from another part of the verse or the song. I believe something like this happens in "False Media," the first track with vocals on *Game Theory*. The track, recorded in the late spring of 2006, is a response to the Iraq War, then growing increasingly deadly for both combatants and Iraqi civilians. It begins with two speech fragments: the first from Walter Lippmann's 1961 *CBS Reports* interview ("I don't think old men ought to promote wars for young men to fight") and the second from the poet and attorney Wadud Ahmad, connecting the Iraq War to previous episodes of American imperialism.

As I will discuss here, the sonic world created by producers ?uestlove, Kamal Gray, and James Poyser is one of sparseness and violence. The instrumental streams consist of only a bass drum and snare drum (with the snares disengaged), a descending whistle that approximates an impending missile strike, and intermittent and menacing low brass hits. Absent are usual components of a beat by The Roots such as keyboards, hi-hat, and bass. Black Thought's flow is sonically sparse as well. The verse includes the longest continuous rhyme class in his corpus: the flow's economy of phonemes parallels the beat's economy of instrumental timbres.

Yet the flow never settles into a pattern that might be compared to the beat in terms of convergence or complementarity. Instead, Black Thought seems mainly interested in the possibilities presented by the low brass. The brass first appear in the fourth beat of the first measure, gaining in volume before disappearing just before the downbeat. This reiterates in the next three measures, softer each time, suggesting that the brass might disappear altogether. Instead, they return just after the downbeat of m. 5 and begin reiterating every 3 positions, ceasing after five such intervals. In measure 11, the brass reenter in earnest, stringing together 3-durations continually until the end of the verse. Example 7.9a 🔊 transcribes the emceeing of the verse and indicates the low brass as well.

Although Black Thought uses 3-durations more than most of his peers, reiterating that duration is problematic because multiples of 3 rarely coincide with multiples of 16. The most 3-durations one can employ within a measure is 4, as in rotations of the groove class <333322>. Yet much of what Black Thought does in "False Media" aspires to saturate his flow with 3-durations, beginning on position 8 of m. 1. First is the reiterated groove of <333322> starting on position 2 in each of the first three measures, a groove class that informs only 5 percent of the genre-wide corpus (see Table 4.3). Keep in mind that this early in the verse, one unfamiliar with the verse does not yet know that 3-durations will be relevant in the brass later on.

The relationship between Black Thought's flow and the brass is clearer when the brass begins reiterating 3-durations in m. 5. But his IAI segment of [3333] does not capture the scope of the commitment to 3-durations the brass will display at the end of the verse. If mm. 1–3 foreshadow the kind of reiterated 3-durations in the brass in mm. 5 and 7, then the rhythm of the lines *nothin' is sacred, we gon' pimp the shit outta nature, send our troops to get my paper* foreshadows the saturation of 3-durations in the brass at the end of the verse. Through those words, Black Thought strings together an IAI segment of [3333333333], ten 3-durations in a row, an extreme rarity in rapping.[11] And to further underline the point, he begins configuring rhymes around 3-beat durations as well, placing a rhyme every three beats beginning with *sacred* in m. 7 and running all the way through m. 13 (see Example 7.9b 🔊). At that point, with the brass reiterating 3-durations at full volume, he returns to a more rhythmically placid flow and consistent 4-beat rhymes. By isolating an important rhythmic feature of one stream in the beat and building his verse around that feature, Black Thought demonstrates how to interact with a prominent feature of a beat—one temporally nonadjacent no less—instead of aligning with or complementing particular sounds.

Another example of convergence with a temporal difference is heard in "Bread and Butter," a bonus track on the UK, Japan, and iTunes versions of the album *Game Theory*. In verses by Black Thought and Truck North, the track addresses the calamity of Hurricane Katrina, which killed an estimated 1,800 people and displaced an additional 400,000 from New Orleans and the Gulf Coast of Louisiana and Mississippi in August 2005, a year before the track was released. In general, the lyrics of the first eight measures of Black Thought's verse are a second-person narrative, asking the reader to imagine finding themselves in the situation confronted by so many residents of New Orleans. And in general, the latter two thirds of the verse abandon this narrative device in order to highlight more abstract causes of the destructive aftermath of the storm. Throughout these measures, Black Thought bemoans leadership failures and the mischaracterizations of the media. He also gives voice to the view that the government "let the levees break," an idea disputed by official reports but resonant with the intentional destruction of black

---

11. See Chapter 4. There is one verse with a longer string of continuous 3-durations (12, in Eminem's "Drug Ballad," verse 2) and a few other verses with strings nearly as long (8 in Jay Rock's "Pay for It" and 7 in the first verse of Eminem's "Stimulate). In contrast, there are more than 3,000 instances of 3-durations in strings of only 1 or 2.

communities in St. Bernard and Plaquemines Parishes during the historic flood of 1927 and that of the Lower Ninth Ward and Chalmette during Hurricane Betsy in 1965 (Davis 2006, p. 34).

Example 7.10a shows the groove segmentation of the verse, and Example 7.10b transcribes the flow of the first eight measures. What is striking about the verse is the way in which it evens out after a chaotic beginning. The first eight measures are unsettled in terms of groove, but the duple groove organizes the remainder. Within the first eight measures, there are suggestions of a more consistent flow. In the first four bars, a rhyme class extends from positions **8** through **11** (*mother is gone, tussling strong,* etc.), coinciding with and highlighting the climax in pitch height of the guitar part (see the transcription in Example 7.10b). Underneath this patterning of inter-rhyme interval is an unpatterned segmentation in terms of line. While *mother is gone* in m. 1 is both a rhyme and line ending, the second line extends past the rhyme with *for his life*. The third line ends with the rhyme *eye of the storm*, but going into m. 4, the reiteration of inter-accent intervals of three positions between the accents *storm / man- / boy / -rive* blurs the line's ending. A possible inspiration for this nonpatterning of line is the beat's unusual bass line, which lands on the tonic E on position **4** of each measure; bass lines nearly always land on the downbeat (position **0**). This undercuts the usual tendency of flow to begin just after the downbeat, and thus pushes the lines well past their typical endpoints near the end of the measure. In the second quatrain (mm. 5–8), even the patterning of inter-rhyme interval falls away. One rhyme class (*spare time, -pare times, headline, bedtime*) establishes a new pattern of three-beat IRIs. The duration of two beats between *bedtime* and the start of the next rhyme class (*head down*) suggests a return to the more typical four-beat IRIs of the beginning of the verse, but the following rhyme (*is now*) reprises the three-beat IRI. Yet starting with m. 9, the flow becomes surprising placid, with rhymes on position **12** of every measure and many measures with only 0_{mod2} accents. In this way, the latter part of the verse converges on the decidedly duple nature of the instrumental parts, save the second guitar part, which I will discuss in a moment.

What might account for the organization of this verse, with its turbulent beginning and staid ending? Perhaps lyrics suggest this structure, pairing the initially unpatterned flow with the mental state of one negotiating a chaotic and dangerous situation and pairing the more direct flow of the latter portion of the verse to the latter lyrics' presentation of an argument. We might also look to the beat to understand the dynamics of the verse. As the transcription shows, this is, for a Roots track, a strikingly duple beat. Only the second guitar part, heard just before Truck North's first verse, presents 1_{mod2} accents, emphasizing positions **1**, **7**, **9**, and **15**. In doing so, it creates an instrumental equivalent of the vocal groove <332_332> beginning on position **1**. Threeness in duration also plays a role in the pitch contour of the line. The guitar starts on G4 on the first beat, reaches B4 on the fourth beat, and returns to A4 on the third beat of the following measure—in terms of round numbers of beats, these inflection points of contour (i.e., those notes locally highest or lowest) are three beats apart. Finally, the second guitar joins the duple first guitar in the second half of the phrase. I believe all these features have correlates in the Black Thought verse. The emphasis on inter-accent intervals of

Example 7.10 The Roots, "Bread and Butter" (2006, second verse, 2:03–3:07): (a) groove segmentation of the verse; (b) flow transcription, mm. 1–8; (c) instrumental streams. From top to bottom, first guitar part (heard throughout), second guitar part (heard in intro at 0:22 and 0:31), bass of intro and hook, bass of verses, and drums throughout.

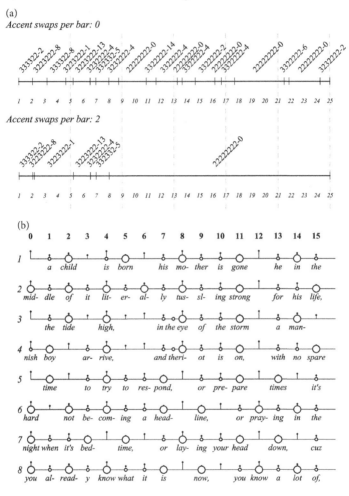

3 mirrors the strings of continuous 3-durations heard in both *child is born, his mother is gone* and *eye of the storm, a mannish boy arrive.* The [323323] groove (a rotation of <332_332>) appears in m. 7, and isolated [323] fragments appear in mm. 6 and 8. At a slightly larger level, the three-beat durations between inflections of contour in the guitar mirror the three-beat inter-rhyme intervals in the flow of mm. 5–8. And at the largest level, and perhaps most speculatively, I hear a connection between the contrast of syncopation in mm. 1–2 vs. 3–4 of the guitar part and the contrast in patternedness of the flow between mm. 1–8 and mm. 9–16. Thus, this verse shows a kind of convergence between the flow and the beat, but a convergence that is temporally dislocated and augmented.

7.5 Cycles of Interaction

In the last section, I detailed how Black Thought constructs flows in response to features of the beat, sometimes converging and aligning, sometimes converging without aligning, and sometimes diverging. Perhaps for some emcees, the trail of interaction would stop with their response to prerecorded or sampled beats. But Black Thought performs as part of a band, and the group dynamic invites analysis of further interactive possibilities. How do other musicians on The Roots's tracks respond to Black Thought's flow, which is itself a response to their playing? If their playing changes substantially, how does Black Though adjust his flow to new musical circumstances?

To address the first question, consider the first half of the third verse of "Long Time," also from *Game Theory*. Example 7.11a transcribes the flow along with a representation of ?uestlove's drumming. Example 7.11b transcribes two of the instrumental streams that repeat every four measures. These measures are an example of Black Thought's capacity for consistent flowing, with a nearly unperturbed <332_2222> groove starting on position 8. This groove includes an accent on position 11, which the guitar and bass drum accent as well (notice the squares above position 11 in Example 7.11a and see Example 7.11b). I imagine Black Thought writing this verse in the way MC Kylea describes: he might have heard a demo of the song, attended to the rhythm of the bass drum and especially the guitar—the only rhythmically active instrumental stream— and crafted a verse converging on that rhythmic particularity. But a few details of the flow diverge from those streams. The first is that the number of syllables at the beginning of the line preceding the downbeat increases incrementally in each of the first four measures, from no anacrusis in the first measure to a three-syllable anacrusis in the fourth (i.e., *clap to* into m. 2, *to the top* into m. 3, *picture the pool* into m. 4). The second is how the location of the rhyme shifts from position 11 (*clap, back, that, at*) in mm. 1–4—convergent with the bass drum and guitar—to position 14 (*-lino, -sino, me though*) in mm. 5–8. And finally, more syncopation is added in mm. 7 and 8, when the groove <333322> underlies, briefly, *sweeping the floors and running to stores, but all them old [heads].*

Example 7.11 The Roots, "Long Time" (2006, 2:40–3:00): (a) flow transcription with percussion. □ = bass drum; × = snare drum; o = tom; • = crash symbol. (b) Instrumental streams (minus percussion) in "Long Time," third verse. Upper line transcribes guitar in mm. 5–15 and strings in mm. 12–16. Lower line transcribes synth throughout and bass in mm. 5–16.

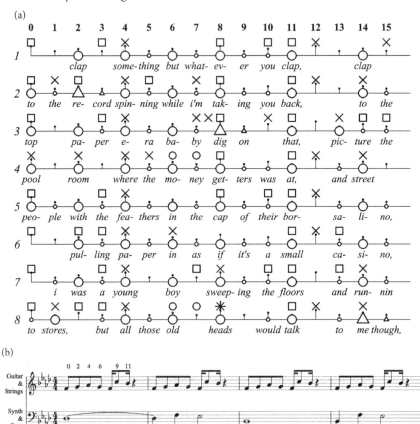

These details, in my view, help explain the particularities of some of ?uestlove's playing and point toward another iteration of interaction between the emcee and the drummer/producer. Black Thought's first four measures increase the expectancy for rhyme by introducing successively longer anacruses. Another process in the instrumental streams also increases expectancy for the essential third beat in the bass drum. Just as the length of anacrusis increases in each measure, so, too, does the incidence of a 3-duration in the bass drum. This IAI happens twice in the first measure (starting on positions 0 and 8) but 3 times each in mm. 2 and 3. In m. 4, unable to pack in more 3-durations into the bass drum part, ?uestlove fills in almost every syllable of the line *picture the pool room where the money getters was at*, moving down through pitch space from the snare, through the toms, to the bass drum.

?uestlove also diverges from his typically patterned playing style to support Black Thought's <333322> groove in mm. 7–8. There, he places snare hits on the syllables *young, sweep-, run-, stores*, and *all. Sweep* falls on position **8**, a position ?uestlove avoids in the snare in the rest of the measures in deference to the bass drum's "boom" of the boom-bap. The groove also prevents him from hitting position **12** with the snare, since *floors* and *run-* surround that beat. I believe that the drumming in these measures shows a process of interaction implying a more involved creation than *Beat to Lyrics*. Instead, I believe the emcee heard the beat and selected features to mimic in his flow. But his flow contains features not suggested by the beat, and these features interactively inform the beat's alterations.

As Adams (2015a) points out, the details of creation in rap music pose problems for traditional music analysis because of rap music's often uncertain authorship. The features of a track are not easily aligned with the creative agents of emcee, producer, performer, and editor. Extensive revisions—with or without the collaboration of the emcee—are possible. Thus, it can be hard to say whether, for example, Black Thought configures his flow to some feature of the beat or whether that feature was added to highlight the flow. But in some cases, such as the foregoing analysis of "Long Time," one can uncover the traces of the process of creation by viewing the final product through an interactive lens.

In some ways, live performance avoids problems of attribution that complicate much of the analysis of rap music. One can assume that alterations to a flow in live performance are the creative provenance of the emcee, and further that they are a response to changes in the beat or, alternatively, evidence of a style change in the emcee him- or herself. As a practical matter, emcees usually try to perform their verses live in a nearly identical manner to the recorded version. In many cases, the audio of the instrumental stream will be very similar, encouraging similarity in the emcee. Furthermore, because the genre relies heavily on fan participation, emcees have a strong incentive to make their live performances maximally predictable by recreating the studio version. The Roots are an exception to these tendencies, and not only because they use live instruments. Many of the musicians on their studio tracks appear as guests and are not available for touring. Furthermore, The Roots frequently invite other musicians to share the stage in concert. Therefore, the instrumental streams of a Roots track might be quite different in different contexts. And examining how Black Thought responds to those differences can illuminate aspects of his creative and interactive practice.

In order to document that response, I collected and transcribed seven performances of the first verse of The Roots's "You Got Me" recorded between 1999 and 2015. These performances are summarized in Table 7.1. The venues of these performances include large outdoor concerts and intimate television programs. There are several advantages to examining performances of "You Got Me" in particular. The track garnered the group's first Grammy award, so it is frequently performed. It also invites instrumental revision in live performance. The hook of the song was written by Jill Scott but performed by Erykah Badu.[12]

---

12. It is frequently asserted (e.g., Harrington 2004) that Scott was omitted from the recording at the request of MCA records because Erykah Badu was at the time a higher-profile singer, but I can find no instance of Scott herself confirming this. In contrast, in one interview, Scott says she only sang the song because Badu was stuck in traffic, but it is unclear which performance this refers to and whether it influenced the studio recording (Martin 2007).

Table 7.1 Live performances of The Roots, "You Got Me," 1999–2015

Index	Year	Venue	Hook performer	BPM
1	1999a	[Studio album]	Erykah Badu	81
2	1999b	Bowery Ballroom, New York	Jill Scott	75
3	1999c	*Nulle part ailleurs*, television program (France)	Jill Scott	75
4	2002	*$2 Bill*, MTV television program	Jill Scott	76
5	2005	Clinton Hill, Brooklyn, featured in film *Dave Chappelle's Block Party*	Jill Scott (prior to verses); Erykah Badu (end of song)	78
6	2008	*Soul Stage*, VH1 television program	"Captain" Kirk Douglas (guitarist for The Roots)	85
7	2010	*AMEX Unstaged*	Estelle	83
8	2015	*Brooklyn Bowl*	Soul Rebels (brass band)	88

Badu rarely performs the song live, but Scott has performed it live many times, and with extensive alterations to the accompanying streams. These alterations may be an attempt to make the song less recognizable and thus available for her to reassert her authorship. Finally, when The Roots perform live with other musicians (e.g., John Legend, Estelle, the Soul Rebels, etc.), they frequently perform "You Got Me," perhaps because it is the song most likely familiar to fans of the other artists.

The first difference among performances of "You Got Me" that impinges on Black Thought's flow is tempo. As Example 7.12 shows, the track, unlike rap music as a whole, is getting faster in live performance.[13] Increasing the tempo increases the difficulty of syncopation for an emcee. The most prominent difference between syncopation and non-syncopation is that syncopation places events (or accents) off the beat. But syncopation also suggests a greater variety of durations. If a non-syncopated rhythm has been displaced by shifting several events back in time by one position (and this, recall, is Temperley's model of syncopation cited in Chapter 4), then the first duration will be shorter than the others and the last will be longer. Because of these additional short durations, the challenge of executing syncopation—which ultimately comes down to moving vocal articulators in an aperiodic fashion—increases as a function of tempo.

The result is that The Roots's fastest performances lead to less syncopation in Black Thought's flow, and this demonstrates how tempo constrains flow more generally. Measures 13–15 are emblematic. In the studio version (Example 7.13a),

13. Year and tempo are strongly correlated in these performances, $r^2(6) = 0.73$, $p < 0.01$.

Example 7.12 Tempo in seven live performances of The Roots, "You Got Me." Numbers refer to "Index" column of Table 7.1.

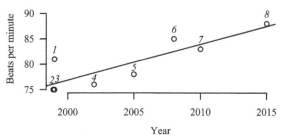

Example 7.13 The Roots, "You Got Me," first verse, mm. 13–15: (a) studio version (1999a, 81 bpm) and (b) live version on VH1's *Soul Stage* (2008, 85 bpm).

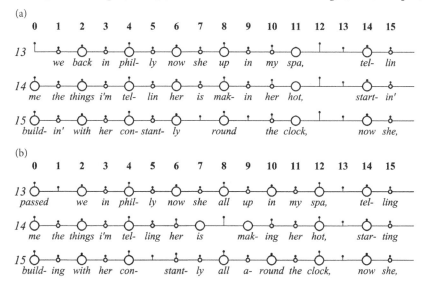

Black Thought accents position **11** in all three measures, ending the phrase *up in my spot, making her hot,* and *round the clock* off the beat. Example 7.13b shows the same measures in the 2008 performance from *Soul Stage*, a VH1 television program. The live version is less than 5 percent faster than the studio version. Yet in all three measures, what was a position **11** accent shifts to land on the beat (i.e., position **12**). In the case of *making her hot*, an entire phrase is shifted one position. In *up in my spot* and *round the clock*, Black Thought inserts other words (*all up in my spot, all around the clock*) in order to avoid syncopation.

These and other alterations dramatically reduce the amount of syncopation in the verse. Example 7.14 plots the percentage of accented syllables on 1_{mod2} positions among the performances against tempo and shows the strong correlation between tempo and the avoidance of syncopation; the plot also suggests that the studio recording

Example 7.14 Percentage of accents on 1_{mod2} positions vs. tempo in seven performances of "You Got Me," verse 1.

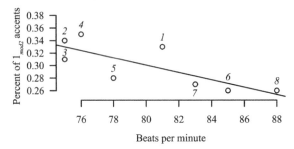

Beats per minute

("1" in the plot) is especially syncopated given its tempo.[14] Especially vulnerable to reduced syncopation are accents on 1_{mod4} positions such as *Queen* in *Ethiopian Queen* in m. 4 and *not* in *shit, you think not?* in m. 11. Example 7.15 🔊 shows the former phrase in the studio version and the three faster versions performed later; the accent on position **1** is removed in two of them. Example 7.16 🔊 illustrates the same for m. 11, where the accent on position **1** (*not*) is altered in all the faster versions. At the other end of the tempo spectrum, slower tempos enable Black Thought to expand on the variety of durations in the flow. In live versions from 1999 and 2002, Black Thought introduces 32nd notes into the flow, a duration otherwise extremely rare for him. He does this by displacing the onset of a syllable that falls on the beat in the recorded version and halving its duration and the duration of the following syllable.

But some alterations to the flow of the recorded version are not easily related to tempo. Versions featuring Jill Scott, particularly the 2002 MTV performance, are especially interesting because of how dramatically the instrumental streams change. When accompanying Jill Scott, the mode of the song changes from minor to what is called a Phrygian or Phrygian dominant scale. This scale has a major triad built on the tonic (like a major scale), but most of the other notes in the scale are lowered (i.e., ♭$\hat{2}$, ♭$\hat{6}$, and ♭$\hat{7}$).[15] Although the main chord remains major, the lowered ♭$\hat{2}$ imparts a sound associated with the exotic and foreboding. Black Thought's response in many ways flips the flow heard on the album. In the recorded version, he accents position **8** ten times and is silent there six times. In contrast, on the album, he accents position **12** seven times and is silent nine. With Scott on stage, these tendencies are reversed and amplified: position **8** is accented three times and silent thirteen, while position **12** is accented fourteen times and silent two.

The tendency toward a silent position **8** in the 2002 live version is a consequence of the shifting many syllables that should fall there to position **9**, a 1_{mod4} position he and other emcees would usually avoid. These shifts result in an

---

14. Year and percentage of accents on 1_{mod2} positions are strongly correlated, $r^2(6) = 0.60$, $p < 0.02$.
15. The "Phrygian dominant" would be familiar to jazz players and likely the musicians of The Roots, and it differs from the Phrygian mode familiar in the classical tradition. Classical-oriented players might call the scale the fifth mode of the harmonic minor scale.

especially disjointed flow because they create phrase endings at odds with syntactical groupings. For example, *Stepped off the stage and took a piece of her heart* becomes *Stepped of the stage and took a . . . piece of her heart*. Similarly, *think that I went home and forgot* becomes *think that I went . . . home and forgot*.

These dramatic alterations to the flow, in my view, are related to the equally dramatic alterations to the accompanying material. When Jill Scott performs "You Got Me," the song transforms into something almost unrecognizable. The mellow, four-note hook, paired with the smooth, descending bass line becomes a reverberated and distorted incantation, stripping away the original suggestions of romance.[16] In a sense, Black Thought's alterations to his flow in the first verse make the verse equally unrecognizable, or at least as unrecognizable as possible given that most of the words are unchanged. A fan attempting to rap along to this verse will fail repeatedly, so often, in fact, it is hard to imagine the fan would continue attempting to synchronize with the emcee on stage. This leaves a listener in a unique position, unable to perform internally music that he or she knows by heart.

Taken together, these examples demonstrate the richness of Black Thought's interactions with other musicians and musical objects. I do not doubt that MC Kylea's description of a one-way exchange from beats to lyrics holds true for some rap music; it is an assertion made too often to be untrue. And, returning to Cale Sampson's view ("To me, it's less about the flow and more about the message"), I do not doubt that some emcees give little thought to musical relations between their flow and the beat. For some, rhyming on position 12 and placing syllable onsets within a recognizable C_{16} metric space are sufficient. And while Black Thought, in my view, is emblematic of the greater coordination that is possible between flows and beats, he is, of course, not the only emcee for a which a study like this one would be fruitful.

Furthermore, I would encourage subsequent studies on flow–beat interaction as a means of addressing questions of music scholarship beyond rap music. Scholars of classical music in recent decades have become increasingly aware of the friction between classical music's score-centered ontology and the experience of musical performance and consumption. Rap music espouses a different ontology, one in which the creative agencies of emcees, producers, and musicians collaborate and revise. Indeed, this ontology itself is little studied and invites greater scrutiny. By examining these cycles of interaction, especially relationships between beats and flows, scholars of a wide range of music might find in rap music a sandbox in which to explore complex issues of authorship, agency, and creative process.

---

16. This sense of disjunction was already present in Scott's work in the original version, where the phrasing of lyrics of the hook contrasts with their syntactic segmentation, as in "if you are worried 'bout where , , , I been or who I so or . . . what club I went to. . . ."

CHAPTER Eight

Flow and Free Rhythm in Talib Kweli

8.1 Does Talib Kweli Rhyme Off-Beat?

In September 2015, Angel Diaz, a staff writer at *Complex* magazine, wrote a blog post defending Drake and Future, two of the biggest emcees of the moment. The two had just released a joint mixtape, *What a Time to Be Alive*, to great commercial success but middling reviews. Diaz defends these contemporary rappers against their unnamed critics, whom he describes as "old head, super lyrical motherfuckers" (Diaz 2015). In short, Diaz advocates for Drake and Future because he likes their music despite (or perhaps because of) its lyrical simplicity, and he resists the idea that rap music should always produce social commentary. As a representation of the kind of emcees these "old heads" would support, Diaz writes that he "can't be listening to Talib Kweli rap off beat and Lupe Fiasco deep cuts at BBQs." Although Kweli is not mentioned again in the article, the sentence is offset in a larger font to the side, the only sentence visible for the scanning reader.

How does an off-hand diss of Kweli arise in a blog post about Drake and Future? For Diaz, Kweli is a metonymy for the so-called conscious rap discussed in connection with Black Thought in Chapter 5, and indeed Kweli has promoted an Afrocentric ideology throughout his career, frequently addressing issues of poverty, mass incarceration, and military intervention. In this sense, Kweli is a reasonable foil for the party rap Diaz champions. But Diaz insults Kweli's ability to flow and stay on-beat, not his subject matter. Why not critique his ideology?

In calling Kweli an "off-beat" rapper, Diaz repeats an accusation as old as Kweli's career, though one that rarely appears in print. While Robert Gabriel (2004) writes of an "ever-hectic flow" in reviewing the 2004 album *The Beautiful Struggle*, most critics of the same album characterize Kweli's rhythm more positively, writing of a "rapid-fire" (Rabin 2004) or "adaptive, veteran flow" (Warren 2004) and praising his "knack for corralling unruly syllables" (Sanneh 2004). Yet many reviews show the trace of a previous reputation, making vague reference to an earlier and less appealing rhythmic style. Sanneh (2002) describes the 2002 album *Quality* as "the first Talib Kweli album on which the beats hold their own against his overstuffed verses. He still likes to smother his songs with syllables, but he now pays more attention to rhythm."

Kweli himself mirrors the mixed reception of his rhythmic abilities. He strenuously defends himself against Diaz's charge, noting that Diaz could not, or did not, cite an objectionable verse (Grant 2015). But earlier, he told Martin Connor (2013) that his earliest verses were written before he had instrumental streams for them (the *Lyrics to Beat* model of Chapter 7). Because of this ordering, he sometimes forced lyrics into a rhythm that did not suit them. By 2015, he morphed his characterization of those early verses, telling Andre Grant that in his earlier material he "found pockets and grooves in the beats that were unorthodox. And to some people it might have sounded off beat." He also acknowledges that his verbosity created rhythmic challenges by "trying to cram a lot of words into smaller spaces than most emcees."

Any time spent listening to Kweli's flow reveals an unusual rhythmic style, one in which syllables often do not fall on expected parts of the beat. Yet neither "complex" nor "off-beat" adequately describes this style. "Complex" is problematic because the style persists even in "simpler" passages with fewer syllables. And the "off-beat" label is problematic because it connotes incompetence. My aim in this chapter is to document the non-alignment between Kweli's flow and his instrumental streams and to contextualize that non-alignment within the genre as a whole. To pursue that contextualization, I will work with two corpora of verse transcriptions in which syllables are not initially quantized to the beat. One of those corpora consists of thirty Kweli verses from across his career; the other is a subset of the genre-wide corpus described in Chapter 2, namely, the verses for which I could acquire the a cappella tracks necessary for non-quantized transcription.[1]

Section 8.2 details how I compile these corpora without the interpretive act of quantizing. In Section 8.3, rather than simply identify non-alignment and label Kweli as off-beat, I will instead propose four processes that shift his syllables away from the beat, which I term phase shift, swing, tempo shift, and deceleration. When his flow can be explained through these processes, I will argue that it should not be characterized as "off-beat." Yet I will also show an example that is off-beat in a clearer sense (Section 8.4). Throughout, I will show that Kweli's use

---

1. A cappella versions of twenty-five of the seventy-five tracks of the genre-wide corpus are available on the Internet through acappellas4u.com; however, many of these are unsuitable for analysis. OJ da Juiceman's "Make Tha Trap," Lupe Fiasco's "The Show Goes On," and Gorilla Zoe's "Lost" have sufficient additional audio that prohibits isolating phonetic features of the flow. Kanye West's "Stronger" and Ghostface Killah's "Mighty Healthy" have heavy clipping in the audio, that is, the outer reaches of the amplitude of the signal have been cut off. This makes determining the midpoint of a vowel's increase in amplitude impossible. Finally, the a cappella for Wise Intelligent's "Steady Slanging'" and Grandmaster Flash's "The Message" does not consistently align with the mixed versions; aligning the two versions at the beginning pushes them out of alignment at the end. It may be that the a cappella is from a different take, or it may be that it has been altered somehow. The remaining thirteen tracks constitute the a cappella genre-wide corpus.

of non-alignment connects his flow to Afro-diasporic rhythmic traditions and hip hop's aesthetics.

8.2 Visualizing and Measuring Flow–Beat Non-Alignment

Example 8.1 🜚 prints the lyrics of the first verse of "Get By," a verse that will serve as a recurring example in this chapter. "Get By" is the highest-charting single from *Quality*, Kweli's first solo album, and remains among his most popular songs. Its sound world bears the mark of its producer Kanye West, still eighteen months away from *The College Dropout*, his breakout album as an emcee. Like other West tracks of the early 2000s, it samples Nina Simone ("Sinnerman") and features gospel-style vocals in the hook. Kweli structures his first verse by introducing a rhythmic motif articulating groove class <332_332> starting on position 0 that recurs throughout the hooks and the looser final section of the song. The two-measure motif, set to the words *just to get by*, recurs three times in the verse, beginning in mm. 5, 9, and 17. I will call these sections the "hook sections" of the verse because they use the rhythm and text of the hook of the song. In between these rhythmically repetitive measures, Kweli addresses themes common in his output, such as poverty, drug trafficking, mass incarceration, materialism, technology, and family. I will call these sections the "flow sections" of the verse. I further segment the flow sections into two-measure groups, matching the length of the hook sections.

Example 8.2 🜚 offers a **combined transcription** that shows both the continuous onsets (i.e., measured in seconds, the upper row of points) and the

Example 8.1 Talib Kweli, "Get By" (2002, 0:10–1:06), lyrics of first verse, segmented into two-measure groups.

Flow 1a and 1b
We sell crack to our own out the back of our homes. We smell the musk of the dusk in the crack of the dawn.
We go through episodes too, like *Attack of the Clones*. Work 'til we break our back, and you hear the crack of the bone.

"Hook" 1
To get by, just to get by, just to get by, just to get by...

Flow 2
We commute to computers, spirits stay mute while you egos spread rumors. We survivalists turned to consumers.

"Hook" 2
Just to get by, just to get by, just to get by, just to get by...

Flow 3a, 3b, and 3c
Askin' why some people got to live in a trailer 'cuz like a sailor I paint a picture with the pen like Norman Mailer.
Mi abuela raised three daughters all by herself, with no help, I think about her struggle and I find the strength in myself.
These words melt in my mouth, they hot, like the jail cell in the south, before my n*gga core bailed me out.

"Hook" 3
To get by, just to get by, just to get by, just to get by...

Flow 4
We do or die like Bed-Stuy, see the red sky out the window of the red eye, let the lead fly, some G Rap shit, livin' to let die.

Example 8.2 "Get By" (2002, 0:21–0:27), Hook 1, combined transcription of continuous onsets (upper row of circles) and quantized onset (lower row of circles).

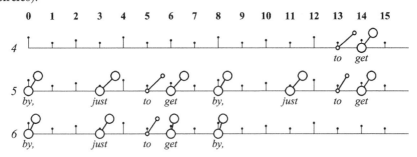

interpreted quantized onsets (i.e., measured in beats, the lower row of points). The slope of the line between the two points of each syllable is an indication of the extent of non-alignment between the flow and the beat. Thus, these lines reveal the "microtiming" or "expressive timing" of Kweli's flow. Studies of microtiming in Afro-diasporic music (e.g., Danielsen 2006, Butterfield 2006, Witek 2017) usually demonstrate how these non-alignments "create forward motion and rhythmic interplay between textural layers" (Witek 2017, p. 140), and I will make similar demonstrations in the discussion that follows, but I am also interested in how Kweli's microtiming approaches the rhythm of speech vs. that of music.

These slopes range from syllables that nearly touch the following position (e.g., the first syllable) to those that are nearly vertical. On the page, at the tempo of "Get By," each position is 166 ms. An accepted figure of the **just-noticeable difference**, the smallest temporal interval that people can perceive as distinct onsets is around 25–40 ms (Levitin et al. 2000).[2] The last *by* in the example falls 51 ms after position 8; even though its slope is nearly vertical, it should be perceptible after the bass drum. Furthermore, the delay is more aurally noticeable than it appears in the transcription. What is needed, then, is a means of showing flow–beat non-alignment as sensitively as aural perception.

Example 8.3 🌑 replots the combined transcription of Example 8.2 🌑 through what I call a **spiral transformation**. The example takes the horizontal lines of previous transcriptions, connects them into a single line, and transforms that line into a spiral originating in the center. Each clockwise rotation around the spiral is one beat (not one measure!), and the spiral is interpreted as a clock face, oriented so that each beat (i.e., 0_{mod4}) occurs at :00. Each of the four *mod* 4 positions are thus "15 minutes" around the spiral if viewed as a clock face. The points along the spiral that represent events are further coded by their quantized position. Thus, *by*, always on a 0_{mod4} position, is plotted with a square point. For comparison, the quantized version of the plot is given in Example 8.4 🌑; by definition, all the points lie at

---

2. The jnd in an isochronous sequence of tones is much smaller, as small as 6 ms at fast tempos and 2.5 percent of a beat at slower tempos (Friberg & Sundberg 1995).

Example 8.3 "Get By" (2002, 0:21–0:27), Hook 1, spiral transformation of continuous transcription. Each clockwise rotation out from the center is one beat. The beat is divided into 60 "minutes," as in a clock face with the beginning of the beat at :00. A syllable's *mod* 4 position in the quantized transcription is given by the shape of its point.

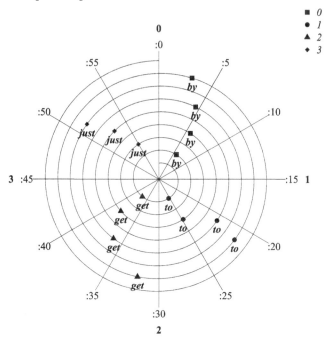

:00, :15, :30, or :45. The spiral plot enables a fine-grained measurement of flow–beat non-alignment. The last syllable of the excerpt, the *by* closest to the top of the plot, appears to be about "3 minutes" after :00 on the clock face. At this tempo, each minute is 11 ms, a duration that would span just 0.02 inches in the linear transcription. (Hereafter, the term "minutes" refers to minutes on the clock face of the spiral representation, not "minutes" of time.) The spiral plot also highlights the similarity in non-alignment among syllables with shared text, which tend to fall within a window of 5–10 minutes. I will return to these systematic displacements in the next section.

Making a combined transcription or its spiral transformation requires three critical pieces of information: the moment of syllable onsets, the moment of beat onsets, and the differences between them. Determining the first two would be much easier if moments of syllable and beat onset appeared undisguised in the audio signal. Usually, both are obscured. The instrumental tracks often visually overshadow syllable onsets in a wave-form image. And the beat itself is abstracted from the onsets of all the sounds heard as coincident with the beat (e.g., drums, bass, etc.). In what follows, I will briefly describe a method for annotating these moments. A more formal description may be found in Appendix 2.

Because the louder components of the instrumental streams obscure syllable onsets, I employ a cappella tracks (i.e., audio of the rapping voice alone) whenever

Example 8.4 "Get By" (2002, 0:21–0:27), Hook 1, spiral transformation of quantized transcription. By definition, each point lies at :0, :15, :30, or :45.

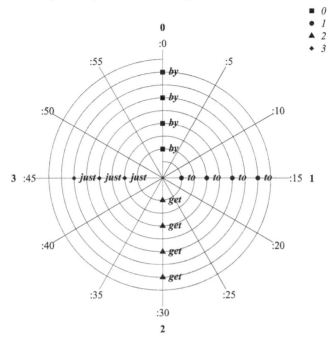

possible. Following a standard though not uncontroversial practice in phonetics research, I define the beginning of a syllable as the moment its vowel reaches half of its maximum amplitude.[3] To speed the annotation of the approximate 6,500 syllables in the Kweli corpus and the approximate 2,220 syllables in the genre-wide corpus, I run the audio through a text-speech forced alignment program, the Penn Phonetics Forced Aligner (P2FA, Yuan & Liberman 2008) discussed in Chapter 2, and manually correct the results. To investigate the error rate of the annotations, I manually corrected the output of the P2FA for one of the tracks twice on different days. More than half of the phones contained the same annotation in both versions, presumably the P2FA output. Of those phones that were adjusted, there was a median difference between vowels in the two versions of 5 ms.[4]

To determine beat onsets, I look for elements of the instrumental streams that have clear attack envelopes (namely, the snare and bass drum) and note the onsets

3. The issue of controversy here is what is referred to in phonetics research as the perceptual center or "p-center" of syllables—the moment at which a syllable is perceived to have started. Many candidates for p-centers have been proposed, including the onset of the initial consonant cluster, the onset of the vowel, and the moment at which the vowel reaches 50 percent of its total amplitude. Some scholars believe that p-centers are contextual, so the perceived onset of a vowel depends on the combination of consonants before it. All this remains unsettled, and my practice of equating p-centers with vowel onsets is a practical heuristic. Villing et al. (2011) provides an overview.

4. See the analysis script. The median difference between adjusted consonants was higher, at 11 ms, though I suspect this is because I am less careful with the annotation of consonants because I know they do not affect syllable placement.

of such events in the first measure and in some much later measure so that any inaccuracy in annotation is divided among many measures. Because I work with a cappella audio, my final step is to align the a cappella and mixed versions. I accomplish this by seeking out a syllable of speech that (1) is near the beginning of the track, (2) has a crisp initial consonant like a plosive "b" or "p" or a sibilant "s," and (3) falls in between events in the mixed audio. I mark the onset of this syllable in both the a cappella and mixed versions. I repeat this process for a syllable toward the end of the track because, bafflingly, I have found through this repeated alignment that a cappella and mixed tracks can differ in duration by as much as 10 milliseconds per second.[5] In other words, 1 second in a mixed track can be shorter than a second in an a cappella track. Though the difference sounds minute, it has the effect of making all the syllables in a transcription appear to drift away from the beat. The repeated annotation produces a multiplier with which to correct this drift.

8.3 Types of Non-Alignment

In discussions of Kweli's flow by Diaz, others, and even Kweli himself, whether or not the emcee is "off-beat" is a binary distinction. A more sophisticated view of Kweli's rhythmic practice would identify the extent to which he is off-beat, the processes pushing him away from alignment, and the expressive affects non-alignment might have on his listeners. In this section, I will describe four processes creating non-alignment: phase shift, swing, tempo shift, and deceleration. Before showing examples of these processes in the "Get By" verse, I will briefly depict them through two visual analogies: coupled waves and the combined transcription.

In thinking about non-alignment, it is useful to think of Kweli's flow and the beat of the instrumental streams as independent waves. Two properties of waves are relevant here: their frequency and their phase. The frequency of a wave is the rate at which it completes a full cycle. Because "frequency" usually refers to pitch in discussions of music, I will refer to the frequency of a flow's wave as its tempo. The phase of a wave is its start point relative to some external event. Example 8.5 shows four pairs of waves (a–d) that demonstrate the effect of changing tempo and phase. Note that although the waves in the lower row differ from the repeated wave of the upper row, by adjusting the tempo or phase, we could make them identical. Kweli's non-alignment with the beat can often be understood in the same way, as a shift in the beat's tempo or phase.

Shifting tempo and shifting phase are two processes misaligning Kweli's flow. Two others are swing, a special case of phase shift, and deceleration, a temporal process more associated with the rhythm of speech than with the rhythm of music. Example 8.6 shows how these non-alignments appear in a hypothetical

5. This discrepancy in duration affects about a quarter of the tracks. It is continuous throughout the tracks and not the result of, say, some portion of the audio being deleted. My suspicion is that this drift arises through conversion between different audio formats, especially between lossless and lossy formats like mp3.

Example 8.5 Four pairs of waves, with points at zero-crossings. From left to right, the pairs have: (a) the same tempo and same phase, (b) the same tempo and different phase, (c) different tempo and same phase, and (d) different tempo and different phase.

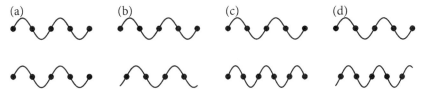

Example 8.6 Visual appearance of four processes of non-alignment in a combined transcription: (a) complete alignment with the beat; (b) phase shift: each syllable is displaced from the beat by the same amount; (c) swing shift: strong-beat syllables (i.e., 0_{mod2} positions) are aligned, weak-beat syllables (i.e., 1_{mod2} positions) are displaced; (d) tempo shift: syllables are equidistant, but at a different tempo (i.e., frequency); (e) deceleration: syllables toward the end of a phrase are progressively longer.

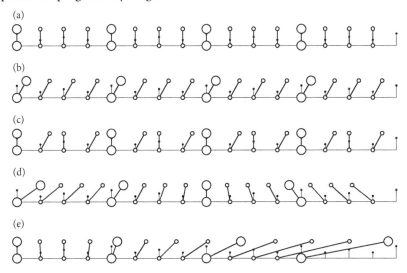

combined transcription. In Example 8.6a, every syllable is directly above its quantized position—in human-generated performance this rarely happens. Example 8.6b shifts every syllable by the same amount (0.1 beats), analogous to a phase shift. Example 8.6c is derived from the same phase shift, but the shift applies only to weak-beat syllables (i.e., 1_{mod2} syllables). As I will next discuss, this selective phase shift is the hallmark of "swing" in jazz and other genres. In Example 8.6d, all the syllables have the same duration, like their quantized equivalents, but those durations are shorter than the tempo of the instrumental streams—this

Example 8.7 "Get By" (2002, 0:21–0:27), Hook 1, spiral transformation of continuous transcription, with average non-alignment of 6.65 minutes.

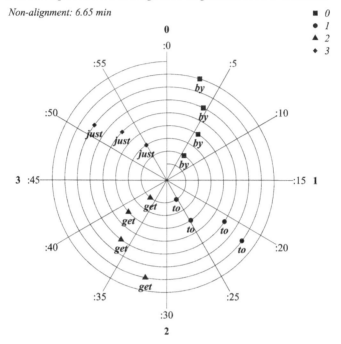

I call tempo shift. Finally, Example 8.6e shows a process of deceleration in which syllables toward the end of the phrase grow gradually longer, even though the tempo of the instrumental streams stays the same.

8.3.1 Phase Shift

Example 8.7 ⬤ reprints the spiral plot of Example 8.3 ⬤. Although all four syllables of *just to get by* tend to fall in consistent locations on the clock face, they are not at the 15-minute intervals the quantization suggests. I call the difference between syllables and their quantization the **average non-alignment** of a span of flow, measured in minutes on the clock face of the spiral representation. Here, the average non-alignment is more than 6 minutes, or 6/60 = 0.1 beats.[6]

Initially striking about the plot are that every syllable is late and half of them are within a narrow band of 6–8 minutes late. This indicates a **phase shift** relative to the instrumental streams. We can compute the **optimal phase adjustment**, defined as the phase shift that results in the lowest average

---

6. This figure is the average absolute value of asynchrony, though in this case every syllable is late and not early.

Example 8.8 "Get By" (2002, 0:21–0:27), Hook 1, spiral transformation. At left, hook without adjustment. At right, hook with phase adjustment of –6.5 minutes.

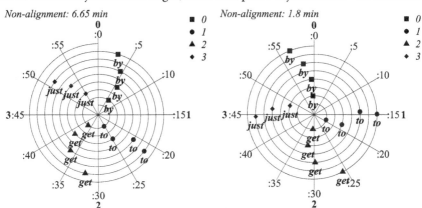

non-alignment in a passage. Example 8.8 🌑 reprints the spiral plot and creates a new one with a phase adjustment of 6.5 minutes—now the on-beat syllables are as close to their quantized positions as a free rotation around the spiral will allow.[7]

Phase shift is the first kind of non-alignment common in Kweli's flow. One can think of phase shift (measured in tens of milliseconds) as the micro-level analogue of the pervasive syncopation common in rap music including Kweli (measured in hundreds of milliseconds). In both phase shift and syncopation, a variety of event onsets saturate musical time, adjacent but not synchronous. This saturation facilitates group interaction by giving multiple voices a chance to cut through. By shifting the location of his own beat, Kweli joins with the instrumental streams but retains his autonomy from them. And from the perspective of the listener, the phase shift heightens involvement by making entrainment more demanding on attention because multiple events must be resolved into a single perceived beat.

Phase shift also connects Kweli's flow to the concept of groove in Afro-diasporic (and other) music discussed in Chapter 4. Alén's study of the *cinquillo* family of rhythms in Cuban music shows that each note of that repeated rhythmic pattern will have a characteristic deviation from an abstract pulse, some ahead, some behind (1995, p. 60). In his analysis of Clyde Stubblefield's drum break on James Brown's "The Funky Drummer," Andrew McGuiness (2006) documents phase relationships among the different instruments of the drum set, mostly behind the beat, but varying in their relationship with the beat by 10–30 ms. Since more than 1,400 songs, mostly hip hop, sample "The Funky Drummer," this analysis is

---

7. Although I am presenting phase shift, swing shift, and tempo shift independently and in order, I intend to combine them. The phase shift of –6.5 is optimal if one only shifts phase. If one shifts swing and tempo as well, the optimal phase shift is lower.

particularly pertinent in establishing phase shift as typical in rap music.[8] In terms of group performance, Mark Doffman's study of a live performance of a London jazz trio shows sustained non-alignment between the rhythm section and soloist, with the rhythm section a little more than 2 minutes behind the soloist (2009, p. 139). Surveying this evidence, Charles Keil declared that "*all* musics have to be out of time to groove" (Keil & Feld 2005, p. 155). His more recent position is largely unchanged: "A groove can happen whenever two or three different personal 'time-feels' or 'intrinsic motive pulses' interact" (Keil 2010).

Keil probably goes too far. For every study documenting non-alignment between different instruments, one can find a study that fails to do so (Butterfield 2010a; Madison et al. 2011). It may be that only certain Afro-diasporic musics value non-alignment, and these values can change over time. For example, Jan Fruehauf, Reinhard Kopiez, and Friedrich Platz (2013, p. 248) cite a number of record producers and studio musicians who argue that the value of synchronicity has dramatically increased since the late 1970s because of the widespread use of looped drum beats, many of which are mechanically quantized. So while Kweli's preference for phase shift might be out of step with much contemporary production, it also connects his flow to an important rhythmic tradition.

Kweli is not alone in employing phase shift, but his use of it is pronounced. To compute phase shifting across an entire verse, I take the optimal phase shift of each complete measure and average them, using absolute values. Kweli shifts his phase by about 4 minutes more than the genre as a whole, and this difference is statistically significant.[9] Example 8.9 shows density estimate plots of the optimal phase adjustments in the two collections of verses. While Kweli uses more phase shift, these two densities overlap, and some of Kweli's verses have optimal phase adjustments lower than the average in the genre-wide corpus.

That some of Kweli's verses have only moderate phase shift suggests to me that phase shifting is a technique Kweli can employ when he feels the instrumental streams call for it. Example 8.10a 📟 🌀 shows a series of spiral representations of "Get By." The first four show different streams of the instrumental track, as they are heard at the beginning of the track before Kweli begins rapping.[10] These instrumental streams are transcribed in conventional music notation in Example 8.10b 📟 🌀. The lowest plot of Example 8.10a 📟 🌀 reprints Kweli's non-alignment in the first hook section. The top of each clock face is the moment that best aligns the bass drum hits on positions **0** and **8** in the first two measures with the meter. That moment also centers the snare drum fairly well, though the snare (which

---

8. See http://www.whosampled.com/James-Brown/Funky-Drummer/, accessed August 1, 2017.
9. The use of phase shift in Kweli's thirty verses ($M = -10.65$, $SD = 3.12$), as compared to the thirteen-verse genre-wide corpus ($M = -6.84$, $SD = 3.78$), is significantly greater [$t(17) = 3.09$, $p < 0.01$]. The measurement of alignment in minutes is tempo-independent, but the range of tempo in these corpora is narrow. Still, there is also a significant difference in the use of phase between Kweli ($M = -0.12$, $SD = 0.03$) and the genre-wide corpus ($M = -0.08$, $SD = 0.04$) when measured in milliseconds and not sixtieths of a beat [$t(17) = 2.80$, $p < 0.015$].
10. The onsets were annotated in Audacity. To verify them, open `Audio/Excerpt.8.a.wav` in Audacity and choose `File/Import/Labels. . .` Then import `SourceData/Other/talibKweli_getBy_loopEvents_forAudacity.txt`.

Example 8.9 Density plots of optimal phase adjustment in twelve verses from the genre-wide corpus and thirty verses of Talib Kweli's.

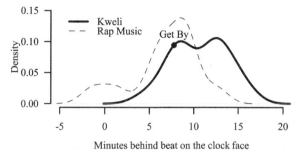

is sampled) appears to shift away from the beat slightly in the second half of the hook. In the second half of the four-measure loop, the bass drum shifts to exclusively 1_{mod2} positions, and also shifts away from the beat it previously established by about 3 minutes.

Human performance varies the placement of events in the other streams (i.e., Nina Simone's piano playing and an uncredited bass guitarist). In comparing Kweli to the instrumental streams, he often places syllables in a portion of the clock face that is unoccupied elsewhere. Thus, the *by* syllables fall after the position articulated by the bass drum and snare. While the piano and bass guitar place 1_{mod4} events between 0:16 and 0:21 minutes, Kweli's *to* syllables fall between 0:20 and 0:25. Similarly, the *get* syllables fall consistently after the piano's 2_{mod4} events, and the *just* syllables are at the outer edge of the space occupied by the piano and bass guitar's 3_{mod4} events. The result of this interaction, then, is that Kweli creates a groove in which nearly every moment is saturated by some kind of onset. It is beyond the scope of this chapter to analyze phase in the instrumental components of Kweli's other tracks or those in the corpus at this level of detail; thus, it is unclear whether the diffuseness of the instrumental streams in "Get By" is typical or not. But this diffuseness and Kweli's relation to it suggest to me that his syllables are not haphazardly late, but rather that they flee from the beat in order to further an objective other creative forces (namely, Kanye West and Nina Simone) have already put in motion—the saturation of musical time.[11]

8.3.2 Swing

There is another kind of non-alignment at work in Groove 1. Even after the optimal phase adjustment is applied, the *just* and *to* syllables (i.e., syllables on 1_{mod2} positions) are still later than the *by* and *get* syllables (i.e., syllables on 0_{mod2}

---

11. Anne Danielsen associates this kind of spreadness in instrumental events with the "wetness" of the "backbeat of a disco groove." Danielsen has explored the expressive affects of intra-ensemble phase relationships in a variety of popular music, including James Brown, Michael Jackson (both found in Danielsen 2012), and Destiny's Child (Danielsen 2016).

positions). This indicates a special case of phase shift in 1_{mod2} positions known as **swing**. Swing is most commonly encountered in jazz music—an entire subgenre of jazz is called "swing music"—and through his use of swing Kweli joins many other rap artists that draw connections between jazz and hip hop.

Justin Williams traces these connections to the so-called "Golden Age" of hip hop in the late 1980s and early 1990s, when a number of rap groups (e.g., A Tribe Called Quest, Digible Planets, De La Soul, etc.) began sampling jazz music in their instrumental streams (2014, pp. 49–51). For Williams, the importation of jazz into hip hop enabled hip hop to trade on jazz's reputation as "high art." More than any other Afro-diasporic music, jazz had, by the 1980s, acquired many of the markers of Western classical music's cultural value. Jazz was presented in concert halls and conservatories, formed the soundtrack for luxury-goods advertising, and featured prominently in the music of *The Cosby Show*, the most visible depiction of the black upper middle class on television.

Earlier "jazz rap" artists associated themselves with jazz's prestige by sampling its music. Kweli's music also does this, but only occasionally.[12] And even when he does, the prestige of jazz only passively transfers to him because he has limited input in the construction of his instrumental streams. A much more direct means of appropriating jazz's status as "high art" is to incorporate swing, its signature rhythmic feature, into the rhythm of his flows. His use of swing also supports the presentation of his ideology. Earlier "jazz rap" was cast as the cultured response to another prevalent subgenre, gangsta rap (Williams 2014, p. 48). A similar opposition plays out in many of Kweli's lyrics, where he sets himself against an array of less cultured competitors. Like jazz artists, and presumably unlike those artists he opposes, Kweli advocates for (lyrical) sophistication (e.g., *let's put more depth in our verses* in "More or Less") and values self-expression over commercial gain (e.g., *You get props off the diamonds you rented / I get my props off the rhymes I invented 'cuz I spoke my mind and I meant it* in "Bright as the Stars"). Thus, referencing the rhythmic markers of jazz music enables Kweli's sound to reinforce his lyrics' message.

The difference between a rhythm with swing and one without has to do with the inequality between on-beat and off-beat durations. Fernando Benadon (2006) coined the term **beat-upbeat ratio** or **BUR** to document these inequalities. BURs are found by dividing the duration of a note on the beat (usually, the longer duration) by the duration of the note off the beat (usually, the shorter one). In a typical swing rhythm, one that might be notated as a quarter note and eighth note under a triplet, the BUR is 2. Research by Benadon, as well as by Anders Friberg and Andreas Sundström (2002), finds BURs in the range of 1:1 at fast

---

12. Four of Kweli's features on other artists' tracks stand out in their sampling of jazz. Asheru's "Mood Swing" samples Duke Ellington and John Coltrane's 1962 recording of "In a Sentimental Mood"; Dela's "Long Life" samples saxophonist Bobby Malach's 1976 solo on Dexter Wansel's "Life on Mars"; "Great Expectations" on DJ Crossfader's 1999 mixtape *The World Traveler* samples "Harvest Time," a 1977 release by saxophonist Pharoah Sanders; and Skyzoo's 2012 "Spike Lee Was My Hero" features trumpeter Freddie Hubbard's 1976 release "Windjammer." In addition, like other hip-hop artists, Kweli often flows to drum beats sampled from jazz recordings. Despite these examples, most samples in Kweli's tracks are drawn from 1960s and 1970s soul and R&B, funk music, or other rap tracks.

tempos and as high as 3.5:1 at slow tempos, equivalent to syllables falling at :23 and :53 on the spiral employed here. (Increasing tempo limits how short the off-beat note can be played; thus, BURs tend to be lower at faster tempos.) BURs also vary by performer and, in the context of jazz, serve as a kind of fingerprint. As Martin Williams says, "Roy Eldridge's triplet doesn't sound like Louis Armstrong's; Miles Davis' didn't sound like Dizzy Gillespie's" (Berendt 1992, p. 192, quoted in Benadon 2006, p. 86).

Differences between jazz and hip hop affect how BURs are measured in rap music. First, BURs, as formulated by Benadon, require three note onsets that de-fine and bisect a beat.[13] Since rap flows can be rhythmically varied (and thus long strings of nominally equivalent durations are relatively rare), it is better to compute swing based on onsets in relation to the beat rather than consecutive durations. Second, because the BUR compares the onsets of on-beat and off-beat events, it is advisable to ensure that the on-beat events indeed align with the beat. In other words, one should account for an optimal phase adjustment before computing swing. Lastly, the metrical level of interest for swing in rap music is the sixteenth note (i.e., between positions 0 and 1, $mod\,2$), since this is the most common quan-tized duration and rap music is usually performed at a moderate tempo. In con-trast, swing in jazz usually happens at the eighth-note level (i.e, between positions 0 and 2, $mod\,2$).[14]

The clock face makes calculating BURs in the hook of "Get By" straightfor-ward. While this is by no means Kweli's most swung performance, the *By* and *get* syllables span an average of 17.2 minutes on the clock face, while *just* and *to* span an average of 12.8 minutes, for a ratio of 17.2/12.8 = 1.34:1. In Friberg and Sundström's study of swing ratios, this BUR is less than would be expected at this tempo and Kweli often exceeds this BUR.[15] As we can compute an optimal phase adjustment, we can similarly compute an **optimal swing adjustment**, the BUR that best minimizes average non-alignment. The upper row of Example 8.11 🔒 🔊 reprints the optimal phase adjustment. The lower row shows both optimal phase and swing adjustments. Admittedly, the effect is subtle, but notice that average non-alignment has decreased and the *just* and *to* syllables are slightly closer to the horizontal axis than with phase adjustment alone. Yet Kweli, like other rap artists, uses swing relatively rarely. The non-alignment of two thirds of the measures in the genre-wide corpus is not improved by adjusting for swing; the same is true of 60 percent of Kweli's measures, and the mean swing adjustment of Kweli is not sig-nificantly different than that of the corpus.[16] The relative paucity of swing is likely

13. Benadon goes considerably further, requiring eight notes of the same nominal duration to compute a BUR.
14. Pressing (2002, p. 303) observes that the sixteenth-note level might be swung in "jazz-rock beats," and rap music would seem to be an extension of this idea.
15. Friberg and Sundström's study of four drummers' swing ratios showed a linear relationship be-tween the tempo and swing ratio that would predict a BUR of 2.2 at 180 bpm (2002, p. 337). The tempo is doubled because Kweli swings sixteenth notes.
16. See the analysis script, where there is also a demonstration that tempo does not affect an emcee's propensity for swing (i.e., BURs are not lower at higher tempos). It should be noted that the range of tempos encountered in rap music is relatively small.

related to the rarity of jazz music in sampling (outside of the repertoire discussed by Williams). At the same time, the rarity of swing in beats or in flow makes their occasional appearance all the more marked.

8.3.3 Tempo Shift

When the "Get By" hook is replotted adjusting for phase and swing, as in Example 8.11 🔊 🔊, non-alignment reduces to 1.64 minutes per syllable, less than a quarter of the non-alignment heard in Kweli's performance. In reading the original plot outward from the center, syllables sharing text seem to shift counterclockwise in relation to each other; in other words, the last *get* is the earliest, and this is true for *by* and *just* as well, and nearly true for *to*. This drift means that the durations between syllables marked with a square are similar— they just are not the durations one would expect from the instrumental streams. It is as though Kweli is flowing at a steady tempo, but a tempo slightly faster than the instrumental streams, making his syllables drift toward earlier positions. I call this kind of non-alignment a **tempo shift**. As with phase and swing shifts, we can compute an **optimal tempo adjustment** to reduce non-alignment. To correct for tempo shift, we can scale the onsets by some constant, likely very close to 1. After the durations are scaled, the onsets are shifted so that the mean onset in the span remains constant. The adjustment thus scales tempo "from the center" of the span. Example 8.12 🔊 🔊 redraws the hook one last time, adding another row of plots representing the optimal adjustment of phase, swing, and tempo. By increasing the tempo by 1 percent, the non-alignment is now less than 1 minute per syllable. Indeed, at this stage, the points of the plot are all quite close to the horizontal and vertical axes.[17]

This reduced non-alignment supports the following claim: in this passage, Kweli's non-alignment with the meter can be characterized as "on-beat," but with moderate amounts of phase shift, swing, and tempo shift. Phase shift and swing are rooted in Afro-diasporic rhythmic practice. Tempo shift would seem to be less so. I suspect it often arises as a function of phrasing, when sneaking a breath requires an acceleration to stay at the global tempo. It is true that Kweli employs tempo shift more than his peers, flowing with durations 99.4 percent as long as the instrumental streams would indicate, but this is a very modest (though significant) difference.[18] Kweli, like Black Thought, does saturate the measure with

---

17. Taken together, these three adjustments (phase, swing, and tempo shift) constitute a **grid search** of the space of transformations a verse might undertake. Because tempo shifts are multiplicative and phase and swing shifts are additive, the transformations are not **commutative**. In other words, one will get different average non-alignments depending on the order in which the adjustments are applied. However, in practice, when the full range of possibilities for each adjustment is compared and an optimal one is selected, the order of executing the adjustments does not matter. As a convention, I compute them in order of tempo, then phase, then swing. This convention respects the conventional order of operations, as tempo adjustments are multiplicative and the others are additive.

18. The tempo adjustment of Kweli ($M = 0.99$, $SD = 0.04$) differs from the genre at large ($M = 1.00$, $SD = 0.03$) by 0.5 percent [$t(45) = -3.04$, $p < 0.003$].

Example 8.13 "Get By" (2002, 0:44–0:54), Flow 3c, combined transcription of continuous and quantized onsets.

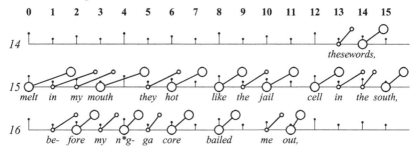

more syllables than his peers.[19] This leaves him with fewer spots to breathe without affecting tempo, so his propensity toward faster delivery may well be explained by his breathing.

8.3.4 Deceleration

A final process that leads to non-alignment is not applicable to the hook section discussed thus far. Example 8.13 ◐ shows the combined transcription of Flow 3c, a span with much greater non-alignment than any of the hook sections. Like the hook section just discussed, many of the syllables do not fall exactly in the metric grid. But this passage is much less easily quantized. The shared rhyme in *melt in my mouth, cell in the south*, and *bailed me out* suggest a shared rhythm and quantization. Earlier in the verse, rhymes like these (e.g., *back of our homes, crack of the dawn, -tack of the clones, crack of the bone*, etc.) map onto positions 0, 1, 2, and 3, *mod* 4. This is a pervasive rhythm for four-syllable rhymes in rap music that we have seen many times before.

The quantized portion of Example 8.13 ◐ reflects this rhythmic structure of the rhyme, but results in much more substantial slopes between points than previously encountered. Furthermore, the lateness of Kweli's syllables with respect to the quantized interpretation is not steady throughout. Note that the first syllable (*melt*) is a half beat late, while the last (*by*) is a quarter beat late. I will return to this trend in a moment. The discrepancy between upper and lower points is borne out by the spiral plot of Example 8.14 ◐, which shows asynchrony as performed on the left and with optimal adjustments on the right. On the left, average non-alignment is nearly 15, which is to say an entire position; note that syllables quantized as 0_{mod4} (i.e., those with square points) range from 0:09 (*n*g-*) through 0:28 (*melt*), a long way from 0:00. Even when the optimal adjustments are applied, the syllables are still diffuse and tend toward a clockwise drift, suggestive of a slower tempo, but tempo has already been optimized.

---

19. Kweli's saturation ($M = 12.52$, $SD = 2.73$) is greater than the genre as a whole ($M = 11.08$, $SD = 2.82$) by 1.44 positions per measure [$t(958) = 9.81$, $p < 0.001$].

Example 8.14 "Get By" (2002, 0:44–0:54), Flow 3c, spiral transformation without adjustment (left) and with phase shift of –14.5 minutes, swing of 1:1, and tempo shift of 5 percent (right).

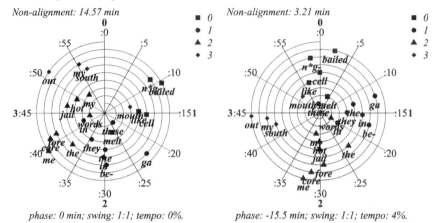

phase: 0 min; swing: 1:1; tempo: 0%.   *phase: -15.5 min; swing: 1:1; tempo: 4%.*

Example 8.15 "Get By" (2002, 0:44–0:54), Flow 3c, syllable durations plotted against onset, with linear regression by phrase.

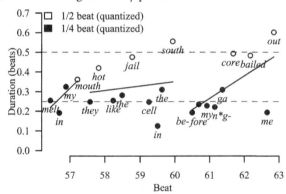

Example 8.15 ⬢ takes a different graphical approach to the passage, plotting the duration of syllable against its onset, segmented into phrases by breaths.[20] The shape of points represents the quantized duration. Each phrase trends toward longer durations, as the regression lines show.[21] Although these regression lines do not distinguish between syllables quantized as different durations (i.e., "sixteenths"

---

20. By "duration of the syllable," I mean the duration between successive vowel onsets. The disjointed *these words* at the beginning of the section are omitted.

21. None of these regressions are statistically significant, though the third is close ($p < 0.07$). The deceleration in the second phrase is not very pronounced, and while the deceleration is pronounced in the first phrase, there are too few syllables to establish significance.

and "eighths"), there is also a tendency to lengthen eighth notes toward the end of the second and third phrases.[22]

Kweli's tendency to lengthen syllables at the end of phrases is a hallmark of rhythm in speech called "phrase-final lengthening" or "boundary-related lengthening" (Lehiste 1977). In speech, such lengthening marks the ends of linguistic segments and is often used to distinguish between ambiguities. The sentence "Pat or Antonia and Dave will help" presents three possible arrangements of helpers: Pat, Antonia and Dave, or Pat and Dave. Boundary-related lengthening clarifies which arrangement is intended. Lengthening also helps distinguish the relative prominence of different segments within an utterance (Fougeron & Keating 1997). It is unsurprising that phrase-final lengthening appears in rap flows, given rap's location at the border of speech and song. Lengthening in rapping does the same work it does in speech—segmenting utterances, resolving ambiguity, and differentiating prominence. Phrase-final lengthening, serving the same aims, is also well documented in performances of classical music whose tempo is not regulated through mechanical means (Todd 1985; Cook 1987; Bowen 1996; Repp 1998; Ohriner 2012, 2018).

On the other hand, there is something distinctly unmusical about boundary lengthening over a beat with fixed tempo. Boundary lengthening replaces the proportional relationships of durations in music (e.g., "quarters" and "eighths") with the more continuously varied durations of speech. This technique differs from those discussed previously in another way as well. Phase and tempo shifts affect durations and onsets uniformly by shifting onsets in the former and scaling durations in the latter. While swing is not a uniform transformation, it does treat syllables sharing *mod* 2 positions equivalently. The deceleration of boundary lengthening, in contrast, affects each syllable differently based on its level of prominence and position in the phrase.

Because the underlying tempo of rap music is constant, Kweli's use of boundary lengthening introduces an element of the rhythm of speech that, in this context, differs from the rhythm of music. But this use of boundary lengthening strengthens the case that he raps off-beat only to the extent that other rappers avoid this technique. In general, that is not the case. One way of comparing Kweli's use of boundary lengthening to the genre-wide corpus goes as follows. First, identify a collection of phrases that end with strings of syllables on successive positions.[23] Then take a linear regression of the continuous duration of those syllables. Since all these syllables should last 0.25 beats, any positive slope in that regression suggests the boundary lengthening common in speech but not in mechanically regulated music. In both these corpora, there is, on average, a positive slope at the end of phrases. But the average slope in the genre-wide corpus

---

22. There is no such tendency to lengthen eighth notes in the first phrase because there is only one eighth note. There is also no clear tendency to lengthen sixteenth notes in any of the phrases.

23. If a minimum cut-off for terminal sixteenth notes is set to four, we can measure the slope of a regression at the end of just under half of Kweli's phrases and just under a third of the phrases in the subset of the genre-wide corpus. The choice of cut-off does not affect the claim I am about to make.

is significantly greater than that of Kweli's verses.[24] In other words, Kweli's use of boundary lengthening does shift some syllables off-beat, and for reasons more re-lated to the rhythm of speech than that of music, but in this respect he hems closer to the beat than his peers.

8.4 An Off-Beat Flow

In the hook sections of "Get By," the flow and the instrumental streams are closely aligned. In the flow section previously discussed, the non-alignment between the two can be largely explained through optimal adjustments of phase, swing, and tempo. At the end of the verse, in the final flow section, Kweli presents a more precarious relationship between the flow and the instrumental streams, one that gives meaning to the term "off-beat." Here, Kweli spins out denser rhymes than at any other point of the verse, rhyming with the title "Get By" 6 times in a little more than two measures. The final line of the verse references Kool G Rap, an emcee said to popularize multisyllabic rhyming, by rhyming the title of Kweli's song and G Rap's third album *Live and Let Die*.

Example 8.16a ◐ and Example 8.16b ◐ show two visualizations of the span, with each highlighting a different aspect of its rhythm. Example 8.16a ◐ offers a combined transcription of syllable onsets and their imputed quantized position. There is limited evidence for the techniques of non-alignment discussed here. The alternating long and short durations of swing can be seen in *red sky out the window*; an increase in tempo can be seen in *the window of the red eye*, which starts slightly ahead of the beat and ends an entire position ahead of it. But much of the passage does not relate to these techniques in an obvious way. The average non-alignment in the passage is 10.32 minutes; applying optimal adjustments—a phase of 11 minutes, nearly a whole position, swing ratio of 1:1.48, no tempo adjustment—brings this down to 4.26 minutes and almost the entire decrease is the result of the phase shift. This adjusted non-alignment is still substantially higher than anything in the hook sections, and it is the result of the continuously varying durations seen in Example 8.16b ◐. There, the syllables quantized as spanning one position (i.e., one quarter beat) range from 0.1 to 0.4 beats, with no clear demarcation between them and those quantized as spanning two positions (i.e., one half beat). Yet Example 8.16b ◐ also illustrates the consistent boundary lengthening associated with timing in speech; notice the deceleration of *we do or die like Bed-Sty, the window of the red eye let the led fly*, and *living to let die*. The durations plotted in Example 8.16b ◐ more closely resemble those of speech than of fixed-tempo music.

This is the kind of flow that, in my view, warrants the label of "off-beat": one in which syllables are substantially non-aligned *and* adjusting the phase, swing, or tempo of the flow does not explain the non-alignment. But calling this snippet

---

24. The genre's average slope ($M = 0.11$, $SD = 0.2$), compared to Kweli's ($M = 0.05$, $SD = 0.11$), is signif-icantly greater [$t(64) = 2.40$, $p < 0.02$]. See the analysis script.

Example 8.16a "Get By" (2002, 0:58–1:06), Flow 4. Combined transcription of continuous and quantized onsets.

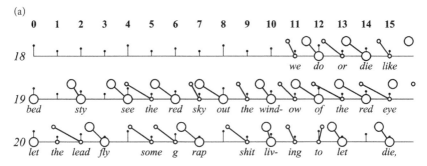

Example 8.16b "Get By" (2002, 0:58–1:06), Flow 4. Syllable durations plotted against onset.

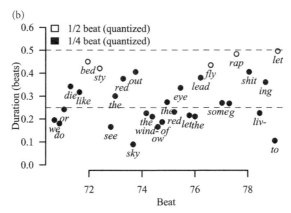

of flow off-beat is different from saying Kweli is an off-beat rapper. The question remaining is how common this kind of non-alignment is in Kweli and the genre at large. For every measure of flow in the thirty Kweli tracks and the thirteen available non-Kweli tracks, I computed the optimal adjustments. Two trends emerge from these data. The first is that before any adjustment is made, Kweli exhibits greater non-alignment with his instrumental streams than do other rappers.[25] Example 8.17 shows the density estimate of this non-alignment in the genre-wide corpus and Kweli.

But does Kweli's greater non-alignment mean he is more often off-beat, or just that he employs greater shifts of phase, swing, and tempo? Example 8.18 addresses this question through boxplots of the percent of unadjusted non-alignment

---

25. Kweli's unadjusted non-alignment ($M = 11.43$, $SD = 4.91$), compared to the genre's ($M = 7.92$, $SD = 5.62$), is significantly greater [$t(350) = 7.87$, $p < 0.001$].

Example 8.17 Density of unadjusted non-alignment in thirty verses by Talib Kweli and thirteen verses from the genre-wide corpus.

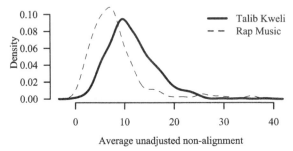

Example 8.18 Unadjusted non-alignment vs. percent of non-alignment explained by optimal adjustments in Talib Kweli (left) and the genre at large (right).

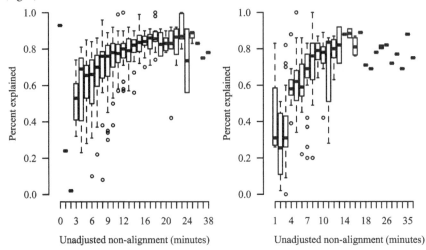

explained through optimal adjustments in the two corpora.[26] In the argument I have made in this chapter, off-beat rapping is rapping whose non-alignment is less well explained by optimal adjustments than is typical. The similarities between these two plots refute this notion in the case of Kweli. Throughout the whole range of potential non-alignment, Kweli performs in a way that affords the same rate of explanation as the corpus. In other words, while Kweli is often further out of alignment than most emcees would venture, his deviations from the beat can be

26. A boxplot shows the median value through the thick bar in the middle. The bounding box shows the middle 50 percent of values, the tick marks show values 1.5 times the interquartile range of the upper and lower quartiles, and the points show values outside the tick marks. Bounding boxes are absent in the higher values of the genre-wide plot because there are too few data points.

explained through the same processes, and to roughly the same extent, as those of other emcees.

As I have demonstrated, Kweli is non-aligned more than is typical for the genre. But as the hook sections of "Get By" demonstrate, he is as capable as anyone of flowing on-beat. Furthermore, he is capable of creating non-alignment through techniques pervasive in Afro-diasporic music, such as phase shifts and swing. Therefore, I would argue that a span like the end of the "Get By" verse could be more closely aligned with the instrumental streams if Kweli desired it to be so, either through a more precise performance or through a reworking of the "unruly syllables." His capacity for flowing on-beat raises an analytical question when we are confronted with a span like the end of the "Get By" verse. What is Kweli's expressive intent in occasionally flowing off-beat?

8.5 Non-Alignment and Rupture

Table 8.1 shows the features of rhythm for each span in the verse. On the whole, the hooks have much higher swing ratios, lower optimal non-alignment, and a high degree of non-alignment explained through adjustment. The hooks are also more self-similar than the flows. In the interior flow sections (e.g., Flow 1b and 2), Kweli is nearly as on-beat as he is in the hooks. And while Flow 3 has higher unadjusted non-alignment, this is mostly explained as phase shift. But these sections are bookended by Flows 1a and 4, sections with high unadjusted non-alignment and the highest optimal alignment of the verse, thus a relatively low percentage of non-alignment explained by adjustment. Because of their placement at the extremes of the verse, thereby surrounded by more rhythmically precise instrumentals, the groove sections of the verse, and the

Table 8.1 Talib Kweli's "Get By," first verse, optimal adjustments, unadjusted and adjusted alignment, and percentage of non-alignment explained by adjustment in two-measure segments

Section	Phase	Swing	Tempo	Unadjusted non-alignment	Optimal non-alignment	Percent explained
Flow 1a	−17.5	none	0.99	18.14	4.07	0.78
Flow 1b	−10.0	1.21	0.99	10.56	1.66	0.84
Flow 2	−11.5	1.21	0.99	11.54	2.08	0.82
Flow 3a	−13.5	none	0.99	14.22	3.61	0.75
Flow 3b	−11.5	none	0.98	11.67	2.14	0.82
Flow 3c	−16.0	none	0.97	15.18	3.32	0.78
Flow 4	−2.5	none	0.97	4.69	3.39	0.28
Hook 1	−8.5	1.21	none	8.94	1.28	0.86
Hook 2	−8.0	none	none	8	1.55	0.81
Hook 3	−9.5	1.10	none	10.01	1.4	0.86

204 ∞ Three Flows

song's actual hook, these sections create maximal contrast with the rhythmic style of surrounding sections. This creation of contrast connects Kweli's flow to essential aspects of hip hop's aesthetics that can be difficult for an emcee to access.

As Tricia Rose (1994, p. 39) and Jeff Chang (2006, p. x) argue, hip hop, in all its expressive manifestations, values flow and rupture in equal measure. Rap music expresses rupture most obviously in the scratches of the instrumental streams or the juxtaposition of divergent sounds within the instrumental streams, and some emcees provide rupture by appropriating these sounds into their rapping (Edwards 2013, pp. 125–129). Another type of rupture in rapping is to dramatically alter the rate of delivery, as Kweli does in the juxtaposition of hook and flow sections in "Get By." This is the kind of rupture Rose refers to when she describes emcees who "stutter and alternatively race through passages" (1994, p. 39). But how can an emcee insert rupture into a flow without dramatically changing the rate of the delivery? In "Get By," Kweli shows a solution by abruptly changing the way his flow relates to the instrumental streams, away from a rhythmic delivery defined by musical phase shifts and the use of swing, and toward a rhythmic delivery that resists explanation in musical terms.

I hope this chapter has presented tools that refine the distinction between "on-beat" and "off-beat" delivery. This contrast pervades the fan culture of rap music and, well beyond Talib Kweli, is frequently used as a weapon. Viewed as a transformation of a quantized rhythmic structure, Kweli's non-alignment with the instrumental streams is a site of rhythmic expression and connection to Afro-diasporic musical practice and not a detrimental feature of his rapping. Indeed, the techniques presented here for annotating syllable onsets and optimizing non-alignment might be useful for other kinds of vocal music with a steady beat and might be applied to correct the underrepresentation of vocal music in studies of Afro-diasporic rhythm. Ultimately, I hope this serves as a final example of how the digital representation of musical features, in rap music and beyond, can support not only wide-ranging descriptions of a genre, but also fine-grained analyses of musical decisions and performances.

APPENDIX 1

Artists in the Genre-Wide Corpus

Below are the 225 artists included in the corpus, 75 of whom were randomly sampled for transcription. "Early," "middle," and "late" designations indicate artists whose careers began before 1992, 2002, and 2013, respectively. Numbers in the last column refer to the presence of an artist on the following "best-of lists," consulted in artist selection:

1. The *Source* magazine (various authors 2012), "Top 50 Lyrical Leaders"
2. *Complex* magazine (Ross 2013), "Best-Selling Albums of All Time"
3. B.E.T. (Gale 2011), "The Fifty Most Influential Rappers"
4. *Complex* magazine (Drake et al. 2012), "Fifty Most Slept-On Rappers of All Time"
5. XXL, "Freshman Class," 2008–2014[1]
6. All albums receiving a score higher than 85 (out of 100) on metacritic. com[2]

Other artists appearing on these lists but not selected for transcription include A.G., Ab-Soul, Ace Hood, Akinyele, André 3000, Andre Nickatina, Angel Haze, Asher Roth, Astronautalis, Azealia Banks, B.O.B., Beastie Boys, Big L, Big Pun, Big Sean, Black Milk, Bun B, Busta Rhymes, Chance the Rapper, Charles Hamilton, Chief Keef, Common, Cormega, Cory Gunz, Curren$y, Cyhi the Prynce, Dizzie Rascal, DMX, Don Trip, Edan, El-P, Eminem, Freddie Gibbs, French Montana, Fugees, Future, Group Home, Guru, Homeboy Sandman, Hopsin, Hyro da Hero, Ice-T, Isaiah Rashad, J Cole, J Dilla, Joell Ortiz, Joey Badass, Jon Conner, Juju, Juvenile, Kendrick Lamar, Kevin Gates, Kid Cudi, Kid Ink, Killarmy, Killer Mike, King Tee, Kool G Rap, Large Professor, Lauryn Hill, Lil Bibby, Lil Twist, Lil Wayne, LL Cool J, M.I.A., Mac Dre, Mac Miller, Macklemore, Marco Polo, Masta Killa,

1. The "Freshman Class" is published in various issues. A list of lists, archived by Wikipedia. org, is available at https://en.wikipedia.org/wiki/XXL_(magazine)#XXL_Annual_Freshman_List.
2. Metacritic aggregates critical reviews and converts their assessments into a percentage. "Metascores" for releases are averages of these percentages, weighted by the site's assessment of the critic's importance. The site allows for filtering by genre and ranking by metascore, which is how the top tier of rap releases was determined. It is likely biased toward more recent reviews that are available online.

Table A1.1 Artists transcribed in the genre-wide corpus

Artist	Era	Region	Lists	Artist	Era	Region	Lists
50Cents	Middle	East	1, 2, 3	Lil Durk	Late	Midwest	5
Action Bronson	Late	East	5	Lil' Boosie	Middle	South	4, 5
August Alsina	Late	South	3	Lil' Kim	Middle	East	1, 3
Big Boi	Middle	South	6	Lizzo	Late	West	6
Big Daddy Kane	Early	East	1, 3	Logic	Late	East	5
Big K.R.I.T.	Late	South	5	Ludacris	Middle	South	1, 2
Black Rob	Middle	East	4	Lupe Fiasco	Middle	Midwest	1, 5
Blu	Late	West	5	Mac Mall	Middle	West	4
Bone Thugs-n-Harmony	Early	Midwest	2, 3	(No)Malice	Late	East	4
Brother Ali	Middle	Midwest	6	Max B	Late	East	4
Bubba Sparxxx	Middle	South	4	Missy Elliott	Early	South	3, 6
Ca$his	Late	Midwest	4	Nelly	Middle	Midwest	2
Canibus	Middle	East	1	OJ da Juiceman	Late	South	5
Casual	Early	West	4	Peedi crakk	Middle	East	4
The Coup	Early	West	6	Phonte	Middle	South	6
Danny Brown	Late	Midwest	5	Pill	Late	South	5
De La Soul	Early	East	3	PMD	Early	East	4
Diggy Simmons	Late	East	5	Queen Latifah	Early	East	1, 3
Dizzy Wright	Middle	West	5	Rick Ross	Middle	South	1
Dr.Dre	Early	West	2, 3	The Roots	Early	East	3
Esham	Early	Midwest	4	Salt-N-Pepa	Early	East	2, 3
Fabolous	Middle	East	1	ScHoolboyQ	Late	West	5
Gang Starr	Early	East	3	Slaughterhouse	Late	Midwest	6
Ghostface Killah	Middle	East	6	Slick Rich	Early	East	1, 3
Grandmaster Flash	Early	East	3	Suga Free	Middle	West	4
Ice Cube	Early	West	1, 3	Three 6 Mafia	Early	South	3
Jadakiss	Middle	East	1	Tim Dog	Early	East	4
Jay Rock	Late	West	5	The Treacherous Three	Early	East	3

Table A1.1 Contd.

Artist	Era	Region	Lists	Artist	Era	Region	Lists
Jay-Z	Middle	East	1, 2, 3	UGK	Early	South	3, 6
Jean Grae	Middle	East	4	Wale	Late	East	5
Kanye West	Late	Midwest	1, 2, 3	Wise intelligent	Early	East	4
Kilo Ali	Early	South	4	Wiz Khalifa	Late	East	5
Kiroko Bangz	Late	South	5	Wu-Tang Clan	Middle	East	2, 3
Kool Keith	Early	East	4	Yelawolf	Late	South	5
KRS-ONE	Early	East	1, 3	YG	Late	West	5
Kurtis Blow	Early	East	3	young Bleed	Middle	South	4
Lil B	Late	West	5				
Gorilla Zoe	Late	South	5	Snoop Dogg	Middle	West	1, 2, 3

Master P, MC Hammer, MC Lyte, Meek Mill, Melle Mel, Memphis Bleek, Method Man, Mickey Factz, Mos Def, N.W.A., Nas, Nature, Nerd, Nipsey Hussle, Obie Trice, Oh No, OutKast, Papoose, Pharoahe Monch, Playa Fly, Plies, Poisonous, Prodigy, Proof, Public Enemy, Puff Daddy, Pusha T, Q-Tip, Quan, R.A. the Rugged Man, Raekwon, Rag Digga, Rakim, Redman, Rich Boy, Rich Homie, Roscoe Dash, Royce da 5'9", Run-DMC, Saigon, Scarface, Schooly D, Sheek Louch, Skyzoo, Soulja Boy, Soulja Slim, Starang Wondah, Statik Selektah, Styles P, T.I., Talib Kweli, Tech N9ne, Tha Liks, The Doc, The Jacka, The Left, The Notorious B.I.G., The Sugerhill Gang, Too Short, Trinidad James, Troy Ave, Tupac Shakur, Ty Dolla $ign, Vanilla Ice, Vic Mensa, Will Smith, Young Dro, and Z-Ro.

APPENDIX 2

Annotating Non-Quantized Flow

For researchers interested in undertaking further studies of non-quantized flow or verifying the work undertaken here, I present my method for calculating the beat index of syllables more formally. To reproduce work like this, one needs to annotate:

- The syllable onsets in an a cappella recording
- Two syllable onsets in the mixed recording, as far apart as possible and with as little interference from the instrumental streams as possible
- Two downbeat onsets in the mixed recording, likely bass drums, as many measures apart as possible

This method is represented graphically in Example A2.1.
Definition of annotated moments in Example A2.1:

e_1^a, e_2^a, e_1^m and e_2^m are two pairs of equivalent points in the a cappella (a) and mixed (m) audio signals, as far apart as possible.

b_1 and b_n are two beat onsets on the mixed signal, n beats apart.

s_a is the onset of a syllable in the a cappella signal, defined as the midpoint of the initial increase in amplitude of the vowel.

Calculation of terms in Example A2.1:

$span_a = e_2^a - e_1^a$, the span of the a cappella track between points of equivalence

$span_m = e_2^m - e_1^m$, the span of the mixed track between points of equivalence. One would expect $span_a$ and $span_m$ to always be equivalent, but I have found they can vary by as much as 5 ms per second.

$offset = e_1^m - e_1^a$, the time offset between the tracks

$beat_{dur} = (b_n - b_1) \div n$, the duration of a beat

$scale = span_m \div span_a$, the scaling factor necessitated by slight differences in the duration of mixed and a cappella tracks

$s_m = s_a + (offset * scale)$, the onset of the syllable in the mixed track

$beat(s_a) = (s_m - b_1) \div beat_{dur}$

Example A2.1 Visual illustration of calculating the (non-quantized) beat index of a syllable in an a cappella audio signal, given an aligned mixed audio signal.

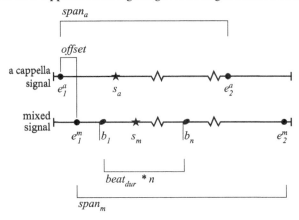

GLOSSARY

Note: Terms that originate with this book or are used differently than their conventional meaning are indicated with an asterisk.

accent The emphasis an emcee places on a syllable. Syllables in rap music accrue emphasis by virtue of vowel length, pitch height, volume, and/or metric position. Furthermore, the words of flow have accents from conversational speech. Generally, accents cannot occur on adjacent positions. See also **limit-3 accent**.

*adaptive vs. persistent listening A persistent listener exerts effort to maintain hearing an existing groove even though some accents are not in his or her expected position. An adaptive listener shifts to a new groove whenever an accent pattern changes. These terms are a renaming of Andrew Imbrie's "conservative vs. radical listening" (1973), applied in the context of groove.

African American Vernacular English A variety of American English that refers to differences in syntactical, phonetic, and phonological features of some African American vernacular speech. Note that speakers of AAVE are not all African American, not all African Americans regularly speak AAVE, and speakers vary the use of AAVE with context and setting.

*average non-alignment The amount of time, on average, that separates the midpoint of the initial increase of the amplitude of a syllable from its purported metric position in the instrumental streams.

*beat-accent type A particular combination of accents and non-accents among the four standard positions of a beat, for example, |1010| or |1001|, where "1" is accented, "0" is unaccented, and each 1 or 0 indexes a $mod\,4$ metric position.

beat index The number of beats that have elapsed since the downbeat of the first measure prior to a syllable onset. A syllable on position **8** of m. 3 in a verse has a beat index of 10. A syllable on position **9** of m. 3 has a beat index of 10.25.

beat-upbeat ratio (BUR) From Fernando Benadon (2006), a measure of the amount of swing, expressed as the ratio of the duration of an on-beat event to that of a successive off-beat event.

Boolean Named for George Boole, a logical value expressed as either true or false.

boom-bap Popularized by the emcee KRS-ONE, a reference to the sounding metrical framework in nearly all rap tracks: the bass drum on beats 1 and 3 (positions 0 and 8) and the snare drum on beats 2 and 4 (positions 4 and 12).

cardinality The number of positions in a **metric cycle**, determined by the fastest division of the measure articulated by the emcee. Most rap music has a cardinality of 16; some has a cardinality of 12 (i.e., "triplet flows," such as Killer Mike's verse on OutKast's "The Whole World"). Cardinality is usually stable within a verse.

central pillar From Dai Griffiths (2003), the point in the measure in which phrases begin and end.

***change in saturation** A change in the number of positions occupied by syllables in successive measures of flow.

***combined transcription** A transcription of a verse showing both the quantized and non-quantized (i.e., "continuous") placement of syllables, for example, Example 8.2.

commutative A property of a mathematical operation wherein the order in which the operation is conducted does not change the outcome. Addition is commutative (3 + 5 = 5 + 3); subtraction is not (3–5 ≠ 5–3).

corpus A collection of texts used in an analysis, usually with an explicit sampling method.

critical analysis vs. style analysis From Leonard B. Meyer (1973), style analysis refers to the process of uncovering the "rules of the game" operative in the works of a circumscribed style. Critical analysis, in contrast, is the process of explaining individual choices made within such a work with reference to the expectations of the style.

density estimate plot An estimate of the distribution of a random sample. Visualized as a curve, the likelihood of any value of the sample is tangent to the curve; the area under the curve is 1. Density estimates are a "continuous" form of histograms and preferable when the variable itself is continuous.

***duple groove** A groove or groove class with no 3-durations.

durational segment (dseg) An ordered string of consecutive durations represented as integers, for example, [323]. In this book, these durations are usually **inter-accent intervals**.

***effort (of hearing a groove)** The rate at which a listener has to swap the accent/non-accent status of contiguous syllables to maintain an existing groove, for example, one swap per measure. See **adaptive vs. persistent listening**.

grid search An exhaustive search of all combinations of a set of parameters to identify the one that performs best according to some metric.

*groove adherence A measure of how closely an emcee hems to an operative groove class. More specifically, the proportion of a verse's grooves heard at an effort rate of zero (i.e., by an adaptive listener) that are the same as those heard at an effort rate of one-swap-per-half-measure (i.e., by a persistent listener).

*groove class One of seven duration segments made up of only 2s and 3s summing to 16, that is, <2222_2222>, <332_2222>, <323_2222>, <3223222>, <333322>, <332_332>, and <333232>. (The underscore indicates a groove class that bisects the measure; groove classes assume rotational equivalence.)

*groove typicality A measure of how common the groove classes of a verse are in comparison to those found in the corpus. Derived through summing the contributions to the first four components of a principal component analysis.

*grooviness A measure of the proportion of a verse that articulates grooves two measures or longer for a persistent listener.

*inner periodicity The sum of the longest substring of a groove (class) consisting of reiterated durations. <332_2222>, with five 2s, has an inner periodicity of 10.

instrumental streams The musical accompaniment of a rap track, usually called "the beat," a term I avoid out of possible confusion with "the [four] beats" of the measure.

inter-accent intervals (IAIs) The duration between consecutive accents, usually expressed as a whole number of metric positions.

inter-rhyme intervals (IRIs) The duration between consecutive rhyme instances, usually expressed as a whole number of metric positions.

inter-syllable intervals (ISIs) The duration between consecutive syllables, usually expressed as a whole number of metric positions.

interval-content histogram From Toussaint (2013), a tabulation of the intervals (durations) among all pairs of onsets in a rhythm. Identical to the "interval class vector" encountered in musical set theory.

just-noticeable difference The smallest distinction that can be perceived as such, for example, the just-noticeable difference for two onsets to be heard as distinct events, estimated at 25–40 ms.

*limit-3 accent A position that carries an accented syllable, or would carry an accented syllable under the stipulation that every two or three positions must be accented. 0_{mod2} positions are limit-3 accents even if they are silent, provided they are not adjacent to other accents.

*line endings Positions that carry the ends of "lines" of rapping, defined as relatively whole grammatical units such that there are as many lines in a verse as there are measures. See also **phrase endings**.

metric accent A kind of emphasis a syllable attains by falling on a relatively strong part of the beat. 0_{mod4} positions (i.e., "on the beat") have the strongest metric accent, followed by 2_{mod4} positions (i.e., "in the middle of the beat"), followed by 3_{mod4} positions (i.e., "just before the beat") and 1_{mod4} positions (i.e., "just after the beat").

*metric saturation The proportion of positions in a measure occupied by rapped syllables.

microtiming The subtle distinctions between an event's quantized position (e.g., "on the beat") and its continuous position (e.g., 25 milliseconds before the beat). Often studied in connection to swing, and also termed "expressive timing."

*nonduple groove A groove or groove class with at least one 3-duration. See also duple groove.

*optimal phase adjustment The amount of phase (measured in "minutes," 1/60th of a beat) added to syllable onsets that would minimize their resulting average non-alignment.

*optimal swing adjustment The amount of swing (measured in the first term of a beat-upbeat ratio) removed from syllable onsets that would minimize their resulting average non-alignment.

*optimal tempo adjustment The amount of change in tempo (measured as a percentage, e.g., 1.01) by which syllable onsets could be multiplied that would minimize their resulting average non-alignment.

*persistent listening See adaptive vs. persistent listening.

*phase shift A consistent displacement of syllable onsets with respect to the beat.

phenomenal accent Emphasis a syllable accrues by virtue of acoustical factors such as vowel length, pitch height, or loudness.

phonological word A segment of speech containing multiple feet, possibly made up of multiple words.

*phrase ending A syllable that precedes a breath taken by the emcee. See also line ending.

position set class A group of metric positions, indicated by parentheses. In the 16-unit metric space of rap music, the positions "on the beat" are (0, 4, 8, 12).

quantization The interpretive act of matching all durations to a limited set of possible durations, for example, durations between whole-number positions within a measure.

*rhyme class A set of words or word groups within a verse that rhyme.

*rhyme instance One statement of a rhyme class.

*rhyme mixture The intermingling of rhyme classes, for example, an instance of a prior rhyme recurring after the initiation of a new rhyme class.

rhythmic contour From Toussaint (2013), an index of whether successive durations in a durational segment are shorter, longer, or equal. The dseg [3, 3, 2] has a rhythmic contour of [0, −1, + 1].

*saturation The average percentage of positions within the measure that are occupied by a syllable.

*spiral transformation A visualization of syllable onsets around a spiral, read out from the center. Each rotation around the spiral is one beat. See, for example, Example 8.3.

statistical significance A determination that the likelihood of a measured relationship (e.g., difference in means, correlation, etc.) occuring by chance is sufficiently low, conventionally less than 1 in 20.

structural accent From Lerdahl and Jackendoff (1983), the emphasis an event accrues through its participation in tonal-syntactical processes.

style analysis See **critical analysis vs. style analysis**.

*swing shift A consistent displacement of syllables on metrically weak positions (i.e., 1_{mod2} positions) with respect to the beat.

syllable speed The rate at which an emcee raps, measured as the inverse of the average **inter-syllable interval**, disregarding **phrase-** and **line endings**.

tactus The metric level at which one naturally taps. In most rap music, the tactus is the tempo that places the bass drum on beats 1 and 3 and the snare drum on beats 2 and 4 (see **boom-bap**).

*tempo shift The performance of a segment of flow at a different tempo than that of the beat.

*unit In this book, a "unit" is a duration, one quarter of a beat or one sixteenth of a measure.

variance From a statistical point of view, variance is the square of the difference between the values of a random variable and the mean of those values.

*vocal groove A reiterating pattern of **inter-accent intervals** (**IAIs**), made up of 2-durations and 3-durations, summing to 16 (one measure).

word accent A syllable in a multisyllabic word that normally carries an accent in conversational speech. Also called the accent of a word's "citation form."

DISCOGRAPHY

This book would not exist without the artistic efforts of countless emcees, producers, and writers. What follows is the most complete discographic information available for the tracks consulted in this project, compiled mainly from discogs.com. Listings are alphabetized by track title because artists might belong to a group or appear as a featured artist. Those tracks mentioned in the text appear before those transcribed in various corpora but not mentioned. Tracks appearing on the same album are listed separately to credit individual artists. Cited lyrics from tracks not transcribed are listed in the bibliography, as are live performances.

Tracks Mentioned in Text

Airplane Mode. Flobots. 2010. *Survival Story.* Universal Republic Records, B0014042-02. Compact disc.

Aston Martin Music. Rick Ross featuring Chrisette Michele and Drake. 2010. *Teflon Don.* Written by Erik Ortiz, Aubrey Graham, and Kevin Crowe. Produced by J. U. S. T. I. C. E. League. Def Jam Recordings, B0014366-02. Compact disc.

Basketball. Kurtis Blow. 1984. *Ego Trip.* Produced by James B. Moore, III. Mercury, 422-822 420-1 M-1. Vinyl.

Black and Yellow. Wiz Khalifa. 2011. *Rolling Papers.* Written by Cameron Thomaz (Wiz Khalifa), Mikkel S. Eriksen, and Tor Erik Hermansen. Produced by Stargate. Atlantic, 527099-2. Compact disc.

Breathe and Stop. Fat Joe featuring The Game. 2006. *Me, Myself & I.* Produced by New Jerzey Devil. Terror Squad Entertainment, 0946 3 81357 2 2. Compact disc.

Business. Eminem. 2002. *The Eminem Show.* Written by Marshall Mathers. Produced by Dr. Dre. Aftermath Entertainment, 694932902. Compact disc.

Don't Get So High (Dancehall Mix). KRS-One. 2008. *Adventures in Emceein.* Produced by QF. Echo-Vista, EV-CD-4073. Compact disc.

Flip Flop Rock. OutKast featuring Jay-Z and Killer Mike. 2003. *Speakerboxxx/The Love Below.* Produced by Mr. DJ, Big Boi. Arista, 82876-50133-1. Vinyl.

Get By [instrumental]. Talib Kweli. 2003. *Get By [single].* Rawkus, 088113938-1. Vinyl.

Go to Sleep. Eminem. 2003. *Cradle 2 the Grave Original Soundtrack.* Written by Simmons, Earl (aka DMX), Luis Resto, Marshall Mathers, Obie Trice, Steve King. Bloodline Records, 063 615-2. Compact disc.

Here Comes the Sun. The Beatles. 1969. *Abbey Road.* Written by George Harrison. Apple Records, PCS 7088. Vinyl.

I Ain't New ta This. Ice-T. 1993. *Home Invasion.* Written by DJ Alladin, Ice-T. Produced by DJ Alladin, Ice-T, and SLJ. Rhyme $yndicate Records, P2 53858. Compact disc.

I Remember. The Roots. 2011. *Undun.* Written by Ahmir Thompson, Khari Mateen, and Tariq Trotter. Def Jam Recordings, B0016282-02. Compact disc.

Instrumental for "Get By." Talib Kweli featuring Kanye West (producer). 2002. *Get By.* Written by Nina Simone, Kanye West. Produced by Joe Nardone. MCA Records, MCAR-25970-2. Compact disc.

Lose Yourself. Eminem. 2002. *Music from and Inspired by the Motion Picture 8 Mile.* Produced by Eminem, Jeff Bass, and Luis Resto. Shady Records, 493 530-2. Compact disc.

Lose Yourself (demo). Eminem. 2014. *Shady XV.* Written by J. Bass, L. Resto, M. Mathers. Shady Records, 2228102. Compact disc.

More or Less. Talib Kweli featuring Dion. 2007. *Eardrum.* Produced by Hi-Tek. Blacksmith Music, 277244-2. Compact disc.

My Crew. Jean Grae. 2003. *The Bootleg of the Bootleg EP.* Babygrande, BBG-CD-13. Compact disc.

Now or Never. The Roots featuring Dice Raw and Phonte. 2010. *How I Got Over.* Written by Jeremy Grenhart, Karl B. Jenkins, Phonte Coleman, and Tariq Trotter. Def Jam Recordings, B0013085-01. Compact disc.

Purple Swag: Chapter 2. A$AP Rocky featuring ASAP Nast and Spaceghost Purrp. 2011. *Live. Love. A$AP.* Produced by ASAP Ty Beats. Unofficial release, Compact disc.

Renegade. Jay-Z featuring Eminem. 2001. *The Blueprint.* Produced by Eminem. Roc-A-Fella Records, 314 586 396-2. Compact disc.

Renegade. Jay-Z featuring Eminem. 2010. *Live performance, recorded June 21, 2010 on the roof of the Ed Sullivan Theater, New York City.*

Say What?. Tung Twista. 1992. *Runnin' Off at da Mouth.* Written by Tung Twista. Produced by DJ Rhythm. Loud Records, 72445-11031-2. Compact disc.

Sing for the Moment. Eminem. 2002. *The Eminem Show.* Produced by Eminem and Jeff Bass. Aftermath Entertainment, 493 290-1. Compact disc.

Sorry. T. I. featuring André 3000. 2012. *Trouble Man: Heavy is the Head.* Grand Hustle, 531304. Compact disc.

Still Got It. Classified. 2009. *Self Explanatory.* HalfLife Records, 88697450092. Compact disc.

Strange. Krizz Kaliko featuring Tech N9ne. 2012. *Neh'mind.* Written by Aaron Yates, Jake McDonough, Manzilla Marquis Queen, Melvin Calhoun, Jr., and Samuel Watson. Produced by Nico Marchese and Tramaine Winfrey. Strange Music, SMI-173. Compact disc.

Take from Me. Bad Meets Evil. 2011. *Hell the Sequel.* Written by Claret Haddon-Jackson, Denaun Porter, Horace Jackson, Marshall Mathers, and Ryan Montgomery. Produced by Mr. Porter and 56. Shady Records, B0015729-02. Compact disc.

The Show Goes On. Lupe Fiasco. 2011. *Lasers.* Written by Dustin William Brower and Jonathan Keith Brown. Produced by Kane Beatz. Atlantic, 7567-89586-5. Compact disc.

The Way I Am. Eminem. 2000. *The Marshall Mathers LP.* Produced by Eminem. Interscope Records, 069490629-1. Compact disc.

Under Pressure. Logic. 2014. *Under Pressure.* Visionary Music Group, B0022126-02. Compact disc.

Walk Alone. The Roots featuring Dice Raw, P. O. R. N., and Truck North. 2010. *How I Got Over.* Written by Greg Spearman, Jamal Miller, Jeremy Grenhart, Karl Jenkins, Rick Friedrich, and Tariq Trotter. Def Jam Recordings, B0013085-01. Compact disc.

Weezy Baby. Lil' Wayne featuring Nikki. 2005. *Tha Carter II.* Written by Dwayne Carter. Produced by Deezie. Cash Money Records, B0005124-02. Compact disc.

You Got Me. The Roots. 1999. *Things Fall Apart.* Produced by The Grand Wizzards and Scott Storch. MCA Records, MCAD-11948. Compact disc.

Mozart, Wolfgang Amadeus. 1986. *Three Piano Sonatas: Klaviersonaten KV 309, 310, & 311.* Written by Mozart, Wolfgang Amadeus, and Mitsuko Uchida. Philips, 412 741-2. Compact disc.

KRS-One. 1993. *Return of the Boom Bap.* Jive Records, 01241-41517-1. Vinyl.

Tracks Transcribed in Corpora

25 Bucks. Danny Brown featuring Purity Ring. 2014. *Old.* Written by Corin Roddick, Daniel Sewell, and Megan James. Produced by Corin Roddick. Fool's Gold Records, FGRLP009. Compact disc.

25 to Life. Eminem. 2010. *Recovery.* Written by Daniel Tanenbaum and Liz Rodrigues. Produced by DJ Khalil. Aftermath Entertainment, B0014411-01. Compact disc.

3am. Eminem. 2009. *Relapse.* Produced by Dr. Dre. Aftermath Entertainment, B0012863-02. Compact disc.

40 Ounce. D12. 2004. *D12 World.* Written by Joe Kent and Mark Williams. Shady Records, B0002404-04. Compact disc.

8 Mile. Eminem. 2002. *Music from and Inspired by the Motion Picture 8 Mile.* Written by Luis Resto, Marshall Mathers. Produced by Eminem. Shady Records, 493 530-2. Compact disc.

Ain't No Half-Steppin'. Big Daddy Kane. 1988. *Long Live the Kane.* Produced by Marley Marl. Cold Chillin', 9 25731-2. Compact disc.

Ambition. Wale featuring Meek Mill and Rick Ross. 2011. *Ambition.* Maybach Music Group, 2-528687. Compact disc.

Amnesia. Blu. 2011. *Her Favorite Colo(u)r.* Written by John Barnes III (Blu). Produced by Blu. Nature Sounds, NSD-146. Compact disc.

Around My Way. Talib Kweli featuring John Legend. 2004. *The Beautiful Struggle.* Written by Henry Charlemagne. Produced by Henry Charlemagne. Rawkus Records, B0003437-02. Compact disc.

Atonement. The Roots featuring Jack Davey. 2006. *Game Theory.* Written by Ahmir Thompson, Colin Greenwood, Ed O'Brien, James Poyser, Jonny Greenwood, Karl. B. Jenkinds, Phil Selway, Thom Yorke, and Tariq Trotter. Produced by The Randy Watson Experience. Def Jam Recordings, "602517001268." Compact disc.

Baby. The Roots featuring John-John. 2006. *Game Theory.* Written by Ahmir Thompson, Frank Walker, John McGlinchey, Kamal Gray, Kirk Douglass, Leonard Hubbard, and Tariq Trotter. Produced by John McGlinchey. Def Jam Recordings, "602517001268." Compact disc.

Baby, Baby Kilo Ali. 1997. *Organized Bass.* Written by Andrell D. Rogers. Produced by Kilo Ali, Kool Ace. Interscope Records, INTD-90128. Compact disc.

Back up Offa Me. Talib Kweli. 2004. *The Beautiful Struggle*. Written by Jason Smith and Tony Cottrell. Produced by Hi-Tek. Rawkus Records, B0003437-02. Compact disc.

Bad Influence. Eminem. 1999. *End of Days Soundtrack*. Geffen Records, 490 508 2. Compact disc.

Bagpipes from Baghdad. Eminem. 2009. *Relapse*. Produced by Trevor Lawrence, Jr. Aftermath Entertainment, B0012863-02. Compact disc.

Batches and Cookies. Lizzo featuring Sophia Eris. 2013. *Lizzobangers*. Written by Sophia Eris and Melissa Viviane Jefferson (Lizzo). Totally Gross National Product, TGNP034. Vinyl.

Bread and Butter. The Roots featuring Truck North. 2006. *Game Theory*. Written by Bonus track, writers uncredited. Def Jam Recordings, "602517001268." Compact disc.

Bright as the Stars. Black Star. 2015. *Train of Thought: Lost Lyrics, Rare Releases & Beautiful B-Sides, Vol. 1*. Produced by Ayatollah. Javotti Media, JAV005. Compact disc.

Broken Anglish. Crunch E. X. featuring Talib Kweli. 2001. *Broken Anglish*. Produced by Jahson. Mission Control, MC-0726. Compact disc.

Business. Eminem. 2002. *The Eminem Show*. Produced by Dr. Dre. Aftermath Entertainment, 493 290-1. Compact disc.

C. R. E. A. M. Wu-Tang Clan. 1993. *Enter the Wu-Tang (36 Chambers)*. Written by The Wu-Tang Clan, David Porter, and Isaac Hayes. RCA, 07863 66336-1. Vinyl.

Cadillactica. Big K. R. I. T. 2014. *Cadillactica*. Def Jam Recordings, B0021368-02. Compact disc.

Can't Stop This. The Roots. 2006. *Game Theory*. Written by Ahmir Thompson, Brian Holland, James Poyser, James Yancey, Karl B. Jenkinds, Michael Lovesmith, and Tariq Trotter. Produced by J Dilla, The Randy Watson Experience, and The Roots. Def Jam Recordings, "602517001268." Compact disc.

Can't Trust'em. Dizzy Wright. 2012. *SmokeOut Conversations*. Funk Volume, Unnumbered. Compact disc.

Candy Shop. 50 Cent faeturing Olivia. 2005. *The Massacre*. Written by Curtis Jack and Scott Storch. Produced by Scott Storch. Aftermath Entertainment, B0004093-02. Compact disc.

Chaos. Relection Eternal featuring Bahamadia. 1999. *Rawkus Presents: Soundbombing II*. Produced by DJ Hi-Tek. Rawkus, P2 50069. Compact disc.

Children's Story. Slick Rick. 1988. *The Great Adventures of Slick Rick*. Written by Richard Walters. Produced by Slick Rick. Def Jam Recordings, 314 527 359-2. Compact disc.

Chillin. Erick Sermon featuring Talib Kweli and Whip Montez. 2004. *Chilltown, New York*. Produced by Erick Sermon. Universal Motown Records Group, B0002716-02. Compact disc.

Country Cousins. Talib Kweli featuring Raheem Devaughn and UGK. 2007. *Eardrum*. Produced by AKidCalledRoots, Sha-La Shakier. Blacksmith Music, 277244-2. Compact disc.

Crack a Bottle. Eminem featuring 50 Cent and Dr. Dr. 2009. *Relapse*. Produced by Dr. Dre. Aftermath Entertainment, B0012863-02. Compact disc.

Dear God 2. 0. The Roots featuring Monsters of Folk. 2010. *How I Got Over*. Written by Ahmir Thompson, Jim James, Pedro Martinez, Richard Nichols, and Tariq Trotter. Def Jam Recordings, B0013085-01. Compact disc.

Deliverance. Bubba Sparxxx. 2003. *Deliverance*. Written by Warren Anderson Mathis, Timonthy Mosley, and Jimmy Douglass. Produced by Timbaland. Interscope Records, B0001147-02. Compact disc.

Dilemma. Nelly featuring Kelly Rowland. 2002. *Nellyville*. Produced by Ryan Bowser. Universal Records, 440 017 747-2. Compact disc.

Dis Aint What U Want. Lil Durk. 2013. *Signed to the Streets*. Produced by Paris Beuller. Only the Family, Unnumbered. Digital mp3 file.

Do It like You. Diggy Simmons featuring Jeremih. 2012. *Unexpected Arrival*. Written by Simmons, Jeremih Felton, john Maultsby, Andrew McGee, Dexter Wansel. Atlantic Records, Unnumbered. Compact disc.

Doin' It Again. The Roots. 2010. *How I Got Over*. Written by Ahmir Thompson, John Stephens, and Tariq Trotter. Def Jam Recordings, B0013085-01. Compact disc.

Don't Let Up. Planet Asia and Talib Kweli. 2000. Non-album single. Produced by 427 and Beats Anonymous. Mona Hip Hop, MONA 1001. Vinyl.

Drank in My Cup. Kirko Bangz. 2011. Non-album single. Digital mp3 file.

Drop It Like It's Hot. Snoop Dogg featuring Pharrell. 2004. *R & G (Rhythm & Gangsta): The Masterpiece*. Produced by The Neptunes. Geffen Records, B0003764-02. Compact disc.

Drug Ballad. Eminem. 2000. *The Marshall Mathers LP*. Produced by Eminem and F. B. T. Interscope Records, 069490629-1. Compact disc.

Dumpin'. Parts Unknown featuring Dirty Dozen. 2006. *Payin' Dues*. Produced by Mr. Porter. Ghosttown Entertainment, Unnumbered. Compact disc.

Easy Rider. Action Bronson. 2015. *Mr. Wonderful*. Written by Action Bronson. Produced by Party Supplies. Atlantic Records, ATL549151CD. Compact disc.

Evil Deeds. Eminem featuring 50 Cent, Obie Trice, and Stat Quo. 2004. *Encore*. Produced by Dr. Dre. Interscope Records, B0003771-71. Compact disc.

False Media. The Roots. 2006. *Game Theory*. Written by Ahmir Thompson, Carlton Ridenhour, Eric Sadler, Hank Schocklee, James Gray, James Poyser, Karl B. Jenkins, and Tariq Trotter. Produced by Kamal Gray and The Randy Watson Experience. Def Jam Recordings, "602517001268." Compact disc.

Feel the Heartbeat. The Treacherous Three. 1981. Non-album single. Written by Bobby Robinson, Kenton Nix, Kevin Keaton, Lamar Hill, and Moe Dewese. Produced by Bobby Robinson. Enjoy Records, ER-6013. Vinyl.

Flash Gordon. Talib Kweli. 2005. *Right about Now: The Official Sucka Free Mix CD*. Written by Dave West. Produced by Dave West. Koch Records, KOC-CD-5963. Compact disc.

Fubba U Cubba Cubba. Eminem. 2005. *Clinton Sparks & Eminem: Anger Management 3*. Produced by Eminem. The Mix Unit, CLIN108. Compact disc.

Fuck Compton. Tim Dog. 1991. *Penicillin on Wax*. Written by Blair, Tim. Produced by Ced Gee and Tim Dog. Ruffhouse Records, CK 48707. Compact disc.

Full Clip. Gang Starr. 1999. *Full Clip: A Decade of Gang Starr*. Written by Elam, Keith and Martin, Christopher. Produced by DJ Premiere and Guru. Virgin Records, 7243 8 47279 2 5. Compact disc.

Game Theory. The Roots featuring Malik B. 2006. *Game Theory*. Written by Ahmir Thompson, Kamal Gray, Khari Mateen, Kirk Douglass, Leonard Hubbard, Smart Abdul-Basit, Tariq Trotter, and Sylvester Stewart. Def Jam Recordings, "602517001268." Compact disc.

Get By. Talib Kweli. 2002. *Quality*. Written by Nina Simone. Produced by Joe Nardone. Rawkus, 088 113 048-1. Compact disc.

Get Em High. Kanye West featuring Common and Talib Kweli. 2004. *The College Dropout*. Produced by Kanye West. Roc-A-Fella Records, DEFF 16021-1. Compact disc.

Get Ur Freak On. Missy Elliott. 2001. *Miss E So Addictive*. Produced by Timbaland. Elektra, 62639-2. Compact disc.

Going through Changes. Eminem. 2010. *Recovery*. Written by Emile Haynie. Produced by Emile Haynie. Aftermath Entertainment, B0014411-01. Compact disc.

Good Mourning. Reflection Eternal. 2000. *Train of Thought*. Written by Talib Kweli Greene and Tony Cottrell. Produced by Hi-Tek. Rawkus, RWK-177. Compact disc.

Headlights. Eminem featuring Nate Ruess. 2013. *The Marshall Mathers LP 2*. Aftermath Entertainment, B0019488-02. Compact disc.

Holy Grail. Jay-Z featuring Justin Timberlake. 2013. *Magna Carta Holy Grail*. Written by Ernest Wilson, Jerome Harmon, Justin Timberlake, Shawn Carter, Terius Nash, and Timothy Mosley. Roc-A-Fella Records, B0018877-02. Compact disc.

Hostile Gospel Pt. 1 (Deliver Us). Talib Kweli. 2007. *Eardrum*. Produced by Just Blaze. Blacksmith Music, 277244-2. Compact disc.

Hot Thing. Talib Kweli featuring Will. I. Am. 2007. *Eardrum*. Produced by Will. I. Am. Blacksmith Music, 277244-2. Compact disc.

How I Got Over. The Roots featuring Dice Raw. 2010. *How I Got Over*. Written by Jeremy Grenhart, Karl Jenkins, Richard Nichols, Rick Friedrich, and Tariq Trotter. Produced by Jeremy Grenhart, Karl Jenkins, Richard Nichols, and Rick Friedrich. Def Jam Recordings, B0013085-01. Compact disc.

Hustla. The Roots featuring STS. 2010. *How I Got Over*. Written by Ahmir Thompson, Don Carlos Price, Tariq Trotter, and Wesley Pentz. Produced by Thomas Pentz. Def Jam Recordings, B0013085-01. Compact disc.

I Try. Talib Kweli featuring Mary J. Blige. 2004. *The Beautiful Struggle*. Written by John Stevens, Kanye West, and Mary J. Blige. Produced by Kanye West. Rawkus Records, B0003437-02. Compact disc.

I'll Hurt You. Busta Rhymes featuring Eminem. 2006. *The Big Bang*. Produced by Dr. Dre and Scott Storch. Unofficial release, Compact disc.

I'm Back. Eminem. 2000. *The Marshall Mathers LP*. Produced by Dr. Dre and Mel-Man. Interscope Records, 069490629-1. Compact disc.

I'm Shady. Eminem. 1999. *The Slim Shady LP*. Produced by Jeff Bass, Mark Bass, and Eminem. Aftermath Entertainment, INTD-90287. Compact disc.

If U Stay Ready. Suga Free featuring Playa Hamm. 1996. *Street Gospel*. Written by Walker, Dejuan and Milo, Bryan. Produced by G-1 and Robert Bacon. Island Black Music, 314-524 385-2. Compact disc.

It was a Good Day. Ice Cube. 1992. *The Predator*. Written by Jackson, O'Shea and Jordan, Mark. Produced by D. J. Pooh. Priority Records, P2-57185. Compact disc.

It's the Pee '97 PMD. 1997. *Bu$ine$$ is Bu$ine$$*. Written by Charity, Chris, Lyric, Derek, and Smith, Parrish. Produced by Solid Scheme. Relativity, 88561-1569-2. Compact disc.

June. No Malice featugin Eric David. 2012. *Hear Ye Him*. Written by Eric David and Gene Thornton [No Malice]. Reinvision, Unnumbered. Digital mp3 file.

Kool On. The Roots featuring Greg Porn and Truck North. 2011. *Undun*. Written by DeWayne Rogers, Porno, Tariq Trotter, and Jamal Miller. Produced by Ahmir Thompson. Def Jam Recordings, B0016282-02. Compact disc.

Lighters Up. Lil' Kim. 2005. *The Naked Truth*. Written by Kimberly Jones [Lil' Kim] and Scott Storch. Produced by Scott Storch. Atlantic, 83818-2. Compact disc.

Lighthouse. The Roots featuring Dice Raw. 2011. *Undun*. Written by Ahmir Thompson, Karl B. Jenkins, Rick Friedrich, and Tariq Trotter. Def Jam Recordings, B0016282-02. Compact disc.

Like Toy Soldiers. Eminem. 2004. *Encore*. Produced by Eminem. Interscope Records, B0003771-71. Compact disc.

Listen!!!. Talib Kweli. 2007. *Eardrum*. Produced by Kwamé Holland. Blacksmith Music, 277244-2. Compact disc.

Lock Shit Down. Chali 2na featuring Talib Kweli. 2009. *Fish Outta Water*. Decon, DCN 772-DLP. Compact disc.

Long Time. The Roots featuring Peedi Peedi and Bunny Sigler. 2006. *Game Theory*. Written by Ahmir Thompson, Bunny Sigler, Darrell Robinson, Kamal Gray, Kerl B. Jenkings,

Kevin Hanson, Kirk Douglass, Leonard Hubbard, Owen Biddle, Pedro Zayas, and Tariq Trotter. Produced by Darryl Robinson, Owen Biddle, and Omar Edwards. Def Jam Recordings, "602517001268." Compact disc.

Lost. Gorilla Zoe. 2008. *Don't Feed da Animals.* Written by Christopher Gholson. Produced by Christopher Gholson. Bad Boy Records, 514278-2. Compact disc.

Love Me. Eminem. 2002. *Music from and Inspired by the Motion Picture 8 Mile.* Produced by Eminem and Luis Resto. Shady Records, 493 530-2. Compact disc.

Make My. The Roots featuring Big K. R. I. T. and Dice Raw. 2011. *Undun.* Written by Ahmir Thompson, Justin Scott, Karl B. Jenkins, Khari Mateen, Raymond Angry, and Tariq Trotter. Produced by Ahmir Thompson, Khari Mateen, and Ray Angry. Def Jam Recordings, B0016282-02. Compact disc.

Make tha Trap Say Aye. OJ Da Juiceman featuring Gucci Mane. 2007. *The Otha Side of the Trap.* Asylum Records, Unnumbered. Digital mp3 file.

Marshall Mathers. Eminem. 2000. *The Marshall Mathers LP.* Produced by Eminem and F. B. T. Interscope Records, 069490629-1. Compact disc.

MC's Act Like They Don't Know. KRS-One. 1995. *KRS-One.* Produced by DJ Premiere. Jive Records, 01241-41570-2. Compact disc.

Me Myself and I. De La Soul. 1989. *3 Feet High and Rising.* Written by Vincent Mason, Paul Huston, Kelvin Mercer, George Clinton, and Dave Jolicoeur. Tommy Boy, TBLP 1019. Vinyl.

Mighty Healthy. Ghostface Killah. 2000. *Supreme Clientele.* Produced by Allah Mathematics. Epic, EK 69325. Compact disc.

Miss January. The Procussions featuring Talib Kweli. 2006. *5 Sparrows for 2 Cents.* Produced by Stro the 89th Key. Rawkus, RKS02. Vinyl.

Mood Swing. Asheru featuring Talib Kweli. 2003. *Heads R Better Than 1: No Edge-Upse in South Africa, Vol. 1.* Produced by Joe Money. Seven Heads, SVH-041-1. Compact disc.

Mosh. Eminem. 2004. *Encore.* Produced by Dr. Dre and Mark Batson. Interscope Records, B0003771-71. Compact disc.

Move Something. Reflection Eternal. 2000. *Train of Thought.* Written by Talib Kweli Greene and Tony Cottrell. Produced by Hi-Tek. Rawkus, RWK-177. Compact disc.

My Chick Bad. Ludacris featuring Nicki Minaj. 2010. *Battle of the Sexes.* Written by Onika Miraj and Samuel Lindley. Produced by The Legendary Traxster. Island Def Jam Music Group, B0014030-02. Compact disc.

My Dad's Gone Crazy. Eminem featuring Hailie Jade. 2002. *The Eminem Show.* Produced by Dr. Dre. Aftermath Entertainment, 493 290-1. Compact disc.

My Darling. Eminem. 2009. *Relapse.* Produced by Dr. Dre. Aftermath Entertainment, B0012863-02. Compact disc.

My Mom. Eminem. 2009. *Relapse.* Produced by Dr. Dre. Aftermath Entertainment, B0012863-02. Compact disc.

My Name Is. Eminem. 1999. *The Slim Shady LP.* Written by Dr. Dre. Produced by Dr. Dre. Aftermath Entertainment, INTD-90287. Compact disc.

My Opinion. Mac Mall. 1993. *Illegal Business?* Produced by Khayree. Young Black Brotha Records, YBBC-2022. Compact disc.

Never Been in Love Before. Talib Kweli. 2004. *The Beautiful Struggle.* Written by Justin Smith. Produced by Just Blaze. Rawkus Records, B0003437-02. Compact disc.

No Love. Eminem featuring Lil Wayne. 2010. *Recovery.* Produced by Just Blaze. Aftermath Entertainment, B0014411-01. Compact disc.

No Love. August Alsina. 2014. *Testimony.* Def Jam Music Group, B0020171-02. Compact disc.

Old Time's Sake. Eminem featuring Dr. Dre. 2009. *Relapse*. Produced by Mark Batson. Aftermath Entertainment, B0012863-02. Compact disc.

One for Peedi Crakk. Peedi Crack, Beanie Sigel, Freeway, & Young Chris. 2002. *Dame Dash Present: Paid in Full Soundtrack*. Produced by Megahertz. Roc-A-Fella Records, B00063201. Compact disc.

One Time. The Roots featuring Dice Raw and Phonte. 2011. *Undun*. Written by Ahmir Thompson, Karl B. Jenkins, Phonte Coleman, Ritz Reynolds, and Tariq Trotter. Def Jam Recordings, B0016282-02. Compact disc.

Pacman. Pill featuring Rick Ross. 2011. *Self Made Vol. 1*. Produced by Young Shun. Maybach Music Group, 527800-2. Compact disc.

Pay for It. Jay Rock featuring Kendrick Lamara and Chantal. 2014. *Kanye West/Kendrick Lamar—Art Represents Life*. Unofficial release, Compact disc.

Pimpin' Ain't No Illusion. UKG featuring Kool-Ace and Too Short. 2001. *Dirty Money*. Produced by Pimp C. Jive Records, 01241-41673-2. Compact disc.

Push Thru. Talib Kweli featuring Curren$y, Glen Reynolds, and Kendrick Lamar. 2013. *Prisoner of Conscious*. Written by Arrow Brown, Glen Reynolds, Kendrick Lamar, and Larry Griffin. Produced by S1. Javotti Media, BSMTK027. Compact disc.

Put ya Stamp on It. Akrobatik featuring Talib Kweli. 2008. *Absolute Value*. Produced by J Dilla. Fat Beats, FB5123. Compact disc.

Radio Daze. The Roots featuring Blu, Dice Raw, and P. O. R. N. 2010. *How I Got Over*. Written by Jeremy Grenhart and Karl Jenkins. Produced by Jeremy Grenhart, John Barns, Karl B. Jenkins, Rick Friedrich, and Tariq Trotter. Def Jam Recordings, B0013085-01. Compact disc.

Ready. Fabolous featuring Chris Brown. 2013. Non-album single. Written by John Jackson, Chris Brown, Andrew Harr, Jermaine Jackson, Andre Davidson, and Sean Davidson. Produced by The Runners and The Monarch. Digital mp3 file.

Revelation. D12. 2001. *Devils Night LP*. Written by Andre Young, Deshaun Holton, Denaun Porter, Marshall Mathers, Mike Elizondo, Ondre Moore, Rufus Johnson, Scott Storch, and Von Carlisle. Shady Records, "0694908972." Compact disc.

Rock On. Talib Kweli. 2005. *Right about Now: The Official Sucka Free Mix CD*. Written by Kevin Resto and Waynne Nugent. Produced by Midi Mafia. Koch Records, KOC-CD-5963. Compact disc.

Say Goodbye Hollywood. Eminem. 2002. *The Eminem Show*. Produced by Eminem. Aftermath Entertainment, 493 290-1. Compact disc.

Say Something. Talib Kweli featuring Jean Grae. 2007. *Eardrum*. Produced by Will. I. Am. Blacksmith Music, 277244-2. Compact disc.

Second-Round K. O. Canibus. 1998. *Can-I-Bus*. Written by Germaine Williams [Canibus], Wyclef Jean, and Jerry Duplessis. Produced by Jerry Wonder, Wyclef Jean. Universal Records, UD 53136. Compact disc.

Self Taught. Brother Ali. 2004. *Champion EP*. Written by Anthony Davis [A. N. T.] and Ali Newman [Brother Ali]. Produced by Ant Turn That Snare Down. Rhymesayers Entertainment, RS0049-2. Compact disc.

Set It Off. Lil Boosie. 2006. *Bad Azz*. Produced by Jeremy Allen. Trill Entertainment, 68587-2. Compact disc.

Sex Style. Kool Keith. 1997. *Sex Style*. Written by Keith Thornton and Kurt Matlin. Produced by Kut Masta Kurt. Funky Ass Records, KTR-006. Compact disc.

Sexy Love. Max B. 2008. *Max B on Demand: Max Payne*. Lazy K Productions, B001NRPQSU. Compact disc.

Shutterbugg. Big Boi. 2010. *Sir Lucious Left Foot: The Son of Chico Dusty*. Written by Antwan Patton, Beresford Romeo, Caron Wheeler, Christopher Carmouche, David Frank,

Michael Murphy, Nellee Hooper, Ricardo Lewis, Scott Storch, and Simon Law. Produced by Scott Storch and Big Boi. Def Jam Recordings, "602527000000." Compact disc.

Sleep. The Roots. 2011. *Undun*. Written by Aaron Livingston, Ahmir Thompson, Nick Koenig-Dzialowski, and Tariq Trotter. Produced by Ahmir Thompson. Def Jam Recordings, B0016282-02. Compact disc.

Soldier. Eminem. 2002. *The Eminem Show*. Produced by Eminem. Aftermath Entertainment, 493 290-1. Compact disc.

Spend Some Time. Eminem. 2004. *Encore*. Produced by Eminem and Luis Resto. Interscope Records, B0003771-71. Compact disc.

Square Dance. Eminem. 2002. *The Eminem Show*. Produced by Eminem. Aftermath Entertainment, 493 290-1. Compact disc.

Stay Fly. Three 6 Mafia featuring Eightball & MJG and Young Buck. 2005. *Ten Toes Down*. Produced by Tony D. Columbia, CK 94724. Compact disc.

Steady Slangin'. Wise Intelligent. 1996. *Killin' U . . . For Fun*. Contract Recording Company, CRC31010. Compact disc.

Still Don't Give a Fuck. Eminem. 1999. *The Slim Shady LP*. Produced by Jeff Bass, Mark Bass, and Eminem. Aftermath Entertainment, INTD-90287. Compact disc.

Stimulate. Eminem. 2003. *Straight from the Lab*. Universal, 4 602912983 1 5. Compact disc.

Stomp. The Roots featuring Greg Porn. 2011. *Undun*. Written by Delano Matthews, Levar Coppin, Porno, and Tariq Trotter. Produced by Sean C & LV. Def Jam Recordings, B0016282-02. Compact disc.

Stronger. Kanye West. 2007. *Graduation*. Produced by Kanye West. Roc-A-Fella Records, B0009541-02. Compact disc.

Studio. Schoolboy Q featuring BJ The Chicago Kid. 2014. *Oxymoron*. Produced by Swiff D. Top Dawg Entertainment, B0020137-02. Compact disc.

Sunshine. Esham. 1993. *KKKill the Fetus*. Overcore, 2066-2. Compact disc.

Take It There. The Roots featuring Wadud Ahmad. 2006. *Game Theory*. Written by Adam Blackstone, Ahmir Thompson, Darrell Robinson, Frank Walker, Kamal Gray, Kevin Hanson, Kirk Douglass, Leonard Hubbard, Pedro Martinez, and Tariq Trotter. Produced by Adam Blackstone, Ahmir Thompson, and Pedro Martinez. Def Jam Recordings, "602517001268." Compact disc.

Takin My Ball. Eminem. 2009. *Relapse: Refill*. Produced by Dr. Dre. Aftermath Entertainment, B0013893-72. Compact disc.

Talkin' 2 Myself. Eminem featuring Kobe. 2010. *Recovery*. Written by Brian Honeycutt and Chin Injeti. Produced by DJ Khalil. Aftermath Entertainment, B0014411-01. Compact disc.

That's How It Is. Casual. 1994. *Fear Itself*. Produced by Del Tha Funkee Homosapien. Jive Records, 01241-41520-2. Compact disc.

The Breaks. Kurtis Blow. 1980. *Kurtis Blow*. Written by Kurtis Blow, Robert Ford, Russell Simmons, and James Biggs Moore III. Produced by Lawrence Smith. Mercury, SRM-1-3854. Vinyl.

The Day. The Roots featuring Blu, Patty Crash, and Phonte. 2010. *How I Got Over*. Written by Ahmir Thompson, Damon Bryson, Frank Walker, James Gray, James Poyser, John Barnes, Karl B. Jenkins, Katrin Newman, Kirk Douglass, Owen Biddle, Phonte Coleman, and Tariq Trotter. Produced by Richard Nichols and The Roots. Def Jam Recordings, B0013085-01. Compact disc.

The Day They Make Me the Boss. Young Bleed. 1998. *My Balls and My Word*. Produced by Nathan Perez. No Limit Records, P2 50738. Compact disc.

The Fire. The Roots featuring John Legend. 2010. *How I Got Over*. Written by Ahmir Thompson, Karl B. Jenkins, Rick Friedrich, and Tariq Trotter. Def Jam Recordings, B0013085-01. Compact disc.

The Good Fight. Phonte. 2011. *Charity Starts at Home*. Written by Patrick Douthit and Phonte Coleman. Produced by 9th Wonder. Hardboiled, HBD-CD-PH1. Compact disc.

The Magic Clap. The Coup. 2012. *Sorry to Bother You*. Anti, 86891-2. Compact disc.

The Message. Grandmaster Flash & The Furious Five. 1983. *Grandmaster Flash & The Furious Five*. Written by Clifton Chase, Ed Fletcher, Melvin Glover, Sylvia Robinson. Sugar Hill Records, 6-25644. Vinyl.

The Monster. Eminem featuring Rihanna. 2013. *The Marshall Mathers LP 2*. Aftermath Entertainment, B0019488-02. Compact disc.

The Next Episode. Dr. Dre featuring Nate Dogg. 1999. *2001*. Aftermath Entertainment, 069490486-2. Compact disc.

The OtherSide. The Roots featuring Bilal and Greg Porn. 2011. *Undun*. Written by Ahmir Thompson, James Poyser, Karl B. Jenkins, Greg Spearman, and Tariq Trotter. Def Jam Recordings, B0016282-02. Compact disc.

The Re-Up. Eminem and 50 Cent. 2006. *The Re-Up*. Shady Records, B0007885-01JK02. Compact disc.

Thug Love. Bone Thugs-n-Harmony. 1997. *Art of War*. Written by Anthony Henderson [Krayzie Bone], Steven Howse [Layzie Bone], Bryon McCane [Bizzy Bone], Charles Scruggs [Wish Bone], Stanley Howse [Flesh-N-Bone], and Tupac Shakur [2pac]. Ruthless Records, 88561-6340-2. Compact disc.

Till I Collapse. Eminem featuring Nate Dogg. 2002. *The Eminem Show*. Produced by Eminem. Aftermath Entertainment, 493 290-1. Compact disc.

Till It's Gone. Yelawolf. 2014. *Love Story*. Produced by WLPWR. Slumerican, 602537811519-1. Compact disc.

Tip the Scale. The Roots featuring Dice Raw. 2011. *Undun*. Written by Ahmir Thompson, Karl B. Jenkins, Raymond Angry, and Tariq Trotter. Def Jam Recordings, B0016282-02. Compact disc.

Tonite. Eminem. 1996. *Infinite*. Web Entertainment, WEB714. Cassette.

U. N. I. T. Y. Queen Latifah. 1993. *Black Reign*. Produced by Kay Gee and Mufi. Motown, 374 636 370-2. Compact disc.

Wages of Sin. Mr. Khaliyl featuring Talib Kweli. 2001. *Wages of Sin/Street Team*. Produced by Mr. Khaliyl. Rawkus Records, RWK-313. Vinyl.

Water Whippin'. Ca$his. 2012. *The Art of Dying*. Written by Ramone Johnson. Produced by Cin-A-Matik the Problem. RBC Records, RBC-277. Compact disc.

We Ain't. The Game featuring Eminem. 2005. *The Documentary*. Written by Jayceon Taylor, Steve King, Luis Resto, and Marshall Mathers. Produced by Eminem and Luis Resto. Aftermath Entertainment, B0003562-02. Compact disc.

We Gonna Make It. Jadakiss featuring Styles. 2001. *Kiss tha Game Goodbye*. Produced by Mahog. Ruff Ryders, 069493011-2. Compact disc.

We Made You. Eminem. 2009. *Relapse*. Produced by Eminem and Doc Ish. Aftermath Entertainment, B0012863-02. Compact disc.

What the Beat. Eminem, Method Man, and Royce The 5'9.". 2001. *DJ Clue?: The Professional 2*. Produced by DJ Clue?. Roc-A-Fella Records, 314 542 325-2. Compact disc.

What They Do. The Roots. 1996. *Illadelph Halflife*. Produced by Brother?uestion, The Grand Negaz, and Raphael Saadiq. Geffen Records, GED 24972. Compact disc.

Whatta Man. Salt 'N' Pepa featuring 3 Feet and En Vogue. 1993. *Very Necessary*. Produced by Herby Azor. Next Plateau Records Inc. 828 392-2. Compact disc.

When I'm Gone. Eminem. 2005. *Curtain Call.* Written by Luis Resto and Marshall Mathers. Produced by Luis Resto and Marshall Mathers. Aftermath Entertainment, "0602498878934." Compact disc.

White America. Eminem. 2002. *The Eminem Show.* Produced by Eminem and Jeff Bass. Aftermath Entertainment, 493 290-1. Compact disc.

Who Do You Love? YG featuring Drake. 2014. *My Krazy Life.* Def Jam Recordings, B0020133-02. Compact disc.

Whoa! Black Rob. 2000. *Life Story.* Written by Anthony Best and Robert Ross. Produced by Buckwild. Bad Boy Entertainment, 78612-73026-2 RE-1. Compact disc.

Without Me. Eminem. 2002. *The Eminem Show.* Produced by Eminem and Jeff Bass. Aftermath Entertainment, 493 290-1. Compact disc.

Wonton Soup. Lil B. 2010. *Blue Flame.* BasedWorld, Digital mp3 file.

Y'all Ready Know. Slaughterhouse. 2015. *Shady XV.* Written by Chris Martin, Dominic Wickliffe, Joe Budden, Joell Ortiz, and Ryan Montgomery. Produced by DJ Premiere. Shady Records, B0022280-01. Vinyl.

Yellin' Away. Zap Mama featuring?uestlove, Common, and Talib Kweli. 2004. *Ancestry in Progress.* Written by Chris McHale, Lonnie Lynn, Marie Daulne, and Talib Kweli Greene. Produced by Anthony Tidd and Marie Daulne. Luaka Bop, WR1027512. Compact disc.

WORKS CITED

Abdul-Lateef, Mahmoud. 1999.The Roots: *Things Fall Apart*. *Vibe Magazine*, March, 162.

Abel, Mark. 2014. *Groove: An Aesthetic of Measured Time*. New York: Brill.

Adams, Kyle. 2008. Aspects of the music/text relationship in rap. *Music Theory Online* 14(2).

Adams, Kyle. 2009. On the metrical techniques of flow in rap music. *Music Theory Online* 15(5).

Adams, Kyle. 2015a. The musical analysis of hip-hop. In *The Cambridge Companion to Hip-Hop*, edited by Justin Williams, 118–134. New York: Cambridge University Press.

Adams, Kyle. 2015b. What did Danger Mouse do? The *Grey Album* and musical composition in configurable culture. *Music Theory Spectrum* 37(1): 7–24.

Agawu, Kofi. 1995. *African Rhythm: A Northern Ewe Perspective*. New York: Cambridge University Press.

Agawu, Kofi. 2014. *Representing African Music: Postcolonial Notes, Queries, Positions*. New York: Routledge.

Agostinelli, Claudio, and Ulric Lund. 2017. R package "circular": Circular statistics (version 0.4–93). https://r-forge.r-project.org/projects/circular/.

Akrobatik. 2004. Lyrics to "U Can't F*ck Wit It." On *The Lost Adats*. Detonator Records DET 130. Compact disc.

Alberti, Gianmarco. 2013. An R script to facilitate correspondence analysis: A guide to the use and the interpretation of results from an archaeological perspective. *Archaeologia e Calcolatori* 24: 25–53.

Alén, Olavo. 1995. Rhythm as duration of sounds in tumba francesa. *Ethnomusicology* 39(1): 55–71.

Alim, H. Samy. 2006. *Roc the Mic Right*. New York: Taylor & Francis.

Alim, H. Samy, Awad Ibrahim, and Alastair Pennycook. 2008. *Global Linguistic Flows: Hip-Hop Cultures, Youth Identities, and the Politics of Language*. New York: Routledge.

Allen, Harry. 2003. The unbearable whiteness of emceeing: What the eminence of Eminem says about race. *The Source*, February, 28–34.

Andrews, Tara. 2015. Software and scholarship—Editorial. *Interdisciplinary Science Reviews* 40(4): 342–348.

Armstrong, Edward G. 2004. Eminem's construction of authenticity. *Popular Music and Society* 27(3): 335–355.

Ashley, Richard. 2014. Expressiveness in funk. In *Expressiveness in Music Performance: Empirical Approaches Across Styles and Cultures*, edited by Dorottya Fabian, Renee Timmers, and Emery Schubert, 154–169. New York: Oxford University Press.

Attridge, Derek. 1995. *Poetic Rhythm: An Introduction*. New York: Cambridge University Press.

Bahamadia. 1996. Lyrics to "3 Tha Hard Way." On *Kollage*. Chrysalis D 112617. Compact disc.

Bailey, Julius. 2014. *Philosophy and Hip-Hop: Ruminations on a Postmodern Cultural Form*. New York: Palgrave Macmillan.

Bakhtin, Mikhail. 1986 (1952). The problem of speech genres. In *Speech Genres and Other Late Essays*, edited by Caryl Emerson and Michael Holquist, 60–102. Austin: University of Texas Press.

Baldwin, Davarian L. 2004. Black empires, white desires: The spatial politics of identity in the age of hip-hop. In *That's the Joint! The Hip-Hop Studies Reader*, edited by Murray Forman and Mark Anthony Neal, 159–176. New York: Routledge.

Bark, Theo. 2009. Easy Mo Bee speaks out about "Notorious" snub. *The Boombox*, January 15. http://theboombox.com/easy-mo-bee-speaks-out-about-notorious-snub-b-i-g-s-death/.

Bartlett, Susan, Grzegorz Kondrak, and Colin Cherry. 2009. On the syllabification of phonemes. In *The Proceedings of the Fifteenth Annual Conference of the North American Chapter of the Association for Computational Linguistics: Human Language Technologies*, 308–316. Cambridge, MA: Association for Computational Linguistics.

Beard, David, and Kenneth Gloag. 2016. *Musicology: The Key Concepts*, 2nd ed. New York: Routledge.

Benadon, Fernando. 2006. Slicing the beat: Jazz eighth notes as expressive microrhythm. *Ethnomusicology* 50(1): 73–98.

Berendt, Joachin Ernst. 1992. *The Jazz Book: From Ragtime to Fusion and Beyond*. Revised by Günther Huesmann, translated by H. and B. Bredigkeit. New York: Lawrence Hill Books.

Biber, Douglas. 1990. Methodological issues regarding corpus-based analyses of linguistic variation. *Literary and Linguistic Computing* 5(1990): 257–269.

Bone, Krayzie, featuring Asu and LaReece. Lyrics to "Ride If Ya Like." On *Thug On Da Line*. Loud Records CK 85784. Compact disc.

Borgman, Christine L. 2015. *Big Data, Little Data, No Data: Scholarship in the Networked World*. Cambridge, MA: MIT Press.

Bowen, José. 1996. Tempo, duration, and flexibility: Techniques in the analysis of performance. *Journal of Musicological Research* 16(2): 111–156.

Bradley, Adam. 2009. *Book of Rhymes: The Poetics of Hip Hop*. New York: Basic Civitas.

Bradley, Adam, and Andrew Lee DuBois, eds. 2010. *The Anthology of Rap*. New Haven, CT: Yale University Press.

Breihan, Tom. 2006. The Roots reconsidered. *The Village Voice*, June 24.

Brogan, Terry V. F. 2012. Rhyme. In *The Princeton Encyclopedia of Poetry and Poetics*, edited by Roland Greene et al., 1182–1192. Princeton, NJ: Princeton University Press.

Burgoyne, John Ashley, Jonathan Wild, and Ichiro Fujinaga. 2013. Compositional data analysis of harmonic structures in popular music. In *Mathematics and Computation in Music*, edited by Jason Yust and Jonathan Wild, 52–63. Heidelberg: Springer.

Butler, Mark Jonathan. 2014. *Playing with Something that Runs: Technology, Improvisation, and Composition in DJ and Laptop Performance*. New York: Oxford University Press, 2014.

Butterfield, Matthew. 2006. The power of anacrusis: Engendered feeling in groove-based music. *Music Theory Online* 12(4).

Butterfield, Matthew. 2010a. Participatory discrepancies and the perception of beats in jazz. *Music Perception* 27(3): 157–176.

Butterfield, Matthew. 2010b. Variant timekeeping patterns and their effects in jazz drumming. *Music Theory Online* 16(4).

Caplan, David. 2014. *Rhyme's Challenge*. New York: Oxford University Press.

Caramanica, Jon. 2017. A jagged ride to fame. *New York Times*, June 22.

Carman, Taylor. 2008. *Merleau-Ponty*. London and New York: Routledge.

Carter, Angela. 2005. Touch and go: How DJ Jazzy Jeff's studio spawned a musical legacy. *Two One Five Magazine* 1(2): 15–20.

Carter, Nick (Murs). 2017. Does hick hop have a right to exist? *The Breakdown* video blog, September 2. https://hiphopdx.com/videos/id.26217/title. the-breakdown-does-hick-hop-have-a-right-to-exist#.

Chalabi, Mona. 2014. The fastest rapper in the game. *Five Thirty Eight*, March 24. https:// fivethirtyeight.com/datalab/the-fastest-rapper-in-the-game.

Chang, Jeff. 2005. An uplifting voice of hip hop. *The Progressive*, October. http://progressive. org/mag_chang1005.

Chang, Jeff. 2006. *Total Chaos: The Art and Aesthetics of Hip Hop*. New York: Basic Books.

Chernoff, John M. 1979. *African Rhythm and African Sensibilities: Aesthetics and Social Action in African Musical Idioms*. Chicago: University of Chicago Press.

Chinen, Nate. 2008. New album, new fears, same old attitude. *New York Times*, March 4.

Chor, Ives. 2010. Microtiming and rhythmic structure in clave-based music. In *Musical Rhythm in the Age of Digital Reproduction*, edited by Anne Danielson, 37–50. Burlington, VT: Ashgate.

Clarke, Stuart Alan. 1991. Fear of a black planet. *Socialist Review* 21(3–4): 37–59.

de Clercq, Trevor, and David Temperley. 2011. A corpus analysis of rock harmony. *Popular Music* 30(1): 47–70.

Clough, John, and Jack Douthett. 1991. Maximally even sets. *Journal of Music Theory* 35(1–2): 93–173.

Cohn, Richard. 1992. Transpositional combination of beat-class sets in Steve Reich's phase-shifting music. *Perspectives of New Music* 30(2): 146–177.

Cohn, Richard. 2012. A Platonic model of funky rhythms. *Music Theory Online* 22(2).

Coleman, Brian. 2005. *Check the Technique: Liner Notes for Hip-Hop Junkies*. Somerville, MA: Wax Facts Press.

Condit-Schultz, Nathaniel. 2016. MCFlow: A digital corpus of rap transcriptions. *Empirical Musicology Review* 11(2): 124–147.

Condry, Ian. 2006. *Hip-Hop Japan: Rap and the Paths of Cultural Globalization*. Durham, NC: Duke University Press.

Conklin, Daniel. 2002. Representation and discovery of vertical patterns in music. In *Music and Artificial Intelligence*, edited by Christina Anagnostopoulou, Miguel Ferrand, and Alan Smaill, 32–42. Berlin: Springer.

Connor, Martin. 2011–2017. *The composer's corner* blog. Renamed *Rap analysis: more than listening*. http://www.rapanalysis.com.

Connor, Martin. 2013. Talib Kweli interview. *The composer's corner* blog, June 13. http:// www.rapanalysis.com/2013/06/talib-kweli-interview.html.

Cook, Nicholas. 1987. Structure and performance timing in Bach's C Major Prelude (WTCI): An empirical study. *Music Analysis* 6(3): 257–272.

Cook, Nicholas. 1999. Analyzing performance and performing analysis. In *Rethinking Music*, edited by Nicholas Cook and Mark Everist, 239–261. New York: Oxford University Press.

Cook, Nicholas, and Mark Everist, eds. 1999. *Rethinking Music*. New York: Oxford University Press.

Cook, Vivian. 1988. Designing a BASIC parser for CALL. *CALICO Journal* 6(1): 50–67.

Costello, Mark, and David Foster Wallace. 1990. *Signifying Rappers: Rap and Race in the Urban Present*. Hopewell, NJ: Ecco Press.

Csikszentmihalyi, Mihalyi. 1991. *Flow: The Psychology of Optimal Experience*. New York: HarperCollins.

Danielsen, Anne. 2006. *Presence and Pleasure: The Funk Grooves of James Brown and Parliament.* Middleton, CT: Wesleyan University Press.

Danielsen, Anne. 2012. The sound of crossover: micro-rhythm and sonic pleasure in Michael Jackson's "Don't Stop 'Til You Get Enough." *Popular Music and Society* 35(2): 151–168.

Danielsen, Anne. 2016. Metrical ambiguity or microrhythmic flexibility? Analysing groove in "Nasty Girl" by Destiny's Child. In *Song Interpretation in Twenty-First-Century Pop Music*, edited by Ralf von Appen, André Doehring, and Allan Moore, 53–72. New York: Routledge.

Davies, Mark. 2013. Google Scholar vs. COCA: Two very different approaches to examining academic English. *Journal for English for Academic Purposes* 12: 155–165.

Davies, Matthew, Guy Madison, Pedro Silva, and Fabien Gouyon. 2013. The effect of microtiming deviations on the perception of groove in short rhythms. *Music Perception* 30(5): 498–511.

Davis, Tom, chairman. 2006. *A Failure of Initiative: The Final Report of the Select Bipartisan Committee to Investigate the Preparation for and Response to Hurricane Katrina.* Washington, DC: Government Printing Office.

Dee, Kool Moe. 2003. *There's a God on the Mic: The True 50 Greatest MCs.* New York: Da Capo Press.

Dehaene, Stanislas. 2011. *The Number Sense: How the Mind Creates Mathematics.* New York: Oxford University Press.

Deleuze, Gilles, and Claire Parnet. 2002. The actual and the virtual. In *Dialogues II*, translated by Eliot Ross Albert, 112–115. New York: Columbia University Press.

DeLuca, Dan. 2012. Prime rhymer. *Philadelphia Inquirer*, August 13.

Demos, Alexander P., Roger Chaffin, Kristen T. Begosh, Jennifer R. Daniels, and Kerry L. Marsh. 2012. Rocking to the beat: Effects of music and partner's movements on spontaneous interpersonal coordination. *Journal of Experimental Psychology: General.* doi:10.1037/a0023843

Devore, Jay. 2000. *Probability and Statistics for Engineering and the Sciences.* Pacific Grove, CA: Duxbury.

DG. 2015. Comment on Ural Garrett, "Black Thought says The Roots are 'kind-of'" without a label." *HIPHOPDX* blog, February 16. http://hiphopdx.com/interviews/id.2690/title. black-thought-says-the-roots-are-kind-of-without-a-label.

Diaz, Angel. 2015. All you "real" rap fans need to stop hating on *What a Time to Be Alive. Complex*, September 21. http://www.complex.com/music/2015/09/ drake-future-what-a-time-to-be-alive.

divine12th. 2014. Comment on Martin Connor, "Black Thought—rap music analysis" (YouTube video). https://www.youtube.com/watch?v=nlVNPR1BYww.

Doffman, Mark. 2009. Making it groove! Entrainment, participation, and discrepancy in the "conversation" of a jazz trio. *Language and History* 52(1): 130–147.

Dougan, John. 2006. Objects of desire: Canon formation and blues record collecting. *Journal of Popular Music* 18(1): 40–65.

Drake, Carolyn, and Caroline Palmer. 1993. Accent structures in music performance. *Music Perception* 10(3): 343–378.

Drake, David, Andrew Martin, Ernest Baker, and Insanul Ahmed. 2012. The fifty most slept-on rappers of all time. *Complex.com*, November 16. http://www.complex.com/ music/2012/11/the-50-most-slept-on-rappers-of-all-time/.

Edwards, Paul. 2009. *How to Rap.* Chicago: Chicago Review Press.

Edwards, Paul. 2010. *How to Rap 2: Advanced Flow and Delivery Techniques.* Chicago: Chicago Review Press.

Edwards, Paul. 2015. *The Concise Guide to Hip-Hop Music: A Fresh Look at the Art of Hip Hop, from Old-School Beats to Freestyle Rap*. New York: St. Martin's Griffin.

Eminem. 2014. Eminem—"Lose Yourself"—the demo (YouTube video) [interview]. November 18. https://www.youtube.com/watch?v=BnH5i5XfpVM.

Enck, Suzanne Marie, and Blake A. McDaniel. 2012. Playing with fire: Cycles of domestic violence in Eminem and Rihanna's "Love the Way You Lie." *Communication, Culture, and Critique* 5(4): 618–644.

Escher, Emcee, and Alex Rappaport. 2006. *The Rapper's Handbook: A Guide to Freestyling, Writing Rhymes, and Battling*. New York: Flocabulary LLC.

Fee, Debi. 1988. Rap producers: Taking on the challenge of creating a sense of longevity amid change. *Billboard*, December 24, R21.

Fink, Robert. 2011. Goal-directed soul? Analyzing rhythmic teleology in African American popular music. *Journal of the American Musicological Society* 64(1): 179–238.

Fitzgerald, Kevin, dir. 2000. *Freestyle: The Art of Rhyme*. VH1 Television.

Fougeron, Cécile, and Patricia A. Keating. 1997. Articulatory strengthening at edges of prosodic domains. *Journal of the Acoustic Society of America* 101(6): 3728–3740.

Francis, W. Nelson, and Henry Kucera. 1964. *Manual of Information to Accompany "A Standard Corpus of Present-Day Edited American English, for Use with Digital Computers."* Providence, RI: Department of Linguistics, Brown University.

Friberg, Anders, and Andreas Sundström. 2002. Swing ratios and ensemble timing in jazz performance: Evidence for a common rhythmic pattern. *Music Perception* 19(3): 333–349.

Friberg, Anders, and Johan Sundberg. 1995. Time discrimination in a monotonic, isochronous sequence. *Journal of the Acoustical Society of America* 98(5): 2524–31.

Friedmann, Michael L. 1985. A methodology for the discussion of contour: Its application to Schoenberg's music. *Journal of Music Theory* 29(2): 223–248.

Frosch, Dan. 2004. The tipping point. *Vibe*, October.

Fruehauf, Jan, Reinhard Kopiez, and Friedrich Platz. 2013. Music on the timing grid: The influence of microtiming on the perceived groove quality of a simple drum pattern preference. *Musicae Scientiae* 17(2): 246–260.

Gabriel, Robert. 2004. Record review: Talib Kweli and Mos Def. *The Austin Chronicle*, November 12. https://www.austinchronicle.com/music/2004-11-12/237288/.

Gale, Alex. 2011. Fifty most influential rappers. *B.E.T.com*, September 23. No longer hosted online. Archived version available at http://web.archive.org/web/20110923144513/http:/www.bet.com/music/photos/2011/09/50-most-influential-rappers.html#!042511-music-soulja-boy-album.

Gale, Alex. 2012. Notorious B.I.G.'s former manager speaks out. *BET News*, March 8. http://www.bet.com/news/music/2012/03/09/notorious-b-i-g-s-former-manager-speaks-outl.html.

Gamer, C. 1967. Deep scales and difference sets in equal-tempered systems. In *Proceedings of the Second Annual Conference of the American Society of University Composers*, 113–122. St. Louis, MI: American Society of University Composers.

Gates, Henry Louis. 1988. *The Signifying Monkey: A Theory of African-American Literary Criticism*. New York: Oxford University Press.

Gaunt, Kyra D. 2006. *The Games Black Girls Play: Learning the Ropes from Double-Dutch to Hip Hop*. New York: New York University Press.

Giorgino, Toni. 2009. Computing and visualizing dynamic time warping alignments in R: The dtw package. *Journal of Statistical Software* 31(7): 1–24. http://www.jstatsoft.org/v31/i07/.

Google Ngram Viewer. 2017. Braggadocio. https://books.google.com/ngrams/graph?content=braggadocio.

Grant, Andre. 2015. Talib Kweli's got something to say. *HipHopDX*, September 30. http://hiphopdx.com/interviews/id.2788/title.talib-kwelis-got-something-to-say.

Grealy, Liam. 2008. Negotiating cultural authenticity in hip hop: Mimicry, whiteness and Eminem. *Continuum* 22(6): 851–865.

Griffiths, Dai. 2003. From lyric to anti-lyric: Analyzing the words in pop song. In *Analyzing Popular Music*, edited by Allan Moore, 39–59. New York: Cambridge University Press.

Gussenhoven, Carlos, and Haike Jacobs. 1998. *Understanding Phonology*. London: Hodder Education.

Hall, T. Alan. 1999. The phonological word: A review. In *Studies on the Phonological Word*, edited by T. Alan Hall and Ursula Kleinhenz, 1–22. Amsterdam: John Jacobs.

Hamanaka, Masatoshi, Keiji Hirata, and Satoshi Tojo. 2006. Implementing "A Generative Theory of Tonal Music." *Journal of New Music Research* 35(4): 249–277.

Handel, Stephen. 1992. The differentiation of rhythmic structure. *Perception and Psychophysics* 52(5): 497–507.

Harrington, Richard. 2004. Jill Scott, "beautifully human." *Washington Post*, July 23.

Harrison, Anthony K. 2008. Racial authenticity in rap music and hip hop. *Sociology Compass* 2(6): 1783–1800.

Hatten, Robert. 1994. *Musical Meaning in Beethoven*. Bloomington: Indiana University Press.

Hayes, Bruce. 1995. *Metrical Stress Theory: Principles and Case Studies*. Chicago: University of Chicago Press.

Heights, Rob, and Les Charles. 2011. Meeting a living legend: Interview with Black Thought. *Life of Kings*, January 9. https://lifeofkings.com/meeting-a-living-legend/.

Hess, Mickey. 2005. Hip-hop realness and the white performer. *Critical Studies in Media Communication* 22(5): 372–389.

Hess, Mickey. 2010. The sound of Philadelphia: Hip-hop history in the city of brotherly love. In *Hip Hop in America: A Regional Guide*, 143–176. Santa Barbara, CA: Greenwood Press.

Hiatt, Brian. 2013. Eminem responds to "Rap God" homophobia accusations. *The Rolling Stone*. http://www.rollingstone.com/music/news/exclusive-eminem-responds-to-rap-god-homophobia-accusations-20131104.

Hirjee, Hussein, and Daniel Brown. 2010. Using automated rhyme detection to characterize rhyming style in rap music. *Empirical Musicology Review* 5(4): 121–145.

Hopsin. 2009. Lyrics to "I'm Here." On *Gazing at the Moonlight*. Ruthless Records EK82952. Compact disc.

Huron, David. 2006. *Sweet Anticipation: Music and the Psychology of Expectation*. Cambridge, MA: MIT Press.

Hurt, Byron, dir. 2006. *Beyond Beats and Rhymes*. Documentary film [DVD]. Media Education Foundation.

Hutchinson, William, and Leon Knopoff. 1987. The clustering of temporal elements in melody. *Music Perception* 4(3): 281–303.

Ice-T, and Andy Baybutt, dir. 2012. *Something from Nothing: The Art of Rap*. Documentary film. Indomina Releasing.

Imbrie, Andrew. 1973. Extra measures and metrical ambiguity in Beethoven. In *Beethoven Studies*, edited by Alan Tyson, 45–66. New York: Norton.

ImTheFxckingPoop. Comment on "Statik Selektah ft. Action Bronson, Royce Da 5'9" and Black Thought—'The Imperial'" (YouTube flash video file). https://www.youtube.com/watch?v=hc-efkXk27w.

Iyer, Vijay. 1998. Microstructures of feel, macrostructures of sound: Embodied cognition in West African and African-American musics. PhD dissertation, University of California, Berkeley.

Iyer, Vijay. 2002. Embodied mind, situated cognition, and expressive microtiming in African-American music. *Music Perception* 19(3): 387–414.

Janata, Petr, Stefan Tomic, and Jason Haberman. 2012. Sensorimotor coupling in music and the psychology of the groove. *Journal of Experimental Psychology: General* 141(1): 54–75.

Jay-Z, and Eminem. 2010. "Renegade." Live performance, recorded June 21 on the roof of the Ed Sullivan Theater, New York City.

Kautny, Oliver. 2015. Lyrics and flow in rap music. In *The Cambridge Companion to Hip Hop*, edited by Justin Williams, 101–117. New York: Cambridge University Press.

Keil, Charles. 1987. Participatory discrepancies and the power of music. *Cultural Anthropology* 2(3): 275–283.

Keil, Charles. 1995. The theory of participatory discrepancies: A progress report. *Ethnomusicology* 39(1): 1–19.

Keil, Charles. 2010. Defining "groove." *PopScriptum*, 11. https://www2.hu-berlin.de/fpm/popscrip/themen/pst11/pst11_keil02.html.

Keil, Charles, and Steven Feld. 2005. *Music Grooves*, 2nd ed. Chicago: University of Chicago Press.

Keller, James. 2003. Shady Agonistes: Eminem, abjection, and masculine protest. *Studies in Popular Culture* 25(3): 13–24.

Kelley, Frannie. 2010. Biggie Smalls: The voice that influenced a generation. *National Public Radio (Morning Edition)*, August 2. http://www.npr.org/2010/08/02/128916682/biggie-smalls-the-voice-that-influenced-a-generation.

Kerman, Joseph. 1980. How we got into analysis. *Critical Inquiry* 7(2): 311–331.

Keyes, Cheryl L. 2002. *Rap Music and Street Consciousness*. Champaign, IL: University of Chicago Press.

Keyes, Cheryl L. 1996. At the crossroads: Rap music and its African nexus. *Ethnomusicology* 40(2): 223–248.

Kilchenmann, Lorenz, and Olivier Senn. 2011. "Play in time, but don't play time": Analyzing timing profiles in drum performances. In *Proceedings of the International Symposium on Performance Science*, edited by Aaron Williamon, Darryl Edwards, and Lee Bartel, 593–598. Brussels: European Association of Conservatories.

Kinetik featuring Tone Richardson. 2013. Lyrics to "London Mornings." On *Hip Hop Is Forever*, Bass and Format. mp3 file.

Kitwana, Bakari. 2017. Hip hop in the halls of the academy. *The 1A* (radio program), April 17. http://the1a.org/shows/2017-04-10/hip-hop-in-the-halls-of-the-academy.

Koetting, James. 1970. Analysis and notation of West African drum ensemble music. *Selected Reports in Ethnomusicology* 1(3): 116–146.

Kopano, Baruti N. 2002. Rap music as an extension of the Black rhetorical tradition: "Keepin' it real." *Western Journal of Black Studies* 26(4): 204–214.

Krebs, Harald. 1999. *Fantasy Pieces: Metrical Dissonance in the Music of Robert Schumann*. New York: Oxford University Press.

Krims, Adam. 2000. *Rap Music and the Poetics of Identity*. New York: Cambridge University Press.

Kweli, Talib, and Planet Asia. 2000. Lyrics to "Don't Let Up." 12" vinyl single. Mona Hip Hop 1001.

Lacasse, Serge. 2006. Stratégies narratives dans 'Stan' d'Eminem: Le rôle de la voix et de la technologie dans l'articulation du récit phonographique. *Protée* 34(2–3): 1–16.

Ladefoged, Peter, and Keith Johnson. 2011. *A Course in Phonetics*, 6th ed. Boston: Wadsworth.

Lambert, Frank L. 2002. Entropy is simple, qualitatively. *Journal of Chemical Education* 79(10): 1241–1296.

Lamere, Paul. 2009. Hottt or Nottt? *Music Machinery* blog, December 9. https://musicmachinery.com/2009/12/09/a-rising-star-or/.

Lehiste, Ilse. 1977. Isochrony reconsidered. *Journal of Phonetics* 5: 253–263.

Lena, Jennifer C., and Richard A. Peterson. 2008. Classification as culture: Types and trajectories of music genres. *American Sociological Review* 73(5): 697–718.

Lenzao, Kevin, and Alex Rudnicky. 2007. *The Carnegie Mellon University Pronouncing Dictionary*, version 0.7a. http://www.speech.cs.cmu.edu/cgi-bin/cmudict.

Lerdahl, Fred, and Ray Jackendoff. 1983. *A Generative Theory of Tonal Music*. Cambridge, MA: MIT Press.

Lester, Joel. 1986. *The Rhythms of Tonal Music*. Carbondale, IL: Southern Illinois University Press.

Levitin, Daniel, Karon MacLean, Max Mathews, and Lonny Chu. 2000. The perception of cross-modal simultaneity. *International Journal of Computing and Anticipatory Systems* 5: 323–329.

Liberman, Mark, and Alan Prince. 1977. On stress and linguistic rhythm. *Linguistic Inquiry* 8(2): 311–313.

Lidov, David. 1979. Structure and function in musical repetition. *Journal of the Canadian Association of University Schools of Music* 8(1): 1–32.

London, Justin. 2004. *Hearing in Time*. New York: Oxford University Press.

Ludacris featuring Playaz Circle, Rick Ross, and Ving Rhames. 2008. Lyrics to "Southern Gangsta." On *Theater of the Mind*. Def Jam Recordings B0012020-02. Compact disc.

Ludacris featuring T-Pain. 2008. Lyrics to "One More Drink." On *Theater of the Mind*. Def Jam Recordings B0012020-02. Compact disc.

Madison, Guy. 2006. Experiencing groove induced by music: Consistency and phenomenology. *Music Perception* 24(2): 201–208.

Madison, Guy, Fabian Gouyon, Fredrik Ullén, and Kalle Hörnström. 2011. Modeling the tendency for music to induce movement in humans: First correlations with low-level audio descriptors across musical genres. *Journal of Experimental Psychology: Human Perception and Performance* 37(5): 1578–1594.

Manabe, Noriko. 2006. Globalization and Japanese creativity: Adaptations of Japanese language to rap. *Ethnomusicology* 50(1): 1–36.

Manabe, Noriko. 2015. *The Revolution Will Not Be Televised: Protest Music after Fukushima*. New York: Oxford University Press.

Mardia, Kanti V., and Peter E. Jupp. 2009. *Directional Statistics*. Hoboken, NJ: John Wiley & Sons.

Marriott, Robert. 2004. Allah's on me. In *And It Don't Stop: The Best American Hip-Hop Journalism of the Last Twenty Five Years*, edited by Raquel Cepeda, 187–201. New York: Faber & Faber.

Marsalis, Wynton. 1988. What Jazz Is—And Isn't. *New York Times*, July 31, 1988. https://www.nytimes.com/1988/07/31/arts/music-what-jazz-is-and-isn-t.html.

Marsden, Alan. 2016. Music analysis by computer: Ontology and epistemology. In *Computational Music Analysis*, edited by David Meredith, 3–28. Cham, Switzerland: Springer International.

Marshall, Wayne. 2006. Giving up hip hop's firstborn: A quest for the real after the death of sampling. *Callaloo* 29(3): 868–892.

Martin, Michel. 2007. "The real thing" according to Jill Scott. *NPR Tell Me More*, September 25.

Mayer, Rudolf, Robert Neumayer, and Andreas Rauber. 2008. Rhyme and style features for musical genre classification by song lyrics. In *ISMIR 2008: Proceedings of the Ninth*

International Conference on Music Information Retrieval, edited by Juan Pablo Bello, Elaine Chew, and Douglas Turnbull. ISMIR.

McGuinness, Andrew. 2006. Groove microtiming deviations as phase shifts. In *Proceedings of the 9th International Conference on Music Perception and Cognition*, 558–565. Bologna: European Society for the Cognitive Sciences of Music.

Mead, Andrew. 1987. About *About Time*'s time: A survey of Milton Babbitt's recent rhythmic practice. *Perspectives of New Music* 25(1–2): 182–235.

Merleau-Ponty, Maurice. 2012 [1945]. *Phenomenology of Perception*. Translated by Donald A. Landes. London and New York: Routledge.

Meyer, Leonard B. 1954. *Emotion and Meaning in Music*. Chicago: University of Chicago Press.

Meyer, Leonard B. 1973. On the nature and limits of critical analysis. In *Explaining Music*, 3–25. Berkeley: University of California Press.

Meyer, Leonard B. 1989. *Style and Music: Theory, History, and Ideology*. Chicago: University of Chicago Press.

Meyer, Leonard B. 2000. Nature, nurture, and convention: the cadential six-four progression. In *The Spheres of Music: A Gathering of Essays*, 226–251. Chicago: University of Chicago Press.

Michaelsen, Garrett. 2013. Analyzing musical interaction in jazz improvisation of the 1960s. PhD dissertation, Indiana University.

Middlebrook v. Knox County School District, 805 F. Supp. 534 (E.D. Tenn. 1991).

Middleton, Richard. 1999. Groove. In *Key Terms in Popular Music and Culture*, edited by Bruce Horner and Thom Swiss, 143. New York: John Wiley & Sons.

Mitchell, Tony. 2002. Doin' damage in my native language: The use of "resistance vernaculars" in hip hop in France, Italy, and Aotearoa/New Zealand. *Popular Music and Society* 24(3): 41–54.

Miyakawa, Felicia M. 2005. *Five Percenter Rap*. Bloomington: Indiana University Press.

Molanphy, Chris. 2014. I know you got soul: The trouble with Billboard's R&B/Hip-Hop chart. *Pitchfork* longform article, April 14. https://pitchfork.com/features/article/9378-i-know-you-got-soul-the-trouble-with-billboards-rbhip-hop-chart/.

Monson, Ingrid. 1996. *Saying Something: Jazz Improvisation and Interaction*. Chicago: University of Chicago Press.

Moore, Allan. 1992. Patterns of harmony. *Popular Music* 11(1): 73–106.

Moore, Allan, ed. 2003. *Analyzing Popular Music*. New York: Cambridge University Press.

N9ne, Tech. 2010. Tech N9ne teaches you how to rap with incredible flows (YouTube video) [interview by Paul Edwards]. March 6. https://www.youtube.com/watch?v=laLco_BrvjI.

Nagle, Aubrey. 2014. Boyz II Men return to their alma mater. *Philadelphia Magazine*, October 13.

Nketia, Joseph H. K. 1974. *The Music of Africa*. New York: Norton.

Ohriner, Mitchell. 2012. Grouping hierarchy and trajectories of pacing in performances of Chopin's mazurkas. *Music Theory Online* 18(1).

Ohriner, Mitchell. 2013. Groove, variety, and disjuncture in the rap of Kanye West, Eminem, and André 3000. Paper presented at the annual meeting of the *Society for Music Theory*, October 28, Charlotte, NC.

Ohriner, Mitchell. 2016. Metric ambiguity and flow in rap music: A corpus-assisted study of Outkast's "Mainstream" (1996). *Empirical Musicology Review* 11(2): 153–179.

Ohriner, Mitchell. 2018. Expressive timing. In *The Oxford Handbook of Music Theory Concepts*, edited by Alexander Rehding and Steven Rings. New York: Oxford University Press. http://www.oxfordhandbooks.com/view/10.1093/oxfordhb/9780190454746.001.0001/oxfordhb-9780190454746-e-33.

238 ～ *Works Cited*

Oliver, Rowan. 2016. Groove as familiarity with time. In *Music and Familiarity: Listening, Musicology, and Performance*, edited Elaine King and Helen Prior, 239–252. New York: Routledge.

Osumare, Halifu. 2003. Phat beats, dope rhymes, and def moves: Hip hop's African aesthetics as signifying intertext. In *Marvels of the African World: Cultural Patrimony, New World Connections, and Identities*, edited by Niyi Afolabi, 371–394. Trenton, NJ: Africa World Press.

Overy, Katie, and Istvan Molnar-Szakacs. 2009. Being together in time: Musical experience and the mirror neuron system. *Music Perception* 26(5): 489–504.

Pardo, Bryan, and William P. Birmingham. 2001. Algorithms for chordal analysis. *Computer Music Journal* 26(2): 27–49.

Pareles, Jon. 1996. Pop review: At an annual festival for jazz, music that strictly isn't. *New York Times*, June 19.

Paté, Alexs. 2009. *In the Heart of the Beat*. Lanham, MD: Scarecrow Press.

Patel, Aniruddh D. 2008. *Music, Language, and the Brain*. New York: Oxford University Press.

Paterson, James Braxton. 2016. *Hip-Hop Headphones: A Scholar's Critical Playlist*. New York: Bloomsbury Academic.

Perchard, Tom. 2015. New riffs on the old mind-body blues: "Black rhythm," "white logic," and music theory in the twenty-first century. *Journal of the Society for American Music* 9(3): 321–348.

Perry, Imani. 2004. *Prophets of the Hood: Politics and Poetics in Hip Hop*. Durham, NC: Duke University Press.

Pihel, Erik. 1996. A furified freestyle: Homer and hip hop. *Oral Tradition* 11(2): 249–269.

Powell, Victor, and Lewis Lehe. 2015. Principal component analysis. *Visually Explained* blog, February 12. http://setosa.io/ev/principal-component-analysis/.

Pressing, Jeff. 2002. Black Atlantic rhythm: Its computational and transcultural foundations. *Music Perception* 19(3): 285–301.

Pressing, Jeff. 1997. Cognitive complexity and the structure of musical patterns. In *Proceedings of the Fourth Conference of the Australasian Cognitive Science Society*. Newcastle, Australia. http://psy.uq.edu.au/CogPsych/Noetica/OpenForumIssue8/Pressing.html.

Quinn, Ian, and Panayotis Mavromatis. 2011. Voice leading and harmonic function in two chorale corpora. In *Mathematics and Computation in Music*, edited by Carlos Agon et al., 230–240. Berlin: Springer.

Rabin, Nathan. 2004. Music review of Talib Kweli: *The Beautiful Struggle. The A.V. Club*, October 4. http://www.avclub.com/review/talib-kweli-emthe-beautiful-struggleem-11254.

Rapsody. 2012. Lyrics to "Believe Me." On *The Idea of Beautiful*. It's a Wonderful World Music Group, ERE-CD-106. Compact disc.

Repp, Bruno H. 1998. A microcosm of musical expression: I. Quantitative analysis of pianists' timing in the initial measures of Chopin's *Etude in E Major*. *Journal of the Acoustical Society of America* 104(3): 1085–1100.

Rodman, Gilbert. 2006. Race . . . and other four letter words: Eminem and the cultural politics of authenticity. *Popular Communication* 4(2): 95–121.

Rodriguez, Jayson. 2015. Jay-Z: Behind the rhymes, part three. *MTV News*, October 10. http://on.mtv.com/1GWm7hD.

Roeder, John. 1995. A calculus of accent. *Journal of Music Theory* 39(1): 1–46.

Roholt, Tiger. 2014. *Groove: A Phenomenology of Rhythmic Nuance*. New York: Bloomsbury.

The Roots featuring "Captain" Kirk Douglas. 2008. "You Got Me." Live performance for taping of VH1 *Soul Stage*, May 12, Until Studios, New York City.

The Roots featuring Estelle. 2010. "You Got Me." Live performance for taping of *VEVO UNSTAGED*, September 23, Terminal 5, New York City.

The Roots featuring Jill Scott. 1999a. "You Got Me." On *The Roots Come Alive*. Recorded February 15, Bowery Ballroom, New York City. MCA Records 111 059–2. Compact disc.

The Roots featuring Jill Scott. 1999b. "You Got Me." Recorded for *Nulle part ailleurs* TV program, April 19, Canal+ Studios, Paris.

The Roots featuring Jill Scott. 2002. "You Got Me." Live performance on the *MTV $2 Bill Tour*, July 2, The 9:30 Club, Washington, DC.

The Roots featuring Jill Scott and Erykah Badu. 2005. "You Got Me." Live performance featured in the film *Dave Chappelle's Block Party*, September 18, 2004, Clinton Hill, Brooklyn, New York City.

Rose, Tricia. 1994. *Black Noise: Rap Music and Black Culture in Contemporary America*. Middletown, CT: Wesleyan Unviersity Press.

Ross, Erik. 2013. The fifty best selling rap albums of all time. *Complex.com*, May 18. http://www.complex.com/music/2013/05/the-50-best-selling-rap-albums/.

Rothstein, William. 1989. *Phrase Rhythm in Tonal Music*. Chelsea, MI: Musicalia Press.

Ryon, Sean. 2012. Kanye West says he didn't physically write his lyrics for first four albums. *Hip Hop DX*, August 15. http://hiphopdx.com/news/id.20809/title.kanye-west-says-he-didnt-physically-write-his-lyrics-for-first-four-albums.

Saigon featuring Jay-Z and Swizz Beatz. 2009. Lyrics to "Come On Baby" (remix). On *The Greatest Story Never Told*. Suburban Noize Records NZE-271. Compact disc.

Sajnani, Damon. 2013. Troubling the trope of "rapper as modern griot." *Journal of Pan African Studies* 6(3): 156–180.

Sampson, Cale. 2013. Lyrics to "Nothing to Prove." On *The Big Picture*. Self-released, mp3 download.

Sanneh, Kelefa. 2002. Music in review, pop: Ernest reasonable rapper who leans to the left. *New York Times*, November 25. http://www.nytimes.com/2002/11/25/arts/music-in-review-pop-earnest-reasonable-rapper-who-leans-to-the-left.html.

Sanneh, Kelefa. 2004. Hip-hop review: A rapping acrobat with lyrics that do back flips and cartwheels. *New York Times*, April 29. http://www.nytimes.com/2004/04/29/arts/hip-hop-review-a-rapping-acrobat-with-lyrics-that-do-back-flips-and-cartwheels.html.

Sanneh, Kelefa. 2006. The Roots, with Nas, Common, and Talib Kweli, at Radio City Music Hall. *New York Times*, May 20. https://www.nytimes.com/2006/05/20/arts/music/20root.html.

de Saussure, Ferdinand. 2013 [1916]. *Course in General Linguistics*, translated by Roy Harris. London: A&C Black.

Schloss, Joseph G. 2014. *Making Beats: The Art of Sample-Based Hip Hop*. Middleton, CT: Wesleyan University Press.

Scholes, Percy, and Judith Nagley. 2017. Syncopation. In *The Oxford Companion to Music*. Oxford Music Online. Oxford University Press.

Selfridge-Field, Eleanor. 1997. Beyond codes: Issues in musical representation. In *Beyond MIDI: The Handbook of Musical Codes*, edited by Eleanor Selfridge-Field, 565–572. Cambridge, MA: MIT Press.

Selkirk, Elizabeth. 1986. *Phonology and Syntax: The Relation between Sound and Structure*. Cambridge, MA: MIT Press,

Small, Christopher. 1998. *Musicking: The Meanings of Performance and Listening*. Middletown, CT: Wesleyan University Press.

The Soul Rebels featuring Black Thought. 2015. "You Got Me." Live performance, February 26, Brooklyn Bowl, Brooklyn, New York City.

Stammen, Dale, and Bruce Pennycook. 1993. Real-time recognition of melodic fragments using the dynamic timewarp algorithm. In *Proceedings of the International Computer Music Conference*, edited by Sadamu Ohteru, 232–235. ICMA.

Stephens, Vincent. 2005. Pop goes the rapper: A close reading of Eminem's genderphobia. *Popular Music* 24(1): 21–36.

stic.man. 2005. *The Art of Emceeing: An Easy to Follow, Step-by-Step Guide for the Aspiring Hip-Hop Artist*. Atlanta, GA: Boss Up, Inc.

Svensson, Patrik. 2016. Humanities computing as digital humanities. In *Defining Digital Humanities: A Reader*, edited by Melissa Terras, Julianee Nyhan, and Edward Vanhoutte, 159–186. New York: Routledge.

Sweatshirt, Earl. 2013. Lyrics to "Hoarse." On *Doris*. Columbia 88883 75170 2. Compact disc.

Swedenburg, Ted. 2004. Homies in the "hood": Rap's commodification of insubordination. In *That's the Joint! The Hip-Hop Studies Reader*, edited by Murray Forman and Mark Anthony Neal, 579–610. New York: Routledge.

Syron. 2013. Freeway declares Black Thought the most underrated emcee. *HipHopDX*, January 13. http://hiphopdx.com/news/id.22490/title.freeway-declares-black-thought-the-most-underrated-emcee.

Temperley, David. 1999. Syncopation in rock: A perceptual perspective. *Popular Music* 18(1): 19–40.

Temperley, David. 2001. *The Cognition of Basic Musical Structures*. Cambridge, MA: MIT Press.

Temperley, David, and Daniel Sleator. 1999. Modeling meter and harmony: A preference-rule approach. *Computer Music Journal* 23(1): 10–27.

Thomas, Erik R. 2015. Prosodic features of African American English. In *The Oxford Handbook of African American Language*, edited by Sonja Lanehart, 420–439. New York: Oxford University Press.

Todd, Neil P. M. 1985. A model of expressive timing in tonal music. *Music Perception* 3(2): 33–57.

Toiviainen, Petri, Geoff Luck, and Marc Thompson. 2010. Embodied meter: Hierarchical eigenmodes in music-induced movement. *Music Perception* 28(1): 59–70.

Toussaint, Godfried T. 2013. *The Geometry of Musical Rhythm: What Makes a 'Good' Rhythm Good?* Boca Raton, FL: CRC Press.

Traut, Don. 2005. "Simply irresistible": Recurring accent patterns as hooks in mainstream 1980s music. *Popular Music* 24(1): 57–77.

Tsagris, Michail, Girgos Athineou, and Anamul Sajib. 2017. *Directional: Directional Statistics*. R package version 2.7. https://CRAN.R-project.org/package=Directional.

Tufte, Edward. 2006. *Beautiful Evidence*. Cheshire, CT: Graphics Press LLC.

Twrocks. 2014. Comment on "Are one of these the best Black Thought verses ever?" *Rap Genius* discussion board thread. https://genius.com/discussions/70915-Are-one-of-these-the-best-black-thought-verses-ever.

various authors. 2012. Top 50 lyrical leaders. *The Source*, June 26, 66–75.

Villing, Rudi C., Bruno H. Repp, Tomas E. Ward, and Joseph M. Timoney. 2011. Measuring perceptual centers using the phase correction response. *Attention, Perception, and Psychophysics* 73: 1614–1629.

Virtuoso. 2004. Lyrics to "Crematorium." On *World War II—Evolution of the Torturer*. Omnipotent Records 692227 0029–2. Compact disc.

VladTV. 2015. Talib Kweli speaks on chances of a Black Star reunion (YouTube video). August 16. https://www.youtube.com/watch?v=uzI15E2JcJI.

Von Appen, Ralf, and Andre Doehring. 2006. Nevermind The Beatles, here's Exile 61' and Nico: "The Top 100 Records of All Time"—A canon of pop and rock albums from a sociological and an aesthetic perspective. *Popular Music* 25(1): 21–40.

Wald, Elijah. 2012. *Talking 'bout Your Mama: The Dozens, Snaps, and the Deep Roots of Rap*. New York: Oxford University Press.

Walser, Robert. 1995. Rhythm, rhyme, and rhetoric in the music of Public Enemy. *Ethnomusicology* 39(2): 193–217.

Warren, Jamin. 2004. Record review of Talib Kweli: *The Beautiful Struggle*. *Pitchfork*, September 24. http://pitchfork.com/reviews/albums/4550-the-beautiful-struggle/.

Weinstein, Susan. 2008. A love for the thing: The pleasures of rap as literate practice. *Journal of Adolescent and Adult Literacy* 50(4): 270–281.

Wells, John. 2007. Multiple-stressed words. *John Wells's Phonetic Blog*, May 29. http://www.phon.ucl.ac.uk/home/wells/blog0705b.htm.

Werd n Deeko. 2007. Lyrics to "Let's Talk." On *S.O.S: Presents Werd n Deeko Vol. 1*. Sons of Scotland. Compact disc.

White, Christopher W. 2013. An alphabet reduction algorithm for chordal *n*-grams. In *Mathematics and Computation in Music*, edited by Jason Yust and Jonathan Wild, 201–212. Heidelberg: Springer.

White, Christopher W. 2014. Changing styles, changing corpora, changing tonal models. *Music Perception* 31(3): 244–253.

Wickham, Hadley. 2014. Tidy data. *Journal of Statistical Software* 59(10): 1–23.

Wiggins, Geraint. 2008. Computer models of musical creativity: A review of *Computer Models of Musical Creativity* by David Cope. *Literary and Linguistic Computing* 23(1): 109–116.

Wiley. 2012. Lyrics to "Welcome to Zion." On *Evolve or Be Extinct*. Big Dada Recordings BD 187. Compact disc.

Williams, Justin. 2009. Beats and flows: A response to Kyle Adams, "Aspects of the music/text relationship in rap." *Music Theory Online* 15(2).

Williams, Justin. 2014. The construction of jazz rap as high art in hip-hop music. In *Rhymin' and Stealin': Musical Borrowing in Hip Hop*, 47–72. Ann Arbor: University of Michigan Press.

Witek, Maria A. G. 2017. Filling in: Syncopation, pleasure and distributed embodiment in groove. *Music Analysis* 36(1): 138–160.

Wyckoff, Geraldine. 2003. Joey DeFrancesco: Philadelphia flyer. *Jazz Times*, December.

Wynn, Karen. 1992. Addition and subtraction by human infants. *Nature* 358(6389): 749–750.

Yasin, Jon A. 1997. In yo face! Rappin' beats comin' at you: A study of how language is mapped onto musical beats in rap music. EdD dissertation, Columbia University.

Yuan, Jiahong, and Mark Liberman. 2008. Speaker identification on the SCOTUS corpus. *Proceedings of Acoustics* 9: 5687–5690.

Zbikowski, Lawrence M. 2004. Modelling the groove: Conceptual structure and popular music. *Journal of the Royal Musical Association* 129(2): 272–297.

Zuckerkandl, Victor. 1973. *Sound and Symbol: Music and the External World*. Princeton, NJ: Princeton University Press.

INDEX